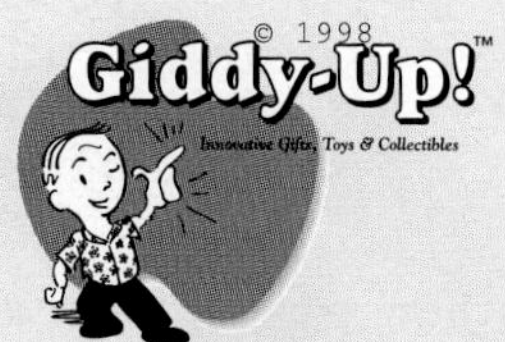

© 1998
Giddy-Up!™
Innovative Gifts, Toys & Collectibles

Contents

OCTOBER 1998

MARY BETH'S BEANIE WORLD MONTHLY OCTOBER 1998 VOL. 2, NO. 1

DEPARTMENTS

FROM THE PUBLISHER

"Mary Beth's Beanie World Monthly" is proud to present this special First Anniversary issue. When we started producing this magazine, no one knew how big a phenomenon it could become. In one short year, we've gone from producing a 72-page magazine on a quarterly basis to creating a 248-page magazine every month! During this period of rapid growth, we have never raised our cover price, opting simply to provide more information and features for the same value. We hope you have enjoyed the improvements in every issue!

As part of our anniversary celebration, we have printed 25,000 copies of this issue in a collectible hardcover format. You can buy these hardcover books while supplies last at selected gift stores and specialty shops and at Beanie shows where "Mary Beth's Beanie World Monthly" has a booth or table set up. We also intend to offer this special edition for sale at our Web site, which now incorporates using secure credit card transactions. Pick up your copy before they disappear!

In addition, only limited quantities remain of the bear designed exclusively for "Beanie World" by renowned artist Sally Winey. Each bear comes with a signed and numbered certificate of authenticity. For more information on ordering this unique collectible, see the advertisement on page 30 of this issue.

Finally, in case you haven't heard, perhaps the biggest news of our first anniversary celebration is the announcement of plans to produce our first "spinoff" magazine: "Mary Beth's Beanie World For Kids." Editor In Chief Sara Nelson – known to many collectors as "Beanie Mom" – has a lot of great ideas for the new publication, and you can take a sneak peek at it in the special, eight-page booklet that came in the polybag with this magazine. Look for the premiere issue of "Mary Beth's Beanie World For Kids" at newsstands everywhere in late October 1998.

Thank you, as always, for your continued support of "Mary Beth's Beanie World Monthly." We are happy to be regarded as the world's No. 1 Beanie Babies magazine!

Michael M. Meyers
Michael M. Meyers
Publisher

Volume 2, Number 1
October 1998

3400 Dundee Road, Northbrook, IL 60062 Phone: (847) 291-1135 • Fax: (847) 291-0612

ABC MEMBERSHIP APPLIED FOR

"Mary Beth's Beanie World Monthly" (USPS #016-284, ISSN #1520-7005) is published monthly by H&S Media, Inc., 3400 Dundee Road, Suite 245, Northbrook, IL 60062. U.S. subscription prices are $59.90 for one year and $107.90 for two years. The Canadian subscription price is $89.90 (U.S. funds) for one year.

Postmaster: Send address changes to:
"Mary Beth's Beanie World Monthly," P.O. Box 500, Missouri, TX 77459.
Periodicals postage paid at Northbrook, IL, and additional mailing offices.

Change of address notice: Please allow 6-8 weeks for an address change to take effect. "Mary Beth's Beanie World Monthly" is not responsible or liable for missed issues due to an address change.

CONTACT INFORMATION

For information about the magazine, **EXCLUDING SUBSCRIPTIONS**, call our 24-hour info line at (847) 291-1135, Ext. 803.

• • •

Direct all **SUBSCRIPTION INQUIRIES** in writing to: McMillen Communications, P.O. Box 500, Missouri City, TX 77459-4052. Or, you can call 1-800-310-7047 or fax to (281) 261-5999. E-mail inquiries about subscriptions only can be sent to sirtm@flash.net.

• • •

We welcome your letters, suggestions, questions, pictures, news, and ideas for future articles of interest. Please write:
Mary Beth's Beanie World Monthly,
P.O. Box 551,
Mt. Prospect, IL 60056-0551.
Make sure to include your full name, postal address, e-mail address (if any), and daytime phone number. Address and phone number are for office use only and will not be published. You can correspond via e-mail by sending to beaniew@interaccess.com.

• • •

If you are a gift or specialty retailer or distributor wishing to carry "Mary Beth's Beanie World Monthly" in your store, call for information:
U.S. – Metro Marketing, (800) 995-7197
Canada – Zibbers Inc., (416) 787-8516
United Kingdom – Honey 'N Lemon, 011 44 0800 146345

• • •

If you are an advertiser wishing to place an ad or business card size classified in an upcoming issue, please call Patrick Julian at (847) 291-1135, Ext. 307, or send e-mail to pjulian@adspub.com.

• • •

For "Mary Beth's Beanie World Monthly" Web site inquiries, send e-mail to Jennifer Coyle at jcoyle@interaccess.com.

• • •

If you would like to list your upcoming Beanie collectibles show, read our procedures listed on in the show section of this issue. Direct any questions to Aileen Cordero at (847) 291-1135, Ext. 326, or send e-mail to acordero@adspub.com.

• • •

We regret that we are unable to answer any mail or phone calls regarding Beanie Baby questions, variations, pricing or where to purchase Beanie Babies in your area. We cannot forward any forms of correspondence to Ty Inc.

From The Editor

Join in the fun as we celebrate the First Anniversary of "Mary Beth's Beanie World Monthly!" We have come a long way during this first year and we appreciate all of your suggestions and support over time. Every month we aim to provide all of the information and exclusive features that Beanie lovers worldwide want. When it comes to Beanie collecting, we want you to feel that "Mary Beth's Beanie World Monthly" is the only publication you need to be informed and entertained.

In honor of our first anniversary, we've packed this issue with many exciting features! For starters, you won't want to miss our exclusive story on page 80 by the "Beanie Mom" herself, Sara Nelson. Sara shares with you how she started collecting Beanies, a hobby that quickly led to the development of her popular Beanie Web site, BeanieMom.com, and her service as editor in chief for our new spinoff magazine, "Mary Beth's Beanie World For Kids."

In addition, check out our EXCLUSIVE interview with vice president of Ty Canada Bill Harlow on page 26. With all the mystique that surrounds Ty Inc., it was quite refreshing to meet with Bill and listen to his perspective on this whole Beanie phenomenon. You will certainly enjoy his candor as he answers many questions about Beanies north of the border.

We launched our Beanies In The News section in our September issue, and already we have received a tremendous amount of positive response. In every issue we aim to get you up to date on news worldwide that relates to Beanies and bean bag toy collecting. In this issue's Beanies In The News you will find updates on Clubby the bear, fake Beanies, sports team giveaways, Beanie-related crime and much more. If you have Beanie news to report, you can send us an e-mail at beaniew@interaccess.com.

I was proud to write this month's Collector Spotlight about one of the world's hottest young actresses, Mae Whitman. You may have seen her in the 1998 summer movie "Hope Floats" with Sandra Bullock, or perhaps you remember her from "Independence Day" or "One Fine Day." This Beanie collector is one special young lady! Read all about her on page 51.

Have you become an Attic Treasures fanatic yet? If not, you may very well become "hooked" after looking through the first published pictorial guide of the entire Attic Treasures Collection. This special section – brought to you with the help of Attics experts Peggy Gallagher and Paula Abrinko – begins on page 59. In an unprecedented move, Ty announced the retirement of 10 members of only the Attic Treasures family on July 31. Say goodbye (or hurry out to buy!) Amethyst, Christopher, Dickens, Ebony, Fraser, Gloria, Morgan, Nicholas, Scotch and Sidney.

Also, we should note that we've followed up the Pillow Pals feature in our September issue with a pictorial in this issue featuring the complete Pillow Pals Collection! The section begins on page 76, immediately after the Attic Treasures section.

Our comprehensive Bean Bag Buyer's Guide has grown to 80 pages in this issue. Due to popular demand, among the new features is a "quick reference guide" that lists all of the Ty Beanies in alphabetical order with prices by hang tag generation. Also, we now feature a single page that lists all current Beanies and retireds organized by retirement date. Use this as a handy reference at Beanie shows or when you're shopping for Beanies on the Internet! All listings for this issue were accurate as of August 10, 1998.

Other new features you will notice are Canadian prices for all Beanies (thanks to our Canadian readers for the suggestion!) and the inclusion of tush tag generation information. Want to know which tush tags you can find on Flutter the butterfly or Peking the panda? The information is now right at your fingertips!

Of course, in this issue you will find all of the regular departments you have come to expect: from Reader Mail to Web Watcher to the ever-popular Odds 'N Ends. Our "Mary Beth's Beanie World For Kids" section continues to grow, and our Bean Bag Bonanza section is spotlighting even more newly released bean bag toys. In this issue you'll find exclusive looks at the Wizard of Oz bean bags from Warner Brothers, Silly Slammers and Salvino's Bamm Beano's. And don't miss our pullout of the hot Mark McGwire Bamm Beano. This bear honoring baseball's super slugger is on the reverse side of the pullout between pages 16 and 17.

All of this and much more await you in this issue as we celebrate our first anniversary. All of us at "Mary Beth's Beanie World Monthly" look forward to many more years with you, our loyal readers. Happy Collecting!

Mary Beth Sobolewski

Mary Beth

Editor-In-Chief

QUESTION:

Dear Mary Beth,

I recently purchased the set of 11 Grateful Dead Bears at a flea market. The tush tags on my bears read: "Steven Smith Stuffed Animals, Inc., Brooklyn, NY 11236" and are made in the Philippines. Each bear has a laminated tag with the bear's name, Tour Memory and birthdate. They appear to be identical to the bears pictured on page 70 of the June 1998 issue of "Beanie World." My concern is that nowhere on either the tag or the bears does the name "Liquid Blue" appear, as mentioned in Claudia Dunne's article. Does this mean my set is fake?

Denise Koveikis
Fountain Hills, AZ

Dear Denise,

Liquid Blue manufactures and distributes the Grateful Dead bears, but the Liquid Blue name does not appear on the tags.

QUESTION:

Dear Mary Beth,

We have a dark Stripes the tiger in our Beanie collection. Although it does not have a fuzzy belly, it does have the fuzzy material on the bottom of the back legs only. We have never heard of any other Stripes having the fuzzy material only on the legs. Is this more rare than fuzzy belly Stripes and/or does it increase the value?

Ally and Jessie Zerbe
Virginia Beach, VA

Dear Ally and Jessie,

The quite rare fuzzy belly Stripes were given this name after collectors noticed a difference in the fabric that was used on the undersides of the old version (black/gold) of Stripes the tiger. All fuzzy belly Stripes have the third generation swing tag and the black-and-white 1995 tush tag, and most also have the extra Canadian tush tag. Several variations exist among the fuzzy belly Stripes: only the belly being fuzzy, only one or more paws being fuzzy, or sometimes only the underside of the chin being fuzzy. Any or all of these variations can be mixed/matched to provide a truly special Beanie!

QUESTION:

Dear Mary Beth,

I would very much like to get a copy of your April 1998 issue that featured the Harley Davidson Cycle Bean Bag Plush Bears and Pigs. I have just purchased a set and was told your magazine had an excellent article on them. Are these available for sale?

Judy M. Fuqua
Shreveport, LA

Dear Judy,

Currently, back issues of "Mary Beth's Beanie World Monthly" are available for sale only through the publisher at Beanie shows = attended by representatives of the magazine. A list of upcoming shows "Mary Beth's Beanie World Monthly" reps plan to attend can be found in the back of every issue or at the "Beanie World" Web site, http://www.beanieworld.net. Also, check at Beanie shows, swap meets or Internet trading sites. Some secondary market dealers may have back issues of "Beanie World" for sale.

(conitnued on page 8)

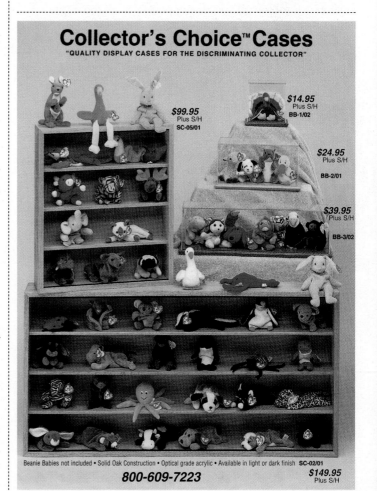

Ask The Editor

QUESTION:

Dear Mary Beth,

According to your August issue, Bessie was not made with a first or second generation hang tag. My daughter's first Beanie was Bessie. She no longer has the hang tag, but the tush tag is black and white. According to pages 145-146 of the same issue, the black-and-white tush tags equal first or second generation hang tag. How can this be? Is there such a thing as a second generation Bessie, or were there black-and-white tags on third generation Beanies?

Julie Perry
Niceville, FL

Dear Julie,

Black-and-white first generation tush tags with dates of either 1993 or 1995 were available with first, second and third generation swing tags. Thanks for helping to clarify this for our readers!

QUESTION:

Dear Mary Beth,

After purchasing the August issue of "Beanie World," I was most disappointed to find that two of the four bonus pullouts were blank. Did this happen to all of the copies of that issue, or is mine unique?

Ginny Shoup
Belle Plaine, IA

Dear Ginny,

In the August issue, we actually had four pullouts. Two were posters (Glory and Wise) with advertising on the back of them, and the other two were just pullouts with a blank backside. One of these special two-page spreads was the Princess Diana special, and the other was Odds 'N Ends. I hope this clears up any confusion.

QUESTION:

Dear Mary Beth,

How can a new collector even begin to collect all of the Beanie Babies in the Ty line? Is is too late to start now with the prices of so many of the retireds so high?

Linda Stringini
Spokane, WA

Dear Linda,

There are thousands of new Beanie Baby collectors that just caught the Beanie fever since the May 1998 McDonald's Teenie Beanie Baby promotion. It is very difficult NOT to be caught up in such excitement! New collectors can find it quite overwhelming to try to collect every Beanie Baby in the entire lineup. It can be both time and cost prohibitive if you set your sights on a full collection. I always encourage people to collect what they like. Collectors are special people who love not only the commodity they are collecting, but also the thrill of the hunt!

Many newer collectors are starting their collections only with the current Beanies, in hopes of finding all of them for the suggested retail of $5-8. Others are beginning their brigade searching only for the 14 newly released Beanies from May 30, 1998. Still others are collecting only the dogs, only the cats or only the new face Teddy Bears. I know one teenager who searched for only the cats with rhyming names ... Zip, Nip, Chip, Flip and Snip!

The recent surge of Beanie Baby Sports Promotions have brought together two very diverse groups of people. Sports memorabilia fanatics have joined forces with Beanie lovers in search of the commemorative cards that so many of the various sports teams are using as promotional give-aways.

Does the thought of owning a complete set of Beanie Babies seem impossible? Look for information at our Web site, http://www.beanieworld.net, for how to win every Beanie Baby ever produced in our exclusive $100,000 giveaway!

QUESTION:

Dear Mary Beth,

I recently purchased a Ty Attic Treasures bear clad in a green/blue clown suit. His hang tag says "SM. BEAR." Yesterday after receiving the August "Beanie World" issue, a picture of my new bear is among the new releases of "Attic Treasures" and his name is Piccadilly. Can you please explain?

Ruby Moss
Chillicothe, MO

Piccadilly

Samuel

Dear Ruby,

It seems the first shipments of both Piccadilly and Samuel had swing tags that say "Sm. Bear" and "Lg. Bear," respectively. Subsequent shipments have correct swing tags.

QUESTION:

Dear Mary Beth,

I must say collecting Beanie Babies is an exciting and fun adventure. I'm having a great time collecting for granddaughters, nieces and myself. Although the Buyer's Guide is wonderful, would you consider including a single-page, up-to-date listing of all current/retired Beanies? If perforated,

conitnued on page 10

this would be so handy to tear out, fold and put into a purse or wallet. It would allow collectors who are on the go to mark which ones they have, write down prices, etc. Handy, handy, handy!

Brenda Vande Voort
Baraboo, WI

Dear Brenda,

We are considering such a pullout for a future issue. For now, we've provided a concise list of all current/retired Beanies by date on one page in our Buyer's Guide. You can find that page after the section that features photos and pricing information for every Ty Beanie Baby.

QUESTION:

Dear Mary Beth,

I noticed that the poem I have read in your August issue for Glory is different than the poem I've seen elsewhere. In your magazine it says:"Wearing the flag for all to see, Symbol of freedom for you and me, Red white and blue — Independence Day, Happy Birthday USA!"

In another place, I've read Glory's poem as: "Oh say can you see, Glory's proud of her country, Born on Independence Day, This bear lives in the USA!"

Can you confirm which one is correct? Is the other poem only on counterfeit Glory bears?

Cary Rivett
Uxbridge, MA

Authentic Glory Swing Tag

Counterfeit Glory Swing Tag

Dear Cary,

The first poem you listed (the one that appeared in our magazine) is the correct poem shown inside the swing tag of the authentic Glory bear. I have found the second poem inside the swing tag of the counterfeit Glorys.

QUESTION:

Dear Mary Beth,

I am not hooked up to the Internet. What is the best way to sell or trade Beanie Babies?

Matt Dixon
Washington, DC

Dear Matt,

As luck would have it, most newspapers carry advertisements in the classified section for collectors looking to buy/sell/trade! Attending a Beanie show might also be a great way to sell your Beanie Babies. Normally, there are many dealers at a Beanie show who are in need of additional merchandise to sell. Do remember, though, when selling to a secondary market dealer, it's quite common to receive only 40 percent to 60 percent of the current market value of the Beanie since the dealer also has to profit on the sale. Good luck!

QUESTION:

Dear Mary Beth,

I recently visited some Buy/Sell/Trade Beanie Baby Boards on the Internet and was surprised by some of the "Beanie Lingo." Can you help the novice collector?

David Hatfield
Palm Beach, FL

Dear David,

It is not surprising that Beanie collecting has developed a language all its own! The major lingo you need to know includes:

• Swing tag: Refers to the lightweight red cardboard heart tag that is attached to a Beanie's ear or foot by a small clear or red plastic connector. Also referred to as "heart tag" or "hang tag," there are currently five different generations available.

• Tush tag: Refers to the sewn-in cloth tag on the bottoms of the Beanie Babies. They are dated and are an important chronological indicator of when the Beanie was produced. There are currently six generations of tush tags available.

• Acronyms depicting the condition of a Beanie Baby advertised for sale:

MWMT – Mint condition Beanie Baby with mint tags.
MWBMT – Mint condition Beanie Baby with Both Mint Tags
MWCT – Mint condition Beanie Baby with Creased Tag
MWM3T – Mint condition Beanie Baby with three mint tags (swing, tush and extra Canadian tush tag)
MIP – Mint in Plastic (applies to the McDonald's Teenie Beanies) in unopened polybags.

WRITE TO US

We welcome your questions about Ty Beanie Babies and other bean bag toys. Please send your questions to: "Ask The Editor," c/o "Mary Beth's Beanie World Monthly," P.O. Box 551, Mt. Prospect, IL 60056-0551. Make sure to include your full name, postal address, e-mail address (if any) and daytime phone number with your correspondence. Address and phone information are for office use only and will not be published. We regret that letters cannot be answered personally.

Retailers Packages available with displays

The Original **Collectors Clipp™**

The Clipp™ remains as the best tag protector for your treasured investment. Clear, acid and wax-free, lightweight and sturdy enough to keep the tag from bending (unlike the sleeves that can scratch and stick to your tag). Shatter proof plastic (unlike brittle off-shore imitators). Made in the U.S.A. and always a money back/replacement guarantee.

NOW AVAILABLE:

Rainbow Collection™ Collectors Clipps™
in shades of purple, red, green, blue and yellow

HOT NEW PRODUCT AVAILABLE NOW:

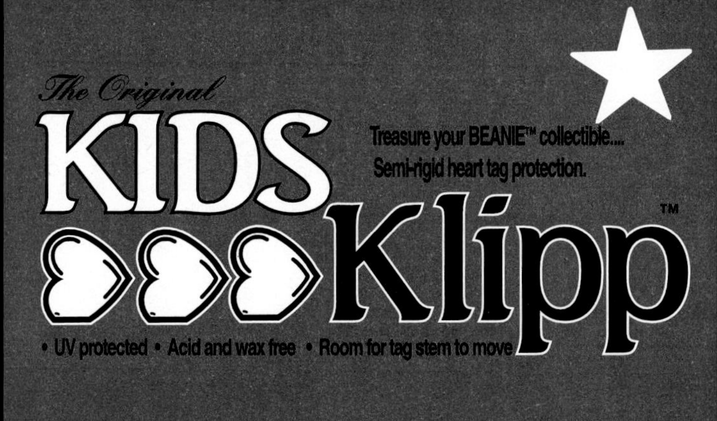

OPEN HERE

Semi-rigid, acid free, UV protected one-piece clear tag protector. Same size as The Clipp™, easy open on top. Best looking semi-rigid, and now lowest price on the market.

WHOLESALE PRICING

(available to businesses only, prices subject to change without notice):

The Original **Collectors Clipp™**	**Suggested Retail: $ 0.99**
Retailer Package:	$150.00 plus Freight*
Collectors Clipps™ individually packaged:	$0.50 plus Freight*
Rainbow Collection™ Collectors Clipps™	$0.50 plus Freight*
100 minimum	
Collectors Cribb™	**Suggested Retail: $ 3.79**
Clipp Designs, Inc. Retailers	$ 1.39 plus Freight
Other Retailers	$ 1.49 plus Freight
75 minimum in 75 count lots	
Kids Klipp™	**Suggested Retail: $ 0.25**
Under 1 case	$0.12 plus Freight*
1 to 4 cases	$0.10 plus Freight*
5 to 9 cases	$0.09 plus Freight*
10 cases	$0.08 plus Freight*

Packaged in in bags of 100 . . . . . 1 case equals 1,500 Klipps™
All prices are per Klipp™

**Freight depends upon your zone. Free freight for orders over $150.00*

We're available in Noodle Kidoodle, Hallmark and other fine gift shops throughout the US, Canada and England.

RETAILERS CALL 1•800•494•3936 and mention this ad, 1•773•594•9727 in Illinois to purchase our Retailer Packages.

Participating distributors: Great Traditions, PA 1-800-309-2211 (sportsnet) and KS Canada 1-888-895-7218.

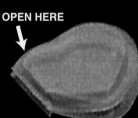

Beanies In The News

Ty has hot products for official retailers

Retailers must be an Official Beanie Babies Headquarters to be able to order any of the new Ty exclusive products. Ty tag protectors, three styles of calendars and Beanie Baby trading cards will be available in October. Retailers will be able to order these products directly through their Ty representatives. In addition, Ty retailers have been encouraged to order their Ty Plush as early as August for the Christmas season. Plush is sure to be a hot seller this Christmas!

Ty relaxes border rules

Ty Inc. and the U.S. Customs Service have eased their one-Beanie-per-family rule at the U.S.-Canadian border. The new rule about bringing Beanies over the border is as follows: 1) No commercial shipments are acceptable for importation without a letter of consent from Ty Inc. 2) Thirty pieces or less are acceptable for importation without a letter from Ty. However, there is a 30-piece-a-month limit. 3) No more than three of any single kind of Beanie Baby is acceptable. Ty had been working with border officials to limit Beanie trafficking, and beanies previously were confiscated and sometimes destroyed at the border.

Update: Valentino goes to Cooperstown!

The Baseball Hall Of Fame in Cooperstown, NY, is Valentino's new home! *(photo courtesy of Hall of Fame)*

In our August 1998 issue, we offered a brief report on the New York Yankees' Beanie Baby day on May 17, 1998. To be sure not to disappoint any young fan, the Yankees purchased enough Valentinos and printed enough commemorative cards to give one to every fan 14 and under. More than 20,000 cards and bears were given to ecstatic children as they entered the park.

But the children at the game got more than just a Valentino – pitcher David Wells treated them to a perfect game (no hits and no walks) that day, too. Jeff Idelson, executive director of communications and education for the Baseball Hall of Fame, happened to be listening to the game as he cleaned out his basement. It is his job to contact clubs to ask for artifacts from current-day players that might be of interest. After the game, Idelson called the Yankees and requested the cap Wells had worn and a ball from the game to display with all the other "perfect game" balls since 1940 that are on display in Cooperstown, NY. He also asked for a Beanie Baby and commemorative card because they helped to explain the attendance of 50,000 for a game in May, which is somewhat unusual.

So, thanks to David Wells, Valentino is enshrined in the Baseball Hall of Fame!

Newspaper's Beanie offer

The Chicago Sun-Times Newspaper is offering a choice of either a Cubbie the bear Beanie Baby or the Sun-Times' own bean bag toy, Sunny The News Hound (sporting a Sun-Times T-shirt), as an incentive to subscribe for 20 weeks of delivery of the daily Sun-Times. Those who subscribe for 26 weeks will get both toys. Subscribers will receive toys only after full payment for the subscription is received. Call 1-888-84TIMES for more information. The offer expires when supply of toys is exhausted, but in no event later than October 31, 1998.

Bankruptcy hoax

Someone on the Internet posted a hoax report credited to the Associated Press that Ty Inc. had filed for bankruptcy. The major reason cited was two major fires in Chinese production plants that had made it impossible to catch up with Beanie production. Rumors such as these are popping up daily, so be cautious about unverified information posted on Internet discussion boards.

Ontario store sets a fine example

Reader J. Raymond from Campbellville, Ontario, sent us a news clipping about the Joseph Brant Memorial Hospital, which received a $10,000 boost courtesy of a local collectibles shop, Dania Unique. The store purchased 100 Princess Beanie Babies and gave them to customers who made $100 donations to the hospital.

Youngster thinking of others first

Julie Dalpiaz Herman reports from Urbana, IL, where her local newspaper featured an 8-year-old boy named Ethan Sanders who is an outpatient at the Shriners Hospital in St. Louis. Although Ethan is able to get in and out of the hospital in just a few hours, he feels very badly that some children have to stay. Ethan and his family have begun to collect Beanie Babies to give to the sick children who must stay in the hospital.

Disney releases more bean bag toys

New Disney Beanie shipments went on sale in the end of July. These new critters include: Pilot Pooh, Pilot Mickey, Toga Mickey, Liberty Minnie, Tourist Mickey and Hula Minnie Set, Black Cauldron, Hamm & Rex and Robin Hood. Check out this month's Bean Bag bonanza section for photos of these hot new items.

One reminder for Disney collectors: if you place any stock in the rumors that Disney will (continued on page 20)

Salvino's INC.
BAMM BEANO'S™
BAMM BEANO'S

Rocket got a Lock–It! I love saying that. He's quick and bright blue and I gave him his very own Lock-It™ for his tag 'cuz it's light and bright like he is. Rocket is a proud bird. And he's handsome. And his tag is so safe.
LOCK-ITS™
The Very Best Beanie Tag Protector
Libearty is my All-American bear. He loves the Cubbie Cube™ I got him 'cuz it helps keep his white fur just perfect. He can see out and knows he can show off a little because he looks so nice. It's his very own home and it keeps him safe and warm.
CUBBIE CUBE™
The Safety of Home for Your Beanies

If you want TagBags or Lock-Its or Cubbie Cubes for your Beanie Buddies, you can get them where you get your beanies. And if they don't have them, ask real nice and they'll get them for you. Or you can call 800-953-6864 and they'll tell you where you can find them.

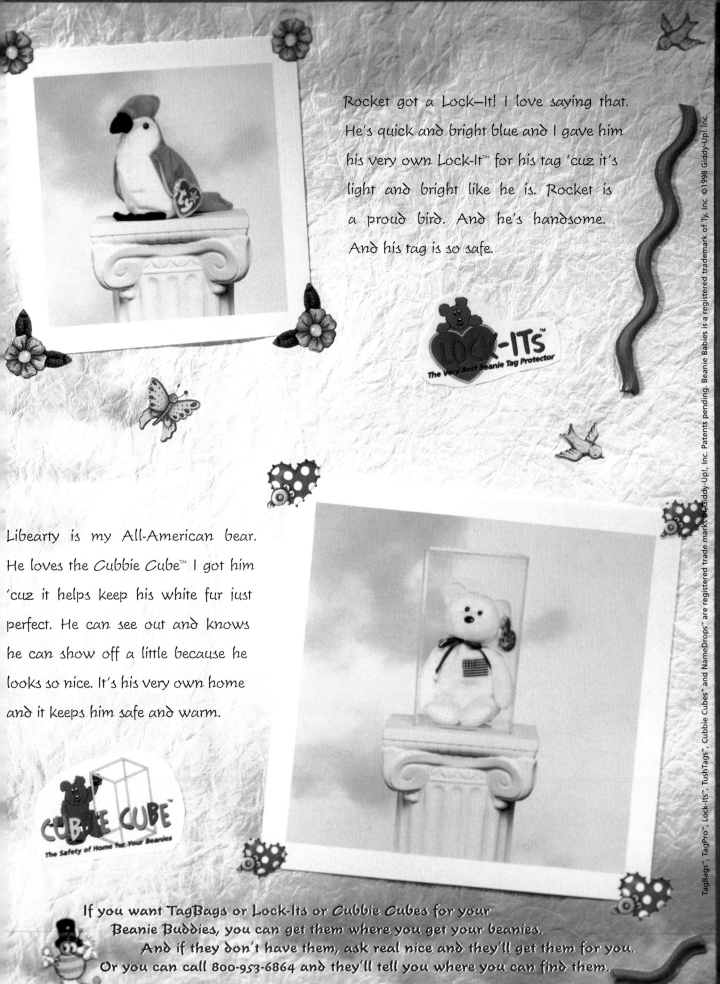

The BEANIE ZONE
COMING SOON
@www.beaniezone.com
The best Beanie auction, ever!

retire a significant number of their Mini Bean Bag Plush this fall, it's best to stock up now!

Mary Beth shows up on 'Home Matters'

Although actually taped in April, the Philadelphia-based Discovery Channel's popular "Home Matters" show will air a Beanie Babies segment with Mary Beth Sobolewski on October 5 at 1 p.m. Central Time. Hosted by Miss America 1981, Susan Powell, "Home Matters" is America's top how-to show on topics such as crafts, home repair, gardening, cooking, hobbies and collectibles. This Beanie Babies segment will be rerun on the Discovery Channel five times a year for three years!

Convention is a huge success

The 19th National Sports Collectors Convention and Beanie Baby Pavilion was held August 6-9 in Rosemont, IL. Many sports celebrities were in attendance, including Karl Malone, Bobby Hull and Joe Montana. The show was a spectacular success, combining sports memorabilia and Beanie Babies collector items. Representatives of the Chicago Bears had a booth where they offered the 1998 Kids Fan Club Kit (which included Ty Beanie Blackie and a commemorative card) in a limited amount per show day.

Corporate sponsor "Mary Beth's Beanie World Monthly" had numerous staff writers and show representatives to greet the tens of thousands of enthusiastic collectors in attendance. Don't miss next year's 19th National event, which will take place in Atlanta.

QVC's Beanie hour

On July 23, 1998, the QVC cable shopping channel became the latest choice available to collectors who prefer to buy their Beanies via television. Slated for a one-hour presentation at 10 p.m. Central Time, show host Mary Beth Roe was visibly surprised when all inventory sold out completely in 27 minutes (rumored to be a sell-out record).

Although priced generally higher than on the Internet or at Beanie shows, the Beanies on QVC were sold in groupings priced somewhat more reasonably than they were on shows by cable competitors. QVC announced on several occasions that the Beanies being sold during this show had been obtained via the secondary market sources.

At press time, two additional Beanie-related shows have aired on QVC with similar results.

Mary Beth Sobolewski, left, appears on "Home Matters," which airs on the Discovery Channel.

This athlete's got heart

Former Chicago White Sox player and current Beanie Baby collector Ron Kittle and children Dylan and Hayley were seen at the Heart to Heart Celebrity Softball Game on June 26. In between innings, Ron shared stories of how Beanie Babies have helped him raise money for the charity that he founded.

Giveaway, heat make for a bad double play

About 30 fans waiting for the Weenie the dog giveaway at the Tampa Bay Devil Rays game on July 26 had to be treated for complications from the sweltering 90-degree temperature. So many paramedics were called to Tropicana Field that fire officials say they fear the rest of the city will be left unprotected and at risk if it happens again, according to an article in the St. Petersburg Times.

Some Beanie enthusiasts camped outside of the stadium overnight despite the fact the giveaway was only for kids age 14 and under. About 6,000 people were outside the gates when the overheating incident occurred.

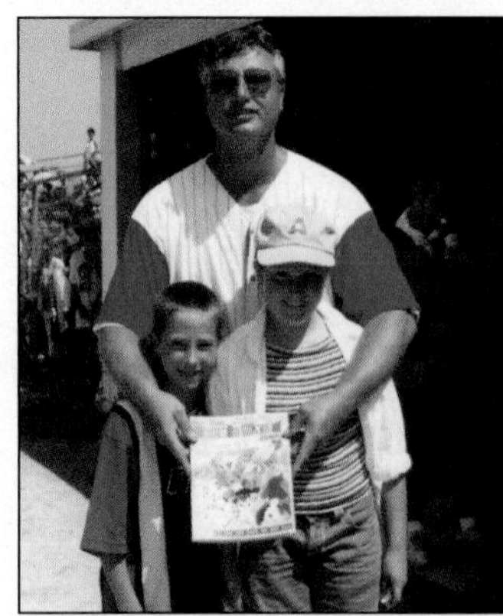

Former Chicago White Sox player Ron Kittle attends the Heart To Heart charity softball event with his children Dylan and Hayley.

Can you DIG it?

Speaking of Disney, the company recently publicized a new Web search engine designed just for kids, Disney's Internet Guide (DIG). DIG – covering such areas as animals, outdoors, games, toys and computing – is presented in easy-to-find sections and sub-categories. Make sure to check out the new site at http://www.dig.com.

Peace lightens up

Lighter colors have been spotted on newer versions of Peace. Several Beanie-based Web sites have reported that it is now difficult to spot any of the browns or darker blues found in the older Peace Beanies. New Rainbows (tagged as Iggy) are also said to have the newer tie-dye colors like Peace.

Bean bags and prescriptions a healthy mix

Pharmaceutical companies are starting to get in on the Beanie craze. Produced only to be distributed to health care providers, 5,000 Cheetah bean bag animals were sent to American doctors to promote Vicoprofen, a combination pain pill containing the pain killer Vicodin and the non-steroidal anti-inflammatory drug Ibuprofen.

In addition, the drug Biaxin used a bean dog resembling the Ty Beanie Wrinkles as a promotion to American Pediatricians. A coupon was given to any child placed on

Biaxin by their doctor. After they finished the drug, they were to send in the coupon to receive the Beanie at their home address directly from the company. The promotion is over, and all of these have already been distributed. Thank you to Dr. Paula Abrinko for this hot tip!

Two exclusive Erin bears!

The Sports Celebrities Festival, the Canadian fundraising organization that benefits Canadian Special Olympics, recently offered a Special Olympics Erin bear on Web site's auction page. The winning bid was $1000 (CDN) for one of only two Erin bears with the Sports Celebrities Festival tag and a letter of authenticity. At press time, plans were pending for the remaining Special Olympics Erin bear, according to a Sports Celebrities Festival source.

Beware fake Glorys

Many Beanie collectors have been reporting spottings of fake Glorys. One collector said that on the Beaniemonium Web site, http://www.geocities.com/~beaniemonium/rumors.html, that the fakes are pretty similar to the real Glorys. He says that,"Even the tush- tag has a stamp inside it ... I'm thinking that (the tush tag) is real, but the hang tag isn't ... If you look in the hang tag, everything is basically double-spaced, and the font's off there, too. The most noticeable thing, though, is the fact that independence is misspelled (spelled indepentence)." Check out our in-depth look at these fake Glorys in the Counterfeits Update of this issue on pages 84 and 85.

Beanie giveaway planned

The group Beanies 4 Charity has announced a contest in which it will give away some of the rarest Beanies, including Peanut the royal blue elephant, Quackers without wings, Spot without a spot, Nana and others, all valued together at more than $30,000! To enter, simply write an essay on why you want to win the rare Beanie collection. The required $10 entry fee will go toward the American Cancer Society. The contest deadline is September 30, 1998.

More information can be found on the Internet at www.beanies4charity.com, or you can send your entry to Beanies 4 All, P.O. Box 505, Lynbrook, NY 11563.

Clubby is coming!

Despite rampant rumors about Clubby's availability (or lack thereof), one reader reports she was told by Ty Inc. that the newest Beanie will indeed be stocked in ample quantities. Because the order forms for the Beanie Babies Official Club (through which you can get Clubby) had been marked "limited offer," many collectors had feared supplies would run out if they didn't mail them in right away.

However, a Ty representative reportedly said the "limited offer" phrase was included only because Ty Inc. was afraid people would hold on to their order form for a year or longer and try to redeem them for a Clubby after Ty had stopped making the bear.

According to Ty, there will be plenty of Clubby bears to go around.

Florida woman's Beanies stolen

A woman in Port Charlotte, FL, decided not to press charges against the six neighborhood children who apparently stole her Beanie Babies, but she said she was surprised the kids' parents hadn't sent them over to apologize, MSNBC reported recently. The suspects, who range in age from 6 to 13, broke into the woman's home and stole $700 worth of Beanie Babies, police said. The victim was on vacation when two teenage girls allegedly broke in through a rear door. Other kids in the neighborhood who heard about the break-in decided to go into the vacant house and get their own Beanies.

Police found the Beanies by going door-to-door in the neighborhood. The theft was reported a week after it occurred when the Beanies' owner returned home after a vacation.

Mary Beth in 'People'

Lots of Mary Beth's wisdom goes into this magazine each month, but it sometimes goes into other magazines as well, such as the August 3, 1998, "People" magazine article on (what else) Beanie Babies. Editor In Chief Mary Beth Sobolewski revealed she has 600 of the creatures in her personal collection and spoke of the high cost and difficulty of collecting Beanies.

Luckily for us, she's stuck with it!

Fake Beanies in Western Canada

Reports of fake Beanies flooding the market in Calgary, Alberta, just keep increasing, according to an August 3 article in the Calgary Sun. The fakes were described as "tiny teddy bears representing Great Britain, the U.S., and Canada" (sounds like Britannia, Glory and Maple, but no details were given).

Dealers are warned to look for some of the telltale signs – harder heads, bright body coloring, missing double tush tags, eyes that are spaced too far apart — that are considered common among fake Beanie Babies. *(continued on page 22)*

ON THE AUCTION BLOCK

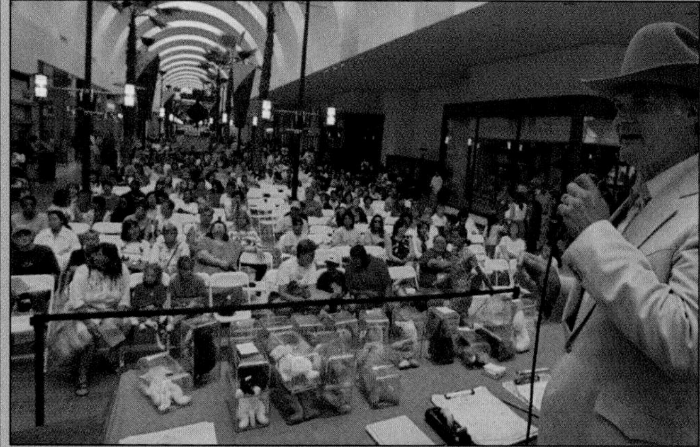

Auctioneer Richard Brewer takes a bid during a Beanie Babies auction at a mall in Cerritos, CA, on Thursday, July 23, 1998. The auction, which raised more than $2,000 for the Make-A-Wish Foundation of Los Angeles, attracted hundreds of people who stood in line starting as early as 3 a.m. for the opportunity to place bids. (AP/Wide World Photo)

Beanies In The News

Beanies stolen from gift store

A thief who broke into a Cheshire, CT, gift shop stole 108 Beanies but barely touched the other merchandise, police said. The Beanies were stolen just a few days before the owners of the Berry Patch were planning to put the new Beanies out for sale, according to an Associated Press article. The shipment included some hard-to-find currents like Princess. The stolen Beanies are worth about $1,500 to 1,700 wholesale, but might go for as much as $7,000 on the secondary market, said Berry Patch co-owner Bob Langhans.

Lucky's new legs?

Some collectors recently reported spotting different legs on Lucky the ladybug. The legs on Luckys purchased in July 1998 are said to be fitted with circular tips, as opposed to the rounded tips on the ones purchased in early 1997.

Beanies hot in Honolulu

Beanie Babies have finally made their way to Hawaii in the past year, according to the Pacific Business News. Local retailers have complained that they were unprepared for the big crowds Beanies seem to bring, but most still stock the fuzzy friends as quickly as they can.

Kraft bean bag update

In our October issue, we spotlighted the Kraft Dairy Fairy Bean Bag, but failed to provide an address for ordering the toy. Available through February 28, 1999, or while supplies last, the toy has its own tush tag that reads "Kraft™ Singles Dairy Fairy."

Mail your name, address, the words "Dairy Fairy Bean Bag Toy" on a 3x5 card and two UPCs from KRAFT™ Singles (12 oz. or larger) and $3.50 (Postage & handling included) for each Dairy Fairy ordered. It takes 10-12 weeks to receive your order; limit three items per address.

If you have the order form, mail to: Kraft Dairy Fairy Bean Bag Toy, P.O. Box 390359, El Paso, TX 88539-0359.

If you do NOT have the order form, mail to: Kraft Dairy Fairy Bean Bag Toy, P.O. Box 390360, El Paso, TX 88539-0360.

The eyes have it

The Eye Centers of Florida are offering a special incentive for back-to-school eye exams – Beanies! In the program, children who need glasses can select Guess frames for just $99 a pair and receive a free Beanie Baby with their purchase. They also can register to win a Princess bear.

Beanie Internet trading may bring junk mail

A recent ABCNEWS.com report on America Online's new privacy policy said that AOL will ensure they won't read your e-mail, but they aren't promising to stop watching how you spend your money on AOL – and that's important news to Beanie lovers who sell and trade on the Web.

Internet Beanie market users may soon be subjected to unwanted ads and marketing because they have bought things from AOL online marketplaces, which reserve the right to later target them based on their purchasing history. The popular Internet provider won't give out your name, credit card or telephone number, but it will fork over your name and address to direct mail and telemarketing companies, according to ABCNEWS.com. You can stop AOL from doing this if you weave your way through the "Marketing Preferences" section of the site, a process that must be done yearly.

NFL starts Beanie giveaways

The Dallas Cowboys are the first NFL team to have a Beanie Baby giveaway. Their Chocolate the Moose giveaway on September 6 at Texas Stadium marks football's first foray into the world of Beanies. Beanies are to be given to the first 10,000 children 14 and under, along with a Cowboys collector card. For more on recent sports Beanie giveaways, see pages 88 and 89 of this issue, and don't forget to consult our Buyer's Guide for prices of sports Beanies and information on future giveaways.

Ty removes link to Web site

Ty Inc. recently announced that it was investigating an adult entertainment Web site that was linked to its popular site at www.ty.com. Ty told MSNBC that it constantly monitors its page because of the high amount of children who regularly view it, and they post warnings online telling children not to give out their address when trading or buying Beanies online. MSNBC described the link as "an ad that appeared on its Web site that promised Beanie Babies for $5.95," but in fact linked to an adult site.

Astro Beanie is out of this world

The Astronaut Hall of Fame is using a new version of Valentino, dubbed Astro Valentino, to raise money for the Astronaut Hall of Fame Scholarship Foundation Fund. Two astronauts, Scott Carpenter and Ed Gibson, signed a limited number of Valentinos that have a swing tag and certificate that are numbered and correspond to one another (see photo, left). The swing tag has a certificate number on one side, and on the other it has a picture of an astronaut looking to Earth. Last we heard, Orlando stores couldn't keep this Beanie in orbit!

– Compiled by Erin Brereton

"ASTRO-VALENTINO"™

LIMITED EDITION SERIES 1
(1000 ISSUED 07/26/98)
THE FIRST ASTRONAUT BEANIE BABIE
Created to Honor All of America's Great Space Pioneers Past, Present and Future.

The history of the Astronaut Hall of Fame (AHOF) begins in 1984 when the original seven Mercury Astronauts formed a foundation to advance space education to affirm this country's achievements in space. Over $10,000 from the sale of Astro Valentino will go to the AHOF Scholarship Foundation Fund for future generations.

SERIAL # 902

The commemorative card that comes with each Astro-Valentino.

WALLOS

BRIAN WALLOS & CO., INC

60 West Ethel Rd. #5
Piscataway, N.J. 08854

(732) 287-54
FAX (732) 287-63

E-mail: info@wallos.com

World's Largest Beanie Selection!!!

Every Beanie in Stock • Great Holiday Gifts

Dear Valued Customer,

Brian Wallos & Co., Inc. has been in the collectibles business for 12 years. We are very happy to be serving all of your Beanie Baby needs. We pride ourselves on fast friendly service and a large selection for you to choose from. Please be advised that due to long advertising lead times and constantly changing market conditions, price often change after publication and sale dates. Please call for up-to-the-minute, rock-bottom prices on all Beanie Babies. Thank you and we look forward to hearing from you.

Sincerely, Brian Wallos & Co., Inc.

Please Note: **This ad was created on July 20, 1998. Prices will change up and down due to the volatile nature of the Beanie market. Please call for current rock-bottom prices on any Beanie you need!**

McDonald's Teenie Beanie Sets All 10 Pieces! $229.00

1998 12pc. Set C

Beanies® • Beanies® • May '98 Retireds

Beanie	Price	Beanie	Price	Beanie	Price
PRINCESS The Bear	Call	PEACE The Bear	29.95	BRUNO the Terrier	6.95
McDonald's Set (10 pc.)	Call	PINKY The Flamingo	4.95	SMOOCHY the Frog	9.95
BATTY The Bat	9.95	POUCH The Kangaroo	6.95	BALDY The Eagle	19.95
BERNIE The St. Bernard	4.95	PUGSLY The Pug	6.95	BLIZZARD The Tiger	19.95
BLACKIE The Bear	9.95	RINGO The Raccoon	6.95	BONES The Dog	16.95
BONGO The Monkey	6.95	ROARY The Lion	6.95	EARS The Bunny	16.95
CHOCOLATE The Moose	9.95	SCOOP The Pelican	6.95	ECHO The Dolphin	19.95
CHIP The Cat	9.95	SEAWEED The Seal	9.95	FLOPPITY The Bunny	19.95
CLAUDE The Crab	9.95	SLY The Fox	4.95	GRACIE The Swan	16.95
CONGO The Gorilla	9.95	SNIP The Cat	6.95	HAPPY The Hippo	24.95
CRUNCH The Shark	4.95	SNORT The Bull	4.95	HIPPITY The Bunny	19.95
CURLY The Bear	19.95	SPINNER The Spider	9.95	HOPPITY The Bunny	19.95
DAISY The Cow	6.95	SPIKE The Rhino	9.95	INCH The Worm	19.95
DERBY The Horse	9.95	STINKY The Skunk	4.95	INKY The Octopus	29.95
DOBY The Doberman	4.95	STRUT The Rooster	14.95	JOLLY The Walrus	19.95
DOTTY The Dalmatian	6.95	TUFFY The Terrier	6.95	LUCKY The Ladybug	22.95
FLEECE The Lamb	4.95	VALENTINO The Bear	19.95	PATTI The Platypus	22.95
FRECKLES The Leopard	5.95	WRINKLES The Dog	5.95	PEANUT The Elephant	19.95
GOBBLES The Turkey	9.95	**January 1998 Releases**		PINCHERS The Lobster	16.95
MEL The Koala	6.95	STRETCH the Ostrich	6.95	QUACKERS The Duck	14.95
MYSTIC The Unicorn Old	29.95	SPUNKY the Cocker Spaniel	6.95	ROVER The Dog	22.95
NEW MYSTIC	9.95	HISSY the Snake	6.95	SCOTTY The Terrier	29.95
NANOOK The Husky	9.95	RAINBOW the Chameleon	9.95	SQUEALER The Pig	26.95
NUTS The Squirrel	6.95	PUFFER the Puffin	6.95	STRIPES The Tiger	19.95
		PRANCE the Cat	6.95	TWIGS The Giraffe	19.95
		POUNCE the Cat	6.95	WADDLE The Penguin	19.95
		IGGY the Iguana	9.95	WAVES The Orca Whale	16.95

OCTOBER RETIRED BEANIES!!!		JANUARY, 98 RETIRED BEANIES		RARE BEANIES, NO SWING T	
TEDDY The Brown Bear	CALL			CHILLY	$6
TANK The Armadillo	CALL	97 TEDDY	CALL	PEKING	$6
SEAMORE The Seal	CALL	SNOWBALL	CALL	BRONTY	$3
BESSIE The Cow	CALL	SPOOK	CALL	REX	$2
SPOT The Dog	CALL	LIZZY	CALL	STEG	$2
FLIP The Cat	CALL	GOLDIE	CALL	HUMPHREY	$7
VELVET The Panther	CALL	BUCKY	CALL	FLUTTER	$3
SPEEDY The Turtle	CALL	MAGIC	CALL	CAW	$2
LEGS The Frog	CALL	NIP	CALL	TRAP	$6
ALLY The Alligator	CALL	CUBBIE	CALL	BUMBLE	$2
HOOT The Owl	CALL			WEB	$4
				TEDDY COLORED	$6
				ORANGE DIGGER	$3
				RARE STRIPES	$1
				MAGENTA PATTI	$2
				TIE-DYE LIZZY	$4
				QUACKERS (NO WINGS)	$9
				SPOT W/O SPOT	$6

Bargain Prices!!

Brian Wallos & Co.
Is not a Direct Account we buy and sell on the secondary market just like you!

BEANIE HEADQUARTERS!!

www.wallos.com

NBC Peacock Beanie
$29.95

Beanie Babies Value Lots
All Guaranteed Authentic Beanie Babies
10 Different (Our Choice) $59.00
25 Different (Our Choice) $125.00
100 Assorted (Our Choice) $499.00
500 Beanie Babies CALL
1000 Beanie Babies CALL

Beanie Protection

Plastic Storage Cases

1 Case	$3.95
10 Cases	$30.00

Swing Tag Rigid Plastic Sleeves

100 ct.	$14.95
10 ct.	$2.00

Heart Savers Soft Clips (Locket Style) $24.95/100ct

Heart Shaped Plastic Locket Cases Hard Plastic "The Collectors Clipp"

1	$.99
10	$7.95
100	$69.00

Beanie Circular Jars W/Lid

1	$3.99
10	$35.00

JANUARY AND MA 1997 RETIREDS!!!

BUBBLES	CALL	FLASH	CA
GARCIA	CALL	SPLASH	CA
CHOPS	CALL	RIGHTY	CA
CORAL	CALL	MANNY	CA
GRUNT	CALL	TUSK	CA
DIGGER	CALL	SPARKY	CA
KIWI	CALL		

Thank you for your business. Please call to reserve. Phone reservations held 7 days. All products carry a 7-day full money back return privilege as long as all items are returned to us in the same condition they were when they left our facility. After 7 days sales are final! No refunds! No cancellations! All returns are subject to a 15% re-stocking fee. Thank you. Due to rapidly changing market conditions and ad lead times, prices are subject to change up and down. Please call for up-to-the-minute, rock-bottom prices on all items. We are not responsible for fluctuating market conditions or typographical errors. No fees for credit card use. No minimum order. Personal checks are held for 14 days. Please call for exact postage, handling & insurance charges. Next day, 2-Day Air and 3-Day Select Service are available. NJ state residents please add 6% sales tax provide your resale certificate. Office hours M-F 11:00-7:00 EST.

ty

Ants
Early
Fortune
Fetch
Rocket
Glory
Jabber
Gigi
Tracker
Stinger
Kuku
Jake
Whisper
Wise

The Right Place at the Right Time

Canada official shares the story of how it all began ... and what's ahead

By Karen Gomes

It's easy to miss. There are no big, flashing red-heart signs or billboards along the highway with Pinky or Bongo proclaiming the remaining mileage to the front door. But the unassuming office/warehouse building on a quiet road on the outskirts of Toronto is the northern home to one of the greatest success stories in toy merchandising history.

Eight years ago, while scouring the New York gift show for new merchandise lines to distribute throughout Canada, Ty Canada Vice President Bill Harlow never could have imagined exactly how pivotal that afternoon would be.

"We just looked at it and knew we had to 'do' Ty in Canada," Harlow recalled. "Ty product wasn't in Canada as all the other plush companies already were, and nobody had what Ty could offer in the way of pricing and quality. We knew if we could get it into Canada we'd have a hit. So, we talked to Ty about it and went from there."

"It's probably easiest to think of Ty Canada as a franchise of Ty Inc.," Harlow said. "We are a separate company, but follow all the rules and guidelines set by Ty Inc. wherever possible. Of course, there are some Canadian regulations that we must also adhere to, but for the most part, we're more than happy to go along with most of Ty's suggestions. Obviously, the man knows what he's doing, and I'm not about to argue with his methods. Quite frankly, I personally think he's a marketing genius, so there's little reason to alter that, although the market in Canada is slightly different."

Ty Canada's Bill Harlow

Beanie Beginnings

Knowing the Canadian market comes naturally for Harlow, who was born and raised in the Don Mills area south of Toronto. When the late-'80s recession hit his small manufacturing company hard, it seemed appropriate to look for other items to distribute through an already established network of gift/specialty stores.

"We knew nothing about plush, nothing about toys," Harlow said. "Plush was probably at the bottom of our list in terms of distribution. At first we thought, 'OK, all the stuffed animals and toys anyone would ever want are probably already in Canada,' but we found the one that wasn't and probably made the biggest success of it." Success indeed. Harlow now co-owns Ty Canada along with Ty Canada's president, Liz Caruth, and two silent partners.

"I remember seeing my first Beanie one afternoon while in Chicago," Harlow recalled. "I was in Ty's office. He handed me a little green frog and said, 'THIS is where you're going to put your money.' That was the beginning of Beanies for me. He knew he had something very special, but I don't think even Ty could have anticipated how enormous Beanie Babies would become – I know I certainly didn't."

Perhaps for the first time publicly, Harlow confirmed that Ty Warner works on all of the initial designs for new Beanie Babies. Furthermore, he suggested that although Warner is very aware of Beanie ideas and suggestions, it is the element of surprise that Ty treasures most.

"But he does listen. For example, Maple was our idea, and it's certainly done well," Harlow said. "I firmly believe that Ty has always been that way in the sense that he's created this, but now he's got his following and understands that it's important to listen to the collectors. With each and every set of new releases, he continues to amaze me with the designs."

Pricing and the Beanie Market

Most collectors agree that the most recent introductions could be the best-designed group of new Beanies to date. Finding them at the suggested retail price, however, is becoming a greater challenge for Canadian and American collectors alike.

"$8.99 to 9.99 is the suggested retail pricing for Canadian Beanies," Harlow explained. "Unfortunately, in Canada we can't actually set a retail selling price, only strongly suggest. So, if a retailer wants to take Maple and sell it for $500, that's his prerogative. I, quite frankly, think it's horrible. I think there are a lot of different ways to go about getting those few pieces out to people. There's a store nearby that has a raffle — a ticket for which is given each time you buy a Beanie. The customer then has an opportunity to place the raffle ticket into a box for Maple or Erin or Princess, and if his name is pulled, is offered the chance to buy the Beanie for $9.99. I think that's a very fair way of doing it.

"We've actually started a policy of 10-to-1 ratio," Harlow said. "Maple comes in a package with 10 other pieces — if the store wants 240 Beanies, within the package will be 24 Maples. Really, it's not to penalize people, but for Princess, Erin, Maple and Peace we could never get enough of those pieces. The need is simply insatiable.

"So, what we're trying to do is stop retailers from just buying those pieces. Anybody can take those four pieces, walk out on the street and sell them. Well, that's not the kind of business we're looking for. We're looking for people to create a display with the Ty products – all of our Ty products – and display it and sell it to the consumers who come in and support their store. There's no doubt we've had some flak over this. A lot of little stores have complained. But we're just trying to make sure if they're going to do it; you're going to do the whole line — not just Beanies. If you're going to be a serious Ty retailer, that's what we want.

"At one time, we were ordering huge amounts and later found out that most were being trucked down to the States.," Harlow said. This does not serve our Canadian collectors in any way, shape or form. It provided a very unrealistic market for us to try and supply. By incorporating some of these policies, we're trying to say, 'This is what Ty Canada's all about.'

"Neither Ty nor myself is interested in 'feeding' each other's markets. I don't think our smaller retailers will get 'caught' with excessive inventory as long as they're smart about it and not get greedy. Unfortunately, there IS a lot of greed out there — at $200 or $300 for a Maple, that takes it right out of the kids' hands. We're trying to give everyone more of a fair chance and even it out a bit. It might not be perfect, but we're trying to do the best we can.

"We're also trying to have our retailers not focus quite so much on Beanies," Harlow noted. (continued on page 28)

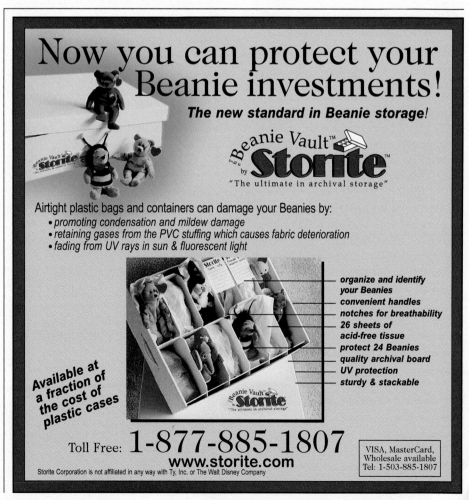

"We're seeing our Plush line has really started to take off. Attics (Ty's Attic Treasures) are literally flying off the shelves; we can't get enough of them. I know they're way oversold in the States."

Harlow agrees, however, that the typical Canadian collector isn't quite as willing to jump on the Beanie/Plush/Attic bandwagon as their American counterparts.

"For some reason, it does seem to take a little longer to come up across the border, but no doubt, the wave has started and the flood will follow," he said. "Of course, everybody keeps asking, 'When are Beanies going to die?' and when that didn't happen last Christmas, they're looking to the summer or fall. I don't have a crystal ball, so I can't tell you for sure. What I can tell you – and it's absolutely true – is that Ty Canada is stronger now than we've ever been. We just can't keep up. As long as Ty keeps coming out with great designs and retires them, it just keeps the hype ongoing."

A Few Frustrations

Of course, any success story still has its share of difficulties. It's no secret, for instance, that Canadian collectors always seem to be waiting for delivery of new or hard-to-get Beanie styles. Harlow explained that all Beanies are ordered through Ty Inc. but shipped directly to the Ty Canada warehouse from China or Indonesia. The delays often stem from the decision to ship nearly complete orders of new designs to the retailers.

"We like to be able to have the retailers place as many of the new styles as possible all at once on their shelves," he said. "It makes it much easier on the consumer. But not all stores will be receiving all the new Beanies at the same time. Honestly, the retailers that are supporting our entire line and being fair with their retail pricing will be shipped sooner than others. I have no problem with that. And because some of the quantities we receive aren't always huge, we have to pick who will be getting the earliest shipments."

Perhaps the most frustrating issue, however, is the growing problem of counterfeit Beanie Babies entering

One bonus for visiting Ty Canada was the rare opportunity to view these prototypes – a tan/pink Ears the rabbit and a bright yellow/brown Bongo the monkey.

Canada. Unlike in the United States, no Customs regulations are available for trademark protection, which means authentic Ty products are coming in from the United States along with thousands of counterfeits directly from Asia.

Harlow said the consumer's best defense against counterfeits is to buy direct from Ty retailers exclusively.

"Certainly grey market distributors purchase goods from Ty retailers, but they also often purchase merchandise from less than reputable sources," he said. "For some of these grey market distributors who have carried Beanies in their stores for only a short time, many don't know the difference and are unknowingly selling illegal merchandise to consumers.

"We're encouraging our retailers to report information to us regarding counterfeits and their origins. It's very frustrating though, and the information is slow in coming. Most of those buying the counterfeits are not the Ty retailers but grey market distributors. We're also looking to eliminate many of these grey market distributors, but it's very difficult — again, because of the greed of many of the retailers. We're taking action to immediately cut off any of these retailers who sell to grey market distributors. We absolutely want to hear from customers about this happening. The retailers WILL be cut off, make no mistake."

It's the Beanies That Matter

Still, no matter what the headaches, working with Ty Canada can be a great experience.

"I take Beanies with me wherever I go," Harlow said, beaming, "especially on planes. "I'm always passing them out to kids. There isn't a birthday party I go to and not give a Beanie. "It doesn't matter how old they are! It's just about the best part."

When prompted to pick out his favorite Beanie, he smiled, paused and explained, "Bones … yes, definitely Bones. I've always had a special place in my heart for him. Ever since he first came out, Bones has just been a really good, fun, all-around dog. He was such a big hit when he first came out, and it was all so new to us then. But I do love them all – there isn't a Beanie in the line that can't capture someone's heart." ❤

Karen Gomes is a a staff writer for "Mary Beth's Beanie World Monthly." She writes features of interest to Canadian Beanie Baby collectors.

We also sell
SPORTSCARDS & SUPPLIES

Ordering Instructions

- ★ $50.00 minimum order
- ★ Call for shipping rates
- ★ CODs welcome to established customers
- ★ Prices may change due to market fluctuations

ORDERS ONLY 1-800-922-FLIP

201 Charles St., Hackensack, NJ 07601 Tel: (201) 488-8885 Fax: (201) 488-5813

LUCITE DISPLAY CASES

★ Lucite Walls ★ UV Stabilized ★ Sliding Doors for Easy Use

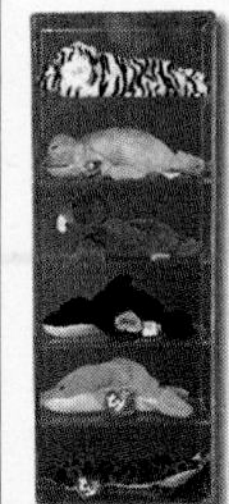

6 Piece Horizontal
Wall Mount
Sliding Front Door
★ 8 1/2" X 24"

$25.00

6 Piece Vertical
Wall Mount
Sliding Front Door
★ 8 1/2" X 24"

$25.00

Holds All Styles of Beanies
Wall Mount
Sliding Side Door

$25.00

- ★ 12 Piece Vertical
- ★ Folds in Half for Easy Carrying
- ★ Great for Home, Show or Store Display
- ★ 18" X 24"

$45.00

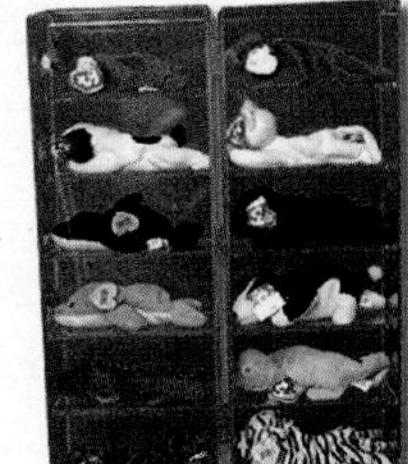

- ★ 12 Piece Horizontal
- ★ Folds in Half for Easy Carrying
- ★ Great for Home, Show or Store Display
- ★ 18" X 24"

$49.00

- ★ 24 Piece Tower
- ★ Folds in Half
- ★ Great for Home, Show or Store Display
- ★ 27" X 32"

$90.00

Tri-Fold Display Tower
★ Holds Up To 24 Beanies
★ 36" X 24"

$110.00

★ These are great for resale at SHOWS AND STORES

HEART GUARD™ Tag Protectors

- ★ Heart Shaped
- ★ Acid Free - Archival Safe
- ★ UV Resistant
- ★ Made in USA
- ★ Double Seal For Extra Strength

Your Tag Slides In Easily And Stays Safe And Snug

100 Per Pack

1 (pack)...................... $10.00 ea.
5 packs......................... 8.00 ea.
25 packs........................ 6.00 ea.
50 packs (case)............. 5.00 ea.
200 packs....................... 4.50 ea.

HEART SHELL

★ Archival Safe ★ Clips Tight ★ Covers Heart Shaped Tag Completely

100	.20 ea.
1,000	.15 ea.
5,000	.12 ea.
10,000	.10 ea.

ENGRAVED NAME PLATES

★ Brass Plates ★ Double Sided Tape ★ Fits great on Beanie Boxes ★ Custom made for your favorite Beanie ★1" x 3"

$2.00ea.

Call for wholesale quantities

SNAP-LOCK Tag Protectors

★ Heart Shaped ★ Thick Plastic ★ Archival Safe

$1.00 ea.	
50	.75 ea.
100	.50 ea.
250	.40 ea.
1,000	.33 ea.

Call for larger quantities

BEANIE BOXES

★ 4" x 4" x 7" ★ Crystal Clear

Each	$3.00
10	2.50 ea.
25	2.00 ea.
100	1.75 ea.
500	1.60 ea.
1,000	1.40 ea.
5,000	Call

SMALL BEANIE BOX

★ 3 3/4" Base, 6 3/4" Tall

Each	$2.00
10	1.75 ea.
25	1.50 ea.
100	1.25 ea.
250	1.10 ea.

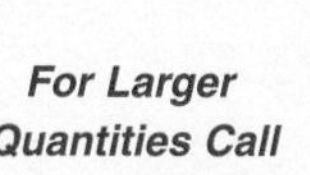

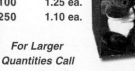

For Larger Quantities Call

BEANIE BABIES

Ally	50.00	Happy	22.00	Seamore	175.00
Baldy	16.00	Hippity	15.00	Snowball	35.00
Bessie	65.00	Hoot	55.00	Sparky	150.00
Blizzard	16.00	Hoppity	16.00	Speedy	33.00
Bones	16.00	Inch	16.00	Splash	125.00
Britannia	450.00	Inky	20.00	Spooky	35.00
Bubbles	160.00	Kiwi	180.00	Spot	50.00
Bucky	40.00	Jolly	20.00	Squealer	26.00
Chops	170.00	Lefty	300.00	Sting	200.00
Coral	175.00	Legs	30.00	Stripes	16.00
Cubbie	25.00	Libearty	400.00	Tabasco	200.00
Curly	15.00	Lizzy	29.00	Tank	75.00
Harry Caray Daisy	350.00	Lucky	25.00	Br. Teddy	95.00
Digger	125.00	Magic	45.00	'97 Teddy	39.00
Doodle	40.00	Manny	190.00	Tusk	140.00
Ears	15.00	Maple	270.00	Twigs	16.00
Echo	15.00	Nip	22.00	Valentino	20.00
Erin	49.00	Patti	25.00	Valentino (Yankee)	200.00
Flash	125.00	Peanut	16.00	Velvet	30.00
Flip	35.00	Peace	25.00	Waddle	16.00
Floppity	16.00	Pinchers	16.00	Waves	16.00
Fortune	Call	Princess	40.00	Weenie	22.00
Garcia	175.00	Quackers	16.00	Wise	Call
Glory	Call	Radar	175.00	Ziggy	16.00
Goldie	45.00	Righty	300.00	Zip	35.00
Gracie	16.00	Rover	20.00	'97 Teenie Beanie Set	199.00
Grunt	175.00	Scottie	25.00	'98 Teenie Beanie Set	60.00

BEANIE TUBES

★ 3 3/4" Base, 6 3/4" Tall

Each	$2.00
10	1.75 ea.
25	1.50 ea.
100	1.00 ea.
250	.90 ea.

For Larger Quantities Call

Sally Winey Bear

Designed Exclusively for Mary Beth's Beanie World

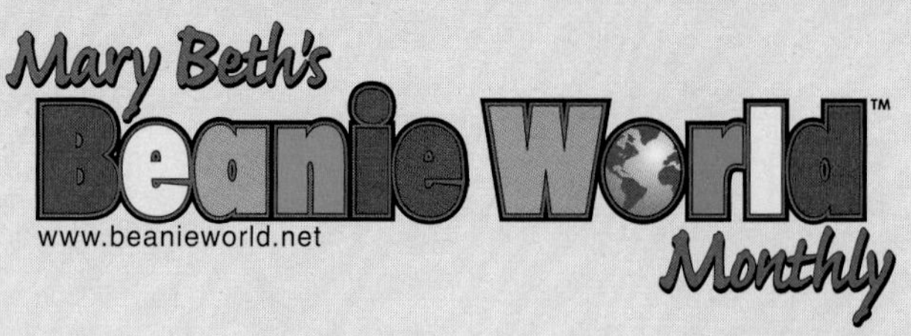

Certificate of Authenticity

Presents the Limited Edition Mary Beth's Beanie World Bear. This is an authentic Sally Winey Baby Bear design.

Created by international bear artist Sally Winey exclusively for Mary Beth's Beanie World Monthly.

Mary Beth's Beanie World Bear comes to you signed and numbered by Sally Winey and complete with this signed and numbered Certificate of Authenticity.

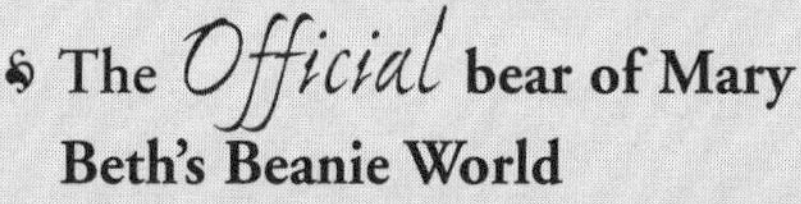

________________ #_____ of 2500

Mary Beth's Beanie World Bear
Distributed by Antiques & More • LaGrange, Illinois, U.S.A.

- The *Official* bear of Mary Beth's Beanie World
- Designed by *Sally Winey* EXCLUSIVELY for Mary Beth's Beanie World
- Limited edition *2,500* produced
- *Only $99* per bear including shipping and handling
- Each bear comes with a signed and numbered certificate of authenticity
- Each bear is signed and numbered by the artist

to order:

Please Note: Bear pictured is the prototype designed by Sally Winey. The actual bear is approximately 8" tall and may vary slightly from this photo.

Sally Winey Bear Is Subject to Availability While Supplies Last

Cost:	$99 per Bear including shipping and handling. *IL residents must add 7.75% sales tax.*
Online orders:	E-mail: AandMore@aol.com Provide your name, address and phone number. State the quantity you desire.
Phone Orders:	Call Antiques and More at 708-352-2214, during business hours Tues.-Sat. 10 a.m. to 5 p.m. CST.
Mail Orders:	Antiques & More, 2 South Stone • LaGrange, IL 60525
Payment:	Either cashier check or money order **ONLY.** Sorry **NO** personal checks or credit card orders will be accepted.

Shipping will take approximately 6 weeks from receipt of your payment.

For more information about the Sally Winey Bear please visit our web site: *www.beanieworld.net*

WHAT A SHOW!

The first Beanie show in the United Kingdom was a learning experience for all involved

By Elaine Smith, Lemon Lainey Design UK

The First UK Beanie Show is over! Nearly 6,000 collectors arrived at the fair in Ascot on Sunday, August 2, many with bags full of Beanies to trade with others. It was a really "interesting" day!

Fortunately, those few thousand people who managed to find the venue (the one we all finally ended up in) seemed to have an enjoyable day, and the weather was really quite good, almost like summertime should be. The weather is just about THE most popular topic of conversation in the UK, so that was kind of important!

Many collectors just gave up in the traffic queues, as the show had been widely advertised at Maidenhead and previously at High Wycombe, but, in the last eight days prior to the event, it was moved to Royal Ascot Racecourse! This is really the most suitable venue in the area, which would have been far better to start out with, but then, who knew? Hundreds of collectors reportedly arrived at the other two venues, only to find that it was not taking place at either, and a great deal of confusion meant that many collectors didn't get to Ascot at all!

The Police Department contacted us eight days before the show to ask us how many people we expected to attend. Based on 5,000 people attending the launch of the new Bees Party World store in Southampton, we figured that 10,000 collectors was a conservative estimate. They told us that no more than 500 people at any one time would be allowed to enter the Leisure Centre at Maidenhead, so we had a choice: cancel the show or move the event to another venue.

Beanies in the UK

We tried our hardest to publicize the venue change on our Web site and BeanieMom's, on local radio and TV, and in as many local and national newspapers as possible. We even called all the stores we could to tell them about the change, and the organizers promised to put road signs up to divert those who hadn't heard about the change. We heard, however, that on the day of the show no road signs were visible at either original venue, so many just turned home when they couldn't find out what was happening!

Most shows and exhibitions take several months to organize in order for them to be a success. We hope that future Beanie shows in the UK will be organized with this in mind, and we thank collectors for their patience as Beanies become even more popular in the UK. We expect the McDonald's Teenie Beanie Babies to debut in the UK in the fall of 1999, and that is bound to bring in vast numbers of new collectors, just as the two McDonald's promotions did in the USA.

Elaine Smith signs a copy of "Beanie World" for a young collector.

Honey 'N' Lemon Marketing, which is already preparing for its first UK Beanie show in association with "Mary Beth's Beanie World Monthly," intends to make it a huge success and is already working very hard to ensure that it will be! Watch for future stories in this magazine as show details become available.

The First UK Beanie Fair in Ascot was a huge learning experience for most of the vendors and collectors who attended. There were a lot more counterfeits than anyone could have imagined there would be, and we were astonished to see fake Britannia bears circulating at the show, including some in the most ridiculous colors, almost the same color as Derby the horse!

Among the counterfeit Beanies spotted at the show were some crazy-looking Royal Blue Peanuts. They were selling for about $800 in supposedly mint condition. They even had a red-and-white tush tag, sewn in the wrong place, with glossy tags, the wrong bar code, and to top it all, the shade of royal blue was at least two shades too light! Counterfeit Humphreys were far too small, a very light beige color, and too overstuffed.

There were some very strange looking fake Beanies, including all black Zip the cat, Flutter, Caw, Bumble, Chilly (with a round nose!), Kiwi, Sting, Web, Maple, Glory, Libearty, and some strange scarlet colored and bright green Teddies that were pretending to be colored Teddies, with really wide ribbons. Although some counterfeits were borderline, such as Radar and Web, the others could never have been made by Ty Inc.

The first Beanie show in the UK proved to be a hectic experience for the "Beanie World" crew.

Look at your authentic Beanie Babies, read and learn, keep studying the pictures, and make sure that you don't buy anything without a proper written receipt and contact details for the vendor. Ask them where the Beanie came from. If the price is a bargain, ask why, or remember that if it's anywhere near too good to be true, then it probably is! You may be buying a Beanie for £500 that isn't even worth £5!

Try to get a potential purchase looked at by an established collector or, if possible, by a Beanie expert. If the expert cannot tell you for sure if a Beanie is authentic or counterfeit, then move on and find another vendor and compare as many Beanies as possible to a genuine collection and the photos in this magazine. Buyer Beware! ❤

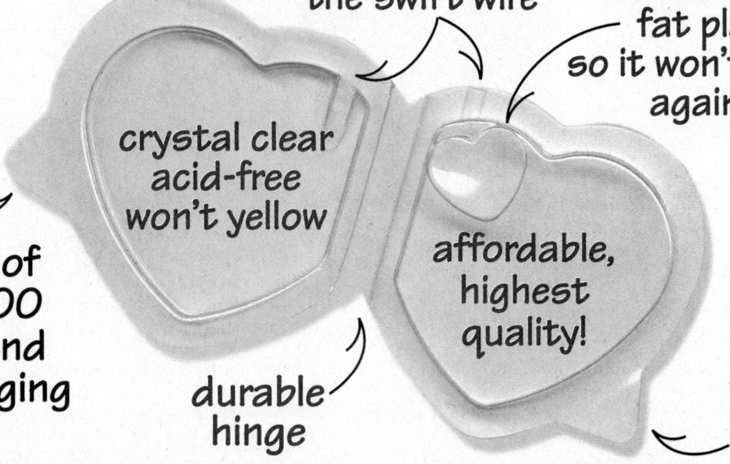

Elaine Smith writes stories of interest to Beanie collectors in the United Kingdom for "Mary Beth's Beanie World Monthly." Visit Lemon Lainey Design's Web site at http://www.lemonlaineydesign.com, or send e-mail to lemon@lemonlaineydesign.com

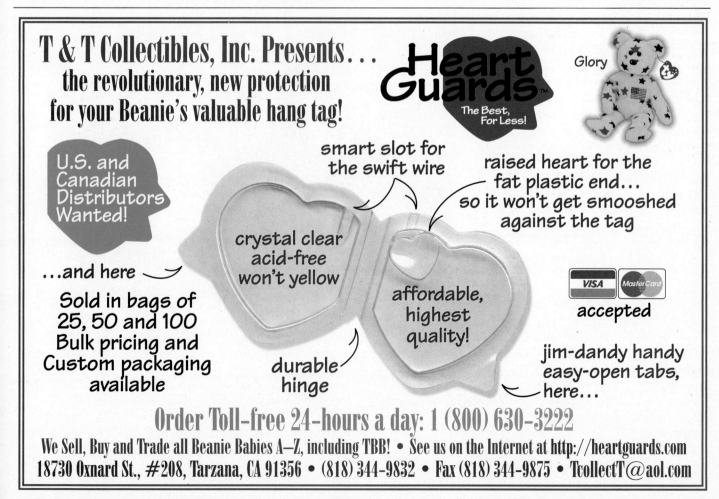

THE UK BEANIE MARKET TAKES FLIGHT

Interest in Ty products is increasing along with charitable work related to the hobby

By Bob Baker

The Beanie market in the United Kingdom is growing as more and more British people become aware of the Ty phenomenon. Despite the extensive information available on the Internet, there is very little national advertising, but the media cannot ignore the occasional five-minute TV documentary that leaves Joe Public saying, "What are Beanie Babies?"

My company recently accessed the Internet through several "service providers." In every instance, each comparatively large UK computer company could not believe the amount of content about Beanie Babies on the various Web sites. Unless one accesses the Ty web site or any of a variety of Beanie-related sites, many in the UK remain naive about American interest in Beanie Babies and still have very little knowledge of the Ty products. This will obviously change as Ty introduces more Beanies in the UK and prepares for its overseas McDonald's Teenie Beanie Babies promotion. That promotion had been slated for late 1998, but indications now are that it will be held in fall 1999.

Ty's Erin bear arrived in UK shops in the middle of June, but as expected the bear's quantity was restricted. Princess is more readily available, but Peace and Valentino remain elusive. Of course, Britannia remains in great demand and is very hard to find – sort of like looking for gold dust scattered in the desert. As of early July, the May retired Beanie Babies could still be found in retail outlets, but retailers were still awaiting the arrival of the 14 newly introduced Ty Beanies.

Some consumers have criticized retailers for inflating the prices of Britannia, Erin and Princess in the UK, but fortunately this practice is occurring only among a few retailers. My company, Pine Secrets, and other Ty-retail-approved outlets actively support local charities and are using profits from Beanie sales to help others. My principal interest is in "The Rocking Horse Appeal," which represents the only children's hospital in the southeast of England, the Royal Alexandra's Children's Hospital. I donate the most sought-after Beanies to the Appeal and have a weekly raffle and auction, with all of the proceeds going to charity. This charity support from retailers not only provides a valuable service to the local community, but also gives a fair opportunity for anyone to obtain Britannia and other rare Beanie Babies.

Charities in the UK rely on public donations, and hospitals such as the Royal Alexandra's Children's Hospital require contributions to ensure its survival. This year is the Alexandra's 130th Anniversary, and the celebration will culminate in October with a very special Beanie promotion. Our charity raffle includes a first prize of Britannia, Erin and Princess; a second prize of Britannia; a third prize of Erin; and a fourth prize of Princess. There may be more than one prize in each category, subject to the stock availability and the amount of interest.

Tickets will be drawn on a weekly basis, and the winning numbers are displayed wherever tickets are purchased or obtained by telephone from my Brighton outlet at 011 44 1273 729271. The auction and the winning numbers will also be displayed on the Internet, and details of the raffle and auctions will be available via e-mail correspondence. Please call for more information.

Beanies in the UK

It was our intention to raffle the prizes on the Internet so these Beanies could be made available to American collectors. Gaming laws, however, prohibit the sale of raffle tickets over the UK via the Internet, though they can be sold to overseas (continued on page 36)

visitors who purchase the tickets directly from retail outlets. However, the auction can accept bids over the Internet from worldwide users, and we hope this ultimately may generate more interest and increase the donations to our local charity. We are therefore eager to encourage American collectors to bid on the Web site for Britannia and other eagerly sought-after Beanie Babies (please call for updated URL information), and all overseas visitors to the United Kingdom are welcome to purchase raffle tickets from my retail outlets, which are all based in the Brighton area. My central retail outlet is Pine Secrets, 65 East Street, Brighton, England, BN1 1HO, and the telephone number once again is 011 44 1273 729271.

My First Taste of the States

In June, I had the honor of attending the "Mary Beth's Beanie World Monthly" Beanie Babies and Collectibles Show in California. After a 16-hour flight from England, I arrived in Los Angeles. This show provided my first real insight into the American Beanie Baby craze. I had read "Mary Beth's Beanie World Monthly" and was amazed at the amount of accessories and the interest in the Beanies, but it's hard to truly grasp until you experience a Beanie show in the States.

Armed with Britannia, Erin and Princess, I was raising money for The Rocking Horse Appeal, but I also wanted to expand my retail business to sell Beanie Baby accessories. I made several interesting contacts, but the most valuable part of the trip was meeting many Americans who continued to fascinate me and my UK counterparts with their dedication and enthusiasm to Beanie collecting. In Britain, we have never experienced such a craze, even from the infamous Teletubbies, which I sell at my retail outlets.

Teletubbies sales hit a peak in December 1997, but supplies are now available, though they will be restricted again during the build-up to Christmas 1998 because of manufacturing shortages. Teletubbies increase in price only during shortages of products, which tend to occur during peak seasons such as holidays. They do not contain identifying tags nor are they retired to enhance the collectibility of these items. The demand for Teletubbies simply stems from children's fascination by the Teletubbies' television show. And, after all, popularity among children is what toys should be all about. ❤

United Kingdom Beanie collector Bob Baker stocks the full range of Ty products at his stores. He is a regular contributor to "Mary Beth's Beanie World Monthly."

Reader Mail

DEAR BEANIE WORLD,

Our local Beanie store created something unique and unusual for the annual Lennoxville Friendship Day parade held June 13, 1998, in Lennoxville, Quebec, Canada. The theme for the parade was "Ocean," but as Beanie Babies are so popular at their store this year they decided to incorporate both themes — the ocean and Beanies. We had the first-ever Beanie Baby Boat Float! The actual float was a yellow boat built on a trailer with water and waves surrounding it. The boat also had life preservers with the name "S.S. Beanie" and bamboo fishing poles off the back with the catch of the day — Pinchers! A great deal of time, effort and imagination went into this creation by the owners of the store, friends and family. It was such a success that we did it again at the Canada Day Parade in Hatley, Quebec, a few weeks later. Fun was had by all, and the S.S. Beanie was a big hit!

The "S.S. Beanie" rolls in the Lennoxville Friendship Day Parade on June 13, 1998, in Lennoxville, Quebec.

The "S.S. Beanie" crew surfaced again for a Canada Day celebration on July 1, 1998.

Luba Wallace
Sherbrooke, Quebec

DEAR BEANIE WORLD,

In all of your Beanie news coverage, I haven't seen much about Bean Sprouts. There are several retired Sprouts and some with Oddities as well. Because Sprouts usually are more easily found, they seem to have become a popular alternative to Ty Beanies, especially when Beanie Babies are so hard to come by.

Barnie
Via E-mail

Editor's note: Thank you for the suggestion! Look for coverage of Bean Sprouts in a future issue.

DEAR BEANIE WORLD,

We have advertised our Beanie Shows in your magazine since late last year. It really helps to get such large coverage from such a respected magazine. Now I read that the same help I was getting will cost me $150. I think that's outrageous. Couldn't you have come up with something a little more reasonable? Maybe $50 and no magazines? I don't mind paying a fee, but my show is the only one in our area, and we attract about 300 to 400 people from a three-state area. We've just had our best show to date, but after expenses, $150 is about all I make on our shows. How about smaller fees for smaller shows?

Correspondence Via E-mail

Editor's note: I am happy that we have been able to advertise your shows in the past and hope we can continue to do so in the future. Yes, we began charging $150 to advertise Beanie Baby shows beginning with the September 1998 issue, but remember, the charge includes printing the show listing in the world's #1 Beanie Baby Magazine (with a circulation now exceeding 1 million every month) and also 25 free copies of the current issue. If you were to sell these magazines at your show for the retail price of $6, your listing would actually be FREE!

DEAR BEANIE WORLD,

I have just recently started collecting Beanies, but will be doing so for many years to come. Recently, I attended a Beanie show in my area where I was able to purchase Princess and Valentino. I enjoyed the show because many of the Beanies were displayed so people could actually pick them up and check them out. I enjoyed the event very much and wanted to tell you about this Canadian Beanie show. Keep up the great work.

Elisabeth Vickers
Etobicoke, Ontario

DEAR BEANIE WORLD,

As my wife and I were traveling this past winter, we were constantly passed by UPS trucks.I made the comment to my wife that they should change the name to BBBB – the Brown Beanie Baby Buggy! She and our granddaughters love to talk about Beanies!

Oliver J. Robinson
Carbondale, IL

DEAR BEANIE WORLD,

In July, we invited six of our dear college friends with all of their families to our summer house on Lake Michigan. Between us, we numbered 21 children (ages 6 months to 14 years). We had a great time jet skiing, swimming and comparing collections of Beanie Babies!! We were surprised to see how many rare ones we had between us. One of the high points of the weekend was passing around your terrific magazine! We never imagined 20 years ago as college coeds that we would be sitting on a beach surrounded by all these kids and Beanies!

It's a reunion complete with Beanie Babies and many good friends!

Sue Condit
Grand Haven, MI
Pam Biasco
Mt. Prospect, IL

DEAR BEANIE WORLD,

I am just thrilled that you are now publishing your magazine on a monthly basis. This way I can keep abreast of the news, gossip, hints and pricing. When I called my insurance company about putting a rider on the Beanies, I was told to us to use the price listing (secondary market price) found in "Mary Beth's Beanie World Monthly." The insurance company

Reader Mail

said that they considered this publication the most accurate one on the market! All of your hard work to publish a top-notch magazine has certainly paid off and been recognized!

Patricia Dwinnells
Loudon, NH

Editor's note: Although no one likes to dwell on the "unthinkable" happening to their Beanie Babies, it is the wise collector who protects the investment of a large and/or valuable selection of Beanies. Check with your insurance agent for further information. Also, some readers have reported using an online service through Collectibles Insurance Agency at: http://www.collectinsure.com. Thanks, Patricia, for writing in about such an important issue!

DEAR BEANIE WORLD,

I'm glad that Ty Inc. is teaming up with Major League Baseball and other professional sports teams to have special promotion days, but in almost every article I've read about such events, there is some discussion about people "cheating." Because of the popularity of Beanie Babies, I'm surprised that the individual teams (or Ty) have not established a system to prevent people from getting multiple Beanies, such a stamping the hands of children and accompanying parents or punching ticket subs, etc. Nothing is foolproof, of course, but systems like these could be done easily and cheaply, and hopefully make the distribution process much more fair.

Laura Hadley
Glendale, AZ

DEAR BEANIE WORLD,

I thought I would send you this interesting picture taken during the 1998 Ty Teenie Beanie craze. A local McDonald's, it seems, prefers to hire Beanie Babies to work for them (well … according to their signage!).

Lin Burnette
Colonial Heights, VA

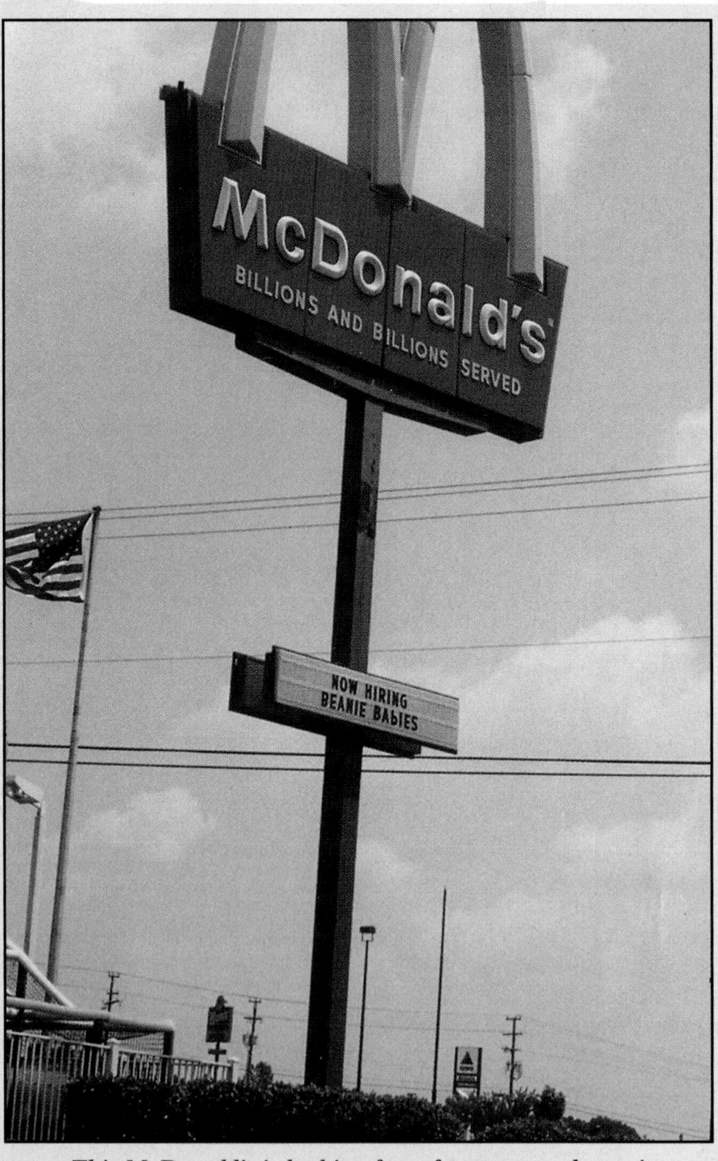

This McDonald's is looking for a few new employees!

DEAR BEANIE WORLD,

After having no luck in obtaining Erin for a cheap price (even "camping out" at 2 a.m. in front of a store), as a last resort I visited a Beanie Babies show. I approached one booth with approximately 20 blue paper bags. I was told they were grab bags, and each contained a bear inside (most of them Peace). I decided to give it a try, handed over $20, and picked a bag. When I opened it, I saw a green face staring up at me! I knew we were meant to be.

Erin Chow
Sacramento, CA

DEAR BEANIE WORLD,

Funny, funny … funny! Just read your article in the August issue about the Teenie Beanie McFrenzy. You have truly captured the excitement and hilarity of the event! I'd race out the door yelling, "Courthouse Road has Scoop!" while my family thought I'd lost my mind. Terrific, great fun!

Kathy Houghton
Stafford, VA

DEAR BEANIE WORLD,

We at Endangered Species have received over 200 letters since your August edition featuring our store came out. Thank you for the opportunity to appear in a national magazine, especially in as special a publication as "Mary Beth's Beanie World Monthly" is. I have read every edition cover to cover, including the very first one last year. The only problem is that most of the local stores run out as soon as they come in. Luckily I have a subscription delivered to my home. I wanted to share one of the letters with your readers:

Meg Roeske
Mall of America
Minnesota

Dear Endangered Species:

I would like to request to be put on your "Beanie List." When I read your article in

"Mary Beth's Beanie World Monthly," it was like a breath of fresh air. Here in Wichita, it is such a mess – filled with greed and profit making. You are all truly "Heroes of Business Values!" Regular prices here are non-existent. My daughters and I are looking for the new Beanie "Glory," but it sells for more than regular price and is doled out in small numbers. Working moms, working grandmothers and working aunts usually miss out – the children, too.

What a genius, to combine caring volunteers and the caring concern for your customers – all of you are on God's team. You will always profit and be in business as you live by the Golden Rule. You treat others first like you want to be treated. I wish there would be more stores like yours everywhere. I am writing Ty Inc. to tell them about you. I am sure Ty Inc. is heartbroken in how this craze has been handled.

Sincerely, a grandmother,
Donna Siniard
Wichita, KS

Turn the page for Reader Poetry – a "Reader Mail Extra" for our first anniversary issue!

Also, for correspondence sent to us by youngsters around the world, see our Kids' Mail page in the "Mary Beth's Beanie World For Kids" section of every issue!

WRITE TO US

We welcome your mail. Please send your correspondence to: "Reader Mail," c/o "Mary Beth's Beanie World Monthly," P.O. Box 551, Mt. Prospect, IL 60056-0551. Make sure to include your full name, postal address, e-mail address (if any) and daytime phone number with your correspondence. Address and phone information are for office use only and will not be published. We regret that letters cannot be answered personally.

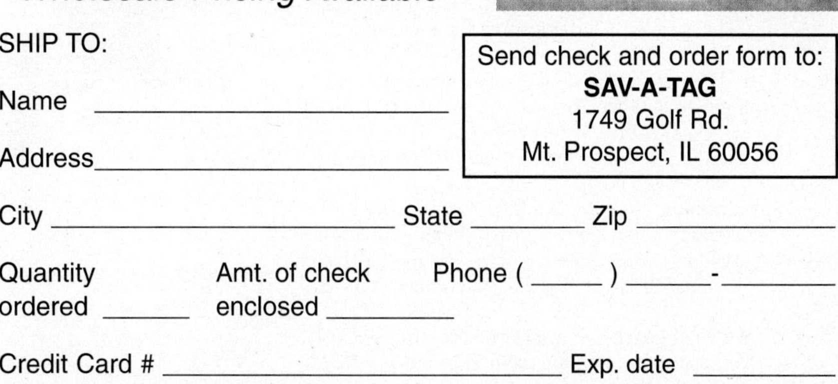

Reader Mail Extra! Extra! Extra!

As a special bonus in our first anniversary issue, we've decided to supplement our regular Reader Mail section with several original poems submitted from readers of all ages. Enjoy!

THE TEENIE BEANIE SEARCH

McDonald's Teenie Beanie Babies have all come and gone.
They didn't hang around for very long.
Getting Inch
was really a cinch.
But, it was quite a trip,
to get a hold of Zip.
I must have put 50 miles on the car,
though I didn't go very far.
Several times through McDonald's loop,
it took to come up with Scoop.
Doby got me all nervous and uptight.
I didn't sleep a wink all night.
When I got a hold of Mel,
it sure did feel swell.
Peanut, Waddle and Bones
now have happy homes.
My husband is sick of burgers and fries,
not to mention chicken McNuggets and apple pies.
But I made him eat some more,
because I still had to get the other four.
I now have Bongo, Twigs, Pinchers and Happy,
The family thinks I'm very "quacky."
I now have gotten them all.
I must admit I had a ball!

Earleen Crowson
Louisville, MS

SCOOP

HIPPITY

BEANIE PEOPLE

Gracing the shelves of shops and boutiques,
those cute little creatures, so quaint and unique.
They arrive quietly with no hint, with no clue,
of the impending chaos that's starting to brew.

"UPS!" yells a woman with hair of silken gray,
whose Cadillac is out back, hiding in the alleyway.
Taking out her binoculars, hands shaking, eyes dart:
"Yippee! It's the box with a big, red TY heart!"

Across town, a young mother is preparing to dine
with her beautiful children, ages two, five and nine.
Then her phone rings, "Hello, Sue? This is Kay.
The store on 82nd got some Beanies today!"

Back at the gift shop the workers prepare.
Says one to another, "Something strange is in the air."
Outside tires squeal and come to a halt,
eyes widen with fright – it's a Beanie Assault!

They swarm in through the entrance, two by two, four by four,
Knocking down shelves, trinkets fall to the floor.
"Calm down, everyone! Can't you be more discreet?
Sir – you with the tie, there's a kid under your feet!"

"We want Peace, we want Princess, Erin or Curly.
You had to have gotten them in by now, surely."
"We don't have them in yet, but they should be here soon.
Check back in a week – Thursday or Friday by noon."

The crowd starts to thin, the workers at ease
"Serenity now," says one quietly, "Please."

The last customer exits, following the mob
his arms full of Beanies, a big guy named Bob.

Erin Whitehouse
Oklahoma City, OK

MY TYS

I collect Beanies, I love each and every one,
I hope that I have hundreds before I am done.

When I first saw Fleece, he melted my heart
I got Blackie, Bones and Bongo – that was only a start.

Then Chocolate, Chip and Congo, I found in a store
then my Mom shocked my by saying, "C'mon, let's get more!"

We were Beanie hunting now and I think we're all hooked,
'cause I saw my Mother hugging little Nanook.

We got Digger, Daisy, Derby and Doodle too,
Beanie Babies everywhere – what shall we do?

We're up to 60 Beanies now, I think we should stop
that's of course until we find another Beanie Baby shop.

We bought Floppity, Freckles, Flip and Gobbles was cute,
Then Happy, Hippity, Hissy and the little owl Hoot.

We found Legs, Lizzy, Lucky and Batty the bat,
Nuts, Nip, Pinky and Prance the cat.

We're up to 100 Beanies now – we can't buy anymore,
because there are Beanies in closets and all over the floor!

There are Beanies in my pockets and Beanies in my bed,
thank goodness they're not real animals, 'cause they'd need to be fed.

My Mom shouts, "It's enough, we're done, that's all!"
But I know we'll buy more Beanies when we go to the mall.

We're addicted to Ty Beanies, hope they never find a cure,
because we love them all so much and we'll always need more!

Aliza Tucker, Age 11
West Orange, NJ

LIZZY

B-E-A-N-I-E-S

B est things ever invented
E xcellent family fun
A mazing values for each and every one
N othing can stop the fans now
I love those Beanies!
E veryone does
S topping the craze now is impossible – it can't be done!

Suzy Mazur, Age 13
Jacksonville, FL

Reader Scrapbook

TO CELEBRATE OUR FIRST ANNIVERSARY, WE AT "MARY BETH'S BEANIE WORLD MONTHLY" ARE PROUD TO SHOWCASE IN THIS READER SCRAPBOOK THE "OTHER" ANIMALS IN OUR LIVES – OUR WONDERFUL PETS!

It looks like "Meeco" Dodge of Spring Hill, FL, has found just the right spot!

Haley Hunsaker's 8-week-old "Penny" loves to snuggle with her Beanies.

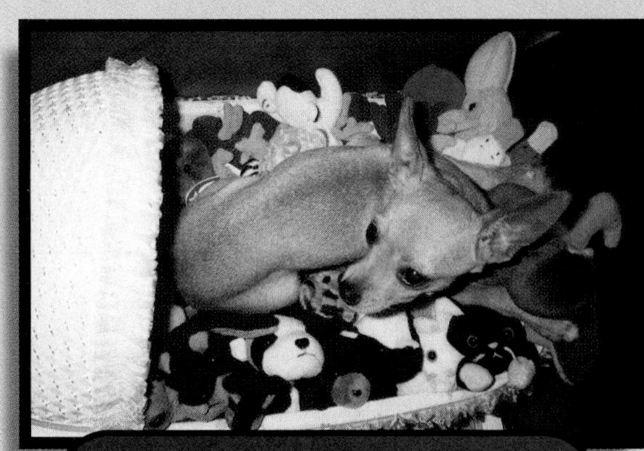

"Lilly" Pollan of Mission Viejo, CA, laments, "C'mon guys, move over a little, would ya?"

Copter the bunny, Lucky the kitten, Needles the hedgehog and Cortney the dog all curl up for an afternoon nap in Zion, IL.

"Hey! It looks just like ME!" thinks "Sydney" Edwards of Palmerstown, Ontario.

This 1997 Christmas portrait features 2-year-old "Scooter" Ellis with all of his Beanie friends!

Reader Scrapbook

"Trinkit" Rozell of Irving, TX, is one proud Mom!

Cool dudes "Terry" Gilbert and Peace say hello from Santa Ana, CA.

Newborn "Oreo" Shelle looks right at home with his Beanie pup pals in Tecumseh, MI.

Matthew Gruntorad of Dwight, NE, sent this photo of his kittens (from left to right): Bobby, Gregg, Peter, Cindy, Jan and Marcia. Their last name should be "Brady," don't you think?!

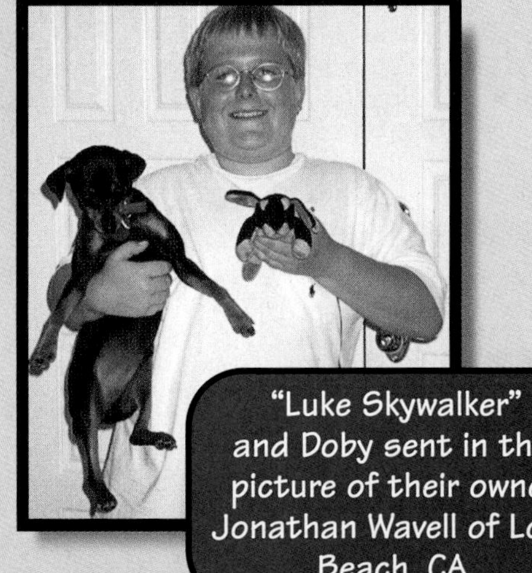

"Luke Skywalker" and Doby sent in this picture of their owner, Jonathan Wavell of Long Beach, CA.

Waiting for treats are "Buffy" Raines and sidekick Spunky of Orange Park, FL.

"Buddy" Hackey from Lake Elmo, MN, proves that Beanies are definitely not just for humans!

We welcome your original pictures. Photos previously submitted to another publication will not be considered. Please send your photos to: "Reader Scrapbook," c/o "Mary Beth's Beanie World Monthly," P.O. Box 551, Mt. Prospect, IL 60056-0551. Make sure to include your full name, postal address, e-mail address (if any) and daytime phone number on the back of each picture. Address and phone information are for office use only and will not be published. We regret that photos cannot be returned.

Mary Beth's Beanie World™ Monthly

www.beanieworld.net

Time Capsule

The first anniversary of "Mary Beth's Beanie World" came very quickly for most of us at the magazine. The premiere issue – all 72 pages of it – was released amid little fanfare in October 1997. Under the expert guidance of Mary Beth Sobolewski, the issue was produced with the help of a few freelance writers and an outside graphics firm that did the layout and design. The issue sold very well, but no one expected that this project would evolve into the massive undertaking it has become.

"Mary Beth's Beanie World" now publishes monthly, with more than 1 million copies of each issue circulating in the United States, Canada and the United Kingdom. A constantly growing production staff generates each issue out of a small office outside Chicago with Mary Beth's oversight and the invaluable help of several excellent staff writers. Every issue has more than 200 pages, including an updated buyer's guide and pullout posters. On this and the following two foldout pages, you can see the front covers from all of our previous issues and get a sense of how we've grown from our humble beginnings. Thanks to you, our readers, "Beanie World" has been a tremendous success!

The First Edition!
This 72-page issue, released in October 1997, started in all, with features on how Beanie Baby collecting got its start and our first buyer's guide.

Special Edition!
This 1998 Buyer's Guide was a huge hit – so much so that we decided to incorporate a comprehensive buyer's guide in every regular issue.

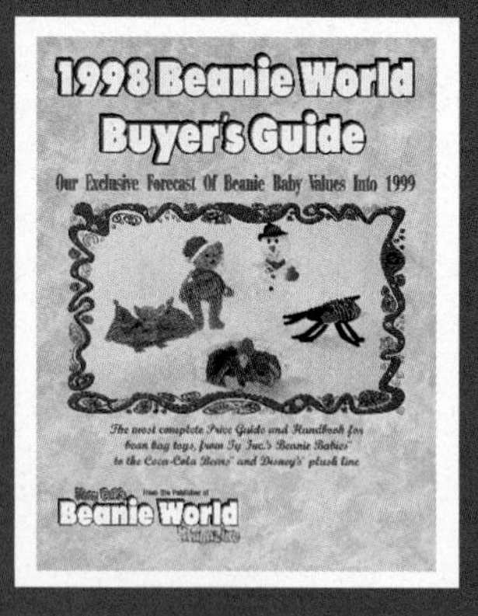

Vol. 1 No. 3
The Princess bear jumped off the cover of our third issue, which had grown to 96 pages and included a pullout poster for the first time.

Vol. 1 No. 2
This holiday-themed issue included new sections on other companies' bean bag toys, Beanie Web sites and letters from readers.

Vol. 1 No. 4
This issue featured another "Beanie World" first – different covers for the United States, Canada and the United Kingdom. The cover image was the same, but each cover had slightly different tag lines.

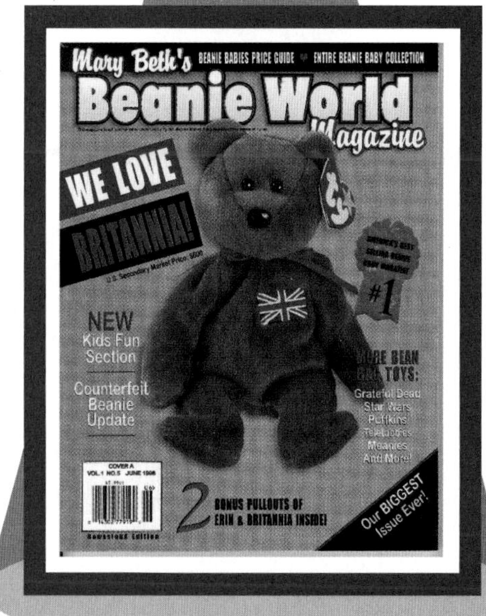

Vol. 1 No. 5
The June 1998
collectible cove
Britannia (left),
Maple the Cana
(above). At 16
far our biggest

Vol. 1 No. 6
"Beanie World" goes monthly! The August 1998 issue was our first with more than 200 pages (224 to be exact) and a foldout front cover.

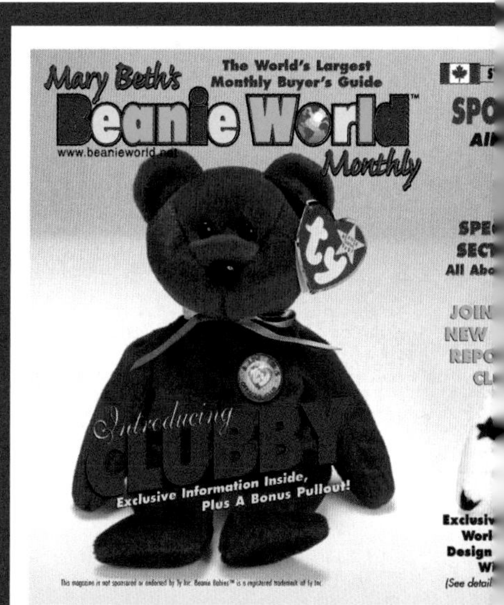

Vol. 1 No. 7
Some trivia for collectors: The Sep
World Monthly" originally had a fo
sports theme. The quick release o
us to change that at the last minut
image ultimately was used inside t
reverse side of not one but both c

ssue had three
's featuring
Erin (right) and
dian teddy
pages, it was by
ssue to date.

Special Edition!
This 32-page special issue was timed to coincide with the May 1998 McDonald's Teenie Beanie Babies promotion in the U.S. It proved to be a quick seller among collectors.

Vol. 2, No. 1
The October 1998 "Anniversary Issue" is our biggest yet – with 248 body pages and four pullouts! We're all looking forward to another exciting year!

tember issue of "Beanie
ldout front cover with a
Clubby, however, forced
e. The original cover
ne magazine on the
f the pullout posters!

AP/Wide World Photo

Mae Whitman with "Hope Floats" co-stars Sandra Bullock and Harry Connick Jr.

Collector Spotlight

A MERRY GIRL NAMED MAE

Actress Mae Whitman proves that Beanies and Hollywood do mix

A "Beanie World" EXCLUSIVE by Mary Beth Sobolewski

SHE is your typical 10-year-old with a beguiling smile and long brown hair who loves to frolic with her dog Lenore, swim and play with her friends. A lover of stuffed animals, her extensive collection of 85 Beanie Babies is a source of great pride for her as they sit carefully placed on shelves in her girlish bedroom. "I keep them in my room on shelves in case I want to play with them," she explains. Her favorite Beanie? "Well, I like Libearty a lot … and Manny, too." A smile comes to her sweet face as she prepares to tell the story of how Manny came into her life.

"Well, I like Libearty a lot … and Manny, too."

This is where everything "typical" ends. After all, this is not just any 10 year old. This is Mae Whitman, a seven-year veteran in the entertainment industry and star of screen and television. And who gave Mae her Manny? "Well, it was my 10th birthday (June 9) and I was (continued on page 52)

Mae Whitman with some of her Beanies

Mae Whitman photographed exclusively for "Beanie World" by Celia Colton Photography

Collector Spotlight

Mae Whitman

(a guest) on'The Rosie O'Donnell Show' and she gave him to me because she knew I wanted him." But the gift giving was not one sided. Rosie, a well-known collector of McDonald's Happy Meal toys, was apparently missing an important one in her collection. "I gave her Pegasus from Disney because it was the one she didn't have."

Mae enjoys going to movies and hanging out with her friends. Her favorite movie is "To Kill a Mockingbird."

Yes, Mae has enchanted the likes of Rosie O'Donnell, David Letterman and Jay Leno. Part of her irresistible charm comes from her ability to ask as many questions of her interviewer as they ask of her. Animated with a sparkling personality, she captures the hearts of young and old alike. It is very easy to forget that with all her poise and maturity, she is really still a kid who loves to roller skate and horseback ride.

Mae enjoys going to movies and hanging out with her friends. Her favorite movie is "To Kill a Mockingbird." She has never seen the smash hit "Titanic," though. "It focuses on just two people," she explains. "I feel bad for all the other people who died, too."

Starring in her first commercial – for Tyson's chicken – at age 3, Mae began her "big screen" career shortly thereafter when she was cast opposite Andy Garcia and Meg Ryan in the 1994 motion picture "When A Man Loves A Woman." She played Matthew Modine's daughter in "Bye Bye Love" and later Bill Pullman's daughter in the colossal 1996 summer hit "Independence Day." More recently, she has been seen in the romantic comedy "One Fine Day" with George Clooney and Michelle Pfeiffer and in "The Gingerbread Man," a Robert Altman thriller based on the book by John Grisham.

Mae was able to work with one of her favorite actresses, Sandra Bullock, along with Harry Connick Jr. and Gena Rowlands in "Hope Floats," a major summer 1998 release. In a June 1998 interview with People Magazine, Sandra Bullock says of Mae, "She's frighteningly gifted. What she does now blows most adults away."

If her movie career doesn't keep her busy enough, Mae's television roles fill in the gaps. She has guest starred as a Girl Scout on "Friends" and is a regular on CBS's critically acclaimed "Chicago Hope" as Dr. Kate Austin's (Christine Lahti's) daughter. She has also acted in three major TV movies. She played young Ashley Judd in "The Judds," co-starred in"Degree of Guilt" and appeared with Meredith Baxter in "After Jimmy."

With all of these great opportunities, one can only assume that her future college tuition has been paid for many times over. All of her earnings are placed in a trust fund and managed by her parents. Mae herself is distanced from the financial aspects of the business.

All of this places great demands on the fifth-grader's time. When she is unable to attend her private school, Mae is tutored three hours a day on the set. Acting "is fun of course," says Mae. "If I didn't like it, I wouldn't do it." On most sets, both her mom Pat Musick (a voice-over artist) and her dad Jeff (a set carpenter) arrange their schedules to accompany Mae. They take an active role in helping her to choose scripts wisely. In a recent interview, her father says, "It's really a luxury to be able *(continued on page 54)*

HOW TO SPOT REAL

High Quality Material - Lean, Mean and Full Of Beans!

Face Detail- Patented Meanies™ brow to convey Bad Attitude!

Painful Attention to Details - From Lucky's Bandage to Bessie's Milk Mustache, we're MAD for the details! It took a lot of research to "Char" Burny properly!

Hang Tags - Made of a high quality space-age paper, each hangtag contains a 100% authentic poem.

Collectibility - You can always come out of retirement. When you're TERMINATED, that's it !

Tongue Detail- Each Meanies™ tongue is planted firmly in its cheek!

To See More Real Meanies™, including the Infamous Meanies™, Visit Our Website @

WWW.MEANIES.COM

ATTENTION RETAILERS

TO PLACE AN ORDER, PLEASE CALL US AT:

1-800-683-7625

We make fun!

the idea factory 1350 Broadway, 24th Floor New York, NY 10018 Tel 212-564-7430 Fax 212-239-0480

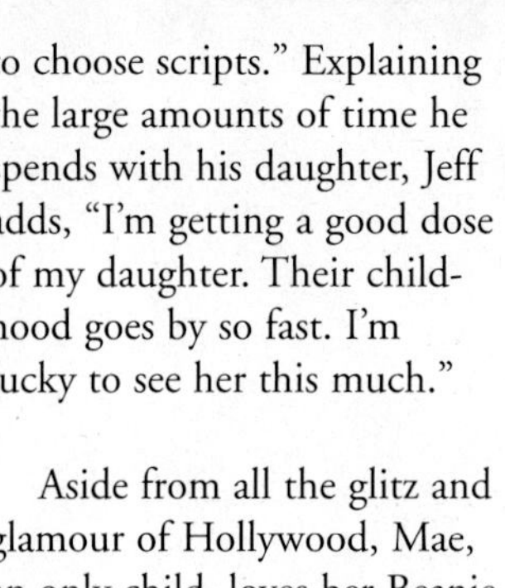

to choose scripts." Explaining the large amounts of time he spends with his daughter, Jeff adds, "I'm getting a good dose of my daughter. Their childhood goes by so fast. I'm lucky to see her this much."

Aside from all the glitz and glamour of Hollywood, Mae, an only child, loves her Beanie Babies.

Lizzy the blue lizard was the first Beanie Baby to make his home with Mae. Filming a scene for "One Fine Day" at an ice cream parlor in New York, Mae just happened to notice that there were Beanie Babies for sale there. Choosing Lizzy from the bunch, she cut off his swing tag (who knew back then?) and brought him back to Los Angeles, where she discovered that most of her friends were becoming Beanie collectors, too. Most of the Beanie Babies in her collection today were gifts throughout the last couple of years. Erin the emerald green bear was given to Mae by an interviewer, and Glory (along with the 1998 All-Star Game commemorative card) was a gift from a friend's mother who attended the baseball game and knew that Mae would love it for her collection. Other favorites include Fortune, Blizzard, Snowball and 1997 Teddy. She has been known to take along a special Beanie on the set of her current production to keep her company between takes.

Mae's wish list? Britannia, Lefty, Waddle ... and an Academy Award someday. The Academy Award seems to be a no-brainer for this budding actress. Britannia, however, may be harder to come by! Good luck, Mae! ❤

Meet the Attic treasures

By Peggy Gallagher and Paula Abrinko

Attic Treasures, part of Ty's Collectibles line, are jointed plush animals that range in height from 6 to 19 inches. The antique-style collection includes animals such as bears, rabbits, hippos, frogs, cats, monkeys, chicks, lions, mice, dogs, lambs, pigs and cows. These cute and cuddly treasures have individual names and facial features and are irresistible to collectors, especially those who are young at heart.

The Attic Treasures first appeared in Ty Inc.'s 1993 catalog. The original collection included 11 creatures from 6 to 12 inches in size. The original Attics, with style numbers in parentheses, were Clifford (6003), Dexter (6009), Fraser (6010), Gilbert (6006), Henry Gold (6005), Reggie (6004), Tyler (6002), Woolie Brown (6012), Woolie Gold (6011), Jeremy (6008) and Sara (6007). All were bears except for the last two, Jeremy and Sara, which were rabbits.

These Attic Treasures came with names and details that created a "personality" for each. Later, the addition of apparel and bows made the Attic characters even more unique.

In addition, Ty changed the name of Attic Treasures to Ty Collectibles in 1995, but the more descriptive name for these animals was restored in 1998, increasing the collectibles' appeal.

The Attic Treasures family grew by nine in the 1994 Ty Catalog. The unique additions to the line were Digby (6013), Emily (6016), Morgan (6018), Nicholas (6015), Nola (6014), Pouncer (6011), Squeaky (6017), Tiny Tim (6001) and Whiskers (6012). These releases introduced cats, a mouse and a monkey to the Attic line.

The 1995 Ty Catalog introduced 20 new Attic Treasures (which in that year began going by the "Ty Collectibles" name). The expanding family included Grover, which at 16 inches was the tallest animal to date. The complete list of additions included Abby (6027), Benjamin (6023), Brewster (6034), Cassie (6028), Checkers (6031), Cody (6030), Grover (6050), Ivan (6029), Lilly (6037), Madison (6035), Malcolm (6026), Mason (6020), Murphy (6033), Oscar (6025), Penelope (6036), Purrcy (6022), Rebecca (6019), Scooter (6032), Shelby (6024) and Wee Willie (6021). Among the new animals represented in 1995 were a dog and a pig.

In 1996, the "family cycle" turned over and produced some second generation counterparts to the original treasures. Some of the new generation Attics were larger in size and wore bows and clothing (as opposed to their "naked" predecessors. Appearing in the 1996 Ty Catalog were Boris (6041), Carlton (6064), Charles (6039), Clyde (6040), Colby (6043), Copperfield (6060), Domino (6042), Ebony (6063), Heather (6061), Ivory (6062), Justin (6044), King (6049), Prince (6048), Priscilla (6045), Tracy (6047), Watson (6065). For the first time, an Attic frog appeared in the catalog.

In 1997, some of the new Attics featured "posh" clothing, but some "old timers" were steadfast and remained as "naked" as their ancestors had been. They were Cody, Ivan, Prince Squeaky. The appearances in this catalog included Chelsea (6070), Christopher (6071), and Frederick (6072).

Finally, 1998 proved to be a great year for this family of collectibles, as Ty Inc. restored the Attic Treasures name. Ivory reappeared in this catalog, but with the new name Amethyst. The new appearances in this catalog were Amethyst (6131), Bearington (6102), Bloom (6122), Bluebeary (6080), Bonnie (6075), Casanova (6073), Grace (6142), Grant (6101), Iris (6077), Ivy (6076), Montgomery (6143), Peppermint (6074), Precious (6104), Rose (6078), Scotch (6103), Scruffy (6085), Sidney (6121), Sire (6141) and Strawbunny (6079). Newly represented animals were the moose, hippo and lion.

This introduction to the Attic Treasures line from Ty is simply that. If you continue collecting these precious animals, it's likely you'll find variations that are not mentioned here. Finding these unique animals is clearly a big part of the fun of collecting!

In addition to the complete lineup of Attic Treasures shown on the following pages, you can find a complete secondary market price guide for Attics beginning on page 161. You can also find photos and descriptions of Attic swing tag generations in the buyer's guide section.

Peggy Gallagher and Paula Abrinko are considered among the world's experts in the area of Ty Plush, Attic Treasures and Pillow Pals. Visit their Web site at www.beaniephenomenon.com.

Abby 8" Teddy Bear
Status: Retired
Abby can be found with only a burgundy ribbon and with clothes. Abby is a smaller version of Cassie.

Amethyst 13"Cat
Status: Retired
Amethyst is a smaller version of Ivory.

Barry 11" Teddy Bear
Status: Retired
Barry never appeared in a Ty catalog. He appeared in a mid-1997 flier, and was retired for the 1998 catalog.

Bearington 14" Teddy Bear
Status: Current
Bearington has a large plaid fabric ribbon. He is a new release as of January 1998.

Benjamin 9" Rabbit
Status: Retired
Benjamin originally wore a pink ribbon, then sported a sweater beginning in the spring of 1996.

Bloom 16" Rabbit
Status: Retired
Bloom is available only with the second type of fourth generation swing tag.

Bluebeary 8" Teddy Bear
Status: Current
Bluebeary's color is not very common among Attic Treasures, and he is very difficult to find.

Bonnie 9" Chick

Status: Current

Bonnie, a hot seller, is a bright yellow chick with a blue gingham bonnet.

Boris 12" Teddy Bear

Status: Retired

Boris is a pot bellied bear that looks almost identical to Charles and Clyde. The only difference is their color.

Brewster 12" Dog

Status: Retired

Brewster looks just like Scooter and Murphy except for the color. He can be found without clothes or with a sweater and coveralls.

Carlton 16" Teddy Bear

Status: Retired

Carlton, a bigger version of Dexter, has nappy fabric like Bluebeary.

Casanova 8" Teddy Bear

Status: Current

Casanova looks like Henry Brown except he is wearing a white sweater with a red heart.

Cassie 8" Teddy Bear

Status: Retired

Cassie, released in 1995, was retired in 1997 and is very difficult to find. A few tags have been found with "Gassie" instead of the correct name.

Charles 12" Teddy Bear

Status: Retired

Charles is the larger version of Dickens. He is a pot bellied bear and can be found wearing buttoned coveralls. His buttons eventually were discontinued.

Checkers 8" Panda

Status: Current

Checkers was introduced in 1995. He originally wore a sweater, but his 1998 catalog appearance shows him without it.

Chelsea 8" Teddy Bear

Status: Current

Chelsea was made available in 1997 and wears a sweater.

Christopher 8" Teddy Bear
Status: Retired
Christopher, released in 1997, is identical to Chelsea except for the fabric color.

Clifford Burgundy Ribbon 12" Teddy Bear
Status: Retired
Clifford with a hump, one of the original Attics, first appeared in the 1993 Ty catalog.

Clifford Green Ribbon 12" Teddy Bear
Status: Retired
Clyde is similar to Boris and Charles. He originally had no clothes, but he eventually acquired a sweater vest.

Clyde 12" Teddy Bear
Status: Retired
Clyde is similar to Boris and Charles. He originally had no clothes, but he eventually acquired a sweater vest.

Cody 8" Teddy Bear
Status: Current
Cody is the smaller version of Clyde.

Colby 11" Mouse
Status: Retired
Colby is the larger version of Squeaky.

Copperfield 16" Teddy Bear
Status: Retired
Copperfield originally sported a brown satin ribbon. He then acquired a blue-and-white sweater.

𝒟exter 9" Teddy Bear

Status: Retired

Dexter was darker when he first appeared with his first generation tag. He later appeared lighter in color and acquired white-and-burgundy-pinstriped coveralls.

𝒟ickens 8" Teddy Bear

Status: Retired

Dickens has the same style as Cody and Ivan, but the color is different.

𝒟igby 12" Teddy Bear

Status: Retired

Digby originally appeared with the hump on his back, but that was changed shortly after its release.

Domino 12" Panda

Status: Retired

Domino, the larger version of Checkers, was released in 1990 and retired in 1997.

Ebony 15" Cat

Status: Retired

Ebony was originally introduced with clothes. He is available with the first style of fourth generation swing tags.

Ebony 13" Cat

Status: Retired

Ebony in the smaller version comes with only the second type of fourth generation swing tag.

Emily Hat and Dress 12" Teddy Bear

Status: Retired

Emily with dress and hat, retired in 1997, is the second version of this Attic Treasure.

Emily Head Bow 12" Teddy Bear

Status: Retired

Emily with head bow is the first version of this Attic Treasure.

(Emily without Head Bow is not picuted)

Eve 12" Teddy Bear

Status: Current

Eve, a spring 1998 release, wears a cape and has a flower halo.

Fraser 8" Teddy Bear

Status: Retired

Fraser is an original Attic Treasure released in 1993. The first version has the very rare white sewn-in tag with red lettering and the artist's signature.

Frederick 8" Teddy Bear

Status: Retired

Frederick was released and retired in 1997 and is very hard to find.

Gilbert Gold 8" Teddy Bear

Status: Retired

Gilbert Gold looks similar to Nicholas and Henry except for the color.

Meet the Attic treasures

Gilbert White 8" Teddy Bear

Status: Retired

Gilbert White is actually Nicholas with a swing tag error. He is extremely rare.

Gloria 12" Rabbit

Status: Retired

Gloria, a spring 1998 release, wears a patriotic jumpsuit.

Grace 12" Hippo

Status: Current

Grace is an adorable hippo dressed as a ballerina.

Grady 16" Teddy Bear

Status: Retired

Grady is actually the same as Grover Gold.

Grant 13" Teddy Bear

Status: Current

Grant is a January 1998 release wearing an American flag sweater.

Grover 16" Teddy Bear

Status: Retired

Grover later appeared with clothes. The earlier releases came with only a green ribbon

Grover 13" Teddy Bear

Status: Retired

Grover was released in 1998 with coveralls.

*G*rover Gold
16" Teddy Bear
Status: Retired

*H*eather 20" Rabbit
Status: Retired
Heather first appeared with a burgundy ribbon.

*H*enry Gold 8" Teddy Bear
Status: Retired
Henry Gold is gold version of Henry Brown.

*H*enry Brown 8" Teddy Bear
Status: Retired
Henry Brown was retired in 1997.

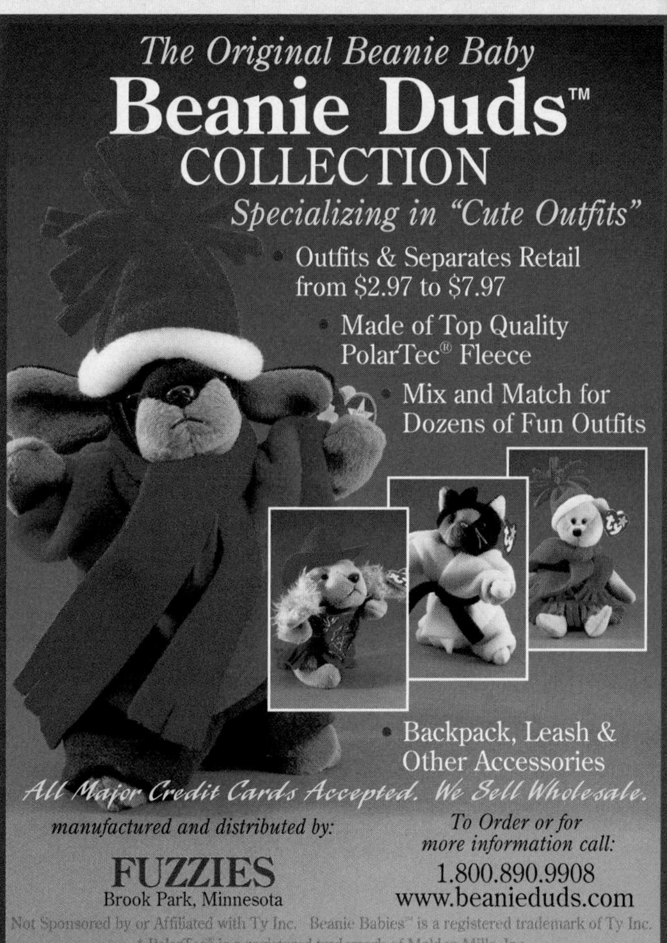

*I*ris 10" Rabbit
Status: Current
Iris was introduced in 1998 wearing a lavender jumpsuit. She looks like Ivy, Shelby and Rose except for color and clothes.

*I*van 8" Teddy Bear
Status: Current
Ivan, introduced in 1995, is similar in style to pot bellied Boris.

*I*vory 15" Cat
Status: Current
Ivory is similar in style to Ebony.

*I*vy 10" Rabbit
Status: Current
Ivy is similar to Iris, Rose and Shelby.

*J*eremy 12" Rabbit
Status: Retired
Jeremy is one of the original Attic Treasures.

*J*ustin14" Monkey
Status: Retired
Justin is a bigger version of Morgan, and he acquired a green sweater in 1996.

*K*ing 11" Frog
Status: Retired
King is a larger version of the two Kings. He has always worn a cape.

*K*ing 9" Frog

Status: Retired

King is a smaller frog introduced in 1996 with no cape. He acquired a cape in the 1997 Ty catalog.

*L*illy 9" Lamb

Status: Retired

Lilly was first seen without clothes, but she acquired her jumpsuit in 1996.

*M*adison 10" Cow

Status: Retired

Madison can be found with all tag types except for the first generation.

Malcolm 12" Teddy Bear

Status: Retired

Malcolm, first seen in the 1995 catalog, is similar to Cassie except for fabric color.

Mason 8" Teddy Bear

Status: Retired

Mason is the larger version of Oscar. He acquired a green striped sweater in mid-1996.

Montgomery 15" Moose

Status: Current

Montgomery was introduced in 1998 wearing his khaki vest with pockets.

Morgan 8" Monkey

Status: Retired

Morgan is a smaller monkey. He originally appeared with a ribbon and later got a lamb's wool vest.

Murphy 9" Dog

Status: Retired

Murphy looks like Brewster and Scooter.

Nicholas 8" Teddy Bear

Status: Retired

Nicholas was first seen in the 1994 Ty catalog without his sweater. He reappeared wearing a red sweater in the 1996 catalog.

Nola No Head Bow 12" Teddy Bear

Status: Retired

Nola was introduced in 1994 with her pink ribbon around her neck. This version is the most difficult to acquire.

Nola Head Bow 12" Teddy Bear

Status: Retired

Nola acquired her floral head bow in the 1995 and 1996 catalogs.

Nola Hat and Dress 12" Teddy Bear

Status: Retired

Nola in its most recent version acquired a jumpsuit.

Oscar 12" Teddy Bear
Status: Retired
Oscar is a small version of Malcolm.

Penelope 9" Pig
Status: Retired
Penelope was first seen without clothes in the 1995 catalog. She obtained her clothes in the mid-1996 Ty flier.

Peppermint 8" Teddy Bear
Status: Current
Peppermint was introduced in the 1998 Ty catalog.

Piccadilly 9" Teddy Bear
Status: Current
Piccadilly is the new colorful bear with the red nose. The current tag calls him "sm. bear."

Pouncer 8" Cat
Status: Retired
Pouncer was first introduced in 1994. He has no white on his face.

Pouncer 8" Cat
Status: Current
Pouncer in this later version acquired white on the face and tip of tail. He is also wearing a sweater.

Precious 12" Teddy Bear
Status: Current
Precious is a unique Attic Treasure introduced in the 1998 catalog.

Prince 7" Frog
Status: Current
Prince, similar to King, has no cape and is the smallest version of the frogs.

Priscilla 12" Pig
Status: Retired
Priscilla is a larger version of Penelope.

Meet the Attic treasures

Purrcy 8" Cat

Status: Current

Purrcy, introduced in 1995 catalog, was released with two different colored ears.

Rebecca 12" Teddy Bear

Status: Retired

Rebecca first appeared in the 1995 catalog. (Rebecca with floral bow not pictured)

Reggie Red Ribbon 8" Teddy Bear

Status: Retired

Reggie with a red ribbon was released in 1993. It has the rarest red ribbon.

Reggie Navy Ribbon 8" Teddy Bear

Status: Retired

Reggie with navy ribbon is another version from Ty. Rumors have circulated about the existence of Reggie with a green ribbon.

Rose 10" Rabbit

Status: Current

Rose looks like Benjamin except for the different clothing.

Samuel 13" Teddy Bear

Status: Current

Samuel is a new patriotic bear wearing striped pants and a hat. The current tag (a mistag) calls him "lg. bear."

Sara 12" Rabbit

Status: Retired

Sara in its original incarnation (1993) was introduced without clothes.

Sara 15" Rabbit
Status: Current
This version of Sara, released later, appeared with clothes.

Scooter 9" Dog
Status: Retired
Scooter is available with a red nose or dark nose. The red-nose version is the rarer of the two.

Scotch 14" Teddy Bear
Status: Retired
Scotch, first seen in the 1998 Ty catalog, is a large bear.

Scruffy 9" Dog
Status: Current

Scruffy, introduced in the 1998 catalog, has no clothes.

Shelby 9" Rabbit
Status: Retired

Shelby, first seen in the 1995 Ty catalog, comes without clothes.

Sidney 15" Rabbit
Status: Retired

Sidney looks like a large Jeremy.

Sire 13" Lion
Status: Current

Sire, introduced in the 1998 catalog, wears a uniform fit for a king!

Spencer 15" Dog
Status: Retired

Spencer, one of the two larger dogs, was released in 1996.

Squeaky Black Nose and Whiskers 8" Mouse
Status: Retired

Squeaky in its original incarnation has a black nose and black whiskers.

Squeaky 8" Mouse
Status: Current

Squeaky released later has a pink nose and a white tail, paws and inner ears.

Strawbunny 10" Rabbit
Status: Current

Strawbunny, introduced in the 1998 catalog, is easily identified by the pink fabric.

Tiny Tim 8" Teddy Bear
Status: Retired

Tiny Tim, first seen in the Ty catalog in 1993, is available with all swing tags except the second version of the fourth generation tag.

Tracy 15" Dog

Status: Retired

Tracey is a larger dog. This Attic Treasures has also changed clothing styles, going from no clothes at all to a pair of coveralls.

Tulip 10" Rabbit

Status: Retired

Tulip is Shelby with clothes. This Attic Treasure appeared in the Ty catalog as Tulip, but never appeared with a Tulip tag.

Tyler 12" Teddy Bear

Status: Retired

Tyler is an old Attic. He originally appeared with a hump back like Clifford. He lost his hump early in his career.

Watson 14" Teddy Bear

Status: Retired

Watson is a larger bear found only with the first version of the fourth generation swing tag.

Wee Willie 8" Teddy Bear

Status: Retired

Wee Willie is same size as Tiny Tim. He is available with second, third and fourth generation (first version only) swing tags.

Whiskers 8" Cat

Status: Retired

Whiskers was first seen in 1994. Later releases included a change of clothes. A few Whiskers have incorrect swing tags naming him Woolie Brown, style number 6012.

Woolie Gold 6" Teddy Bear

Status: Retired

Woolie Gold is a small, 100% wool teddy bear. He is very rare.

Woolie Brown 6" Teddy Bear

Status: Retired

Woolie Brown apparently was a prototype teddy never released for public sale. The prototype is on display at the W.H. Smith Tyrrific store in Chicago's O'Hare Airport.

The Ty PILLOW

BY PEGGY GALLAGHER AND PAULA ABRINKO

In the September issue of "Mary Beth's Beanie World Monthly," we previewed Ty's exciting lineup of Pillow Pals. In this issue, we're happy to give you a complete lineup of Pillow Pals! On this and the next two pages, you'll find photos of each Pillow Pal, along with collector trivia and other basic information. For a complete list of Pillow Pals with median market prices for each, consult the Bean Bag Buyer's Guide in the center of this issue.

BABA THE LAMB #3008

Introduced: January 1997
Status: Current
Collector Trivia: BaBa is "Mom" to Fleece the Beanie Baby.

BRUISER THE BULLDOG #3018

Introduced: September 1997
Status: Current
Collector Trivia: Shortly after his release, the shade of blue on his ribbon was changed. Bruiser is "Dad" to Wrinkles the Beanie Baby.

CARROTS THE PINK RABBIT #3010

Introduced: January 1997
Status: Current
Collector Trivia: Carrots is one of two rabbits in the Pillow Pals line.

CLOVER THE WHITE RABBIT #3020

Introduced: January 1998
Status: Current
Collector Trivia: There was a style change from black eyes to blue eyes in May 1998. Some collectors regard the black-eyed Clover as retired.

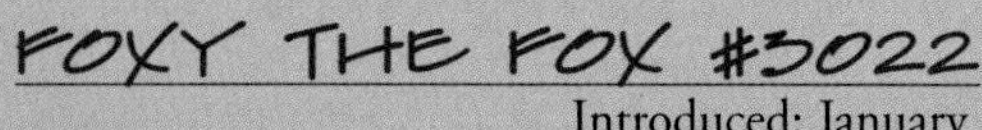

FOXY THE FOX #3022

Introduced: January 1998
Status: Current
Collector Trivia: Foxy is "Dad" to Sly the Beanie Baby.

GLIDE THE DOLPHIN #3025

Introduced: January 1998
Status: Current
Collector Trivia: Glide is "Mom" to Echo the Beanie Baby.

HUGGY THE BLUE BEAR #3002

Introduced: January 1995
Status: Retired January 1, 1998
Collector Trivia: Huggy was first introduced with a blue ribbon tied around his neck. In the fall of 1997, this ribbon's color was changed to pink.

MEOW THE GRAY CAT #3011

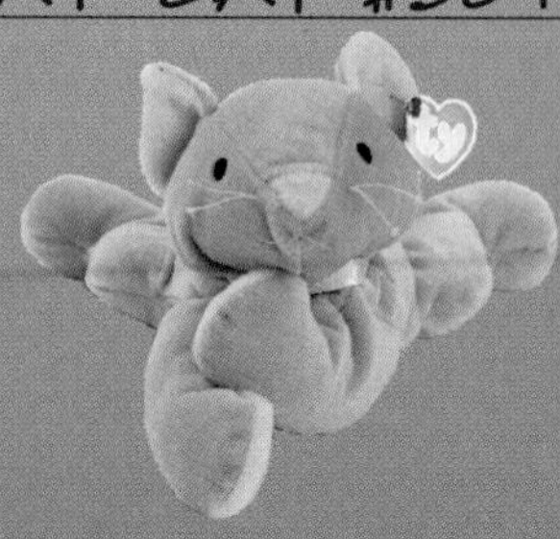

Introduced: January 1997
Status: Retired May 1997
Collector Trivia: This early version of Meow was very drab and almost resembled a mouse more than it did a cat.

PALS Line Up

MEOW THE SIAMESE CAT #3011

Introduced: May 1997
Status: Current
Collector Trivia: This version of Meow is "Mom" to Snip the Beanie Baby.

OINK THE PIG #3005

Introduced: January 1995
Status: Current
Collector Trivia: Oink is "Dad" to Squealer the Beanie Baby

PURR THE TIGER #3016

Introduced: January 1997
Status: Retired May 1, 1998
Collector Trivia: Although there have been two tigers in the Beanie Baby line, Purr has a completely different coloring than either of them.

RIBBIT THE YELLOW AND GREEN FROG #3009

Introduced: January 1997
Status: Current
Collector Trivia: This Pillow Pal replaced the previous all-green frog.

SHERBERT THE TIE-DYED TEDDY BEAR #3027

Introduced: May 30, 1998
Status: Current
Collector Trivia: The tie-dyed fabric used on this Pillow Pal is much more pastel than the fabric used on Ty Beanie Babies.

MOO THE COW #3004

Introduced: January 1995
Status: Current
Collector Trivia: Moo resembles Daisy the Beanie Baby with reversed coloring.

PADDLES THE PLATYPUS #3026

Introduced: May 30, 1998
Status: Current
Collector Trivia: Paddles is "Mom" to Patti the Beanie Baby. There is also a McDonald's Teenie Beanie Baby to match!

RED THE BULL #3021

Introduced: January 1998
Status: Current
Collector Trivia: Red is "Dad" to Tabasco the Beanie Baby.

RIBBIT THE GREEN FROG #3006

Introduced: January 1995
Status: Retired Summer 1996
Collector Trivia: Ribbit is "Dad" to Legs the Beanie Baby.

SNAP THE YELLOW TURTLE #3007

Introduced: January 1995
Status: Retired Summer 1996
Collector Trivia: This version of Snap is the most valuable of all the Pillow Pals. The estimated secondary market value is $400.

The Ty PILLOW PALS Line Up

SNAP THE GREEN AND YELLOW TURTLE #3015

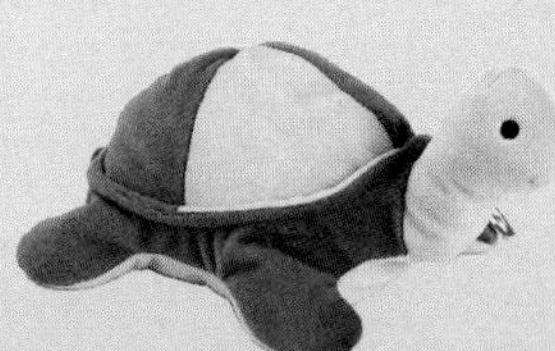

Introduced: January 1997
Status: Retired January 1, 1998
Collector Trivia: Although they do not have the same style numbers, both Pillow Pal turtles have the same name.

SPECKLES THE LEOPARD #3017

Introduced: May 1997
Status: Current
Collector Trivia: Speckles is "Dad" to Freckles the Beanie Baby.

SQUIRT THE ELEPHANT #3013

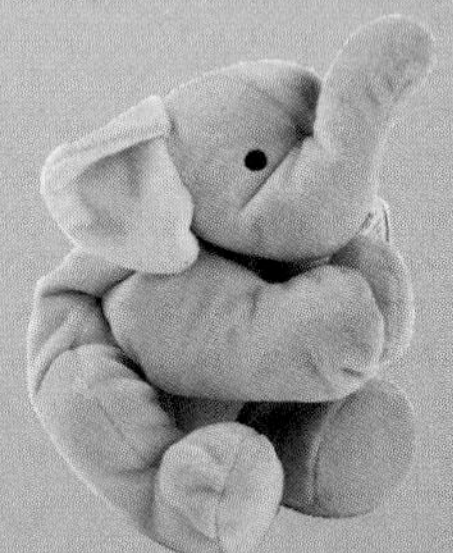

Introduced: January 1997
Status: Current
Collector Trivia: Squirt is "Mom" to Peanut the Beanie Baby. There is also a McDonald's Teenie Beanie Baby to match!

TIDE THE WHALE #3024

Introduced: January 1998
Status: Current
Collector Trivia: Although the Beanie Babies line includes the whales Splash and Waves, Tide does not match either of them.

WOOF THE DOG #3003

Introduced: January 1995
Status: Current
Collector Trivia: Woof is "Dad" to Bones the Beanie Baby.

SNUGGY THE PINK BEAR #3001

Introduced: January 1995
Status: Retired January 1, 1998
Collector Trivia: Snuggy was first introduced with a pink ribbon tied around her neck. In the fall of 1997, this ribbon's color was changed to blue.

SPOTTY THE DALMATIAN #3019

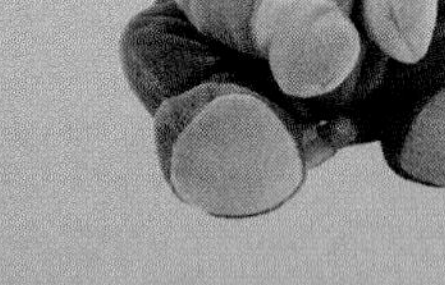

Introduced: January 1998
Status: Current
Collector Trivia: Spotty is "Mom" to Dotty the Beanie Baby. Some "Spotty" tags are misspelled "Sotty."

SWINGER THE MONKEY #3023

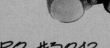

Introduced: January 1998
Status: Current
Collector Trivia: Swinger is "Dad" to Bongo the Beanie Baby. There is also a McDonald's Teenie Beanie Baby to match!

TUBBY THE HIPPO #3012

Introduced: January 1997
Status: Current
Collector Trivia: Tubby is "Dad" to Happy the Beanie Baby. There is also a McDonald's Teenie Beanie Baby to match!

ZULU THE ZEBRA #3014

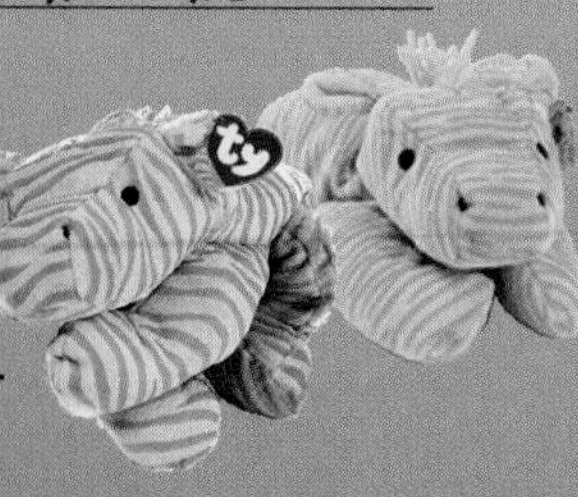

Introduced: January 1997
Status: Retired May 30, 1998
Collector Trivia: Zulu was first introduced with thin stripes. In May of 1997, Zulu's fabric was changed to feature wide stripes.

Beanie MOM'S Story

Sara Nelson, one of the world's best-known Beanie collectors, reflects on how it all began.

I began my Beanie collection quite innocently ... the way most people do. My three girls each received a Beanie Baby as a gift from a special friend in Chicago the "hotbed of Beanie Babies." My girls would play with their new Beanies for hours, and I enjoyed watching all of the creative things they did with them throughout the day.

Once I learned there were more styles available than just Quackers, Coral and Squealer, my "collector mentality" kicked in, and I began searching high and low for other Beanie styles to add to their collection. I didn't realize at that time how difficult it would be to find Beanie Babies. They did not seem to be available in our local stores (in Virginia), so I began to search the Internet for possible sources of Beanie purchases. This was in the early summer of 1996 and there were very few Beanie Web sites established, although I did find a few.

...so I began to search the Internet for possible sources

The rest I can blame on my husband. He encouraged me to begin my own collection separate from the kids. Little did my husband know what a monster he would create. I was able to amass my own first complete collection relatively quickly using the sources I had used to complete my girls' collection.

Around that time, Ty Inc. changed the swing tags on the Beanie Babies to include the star (fourth generation) and I began collecting another set all over again. With the fourth generation swing tags came the opening of the Ty Web site, and that brought a whole new dimension to my collecting ability. Through the Ty Guestbook, I was able to contact women much like myself who had already been collecting Beanies for several years. It was through them that I realized that while I thought I had a complete collection, my search had only just begun. I was introduced to the concept of "retired" Beanie Babies, and my hunt began anew.

Scouring the Ty Guestbook became one of my favorite activities in the fall of 1996. Several times a day I would pull up the Ty Guestbook to see who was selling their retired Beanies and at what prices. Did I really want to pay $25 for a Bumble? How about a gray Happy for $45? These were all decisions I had to make. Which Tank did I really want, the 9-lined or the 7-lined version? Could I still afford the Dino SET for $100? Looking back now, it is amazing how I struggled over these choices.

Soon I moved into the hard stuff ... the really old retireds such as Slither, Humphrey and the colored bears, to name just a few. Dealers were becoming more sophisticated and holding online auctions rather than selling at a set price. All bidding for these auctions occurred via private e-mail. The use of online auction services such as E-bay and Auction Universe did not exist yet in our small Beanie community. I think my best auc- *(continued on page 82)*

Scratch & Win!

Scratch &
Win!
cratch off the card to see what you ve
then go to the nearest participating
that carries the very best in Beanie
ction products and redeem your winning
n for a genuine GiddyUp! Lock-It".*
t no Substitutes!
Face Value 50¢.
LOCK-ITS
The Very Best Beanie Tag Protector
© 1998
Giddy-Up!
While you re there, register to win a complete set of Ty" Beanie Babies* in the Beanie Dream Sweepstakes!
Play Beanie Trivia TAG! Then register to Win on-line at www.beaniedreams.com
Giddy-Up!, Inc. Cubbie Cubes, Lock-Its, TagPro, TushTag, TagBag and NameDrops are registered trademarks of Giddy-Up!, Inc. Ty and Beanie Babies are registered trademarks of Ty, Inc.
Coupon expires 12/31/98

Just scratch off the card to see if you're a winner. Then go to the nearest store that carries the very best in Beanie™ protection products, and redeem your winning coupon for a genuine Giddy-Up! Lock-It™.* Accept no Substitutes! Plus, it's where you'll find entry forms so you can...

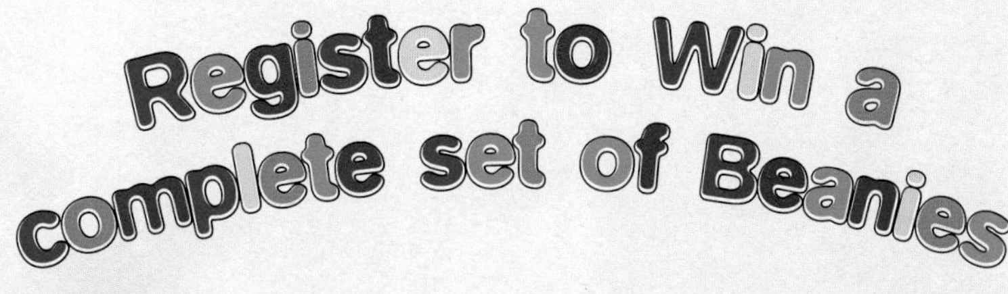

Register to win a complete set of Ty™ Beanie Babies™ or one of hundreds of other prizes with a total value of over **$150,000.00!!**

Grand Prize!	• One Complete Set of Ty™ Beanie Babies™†
1st Prizes	• 10 Sets of retired Beanies, each Set Valued at $1,000
2nd Prizes	• 100 Sets of 100 Cubbie Cubes™ and 100 Lock-Its™
3rd Prizes	• 250 Sets of 100 Lock-Its and 100 TushTags™
4th Prizes	• 500 Sets of 100 TagPros™ and 100 TushTags

Over $150,000 in prizes!

If you don't enter, you can't win, so enter today!

Get Your Entry

when you redeem your winning scratch off coupon wherever Cubbie Cubes™, Lock-Its™, TagPros™, TushTags™, TagBags™ and NameDrops™ are sold!

Call us today for the store nearest you!

1-800-953-6864

Play Beanie Trivia Tag! Then register to Win on-line at www.beaniedreams.com

NO PURCHASE NECESSARY. Complete rules for the Beanie Dream Sweepstakes are available on the official entry form and wherever Cubbie Cubes™, Lock-Its™, TagPros™, TushTags™ and TagBags™ are sold, or on-line at www.beaniedreams.com, or you can send a self-addressed, stamped envelope to: Rules, Beanie Dream Sweepstakes, P.O. Box 8130, Grand Rapids, MN 55745-8130. (Residents of WA and VT may omit return postage when requesting rules or an official form).
*Coupon expires 12/31/98

†Tag Bags™, TushTags™, TagPros™, Lock-Its™, Cubbie Cubes™ and NameDrops™ are registered trademarks of Giddy-Up!, Inc. Patents pending. Beanie Babies is a registered trademark of Ty, Inc.

601 Carlson Parkway, Suite 490
Minnetonka, MN 55305
612-404-6400

tion purchase – although I didn't know it at the time – was the $260 I spent for Tie-Dyed Lizzy and Humphrey COMBINED. I bet the seller wishes she had both of those pieces back to sell again. I was buying only one of each piece, but occasionally purchased duplicates when the deal was right.

I can't tell you how many friends I have made and kept from my early dealings on the Ty Guestbook. We all shared our "Looking For Lists" and would help each other track down affordable Beanie Babies. I remember being able to pay for Beanies in installments; there was no Visa/MasterCard buying back then. If it weren't for the layaway/installment plan, I wouldn't own my Teddy New Face Violet for $350, my All Gold Nip for $400 or my last retired purchase in December 1996 – Royal Blue Peanut for $600.

There was a time not long ago that more people knew me as "Sara" instead of "Beanie Mom."

Beginning with the 1997 New Year's Day retirement, the first on the official Ty Web site, the prices for all retired pieces began to skyrocket. I could no longer afford to pay these higher prices, and my collection remains incomplete, but my fond memories of the "old days" will stay with me forever.

There was a time not long ago that more people knew me as "Sara" instead of "Beanie Mom." Today, I continue to operate my Beanie Web site at http://www.beaniemom.com, and my involvement with "Mary Beth's Beanie World Monthly" has made me even more visible in the Beanie collecting community.

What's next? I'm happy to say that I've been named editor in chief for a new spinoff publication called "Mary Beth's Beanie World For Kids." It's the perfect job for someone known worldwide as "Beanie Mom!" ❤

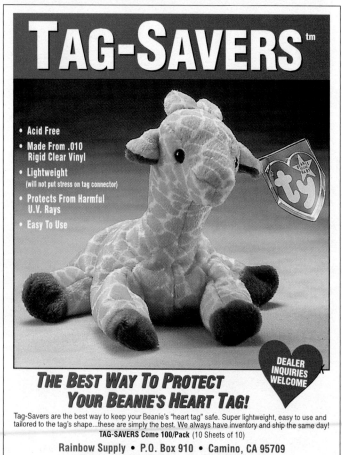

Sara Nelson, also known as "Beanie Mom," is a regular contributor to "Mary Beth's Beanie World Monthly" and is the editor in chief of the new bimonthly magazine "Mary Beth's Beanie World for Kids."

Counterfeit UPDATE

By Claudia Dunne

The special, 16-page supplement to our September issue provided a closer look at counterfeit Beanies in an effort to educate and protect you, the consumer and collector. We will be providing periodic updates as we encounter examples of counterfeit Beanies in the marketplace.

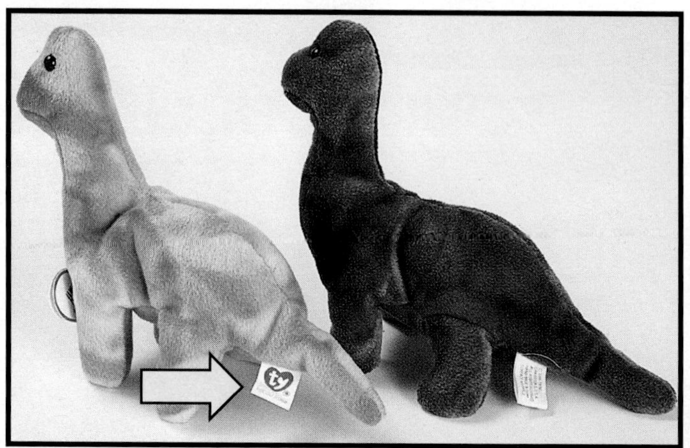

GLORY THE BEAR

In this photo, the counterfeit Glory is on the left, and the authentic Glory is on the right. The fake's eyes are too close together and the nose is brown when it should be black.

On the fake's swing tag, "Original" in the yellow star is scrunched together, the font is wrong for "Original Beanie Baby," and "Independence" in the poem is spelled "Indepentence."

On the fake's tush tag, there is a Chinese stamp on the inside, which is supposed to helping to curb counterfeits. The presence of this stamp on a fake is alarming, but not surprising. The tush tag looks genuine on this one. It's possible that because of "defects" in production (brown nose, eyes too close, etc.), this was thrown in the reject pile, and someone picked it up, put a fake swing tag on it, and went on to sell it as if it were an authentic Beanie.

BRONTY THE BRONTOSAURUS

In the top right hand photo, the counterfeit Bronty is on the left, and the authentic Bronty is on the right. The fake Bronty was sold as a production error/prototype. Note, however, that prototypes will not have tags and they will have swatches of color attached to them.

Other problems with the fake Bronty include: the fabric is the color of Strut's, the eyes are uneven, the head is a bit too small, and the tush tag is red and white. In addition, the swing tag is an orange-red rather than blue-red. The gold looks too bronze, and the font used is incorrect. If this Bronty was going to be sold in Europe, the tag should have had a "CE" on it, which it did not.

"DOCTORED" SNORT THE BULL

This Snort was found in a California flea market and being sold as a "Chicago Bulls Beanie." This is an authentic Snort with authentic tags, but it has been doctored. There is no such things as a "Chicago Bulls Beanie," so buyer beware! Thanks to Felicia Carlucci and Ian Trotter for providing the photos of this doctored Snort.

A TRUE STORY

Many Beanie collectors have the same dream. You find yourself in a small town in the middle of nowhere whose little neighborhood store has a cache of OLD Beanie Babies that no one ever knew about. This was the scenario for a couple of neophyte Beanie Babies collectors. The smalltown store was in Germany, and they thought they had found a hidden treasure when they purchased everything in the top picture, on the next page. As you can see, this was a real find, with Royal Blue Peanut, All Black Zip, Spotless Spot, Peking, Humphrey and Trap, just to name a few.

Q: What is wrong with this picture? A: EVERYTHING!

The man who owned the store told them that he used to work for Ty, and that the Pink Bronty was a production error in the beginning and that it was more rare than Royal Blue Peanut. Since the Beanie Baby craze had not hit Germany yet, he told them he had just been sitting on these and would be willing to sell the whole set for $10 each if they bought them all.

This couple is new to collecting, and the fakes are some of the best around. But the first noticeable problem is the tags. Humphrey, Bronty, Peanut, Zip and Peking should all have black-and-white first generation tush tags, but they don't.

These Beanies should not have red and white tush tags

When looking at a potential purchase that seems too good to be true, look for telltale signs of a fake. Check out the fabric to see if it is too rough or the wrong color. Check the tags – know which should have black and white and which should have red and white tush tags. Check the swing tag to make sure the color is correct, the printing is clear, and the yellow star has a color like sunshine. Remember that misspelled words are not always a sign of a counterfeit Beanie Baby and should never be taken as the ONLY sign that a Beanie is counterfeit. Beanies' tags have been known to come out of the factory with typos. ❤

Claudia Dunne is a staff writer for "Mary Beth's Beanie World Monthly." She is an expert on counterfeit Beanies and other issues of general interest to Beanie collectors.

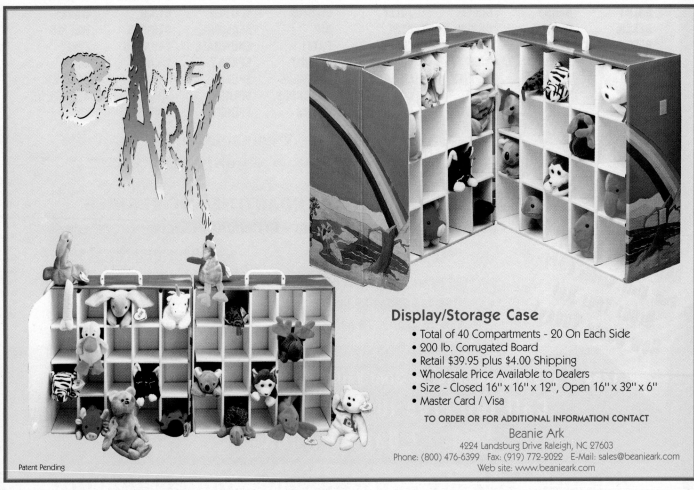

We Carry Limited Treasures!

Authorized Dealer

"Elvis"- the Blue Suede Bear

"Gordon"- the Racing Bear

"Sam"- the All-American Bear

"The Mystery Bear" - call to find out who the Mystery Bear is

Each bear is a limited production

Call Now for Today's Special Price

- Limited production (only 36,000)
- Each hangtag sequentially numbered
- Each hangtag has a hologram to ensure authenticity

Beanie Connection

1268 E. Los Angeles Ave.

Simi Valley, CA 93065

1-888-739-3819 (Toll Free)

Fax: 805-577-8291

E-mail: mark01@unidial.com

Visit our Web site: www.beanieconnection.com

Authorized Dealer

Supplies are limited!

Sports Beanie Promotions

A monthly look at sports teams' Beanie Baby giveaways

Compiled by John Delavan

WNBA: Charlotte Sting vs. Washington Mystics
Friday, July 17, 1998
Giveaway: Bongo the monkey

In the wake of a very successful Beanie Baby giveaway in June, the WNBA's Charlotte Sting decided to hold another Beanie promotion the next month! The first 3,000 youngsters ages 14 and under entering the gates for the Sting's game against the Washington Mystics on July 17, 1998, received an authentic Bongo Beanie Baby and a commemorative card. The Sting went on to thrash the Mystics, 86-56, before a crowd of 7,665 at Charlotte Coliseum.

T.W. Teague poses with the Charlotte Sting's Sharon Manning and Beanie Baby Bongo.

T.W. Teague, who sent a report to "Beanie World" after the Sting's June Beanie giveaway, said the event was run very well. Young fans received a coupon upon entering that could be redeemed inside for the Beanie and commemorative card. Before the game, fans were able to get autographs from Sting players, and T.W. was able to get a photo with of his favorite players, forward Sharon Manning. Thanks, T.W., for sharing your story and photo!

MLB: Tampa Bay Devil Rays vs. Oakland A's
Sunday, July 26, 1998
Giveaway: Weenie the dachshund
Attendance: 37,194 at Tropicana Field

Like any baseball game, there were plenty of hot dogs available at the Tampa Bay Devil Ray's game against Oakland on July 26. On this day, however, the hottest dogs in the park had beans inside them instead of next to them on picnic plates.

Yes, Beanie Baby Day at Tropicana Field featured Weenie the dachshund. The coveted Weenies – plus a commemorative card – were given to the first 15,000 youngsters age 14 and under who entered the gates, which opened at 11:35 a.m., two hours before the game. The fact that Weenie is one of the May 1st retireds made the giveaway even more popular.

Reports said eager collectors lined up as early as 11 p.m. the night before to secure a place in line for the game.

During and after the game, fans reported that they being offered up to $200 each for the Beanie with its commemorative card.

The Weenies were so popular that the Devil Rays reported that they fielded up to 100 telephone calls a day for about six weeks about the giveaway. The team's next Beanie giveaway is planned for August 23, when 10,000 youngsters 14 and under will get a Pinky the flamingo with commemorative card.

MLB: Minnesota Twins vs. Toronto Blue Jays
Friday, July 31, 1998
Giveaway: Lucky the ladybug
Attendance: 26,054 at the Hubert H. Humphrey Metrodome

The crowd gathers for the Minnesota Twins' Beanie giveaway on July 31, 1998.

Jolanta Horzely Urosevich reports that the Twins' game against Toronto on July 31 at the Hubert H. Humphrey Metrodome drew 26,100 fans. Fans started lining up at 11:30 a.m. for the 7 p.m. game, and the park opened as scheduled at 5:30 p.m. Within 45 minutes,10,000 Lucky the ladybug Beanies were distributed through eight gates to fans 14 and under. The "Minnesota nice" crowd was polite and orderly.

Some secondary market entrepreneurs offered $20 just for the commemorative cards, while other collectors sprawled Beanies out on top of trash receptacles inviting trades for Peace, Princess and some new releases. Two days after the game, the commemorative Lucky appeared at flea markets and in secondary market stores for $100 to $150.

Thanks, Jolanta, for your on-the-scene report!

MLB: Oakland A's vs. Cleveland Indians
Saturday, August 1, 1998
Giveaway: Peanut the light blue elephant
Attendance: 48,241 at Oakland Coliseum

Fans began arriving before 6 a.m. to wait in line for the Oakland Athletics' Beanie Baby Day featuring Peanut the light blue elephant. The lines were so long, reports said, that the team opened the gates at 10:40 a.m. – about 20 minutes early – to accommodate the crush.

Roving reporter Erin told us via e-mail that she got there at about 10 a.m. and found herself at the end of what seemed like an enormous line. But the gates opened early, the line moved quickly, and she received her Peanut.

Another roving reporter, Cyndi King, told "Beanie World" that Oakland A's officials handed out fliers to fans in line. The fliers said the A's planned to have another Beanie giveaway on Sunday, September 6. Peanut is the giveaway Beanie for that game as well.

Thanks to Erin and Cyndi for their stories!

MLB: Texas Rangers vs. Toronto Blue Jays
Tuesday, August 4, 1998
Giveaway: Pugsly the pug dog
Attendance: 45,213 at The Ballpark In Arlington

Joshua Williams, 9, was among the thousands who waited in line before the Texas Rangers' Beanie giveaway on Tuesday, August 4, 1998. (AP/Wide World Photo)

The Rangers' Beanie giveaway was a smash hit, with the team recording its 11th sellout crowd of the year for the promotion. The Dallas Morning News reported that collectors started lining up at 6 a.m., spreading out blankets and lawn chairs to settle in for the long haul. Gates were scheduled to open at 4:30 p.m. for the evening game.

Rangers spokesman John Blake said, " I've never seen anything like this just for a promotion." The first 10,000 kids ages 13 and under to enter the park received an official Ty Pugsly the pug dog with a commemorative card. Some problems reportedly occurred with the distribution of wristbands that were to be given to kids to ensure each got a Beanie. Some youngsters reportedly never got the wristbands and were turned away at the gate and told to go to the end of the line. Indelible markers were used to mark the hands of those kids who had received their Beanie.

WNBA: Houston Comets 75, Phoenix Mercury 64
Thursday, August 6, 1998
Giveaway: Scoop the pelican
Attendance: 16,285 at Compaq Center

Very special thanks go out to Susan Sternberg of Sugar Land, TX, who took the time to give "Beanie World" this exclusive report from the Houston Comets' Beanie giveaway:

The WNBA Houston Comets had their first Beanie Baby giveaway on August 6 when they played archrival Phoenix. Scoop (probably chosen to honor Comets star Cynthia "Coop" Cooper) the pelican and a commemorative card were given to the first 5,000 kids ages 14 and under to enter the game.

My two sons and I got to the game site, the Compaq Center, at around 5:45 p.m. The doors were to open at 6:30 p.m., with the game starting at 7:30 p.m. There already was quite a crowd of parents and kids. At about 6 p.m., a Compaq Center official came out with a bullhorn and told us we would all get a Beanie Baby, so just stay calm when the doors open.

Finally we saw the security massing inside by the doors and a ripple of excitement went through the crowd. The doors were finally open! Once inside, we saw signs that indicated the Beanies were being given out in two locations to our right. We followed the crowd and waited in a very slow-moving line. It must have taken almost 10 minutes to finally get to the important table (but it always seems longer with two little kids).

Close to the table, the officials told us that the kids should stand in line with their ticket stubs, while the parents wait on the other side. Since one of my sons, C.J., is age 3, they let me stay with both of them (the other one, Jake, is 6). We finally made it to the table, where there were three or four people marking the kids' hands and giving them the card (which wasn't in plastic) and the standard Scoop. I, of course, grabbed the stuff, and we got out of the area. I quickly put the cards and our ticket stubs into a plastic bag I had brought and put the Scoops in my backpack. Then we found our seats and eventually got to enjoy a thrilling 75-64 Comets victory!

There were several announcements during the first half that if any child age 14 or under who had not gotten a Beanie, they could come and get one. I don't know if they had extras or if there just weren't 5,000 kids among the crowd of more than 16,000.

ARENA FOOTBALL: Orlando Predators vs. Nashville Kats
Friday, August 7, 1998
Giveaway: Crunch the shark
Attendance: 12,766 at Orlando Arena

The Beanie Baby craze came to the Orlando Arena on August 7 as the Orlando Predators presented "Crunch the Shark Night" when the Predators played host to the Nashville Kats in the opening round of the 1998 AFL playoffs.

For the event, co-sponsored by the Orlando Sentinel, all children 14 and under with a game ticket received a free Crunch the shark Beanie Baby when they presented a Crunch The shark coupon that could be found in the preceding Thursday and Friday editions of the newspaper.

"A shark is often described as the perfect Predator, so we felt that if we were going to do a Beanie Baby night it should relate to the team," Predators President Jack Youngblood said. "According to the literature we received, Crunch eats everything in sight ... so it sounded perfect to us."

The Predators, who are the first Arena Football League team to do a giveaway with the stuffed toys from Ty, won the game 58-43.

WRITE TO US

We welcome your news and photos from sports giveaways. Please send your questions to: "Sports Giveaways," c/o "Mary Beth's Beanie World Monthly," H&S Media Inc., 3400 Dundee Road, Suite 245, Northbrook, IL 60062. Make sure to include your full name, postal address, e-mail address (if any) and daytime phone number with your correspondence. Address and phone information are for office use only and will not be published. You may also send news via e-mail to beaniew@interaccess.com. Please put "Sports Giveaway News" in the subject line when sending material via e-mail.

Beanie Cooking Corner

BY CHEF TERESA TREMBLAY SHANK

In each issue of "Mary Beth's Beanie World Monthly," one of our Beanie friends will share a recipe unique to that Beanie and his or her family. With our ever-growing world-wide Beanie gang, we have some fun recipes to share with you in the upcoming months. Enjoy!

Since I, Peanut, have the honor of presenting the charter recipe for this column, I simply had to include my favorite food, PEANUTS!! Actually, in this case, it's peanut butter chips, and I managed to slip in some nuts, as well. You can enjoy these special treats at work during your coffee break or after school with a tall glass of milk. I hope you like them because they are named after me!

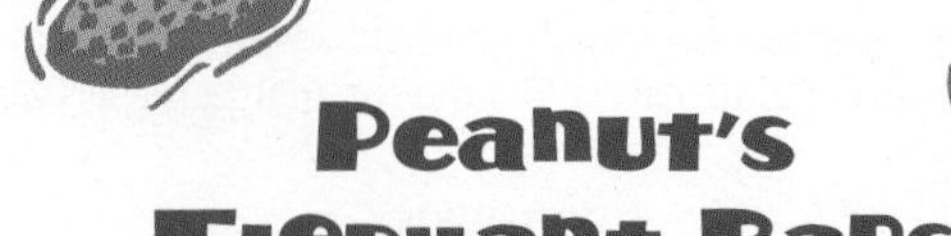

Peanut's Elephant Bars

INGREDIENTS

- 1/2 cup melted butter or margarine (1 stick)
- 1 1/2 cups crushed graham cracker crumbs
- 1 cup chopped walnuts
- One 6-ounce bag of peanut butter chips
- 1 1/3 cups shredded coconut
- One 5-ounce can sweetened condensed milk (not evaporated milk)

Directions

- Melt butter. Pour into a 9 x 13-inch pan.
- Sprinkle the graham cracker crumbs evenly over the top of the butter.
- Continue to do the same with the walnuts, peanut butter chips, and the coconut.
- Pour the condensed milk over the enitre pan of ingredients.
- Bake in an oven at 350 degrees for 20 minutes or until done.
- Cut into 32 squares unless you REALLY want elephant-size bars, and in that case cut them into 16 squares.

Teresa Tremblay Shank is an avid Beanie collector from Idaho. This is her first contribution to "Mary Beth's Beanie World Monthly."

From Here to Eternity

Preserving Your Beanie Collection

By Linda Sigrist

As Beanie Baby collecting becomes an even bigger hobby, more and more people are seeking the safest and most economical way to store Beanies. With a little foresight and care, it is possible to keep your treasures and their tags looking new for years to come.

Potential dangers include moisture, light, smoke, extreme temperatures, insects, chemical pollution, odors, dust and even your hands. Before handling your Beanies, be sure your hands are clean and dry. In addition, store only items that are clean and dry. Soil will cause the fabric to deteriorate, as can vapors from hair spray, paint and paint solvents.

Experts advise individually wrapping overlapping Beanie body parts with acid-free tissue paper.

Moisture and heat may cause fabric to mildew, so you will want to choose a dry location, protected from bright light and between 60 and 72 degrees Fahrenheit. Attics are generally too warm, and basements are often damp. Temperature and humidity levels that are right for you are also good for your Beanies.

There are many excellent products on the market to help with long term storage. Sally Carpenter of the Michigan State University Extension Service offers the following advice for storing Beanie Babies.

Although many people rely on plastic bags for storage, this may not be the wisest choice because plastic does not permit air to circulate freely and may retain dampness. Carpenter recommends that fabric items be wrapped in an acid-free tissue paper during long periods of disuse. When wrapping, flatten tails, ears, beaks and other appendages as much as possible, and wrap separately. Once wrapped with a label attached for easy identification, the items should then be placed in a single layer into an acid-free box.

Because of the porous nature of these items, moisture is not trapped as it would be with plastic bags, and your Beanies can "breathe." This method also protects them from the threat of fading due to sunlight or even fluorescent lighting. Good sources for acid-free storage products are dry cleaners specializing in wedding gown preservation and specialty quilt shops.

A cedar chest may seem to be an obvious choice for storage because the scent of the cedar discourages insects from making a meal of your Beanies. However, while the cedar may deter moths, it does not destroy them in all stages of their development and does not affect many other insects at all. It is also important not to let the fabric come in direct contact with the wood. There are acids in the wood that may leach into the fibers and cause damage. If you choose this option, make sure your pieces are securely wrapped as previously described.

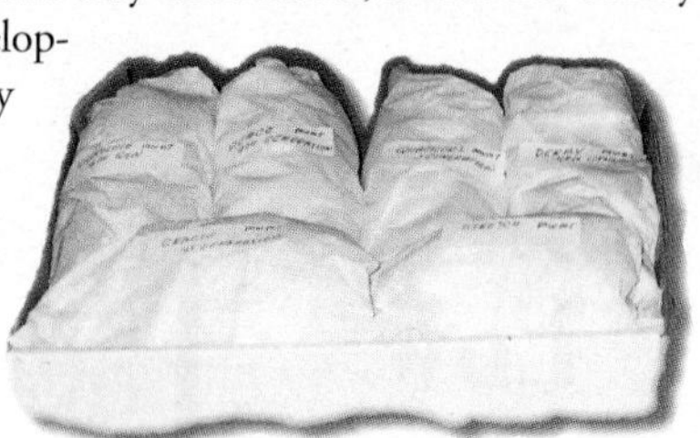

Beanies can be wrapped completely in acid-free paper prior to their placement in plastic containers such as a Rubbermaid storage box (with fresh scent compartment for baking soda).

Collectors may prefer to take advantage of many plastic storage systems available. Any of a variety of see-through products with snap-fit lids are good choices. Before closing your container, it is a good idea to include a small desiccant packet, often referred to as silica gel. The silica will dehumidify your container and protect your items from any damage caused by excess humidity. You may have seen these packets before in boxes containing new shoes. An inexpensive, 2-ounce packet will dehumidify a sealed container up to 6.5 gallons in size. These packets are readily available for sale via the Internet.

The ever-present threat of insects also must be taken into account. Moth control is available in several forms. If you choose to use moth control products, they should be placed at the highest level of the closet or storage area as the vapor travels downward. They should never come into direct contact with your Beanies. Most of these products are toxic and should be kept well out of the reach of children. Often the odor of these products is overpowering and may even be as distasteful as smoke or other odors that permeate fabric. A more natural and pleasant solution might be to crush some bay leaves and scatter them throughout the storage area.

You will want to store your collection far from any areas where people smoke. Smoke and other odors are easily absorbed by fabrics and can detract from the value of your items and may even damage the fibers. If you notice that some of your items have acquired an unpleasant aroma, one popular solution is to put some household baking soda into a muslin pouch and enclose the unwrapped Beanies with the soda for a week or two. This will restore their freshness.

Finally, it is very important to keep your Beanie's swing tag like new. Potential dangers to the tag are tears, creasing, fading, dirt and compression marks. When choosing tag protection, the factors to consider are fit, ease of application, UV protection, lack of acidity, and protection from compression of the broad end of the plastic attacher against the tag.

Before purchasing your Beanie, check to be sure the tag is securely attached and in excellent condition. There are conflicting opinions regarding the existence of price *(continued on page 93)* stickers on tags. Most collectors prefer tags that have never had a price sticker on them, while some feel that the sticker does not devalue the item. If the tag does have a sticker, it is safer not to try to remove it. Sticker removal is a risky business and can cause irreparable damage if not successfully accomplished.

Tag protectors have become an essential ingredient in the long-term protection of any Beanie Baby.

Choose a protector that most closely corresponds to the size and shape of the tag on your item. Tag protectors come in all sizes to accommodate a wide variety of Beanies, from very large to fit the larger plush items down to sizes suitable for your Teenies.

The protector should be lightweight and able to be easily applied with a minimum of handling. Look for a protector that provides room for the wide end of the attacher so that the plastic is not compressed against the tag because this could cause an indentation in the tag. The heart-shaped styles are especially attractive. The tag should be easy to remove from the protector to check information as necessary. Some tags are designed to allow all surfaces of the swing tag to be visible at once. Check to be sure the protector is acid free or that it is "archival" quality and UV protected. Plastics that are not acid free will eventually erode the print and the color on the tag.

No matter which storage method you choose, it is important to remove your Beanies every few months to check them for possible unseen damage and to allow them exposure to the air. You can take advantage of this time to rotate your display if you wish, or take some time to simply enjoy your collection. While on display, remember to keep the display area free from dust. Encasing the Beanie in one of the many available types of attractive display cases will minimize the amount of dust that comes into contact with your treasures. Remember to display in an area of low light and moderate temperature and out of the reach of inquisitive pets. ❤

Linda Sigrist is a freelance feature writer. This is her first contribution to "Mary Beth's Beanie World Monthly."

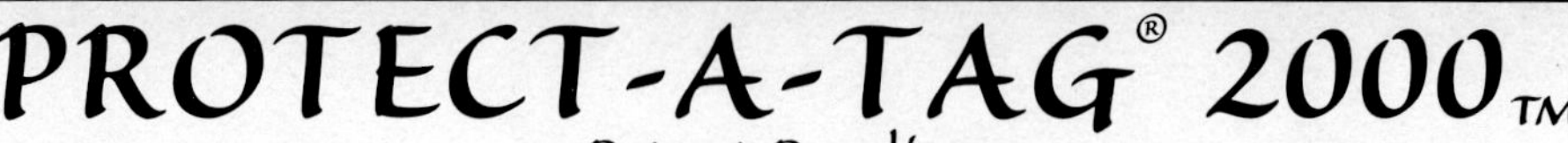

Patent Pending

The Limited Connection, Inc.
The Originators in Swing Tag Protection

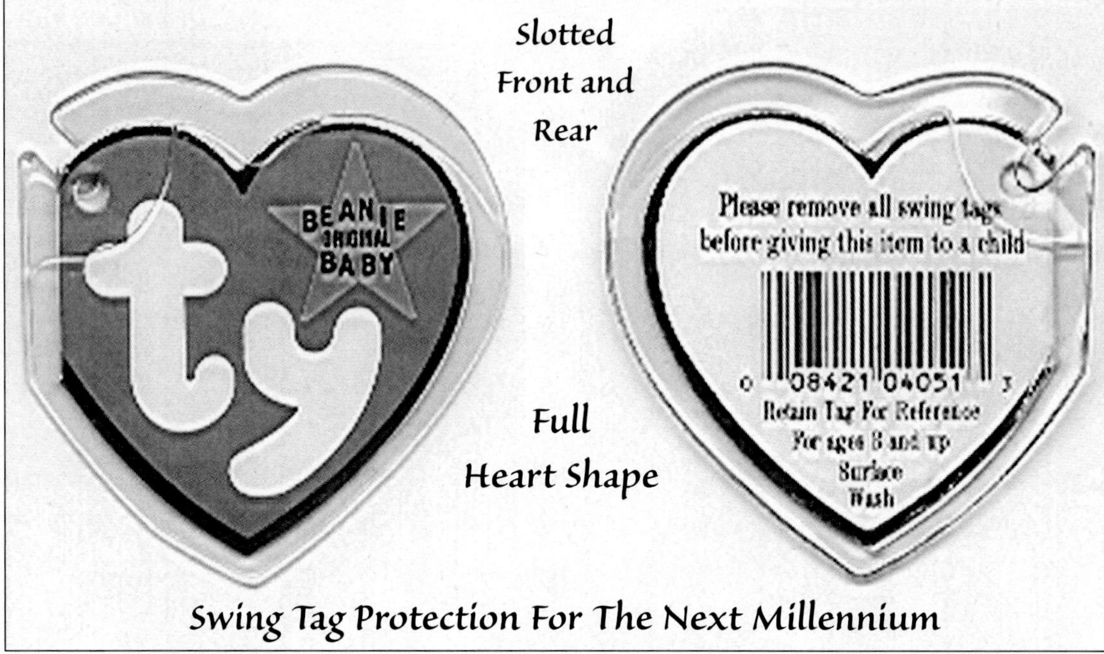

The ultimate "slide on" protector for Beanies • Archival Safe
Easy on and off installation • No pressure on tags • Lightweight
Practically Invisible • Extra stiff material for added strength
Uncompromised quality

PROTECT-A-TAGS® for other collectibles

Disney • Coke • Nintendo • Puffkins
Harley • Meanies • Disneyland • Large Ty Plush
Ty Teenies • Pillsbury Dough Boys

Other Products Available:
Hard Gard™ Rigid, Crystal Clear Acrylic, also available in four new colors: Amber, Green, Red, Purple
Blister Gard™ Clam shell style, semi rigid protector
Display Boxes, The standard, clear 4x4x7¼" box
Visit us at: www.thelimitedconnection.com

Dealer inquiries welcome
For a free sample, please send
a large SASE to:

The Limited Connection, Inc.
P.O. Box 538
Central Islip, N.Y. 11722

516-232-3091
Fax: 516-232-3809

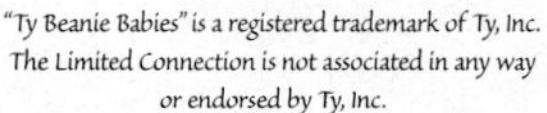

All PROTECT-A-TAG products are
MADE IN THE USA

PROTECT-A-TAG is a registered trademark & 1997 Patent Pending, owned exclusively by The Limited Connection, Inc.

Mary Beth's Beanie World Monthly™
www.beanieworld.net

Comprehensive Bean Bag Buyer's Guide

October 1998

Contents

Page

MARY BETH'S BEANIE WORLD MONTHLY

Bean Bag Buyer's Guide – OCTOBER 1998

About This Guide

Our team of Beanie experts has compiled the information in this exclusive 80-page buyer's guide from a variety of sources, including Internet sites, Beanie dealers and a large sampling of Beanie retailers. Many hours are spent every month translating this data so that the information is as up-to-date and accurate as possible. We have listed prices for all Ty products – including Beanie Babies, Attic Collectibles, Pillow Pals and Ty Plush – and for non-Ty products ranging from the Disney Mini Bean Bag Plush to Meanie Beanies to Warner Brothers Bean Bags. **For Ty Beanie Babies we list median United Kingdom prices and – for the first time – median Canadian prices for each toy.**

The United Kingdom and Canadian median market prices for the Ty Beanie Babies were calculated using the exchange rate from U.S. dollars to British Sterling and Canadian dollars, respectively, obtained from LaSalle National Bank's Exchange Department on July 29, 1998. These median prices represent only the conversion from the U.S. price and in no way reflect the relative scarcity of a particular Beanie in the United Kingdom or Canada.

Many factors affect these prices, including geographical area. If you are able to find the current Ty Beanies in a retail store, you will most likely pay $5 to $8 each. The prices listed for current Beanies in this guide reflect the secondary marketer who buys at retail and resells at a slightly higher price. This listing should be used only as a guide, as your experience may vary by individual transaction.

Please note that values of current Beanies are valid only as long as that Beanie remains "current." Retirement announcements immediately affect the value of a Beanie. **All current/retired designations in this guide are considered accurate as of August 7, 1998.**

Also, some Beanies display a large range of values. We are seeing wide variances as flea market vendors, Internet auctions and TV shopping programs sell the identical item. The *median price* listed is the value used most often.

The prices listed are for MINT condition Beanie Babies with both MINT hang tags and tush tags. A creased or bent hang tag may devalue a retired Beanie Baby up to 40 percent. A Beanie missing a hang tag is devalued roughly 50 percent. A missing tush tag generally translates into 75 percent reductions. Price stickers on the back of a tag usually do not affect pricing, but should be noted to the buyer. A Beanie Baby that has been handled or played with suffers a significant loss in value. Writing on the hang or tush tag (such as a child's initials) also needs to be taken into consideration.

Bronty the brontosaurus

Retired

Fast Facts
Style Number: 4085
Introduced: 1995
Status: Retired 1996
Birthday: Unknown

Collector Trivia
Bronty, the rarest of the three dinosaurs in the Beanie Baby line, shares fabric with Sting the stingray.

Median U.S. Prices By Hang Tag

1st	2nd	3rd	4th	5th
N/A	N/A	$900-1100	N/A	N/A

Available Tush Tag Generations: 1st, 2nd

Median U.S. Prices Over Time

BWM Vol. 1 No. 5 6/98	BWM Vol. 1 No. 6 8/98	BWM Vol. 1 No. 7 9/98	BWM Vol. 2 No. 1 10/98	BWM Projected price 3/99
$1100	$1400	$1100	$1000	$1600

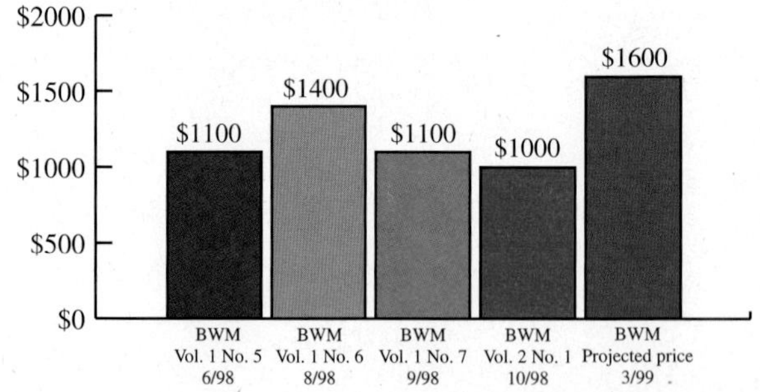

Median U.K. Price: £607.90 Median Canadian Price: $1503.50

We have had many requests for pricing by generation of hang tag, and we are happy to provide updated information each month in this fashion. You may notice that the older hang tags, most notably the first generation of the "Original Nine" Beanies, are quite sought after and command a high value. **In addition, starting with this issue we provide a list of available tush tag generations for each Beanie Baby.** To take a quick look at a chart showing which Beanie hang tag generations correspond to which tush tag generations, see page 150 of this issue. The sample entry above for Echo the dolphin shows you how the information is organized, with headers such as "Fast Facts," "Collector Trivia" and "Median U.S. Prices Over Time." You will notice, also, that we have expanded the graphs to provide more historical pricing information for each Beanie. In addition, the projected prices for each Beanie Baby are for March 1999, two months after the projected prices listed in our previous issue.

We also hope you find our other buyer's guides in this section helpful. We have gotten many requests for all of the promotional Beanies, especially sports giveaways, which are very "hot" due to their limited production. We have also included the major Ty "Odds 'N Ends" and common mistags for your convenience. Remember that all Beanies, but especially oddities, are valued at what they mean to a particular buyer, and prices sometimes vary greatly. Keep in mind that most mistags (other than the ones listed in this price guide) are actually worth about 25 percent less than a correctly tagged Beanie.❤

Ally the alligator

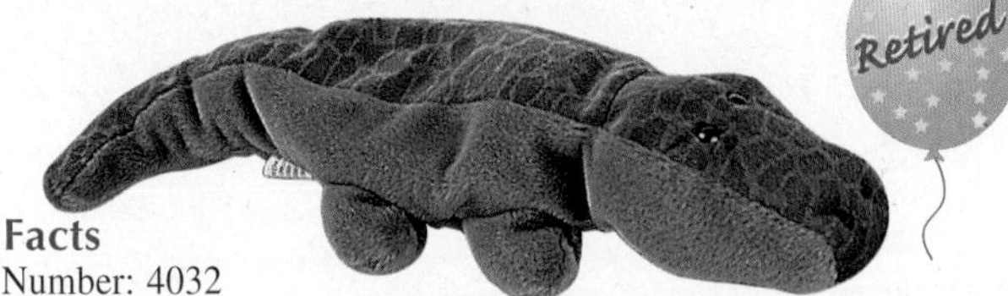

Fast Facts
Style Number: 4032
Introduced: 1994
Status: Retired 10-1-97
Birthday: 3-14-94

Collector Trivia
Ally has the same fabric used for Speedy's shell.

Median U.S. Prices By Hang Tag

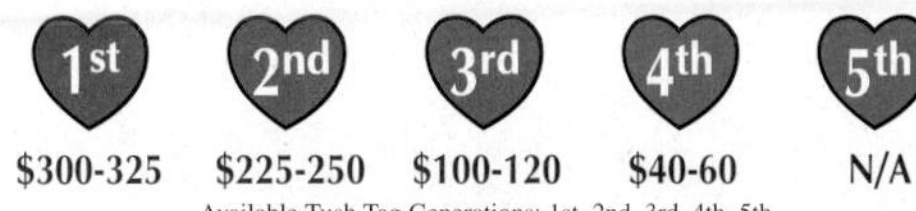

1st	2nd	3rd	4th	5th
$300-325	$225-250	$100-120	$40-60	N/A

Available Tush Tag Generations: 1st, 2nd, 3rd, 4th, 5th

Median U.S. Prices Over Time

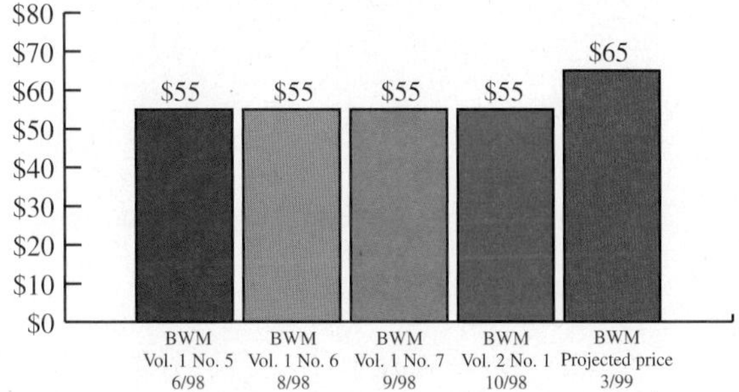

Median U.K. Price: £33.43 **Median Canadian Price: $82.69**

Ants the anteater

Fast Facts
Style Number: 4195
Introduced: 5-30-98
Status: Current
Birthday: 11-7-97

Collector Trivia
Ants was one of 14 new Beanie Babies announced by Ty Inc. on May 30, 1998.

Median U.S. Prices By Hang Tag

1st	2nd	3rd	4th	5th
N/A	N/A	N/A	N/A	$10-20

Available Tush Tag Generations: 6th

Median U.S. Prices Over Time

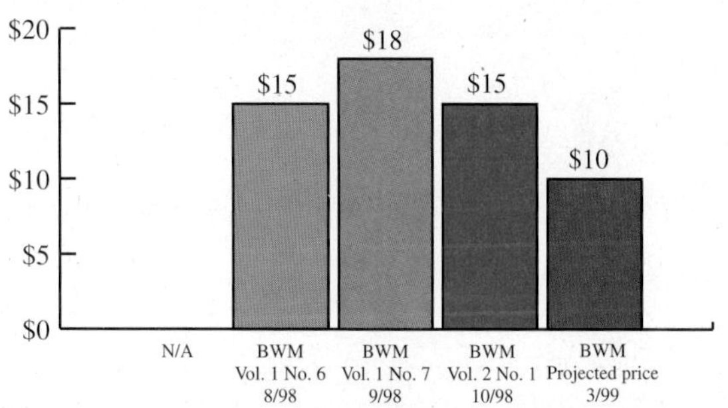

Median U.K. Price: £9.11 **Median Canadian Price: $22.55**

Baldy the eagle

Fast Facts
Style Number: 4074
Introduced: 5-11-97
Status: Retired 5-1-98
Birthday: 2-17-96

Collector Trivia
5,000 Baldys with a commemorative card were given away at the Philadelphia 76ers-Golden State Warriors game on January 17, 1998.

Median U.S. Prices By Hang Tag

1st	2nd	3rd	4th	5th
N/A	N/A	N/A	$15-20	$15-20

Available Tush Tag Generations: 3rd, 4th, 5th, 6th

Median U.S. Prices Over Time

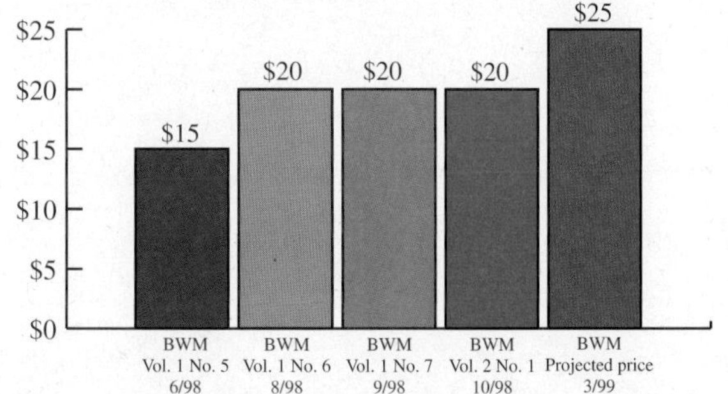

Median U.K. Price: £12.15 **Median Canadian Price: $30.07**

Batty the bat

Fast Facts
Style Number: 4035
Introduced: 10-1-97
Status: Current
Birthday: 10-29-96

Collector Trivia
Batty the bat was part of the Beanie Baby giveaway at a Milwaukee Brewers game on May 31, 1998.

Median U.S. Prices By Hang Tag

1st	2nd	3rd	4th	5th
N/A	N/A	N/A	$10-15	$10-15

Available Tush Tag Generations: 5th, 6th

Median U.S. Prices Over Time

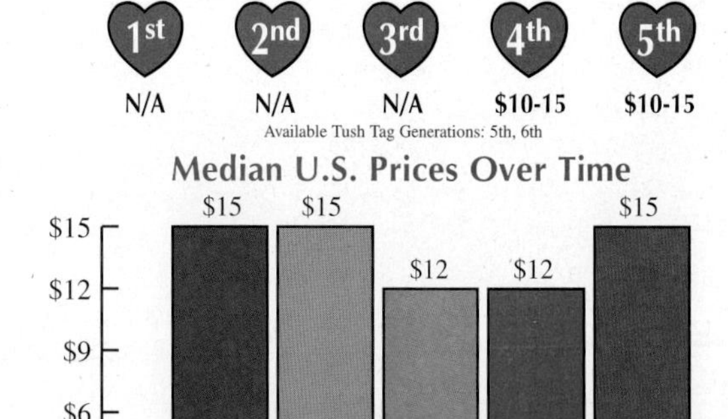

Median U.K. Price: £7.29 **Median Canadian Price: $18.04**

Bernie the St. Bernard

Fast Facts
Style Number: 4109
Introduced: 1-1-97
Status: Current
Birthday: 10-3-96

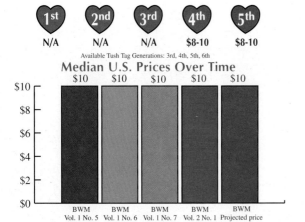

Collector Trivia
Bernie was one of two dogs introduced in the Ty Beanie Baby line on New Year's Day 1997.

Median U.S. Prices By Hang Tag

1st	2nd	3rd	4th	5th
N/A	N/A	N/A	$8-10	$8-10

Available Tush Tag Generations: 3rd, 4th, 5th, 6th

Median U.S. Prices Over Time

Median U.K. Price: £6.07 **Median Canadian Price: $15.03**

Bessie the brown and white cow

Fast Facts
Style Number: 4009
Introduced: 1995
Status: Retired 10-1-97
Birthday: 6-27-95

Collector Trivia
Collectors reportedly have found Bessies with horns in two different colors.

Median U.S. Prices By Hang Tag

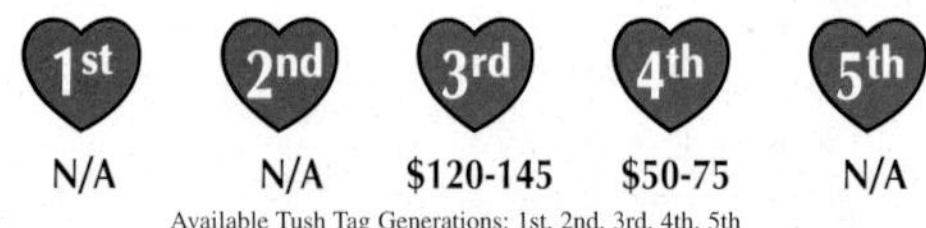

1st	2nd	3rd	4th	5th
N/A	N/A	$120-145	$50-75	N/A

Available Tush Tag Generations: 1st, 2nd, 3rd, 4th, 5th

Median U.S. Prices Over Time

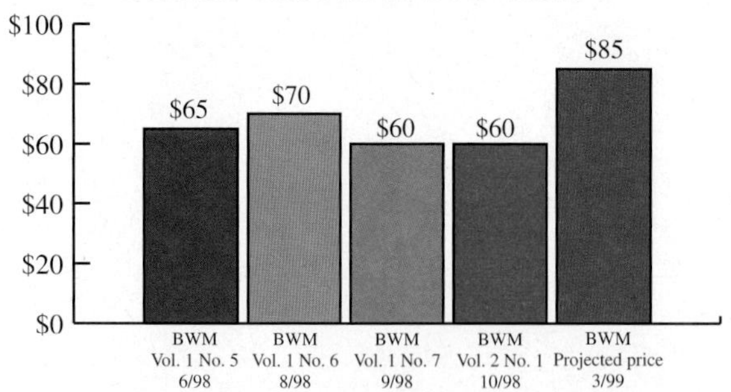

Median U.K. Price: £36.47 **Median Canadian Price: $90.21**

Blackie the black bear

Fast Facts
Style Number: 4011
Introduced: 1994
Status: Current
Birthday: 7-15-94

Collector Trivia
Blackie is one of only a few Beanie Babies to be produced with all five generations of heart hang tags.

Median U.S. Prices By Hang Tag

1st	2nd	3rd	4th	5th
$300-325	$200-225	$70-95	$8-10	$8-10

Available Tush Tag Generations: 1st, 2nd, 3rd, 4th, 5th, 6th

Median U.S. Prices Over Time

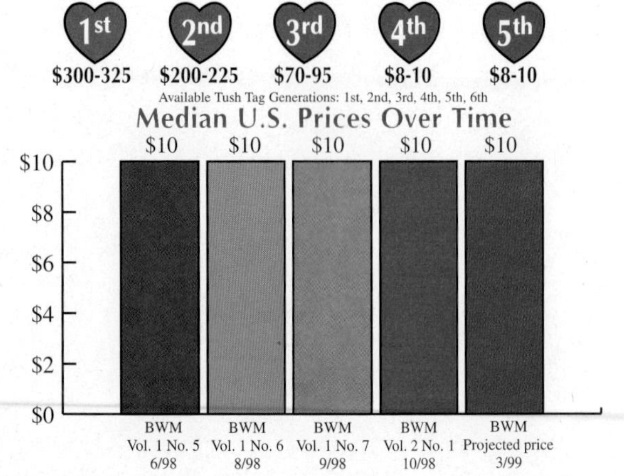

Median U.K. Price: £6.07 **Median Canadian Price: $15.03**

Blizzard the black and white tiger

Fast Facts
Style Number: 4163
Introduced: 5-11-97
Status: Retired 5-1-98
Birthday: 12-12-96

Collector Trivia
Blizzard was part of the Beanie Baby giveaway at a Chicago White Sox game on July 12, 1998.

Median U.S. Prices By Hang Tag

1st	2nd	3rd	4th	5th
N/A	N/A	N/A	$15-20	$15-20

Available Tush Tag Generations: 3rd, 4th, 5th, 6th

Median U.S. Prices Over Time

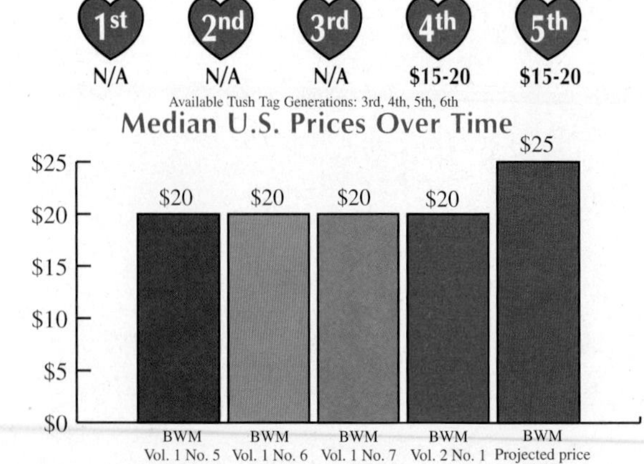

Median U.K. Price: £12.15 **Median Canadian Price: $30.07**

Bones the brown dog

Fast Facts

Style Number: 4001
Introduced: 1994
Status: Retired 5-1-98
Birthday: 1-18-94

Collector Trivia

Bones is the second-oldest dog in Ty's Beanie Baby line. Spot is the oldest.

Median U.S. Prices By Hang Tag

1st	2nd	3rd	4th	5th
$300-325	$200-225	$90-110	$12-20	$10-20

Available Tush Tag Generations: 1st, 2nd, 3rd, 4th, 5th, 6th

Median U.S. Prices Over Time

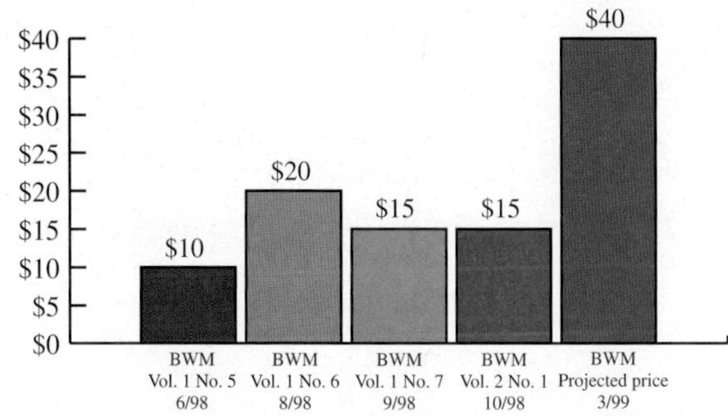

Median U.K. Price: £9.11 Median Canadian Price: $22.55

Bongo the brown monkey with the brown tail

Fast Facts

Style Number: 4067
Version #1: 3rd Generation Tag
Introduced: 1996 - Retired: 1996
Version #2: 4th Generation Tag
Introduced: 1997 - Retired: 1997
Birthday: 8-17-95

Collector Trivia

Bongos have alternated between tan and brown tails several times. The Bongo currently on store shelves has a tan tail.

Median U.S. Prices By Hang Tag

1st	2nd	3rd	4th	5th
N/A	N/A	$125-135	$40-50	N/A

Available Tush Tag Generations: 3rd, 4th, 5th

Median U.S. Prices Over Time

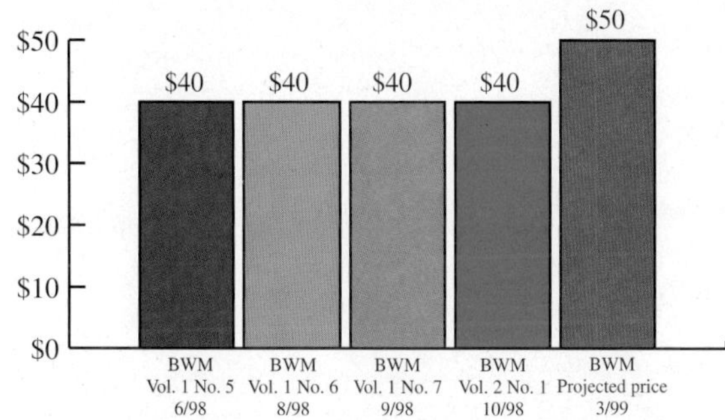

Median U.K. Price: £24.31 Median Canadian Price: $60.14

Bongo the monkey with the tan tail

Fast Facts

Style Number: 4067
Version #1: 3rd Generation Tag;B/W tush tag
Introduced: 1995 - Retired: 1995
Version #2: 3rd Generation Tag; R/W tush tag
Introduced: 1996 - Status: Retired 1996
Version #3: 4th Generation Tag
Introduced: 1996 - Status: Current
Birthday: 8-17-95

Collector Trivia

5,000 Bongos with a commemorative card were given away at the Cleveland Cavaliers-Los Angeles Clippers game on April 5, 1998.

Median U.S. Prices By Hang Tag

1st	2nd	3rd	4th	5th
N/A	N/A	$100-150, b&w $75-100, red tush	$8-10	$8-10

Available Tush Tag Generations: 1st, 4th, 5th, 6th

Median U.S. Prices Over Time

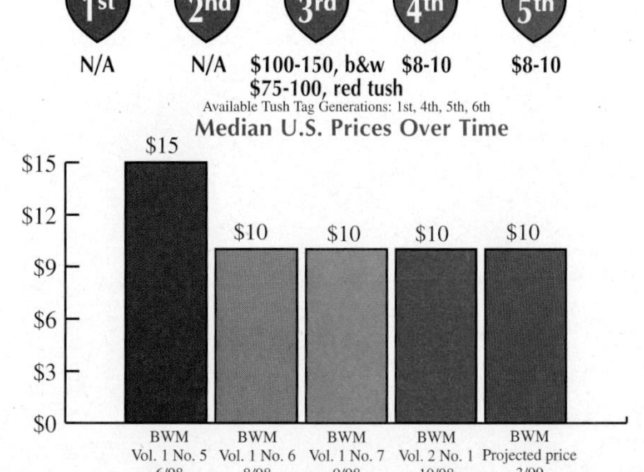

Median U.K. Price: £6.07 Median Canadian Price: $15.03

Britannia the British Bear (Ty Europe Exclusive)

Fast Facts

Style Number: 4601
Introduced: 12-31-97
Status: Current
Birthday: 12-15-97

Collector Trivia

U.S. Customs regulations have kept Britannia from becoming widely available in the United States, and Britannias are also becoming scarce in the United Kingdom.

Median U.S. Prices By Hang Tag

1st	2nd	3rd	4th	5th
N/A	N/A	N/A	N/A	$385-500

Available Tush Tag Generations: 6th

Median U.S. Prices Over Time

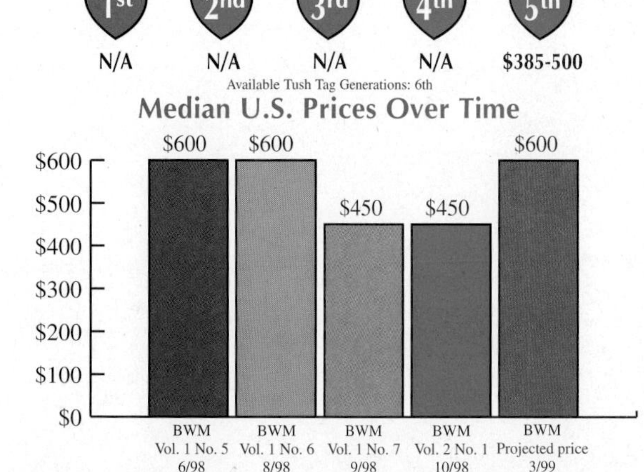

Median U.K. Price: £273.55 Median Canadian Price: $676.57

Bronty the brontosaurus

Fast Facts

Style Number: 4085
Introduced: 1995
Status: Retired 1996
Birthday: Unknown

Collector Trivia

Bronty, the rarest of the three dinosaurs in the Beanie Baby line, shares fabric with Sting the stingray.

Median U.S. Prices By Hang Tag

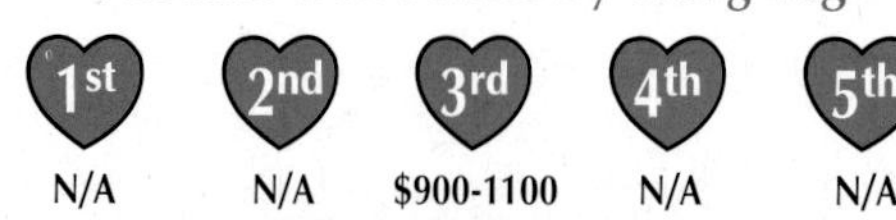

1st	2nd	3rd	4th	5th
N/A	N/A	$900-1100	N/A	N/A

Available Tush Tag Generations: 1st, 2nd

Median U.S. Prices Over Time

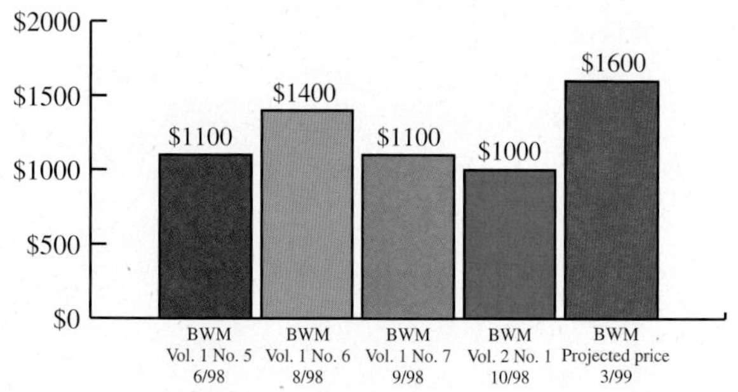

Median U.K. Price: £607.90 Median Canadian Price: $1503.50

Brownie the brown bear

Fast Facts

Style Number: 4010
Introduced: 1993
Status: Retired 1993
Birthday: Unknown

Collector Trivia

The original "Cubbie," Brownie is produced only with a first generation tag.

Median U.S. Prices By Hang Tag

1st	2nd	3rd	4th	5th
$3600-4200	N/A	N/A	N/A	N/A

Available Tush Tag Generations: 1st

Median U.S. Prices Over Time

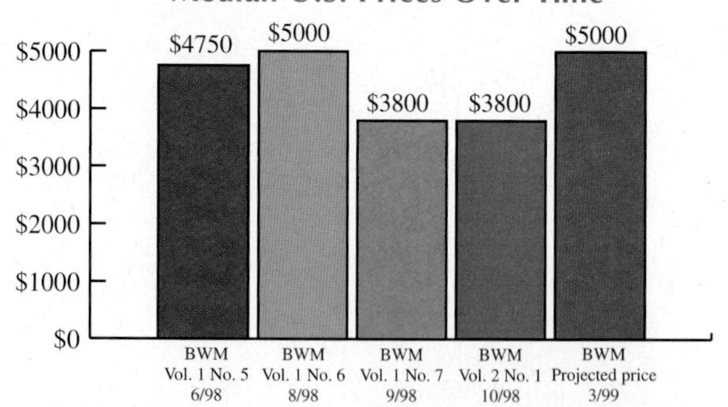

Median U.K. Price: £2310.02 Median Canadian Price: $5713.30

Bruno the terrier

Fast Facts

Style Number: 4183
Introduced: 12-31-97
Status: Current
Birthday: 9-9-97

Collector Trivia

Bruno was one of two dogs announced among the new Beanie Baby releases on January 1, 1998. The other was Spunky.

Median U.S. Prices By Hang Tag

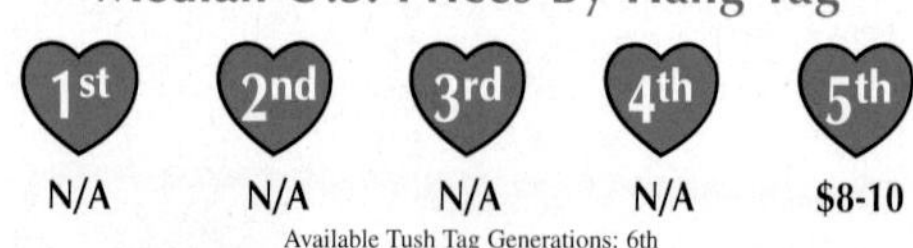

1st	2nd	3rd	4th	5th
N/A	N/A	N/A	N/A	$8-10

Available Tush Tag Generations: 6th

Median U.S. Prices Over Time

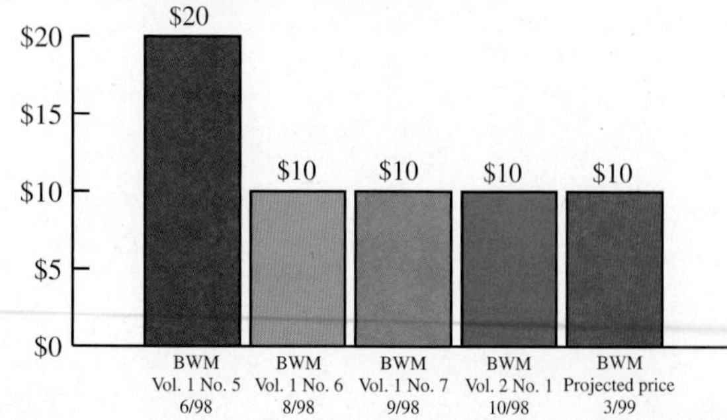

Median U.K. Price: £6.07 Median Canadian Price: $15.03

Bubbles the black and yellow fish

Fast Facts

Style Number: 4078
Introduced: 1995
Status: Retired 5-11-97
Birthday: 7-2-95

Collector Trivia

One of three colorful, tropical fish in the Beanie Baby line, Bubbles was the second to be retired.

Median U.S. Prices By Hang Tag

1st	2nd	3rd	4th	5th
N/A	N/A	$175-205	$150-175	N/A

Available Tush Tag Generations: 1st, 2nd, 3rd

Median U.S. Prices Over Time

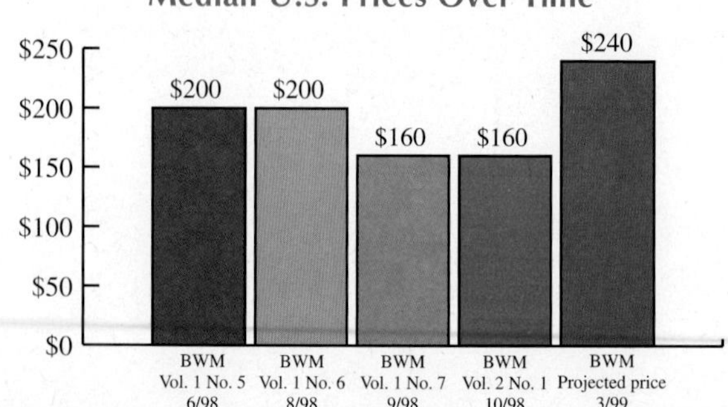

Median U.K. Price: £97.26 Median Canadian Price: $240.56

Bucky the beaver

Fast Facts
Style Number: 4016
Introduced: 1996
Status: Retired 12-31-97
Birthday: 6-8-95

Collector Trivia
Bucky is one of more than 30 Beanie Babies with brown as its primary color.

Median U.S. Prices By Hang Tag

1st	2nd	3rd	4th	5th
N/A	N/A	$100-125	$30-45	N/A

Available Tush Tag Generations: 2nd, 3rd, 4th, 5th

Median U.S. Prices Over Time

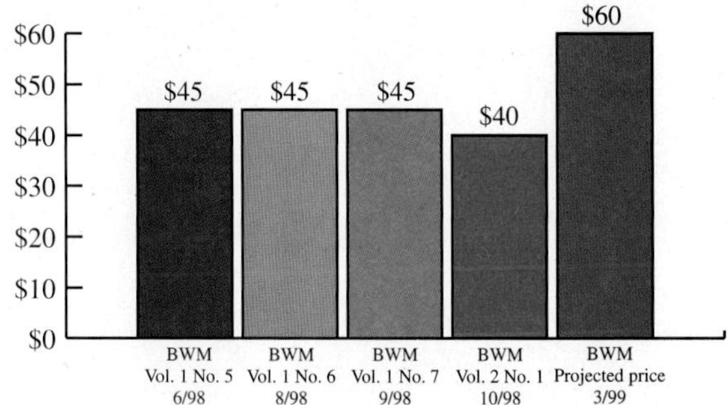

Median U.K. Price: £24.31 Median Canadian Price: $60.14

Bumble the bee

Fast Facts
Style Number: 4045
Introduced: 1996
Status: Retired 1996
Birthday: 10-16-95

Collector Trivia
Bumble is the only Beanie Baby for which the fourth generation heart hang tags commands a higher price than the third generation tag.

Median U.S. Prices By Hang Tag

1st	2nd	3rd	4th	5th
N/A	N/A	$535-560	$600-625	N/A

Available Tush Tag Generations: 1st, 2nd, 3rd

Median U.S. Prices Over Time

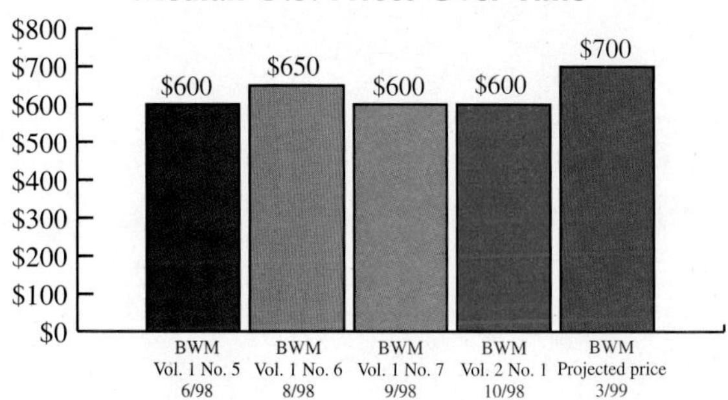

Median U.K. Price: £364.74 Median Canadian Price: $902.10

Caw the crow

Fast Facts
Style Number: 4071
Introduced: 1995
Status: Retired 1996
Birthday: Unknown

Collector Trivia
Caw is nearly identical in body type to Beanie pal Kiwi.

Median U.S. Prices By Hang Tag

1st	2nd	3rd	4th	5th
N/A	N/A	$600-650	N/A	N/A

Available Tush Tag Generations: 1st, 2nd

Median U.S. Prices Over Time

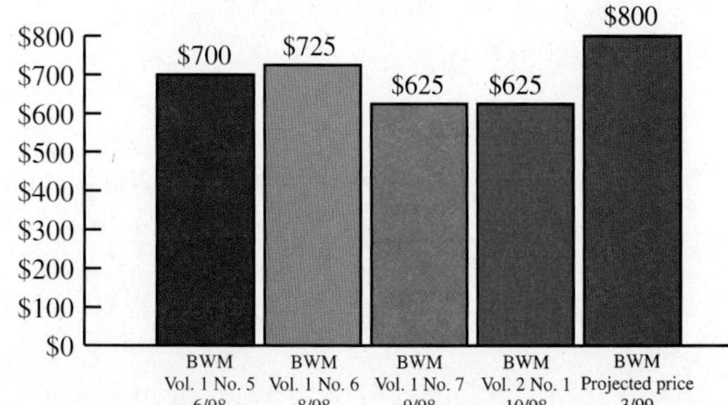

Median U.K. Price: £379.93 Median Canadian Price: $939.68

Chilly the polar bear

Fast Facts
Style Number: 4012
Introduced: 1994
Status: Retired 1995
Birthday: Unknown

Collector Trivia
Chilly should be kept in a dust-free environment because settling dust quickly makes its white coat look old and dingy.

Median U.S. Prices By Hang Tag

1st	2nd	3rd	4th	5th
$2400-3000	$2300-2700	$2000-2400	N/A	N/A

Available Tush Tag Generations: 1st

Median U.S. Prices Over Time

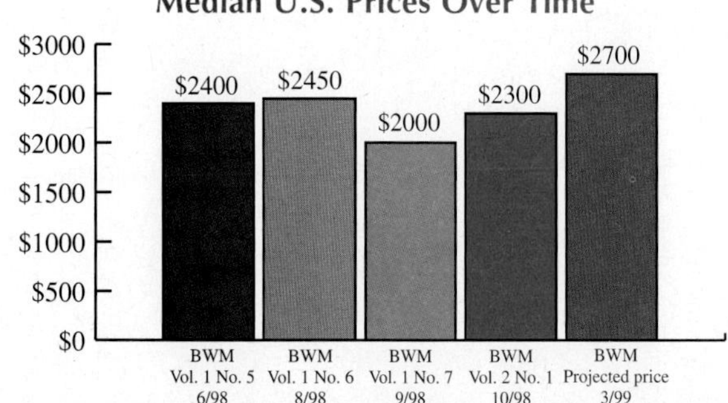

Median U.K. Price: £1398.17 Median Canadian Price: $3458.05

Chip the calico cat

Fast Facts

Style Number: 4121
Introduced: 5-11-97
Status: Current
Birthday: 1-26-96

Collector Trivia

Chip was the last of the rhyming cats (Chip, Flip, Nip, Snip, Zip) to be introduced in the Beanie Baby line.

Median U.S. Prices By Hang Tag

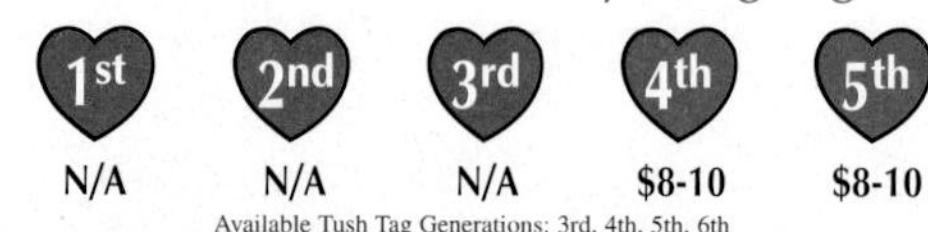

1st	2nd	3rd	4th	5th
N/A	N/A	N/A	$8-10	$8-10

Available Tush Tag Generations: 3rd, 4th, 5th, 6th

Median U.S. Prices Over Time

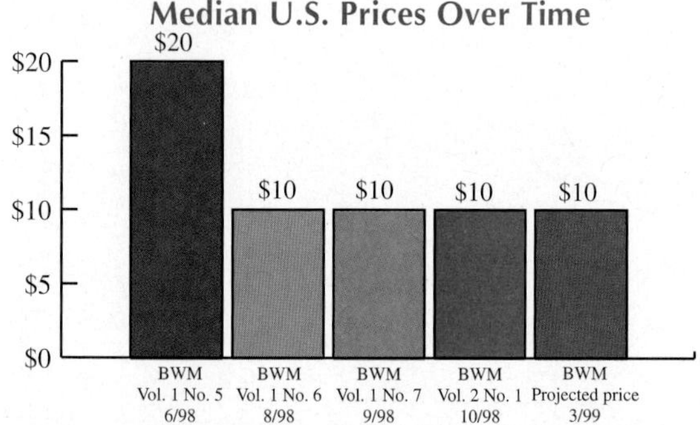

Median U.K. Price: £6.07 **Median Canadian Price: $15.03**

Chocolate the moose

Fast Facts

Style Number: 4015
Introduced: 1994
Status: Current
Birthday: 4-27-93

Collector Trivia

5,000 Chocolates with a commemorative card were given away at the Denver Nuggets-Portland Trail Blazers game on April 17, 1998.

Median U.S. Prices By Hang Tag

1st	2nd	3rd	4th	5th
$700-900	$425-500	$165-185	$10-15	$10-15

Available Tush Tag Generations: 1st, 2nd, 3rd, 4th, 5th, 6th

Median U.S. Prices Over Time

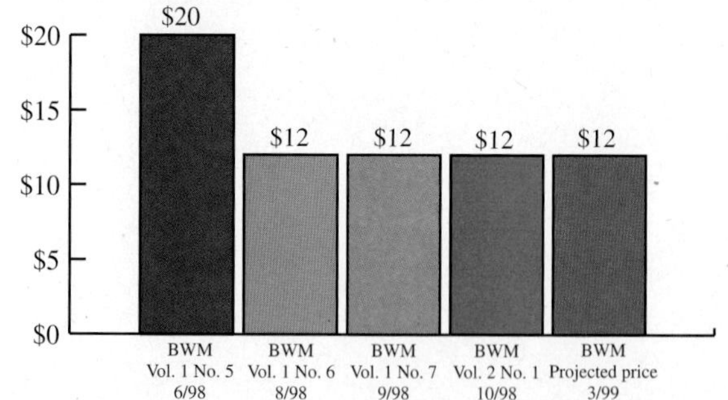

Median U.K. Price: £7.29 **Median Canadian Price: $18.04**

Chops the lamb

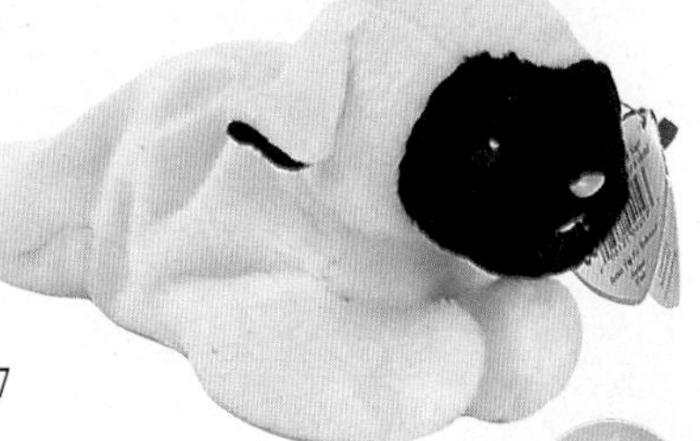

Fast Facts

Style Number: 4019
Introduced: 1996
Status: Retired 1-1-97
Birthday: 5-3-96

Collector Trivia

Chops was replaced in the Beanie Baby line by another lamb, Fleece, on January 1, 1997.

Median U.S. Prices By Hang Tag

1st	2nd	3rd	4th	5th
N/A	N/A	$235-260	$150-195	N/A

Available Tush Tag Generations: 2nd, 3rd

Median U.S. Prices Over Time

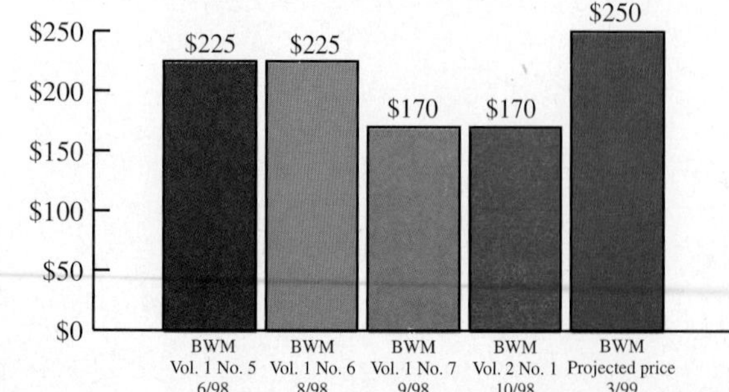

Median U.K. Price: £103.34 **Median Canadian Price: $255.59**

Claude the tie-dyed crab

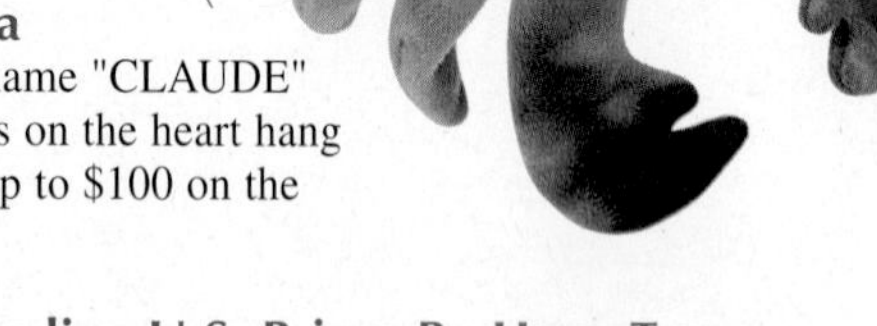

Fast Facts

Style Number: 4083
Introduced: 5-11-97
Status: Current
Birthday: 9-3-96

Collector Trivia

Claudes with the name "CLAUDE" in all capital letters on the heart hang tag can be worth up to $100 on the secondary market.

Median U.S. Prices By Hang Tag

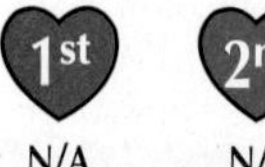

1st	2nd	3rd	4th	5th
N/A	N/A	N/A	$10-15	$10-15

Available Tush Tag Generations: 3rd, 4th, 5th, 6th

Median U.S. Prices Over Time

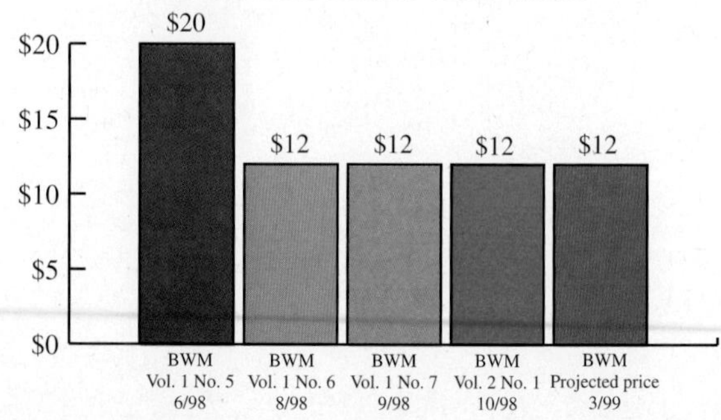

Median U.K. Price: £7.29 **Median Canadian Price: $18.04**

Clubby the bear

Fast Facts
Style Number: None
Introduced: 1998
Status: Current
Birthday: 7-7-98

Collector Trivia
Clubby is the first exclusive Beanie to be offered through Ty Inc.'s Beanie Babies Official Club.

Median U.S. Prices By Hang Tag

1st	2nd	3rd	4th	5th
N/A	N/A	N/A	N/A	$10

Available Tush Tag Generations: 6th

Median U.S. Prices Over Time

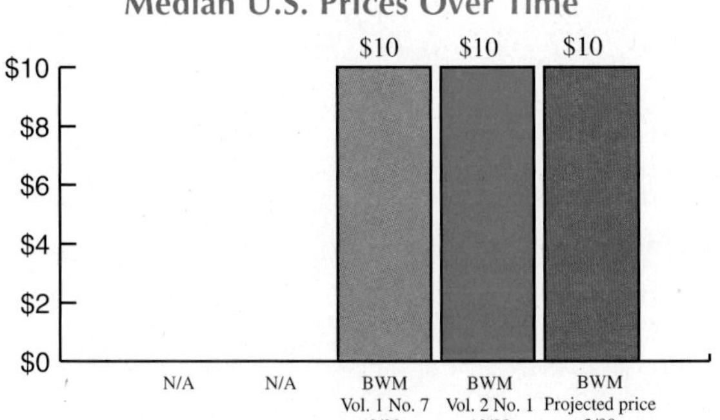

Median U.K. Price: £6.07 Median Canadian Price: $15.03

Congo the gorilla

Fast Facts
Style Number: 4160
Introduced: 1996
Status: Current
Birthday: 11-9-96

Collector Trivia
Congo has often been considered a "hard-to-find" Beanie Baby because of a supply shortage that occurred in the summer of 1997.

Median U.S. Prices By Hang Tag

1st	2nd	3rd	4th	5th
N/A	N/A	N/A	$8-10	$8-10

Available Tush Tag Generations: 3rd, 4th, 5th, 6th

Median U.S. Prices Over Time

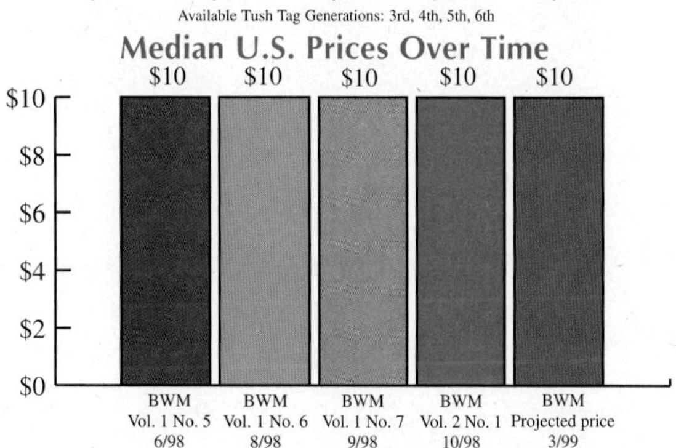

Median U.K. Price: £6.07 Median Canadian Price: $15.03

Coral the tie-dyed fish

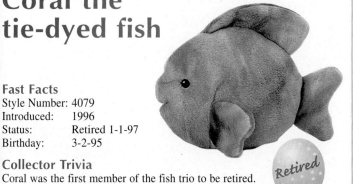

Fast Facts
Style Number: 4079
Introduced: 1996
Status: Retired 1-1-97
Birthday: 3-2-95

Collector Trivia
Coral was the first member of the fish trio to be retired.

Retired

Median U.S. Prices By Hang Tag

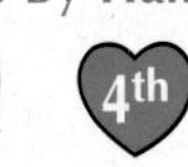

1st	2nd	3rd	4th	5th
N/A	N/A	$250-285	$165-200	N/A

Available Tush Tag Generations: 1st, 2nd, 3rd

Median U.S. Prices Over Time

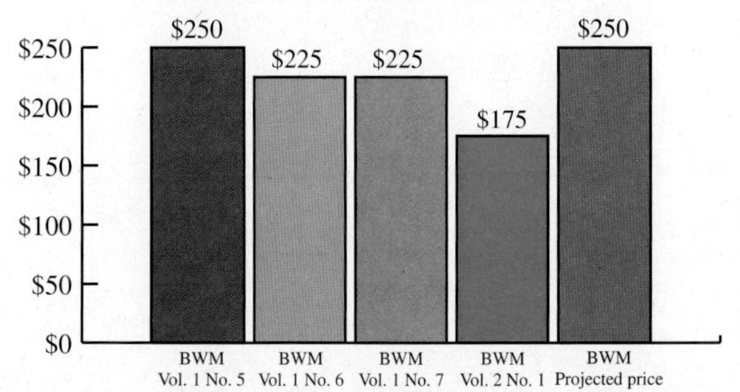

Median U.K. Price: £106.38 Median Canadian Price: $263.11

Crunch the shark

Fast Facts
Style Number: 4130
Introduced: 1-1-97
Status: Current
Birthday: 1-13-96

Collector Trivia
A somewhat slow seller, Crunch has long been rumored for retirement, but he remains current.

Median U.S. Prices By Hang Tag

1st	2nd	3rd	4th	5th
N/A	N/A	N/A	$8-10	$8-10

Available Tush Tag Generations: 3rd, 4th, 5th, 6th

Median U.S. Prices Over Time

BWM Vol. 1 No. 5 6/98	BWM Vol. 1 No. 6 8/98	BWM Vol. 1 No. 7 9/98	BWM Vol. 2 No. 1 10/98	BWM Projected price 3/99
$10	$10	$10	$10	$10

Median U.K. Price: £6.07 Median Canadian Price: $15.03

Cubbie the brown bear

Fast Facts
Style Number: 4010
Introduced: 1994
Status: Retired 12-31-97
Birthday: 11-14-93

Collector Trivia
In 1997, the Chicago Cubs made Cubbie the first Beanie to be part of a sports team giveaway.

Median U.S. Prices By Hang Tag

1st	2nd	3rd	4th	5th
$700-750	$450-495	$160-180	$25-40	$25-40

Available Tush Tag Generations: 1st, 2nd, 3rd, 4th, 5th, 6th

Median U.S. Prices Over Time

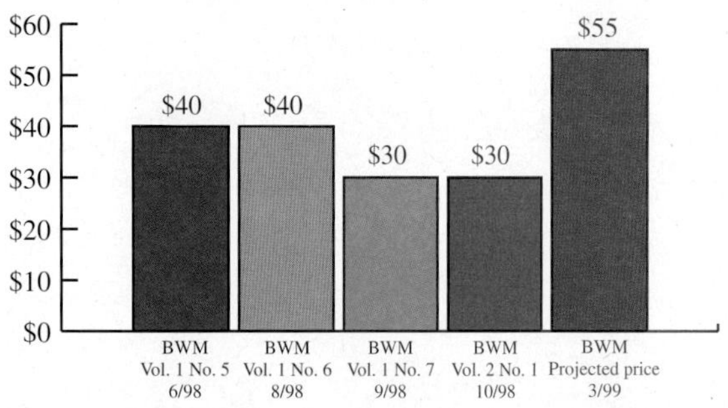

Median U.K. Price: £18.23 **Median Canadian Price: $45.10**

Curly the brown napped teddy

Fast Facts
Style Number: 4052
Introduced: 1996
Status: Current
Birthday: 4-12-96

Collector Trivia
"Ragtime Curly" is a regular Curly Beanie Baby with a special ribbon that could be purchased at Broadway performances of the musical "Ragtime."

Median U.S. Prices By Hang Tag

1st	2nd	3rd	4th	5th
N/A	N/A	N/A	$15-35	$15-35

Available Tush Tag Generations: 3rd, 4th, 5th, 6th

Median U.S. Prices Over Time

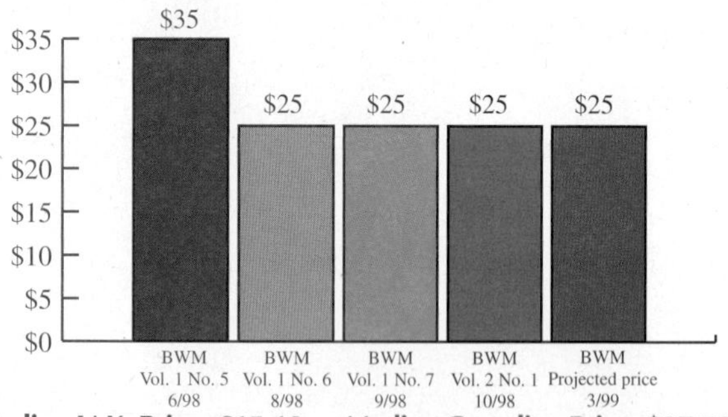

Median U.K. Price: £15.19 **Median Canadian Price: $37.58**

Daisy the black and white cow

Fast Facts
Style Number: 4006
Introduced: 1994
Status: Current
Birthday: 5-10-94

Collector Trivia
Daisy is the only Beanie for which Ty Inc. has produced a new, special heart hang tag. The fifth generation tag for the May 1998 Chicago Cubs Daisy giveaway includes a caricature of and poem to honor broadcaster Harry Caray.

Median U.S. Prices By Hang Tag

1st	2nd	3rd	4th	5th
$300-325	$200-225	$75-100	$10-15	$10-15

Available Tush Tag Generations: 1st, 2nd, 3rd, 4th, 5th, 6th

Median U.S. Prices Over Time

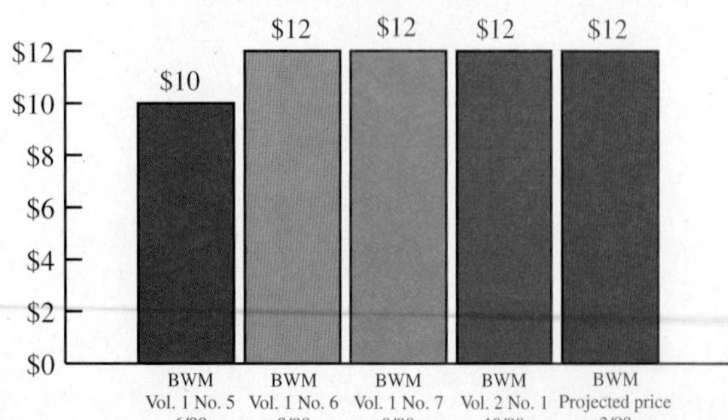

Median U.K. Price: £7.29 **Median Canadian Price: $18.04**

Derby the coarse mane horse with a forehead star

Fast Facts
Style Number: 4008
Introduced: 12-31-97
Status: Current
Birthday: 9-16-95

Collector Trivia
It was quite a surprise when a Derby with a star on its forehead started appearing in stores in 1997.

Median U.S. Prices By Hang Tag

1st	2nd	3rd	4th	5th
N/A	N/A	N/A	N/A	$10-15

Available Tush Tag Generations: 6th

Median U.S. Prices Over Time

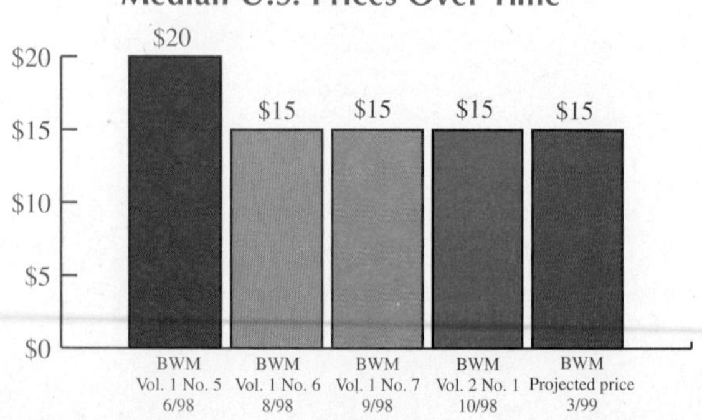

Median U.K. Price: £9.11 **Median Canadian Price: $22.55**

Derby the coarse mane horse without a forehead star

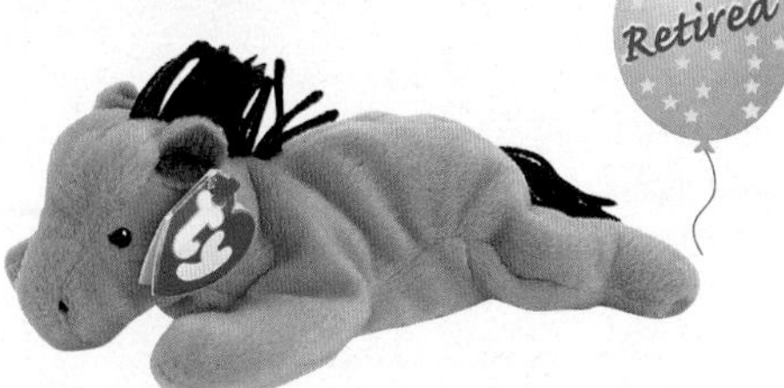

Fast Facts
Style Number: 4008
Introduced: 1996
Status: Retired
Birthday: 9-16-95

Collector Trivia
The high price of this Beanie with a third generation swing tag stems from the fact that it is identical to the tag on Derby the fine mane horse.

Median U.S. Prices By Hang Tag

1st	2nd	3rd	4th	5th
N/A	N/A	$365-450	$20-35	$20-35

Available Tush Tag Generations: 1st, 2nd, 3rd, 4th, 5th, 6th

Median U.S. Prices Over Time

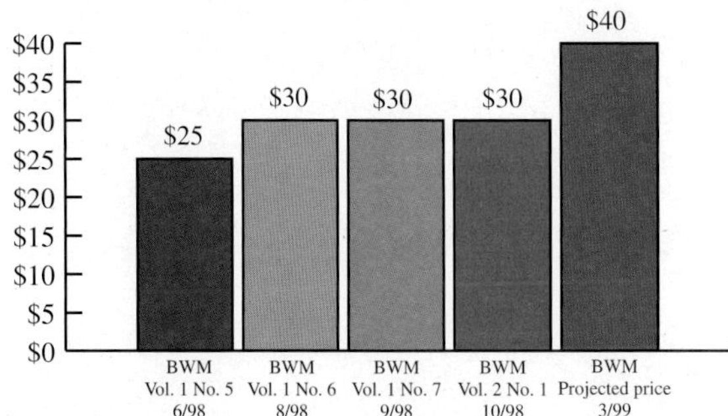

Median U.K. Price: £18.23 Median Canadian Price: $45.10

Derby the fine mane horse

Fast Facts
Style Number: 4008
Introduced: 1995
Status: Retired 1995
Birthday: Unknown

Collector Trivia
This very limited edition Derby was later changed because the fine yarn in the mane had a tendency to unravel.

Median U.S. Prices By Hang Tag

1st	2nd	3rd	4th	5th
N/A	N/A	$3200-3900	N/A	N/A

Available Tush Tag Generations: 1st, 2nd

Median U.S. Prices Over Time

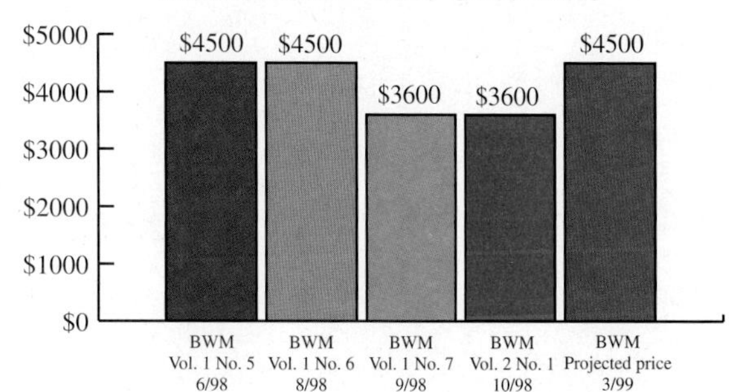

Median U.K. Price: £2188.44 Median Canadian Price: $5412.60

Digger the orange crab

Fast Facts
Style Number: 4027
Introduced: 1994
Status: Retired 1995
Birthday: Unknown

Collector Trivia
Orange Digger is the rarest of the three crabs (orange Digger, red Digger and Claude) in the Beanie family.

Median U.S. Prices By Hang Tag

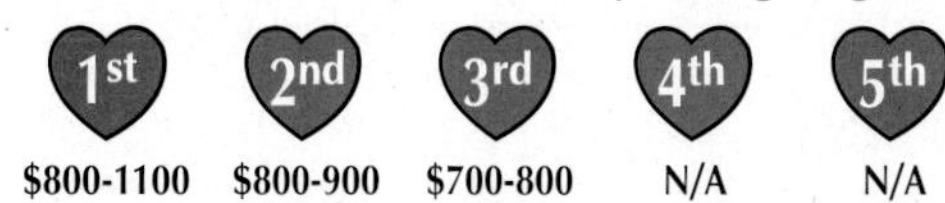

1st	2nd	3rd	4th	5th
$800-1100	$800-900	$700-800	N/A	N/A

Available Tush Tag Generations: 1st

Median U.S. Prices Over Time

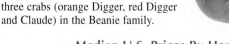

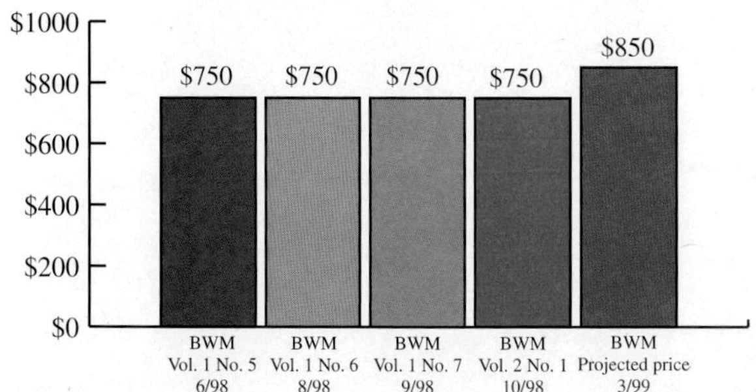

Median U.K. Price: £455.92 Median Canadian Price: $1127.62

Digger the red crab

Fast Facts
Style Number: 4027
Introduced: 1995
Status: Retired 5-11-97
Birthday: 8-23-95

Collector Trivia
Red Digger has the same style number as his predecessor, orange Digger.

Median U.S. Prices By Hang Tag

1st	2nd	3rd	4th	5th
N/A	N/A	$225-250	$110-150	N/A

Available Tush Tag Generations: 1st, 2nd, 3rd, 4th

Median U.S. Prices Over Time

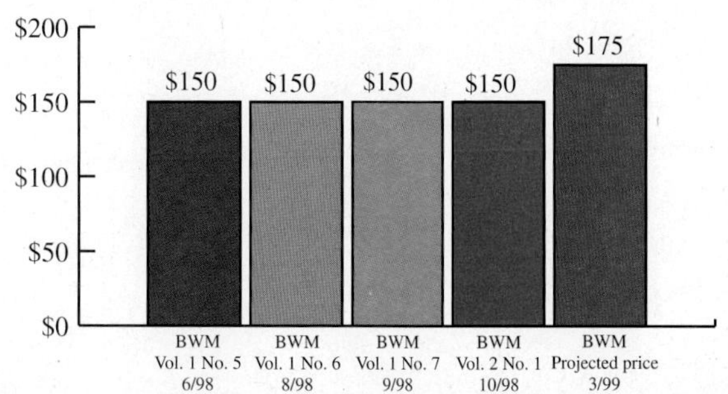

Median U.K. Price: £91.18 Median Canadian Price: $225.52

Doby the doberman

Fast Facts
Style Number: 4110
Introduced: 1-1-97
Status: Current
Birthday: 10-9-96

Collector Trivia
Doby was the first of 12 Beanie Babies in the 1998 lineup of McDonald's Teenie Beanie Babies.

Current

Median U.S. Prices By Hang Tag

Available Tush Tag Generations: 3rd, 4th, 5th, 6th

Median U.S. Prices Over Time

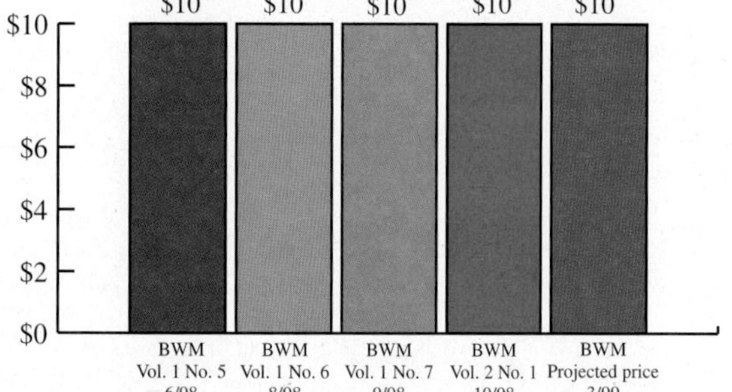

Median U.K. Price: £6.07 **Median Canadian Price: $15.03**

Doodle the rooster

Retired

Fast Facts
Style Number: 4171
Introduced: 5-11-97
Status: Retired 1997
Birthday: 3-8-96

Collector Trivia
Doodle was retired due to a copyright infringement case involving a Southern fast food chain. Its replacement, Strut, looks identical to Doodle.

Median U.S. Prices By Hang Tag

Available Tush Tag Generations: 3rd, 4th

Median U.S. Prices Over Time

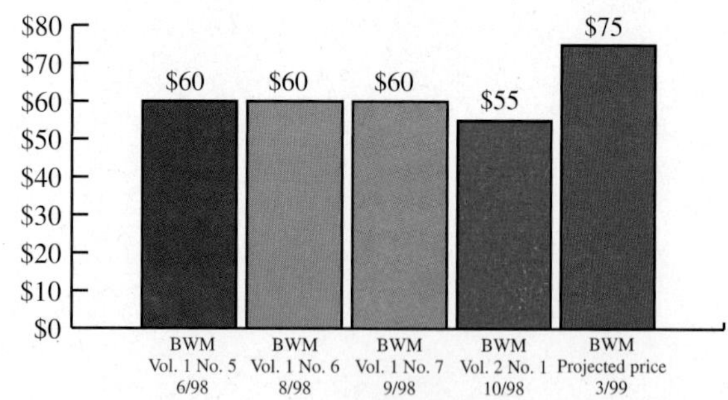

Median U.K. Price: £33.43 **Median Canadian Price: $82.69**

Dotty the Dalmatian with black ears

Fast Facts
Style Number: 4100
Introduced: 5-11-97
Status: Current
Birthday: 10-17-96

Current

Collector Trivia
Dotty replaced the prematurely retired Sparky. Some Sparkys with Dotty tush tags showed up in the marketplace before the official retirement announcement.

Median U.S. Prices By Hang Tag

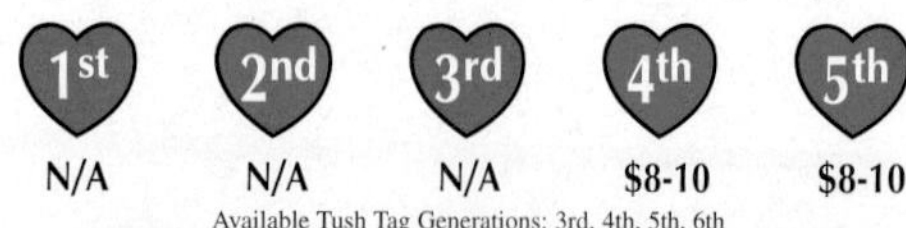

Available Tush Tag Generations: 3rd, 4th, 5th, 6th

Median U.S. Prices Over Time

$10 $10 $10 $10 $10

$10 / $8 / $6 / $4 / $2 / $0

BWM Vol. 1 No. 5 6/98 · BWM Vol. 1 No. 6 8/98 · BWM Vol. 1 No. 7 9/98 · BWM Vol. 2 No. 1 10/98 · BWM Projected price 3/99

Median U.K. Price: £6.07 **Median Canadian Price: $15.03**

Early the robin

Fast Facts
Style Number: 4190
Introduced: 5-30-98
Status: Current
Birthday: 3-20-97

Collector Trivia
Early was one of 14 new Beanie Babies announced by Ty Inc. on May 30, 1998.

Median U.S. Prices By Hang Tag

Available Tush Tag Generations: 6th

Median U.S. Prices Over Time

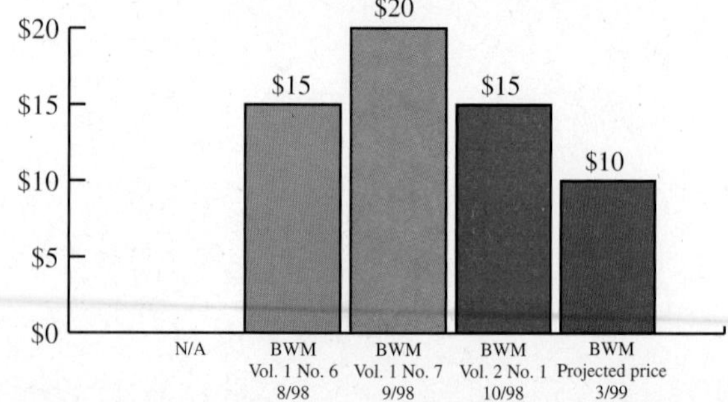

Median U.K. Price: £9.11 **Median Canadian Price: $22.55**

Ears the brown rabbit

Fast Facts

Style Number: 4018
Introduced: 1996
Status: Retired 5-1-98
Birthday: 4-18-95

Collector Trivia

5,000 Ears with a commemorative card were given away at an Oakland A's Spring Training baseball game on March 15, 1998.

Median U.S. Prices By Hang Tag

1st	2nd	3rd	4th	5th
N/A	N/A	$100-125	$15-25	$15-25

Available Tush Tag Generations: 2nd, 3rd, 4th, 6th

Median U.S. Prices Over Time

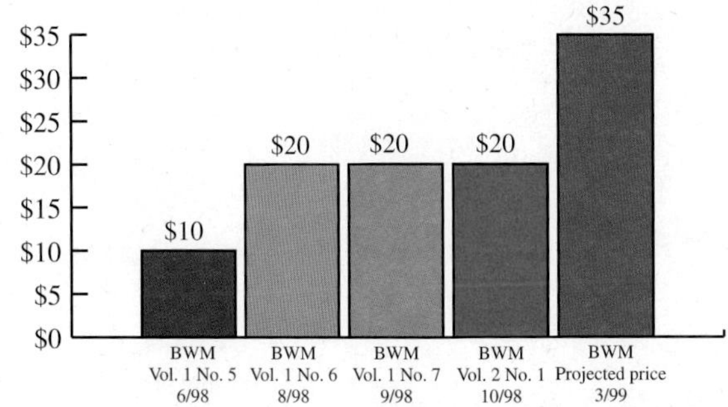

Median U.K. Price: £12.15 Median Canadian Price: $30.07

Echo the dolphin

Fast Facts

Style Number: 4180
Introduced: 5-11-97
Status: Retired 5-1-98
Birthday: 12-21-96

Collector Trivia

Echo was introduced on the same day that fellow dolphin Flash was retired.

Median U.S. Prices By Hang Tag

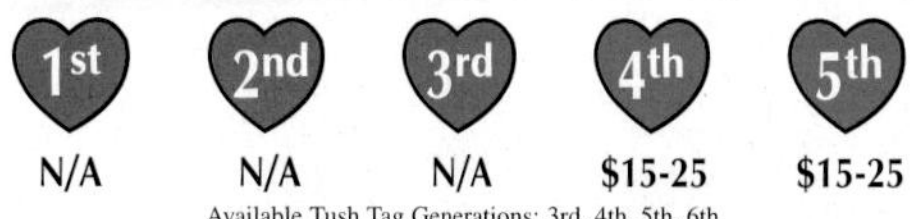

1st	2nd	3rd	4th	5th
N/A	N/A	N/A	$15-25	$15-25

Available Tush Tag Generations: 3rd, 4th, 5th, 6th

Median U.S. Prices Over Time

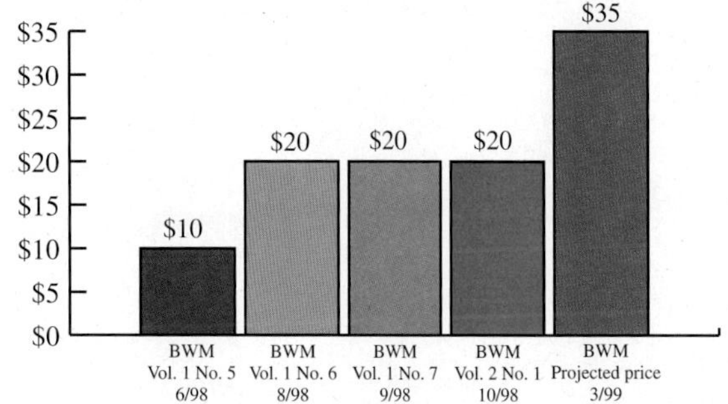

Median U.K. Price: £12.15 Median Canadian Price: $30.07

Erin the emerald green bear

Fast Facts

Style Number: 4186
Introduced: 1998
Status: Current
Birthday: 3-17-97

Collector Trivia

A favorite of Ireland-lovers worldwide, this Beanie originally was very hard to find.

Median U.S. Prices By Hang Tag

1st	2nd	3rd	4th	5th
N/A	N/A	N/A	N/A	$25-50

Available Tush Tag Generations: 6th

Median U.S. Prices Over Time

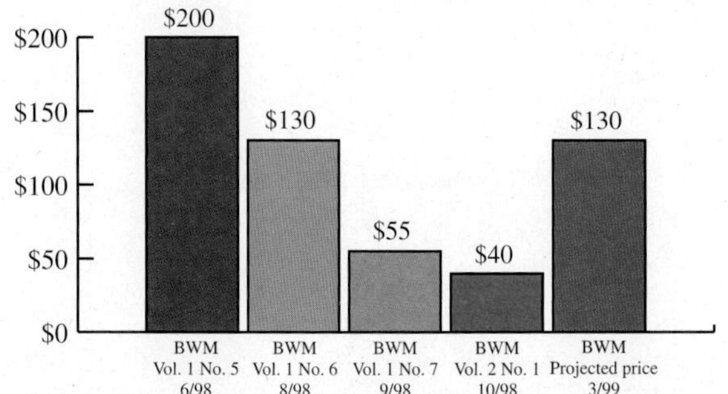

Median U.K Price: £24.31 Median Canadian Price: $60.14

Fetch the golden retriever

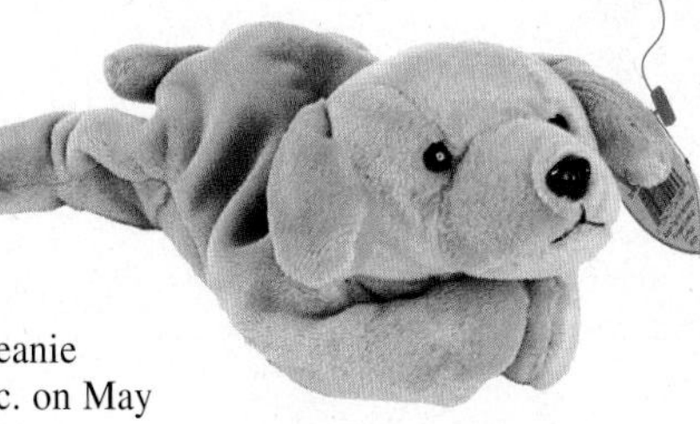

Fast Facts

Style Number: 4189
Introduced: 5-30-98
Status: Current
Birthday: 2-4-97

Collector Trivia

Fetch was one of 14 new Beanie Babies announced by Ty Inc. on May 30, 1998.

Median U.S. Prices By Hang Tag

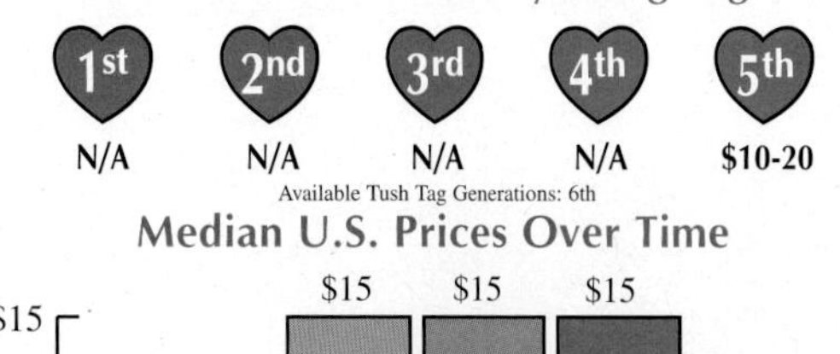

1st	2nd	3rd	4th	5th
N/A	N/A	N/A	N/A	$10-20

Available Tush Tag Generations: 6th

Median U.S. Prices Over Time

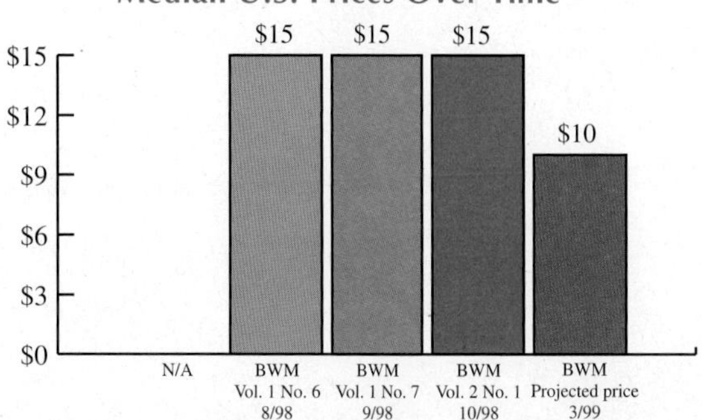

Median U.K. Price: £9.11 Median Canadian Price: $22.55

Flash the dolphin

Fast Facts
Style Number: 4021
Introduced: 1994
Status: Retired 5-11-97
Birthday: 5-13-93

Collector Trivia
When Flash was first retired, its secondary market value was flat for the first few months.

Median U.S. Prices By Hang Tag

1st	2nd	3rd	4th	5th
$800-950	$700-850	$225-250	$110-150	N/A

Available Tush Tag Generations: 1st, 2nd, 3rd

Median U.S. Prices Over Time

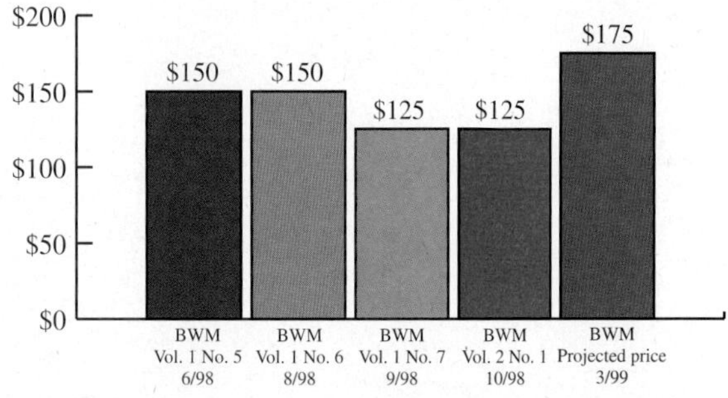

Median U.K. Price: £75.98 **Median Canadian Price: $187.93**

Fleece the napped lamb

Fast Facts
Style Number: 4125
Introduced: 1-1-97
Status: Current
Birthday: 3-21-96

Collector Trivia
Fleece is one of four Beanies with napped fabric. The others are Curly, Scottie and Tuffy.

Median U.S. Prices By Hang Tag

1st	2nd	3rd	4th	5th
N/A	N/A	N/A	$8-10	$8-10

Available Tush Tag Generations: 3rd, 4th, 5th, 6th

Median U.S. Prices Over Time

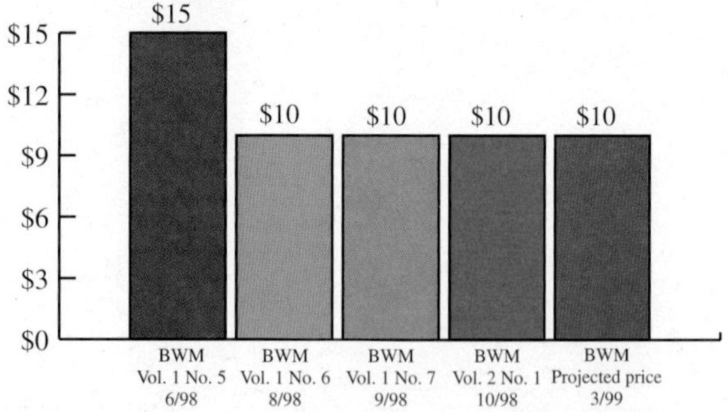

Median U.K. Price: £6.07 **Median Canadian Price: $15.03**

Flip the white cat

Retired

Fast Facts
Style Number: 4012
Introduced: 1996
Status: Retired 10-1-97
Birthday: 2-28-95

Collector Trivia
Flip was the first member of the cat family to be retired.

Median U.S. Prices By Hang Tag

1st	2nd	3rd	4th	5th
N/A	N/A	$100-125	$25-40	N/A

Available Tush Tag Generations: 2nd, 3rd, 4th, 5th

Median U.S. Prices Over Time

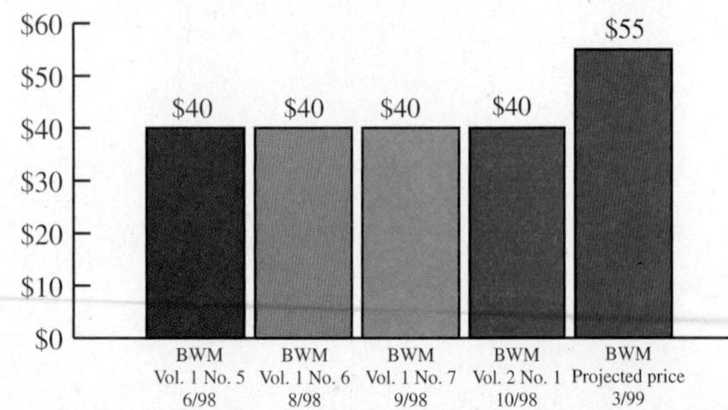

Median U.K. Price: £24.31 **Median Canadian Price: $60.14**

Floppity the lavender bunny

Retired

Fast Facts
Style Number: 4118
Introduced: 1-1-97
Status: Retired 5-1-98
Birthday: 5-28-96

Collector Trivia
The three bunnies – Floppity, Hippity and Hoppity – were selling as a set for $75 to $90 a set when supplies were scarce in the summer of 1997.

Median U.S. Prices By Hang Tag

1st	2nd	3rd	4th	5th
N/A	N/A	N/A	$15-25	$15-25

Available Tush Tag Generations: 3rd, 4th, 6th

Median U.S. Prices Over Time

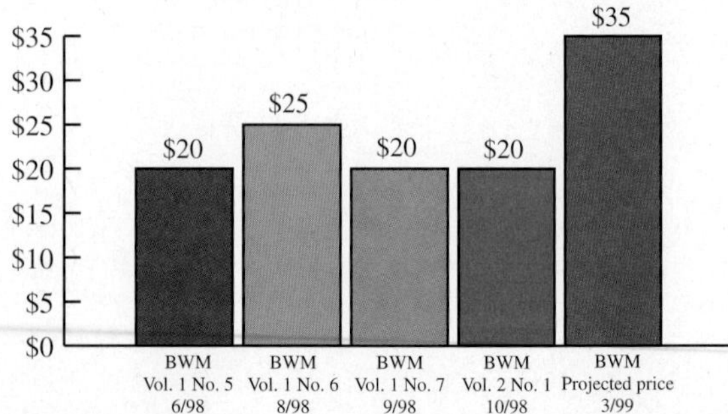

Median U.K. Price: £12.15 **Median Canadian Price: $30.07**

Flutter the butterfly

Fast Facts

Style Number: 4043
Introduced: 1995
Status: Retired 1996
Birthday: Unknown

Collector Trivia

The range of values for Flutter reflects color variations. Flutters with brighter coloring generally command higher prices.

Median U.S. Prices By Hang Tag

Median U.S. Prices Over Time

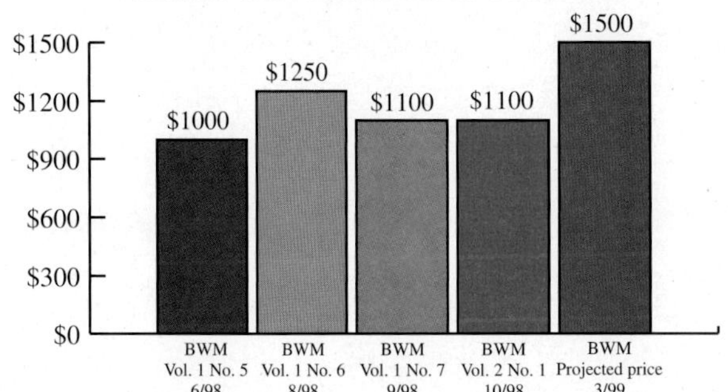

Median U.K. Price: £668.69 Median Canadian Price: $1653.85

Fortune the panda

Fast Facts

Style Number: 4196
Introduced: 5-30-98
Status: Current
Birthday: 12-6-97

Collector Trivia

Although Fortune was released only recently, counterfeit Fortunes have already been spotted on the secondary market.

Median U.S. Prices By Hang Tag

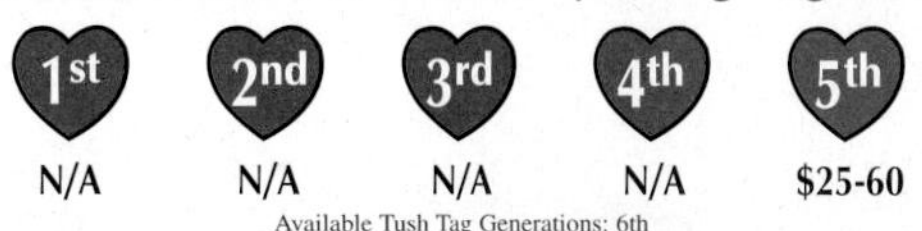

Median U.S. Prices Over Time

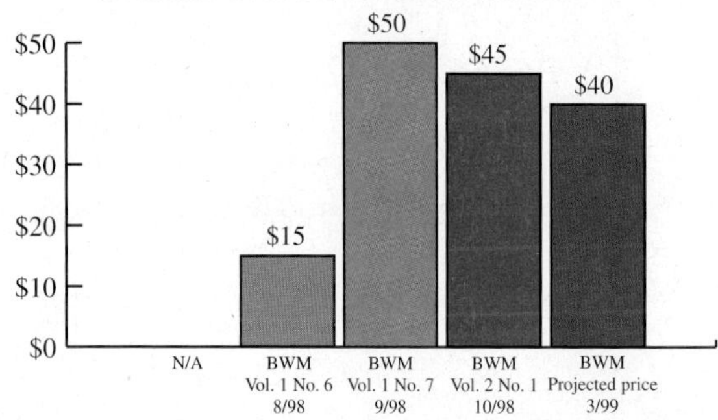

Median U.K. Price: £27.35 Median Canadian Price: $67.65

Freckles the leopard

Fast Facts

Style Number: 4066
Introduced: 1996
Status: Current
Birthday: 6-3-96

Collector Trivia

Freckles originally had a flat tail with a seam on the outside. Current versions have a rounded tail with a seam on the inside.

Median U.S. Prices By Hang Tag

Median U.S. Prices Over Time

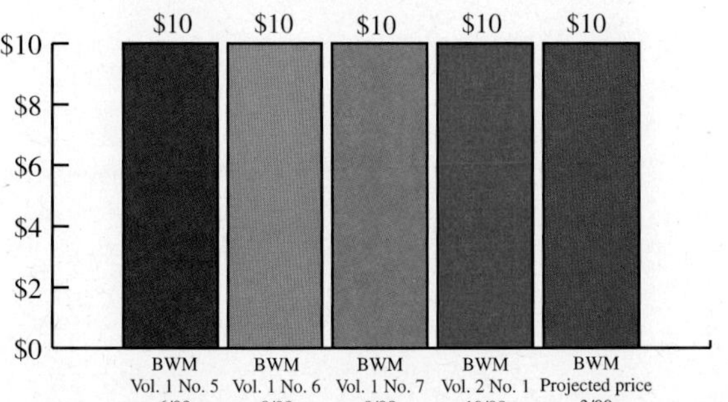

Median U.K. Price: £6.07 Median Canadian Price: $15.03

Garcia the tie-dyed teddy

Fast Facts

Style Number: 4051
Introduced: 1996
Status: Retired 5-11-97
Birthday: 8-1-95

Collector Trivia

Collectors are beginning to ask for specific color combinations in Garcias to meet individual preferences.

Median U.S. Prices By Hang Tag

1st N/A
2nd N/A
3rd $250-300
4th $170-200
5th N/A
Available Tush Tag Generations: 2nd, 3rd

Median U.S. Prices Over Time

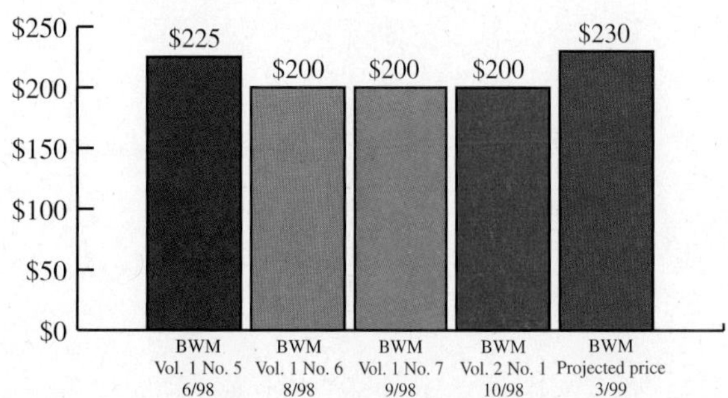

Median U.K. Price: £121.58 Median Canadian Price: $300.70

Gigi the poodle

Fast Facts

Style Number: 4191
Introduced: 5-30-98
Status: Current
Birthday: 4-7-97

Collector Trivia

Gigi was one of 14 new Beanie Babies announced by Ty Inc. on May 30, 1998.

Median U.S. Prices By Hang Tag

Median U.S. Prices Over Time

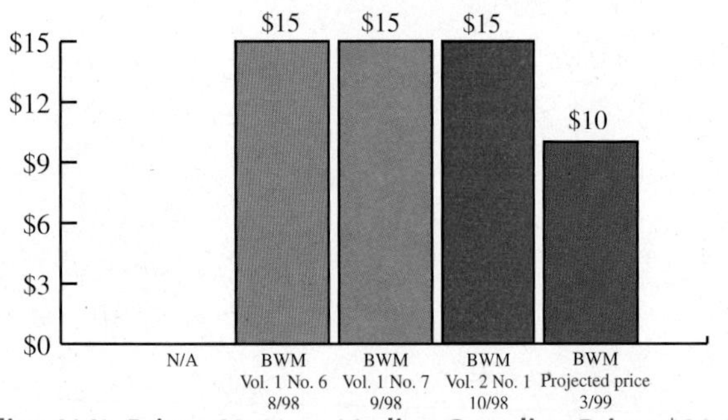

Median U.K. Price: £9.11 **Median Canadian Price: $22.55**

Glory the bear

Fast Facts

Style Number: 4188
Introduced: 5-30-97
Status: Current
Birthday: 7-4-97

Collector Trivia

A Glory with a commemorative card was given away to fans at the Major League Baseball All-Star Game on July 7, 1998, at Coors Field in Denver.

Median U.S. Prices By Hang Tag

Median U.S. Prices Over Time

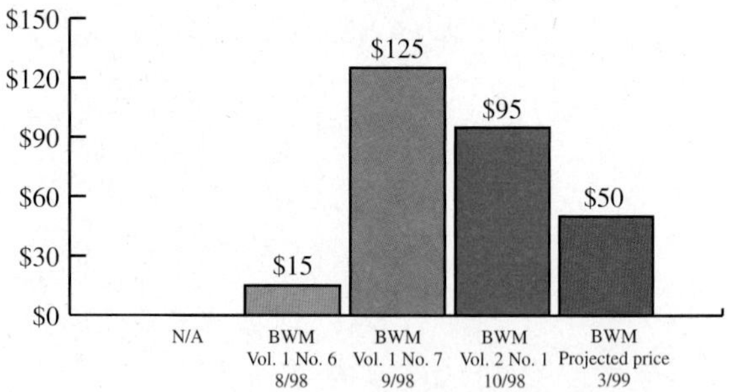

Median U.K. Price: £57.75 **Median Canadian Price: $142.83**

Gobbles the turkey

Fast Facts

Style Number: 4034
Introduced: 10-1-97
Status: Current
Birthday: 11-27-96

Collector Trivia

Many collectors think Gobbles is the cutest and most intricate member of the entire Ty Beanie Baby collection.

Median U.S. Prices By Hang Tag

Median U.S. Prices Over Time

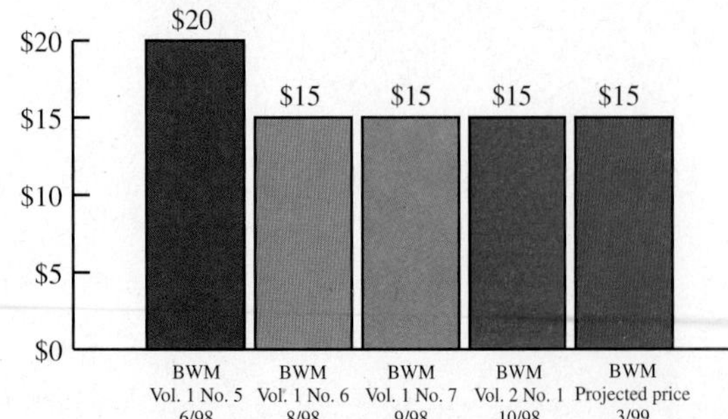

Median U.K. Price: £9.11 **Median Canadian Price: $22.55**

Goldie the goldfish

Fast Facts

Style Number: 4023
Introduced: 1994
Status: Retired 12-31-97
Birthday: 11-14-94

Collector Trivia

Although rumored to be a retirement candidate early in 1997, Goldie was the last fish to bow out, retiring on December 31, 1997.

Median U.S. Prices By Hang Tag

Median U.S. Prices Over Time

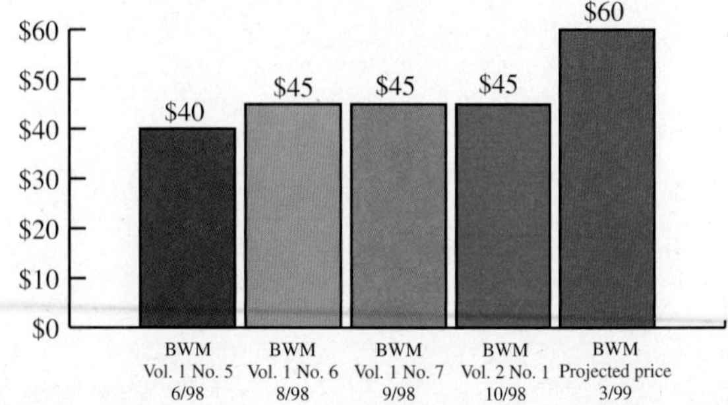

Median U.K. Price: £27.35 **Median Canadian Price: $67.65**

Gracie the swan

Retired

Fast Facts

Style Number: 4126
Introduced: 1-1-97
Status: Retired 5-1-98
Birthday: 6-17-96

Collector Trivia

The Gracie the swan giveaway at the Chicago Cubs game on September 13, 1998, will honor popular Cubs first baseman Mark Grace.

Median U.S. Prices By Hang Tag

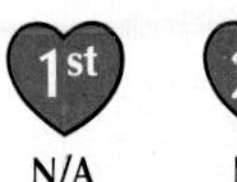

1st	2nd	3rd	4th	5th
N/A	N/A	N/A	$12-18	$12-18

Available Tush Tag Generations: 3rd, 4th, 5th, 6th

Median U.S. Prices Over Time

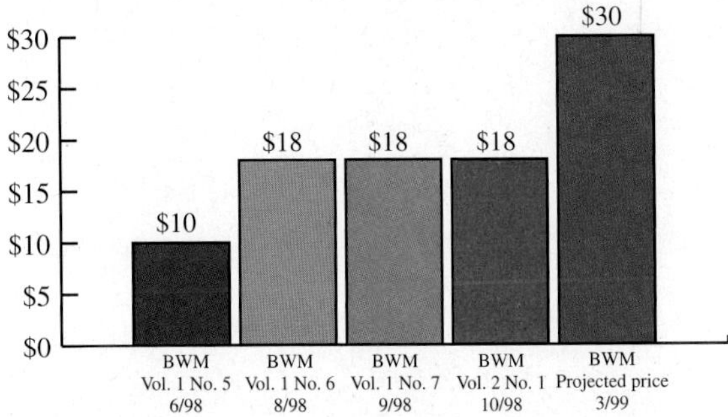

Median U.K. Price: £10.94 **Median Canadian Price: $27.06**

Grunt the red razorback

Retired

Fast Facts

Style Number: 4092
Introduced: 1996
Status: Retired 5-11-97
Birthday: 7-19-95

Collector Trivia

In fall 1997, counterfeit Grunts with cheaper material, less space between the eyes and a smaller overall size began appearing on the secondary market.

Median U.S. Prices By Hang Tag

1st	2nd	3rd	4th	5th
N/A	N/A	$235-260	$160-185	N/A

Available Tush Tag Generations: 2nd, 3rd, 4th

Median U.S. Prices Over Time

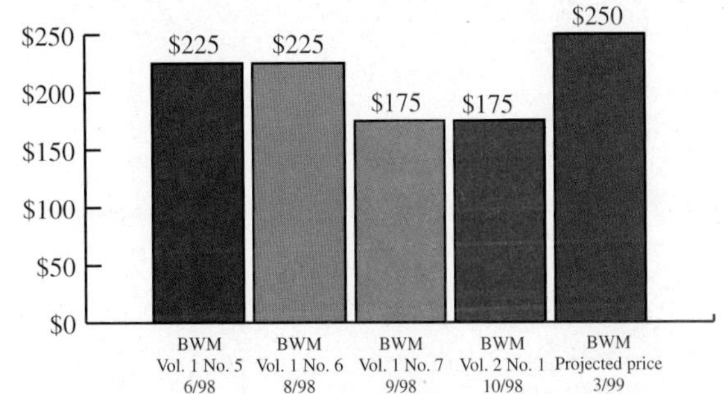

Median U.K. Price: £106.38 **Median Canadian Price: $263.11**

Happy the gray hippo

Fast Facts

Style Number: 4061
Introduced: 1994
Status: Retired 1995
Birthday: Unknown

Collector Trivia

This version of Happy is slightly larger than its replacement version in lavender.

Median U.S. Prices By Hang Tag

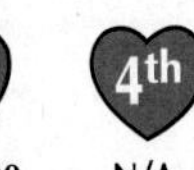

1st	2nd	3rd	4th	5th
$1100-1200	$850-950	$700-800	N/A	N/A

Available Tush Tag Generations: 1st

Median U.S. Prices Over Time

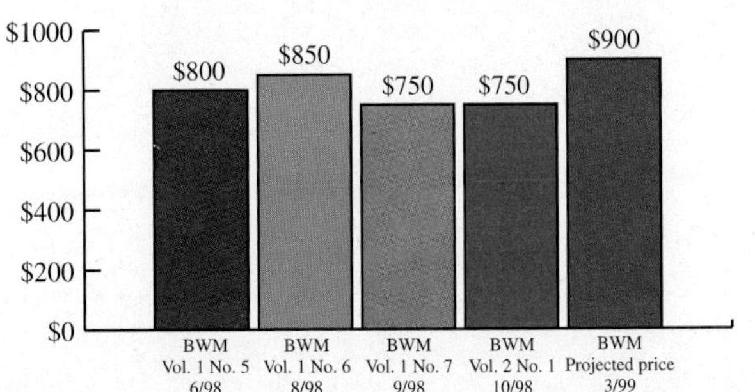

Median U.K. Price: £455.92 **Median Canadian Price: $1127.62**

Happy the lavender hippo

Retired

Fast Facts

Style Number: 4061
Introduced: 1995
Status: Retired 5-1-98
Birthday: 2-25-94

Collector Trivia

Happy has always been a popular "Happy Birthday" gift for collectors young and old.

Median U.S. Prices By Hang Tag

1st	2nd	3rd	4th	5th
N/A	N/A	$250-325	$15-25	$15-25

Available Tush Tag Generations: 1st, 2nd, 3rd, 4th, 5th, 6th

Median U.S. Prices Over Time

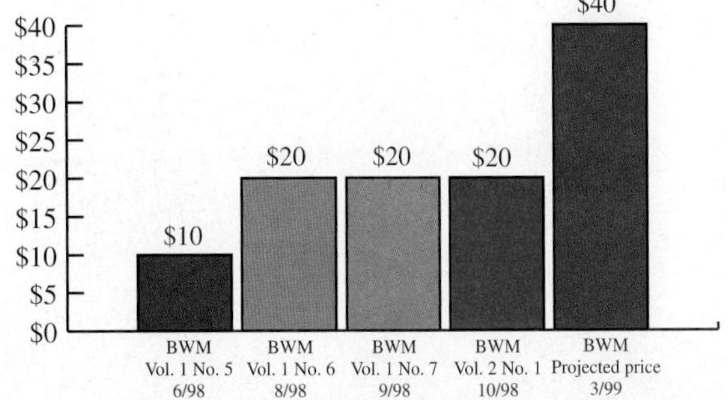

Median U.K. Price: £12.15 **Median Canadian Price: $30.07**

Hippity the mint green bunny

Fast Facts
Style Number: 4119
Introduced: 1-1-97
Status: Retired 5-1-98
Birthday: 6-1-96

Collector Trivia
During the first six months of production, this bunny was often thought to be one of the most difficult for collectors to locate.

Median U.S. Prices By Hang Tag

Available Tush Tag Generations: 3rd, 4th, 6th

Median U.S. Prices Over Time

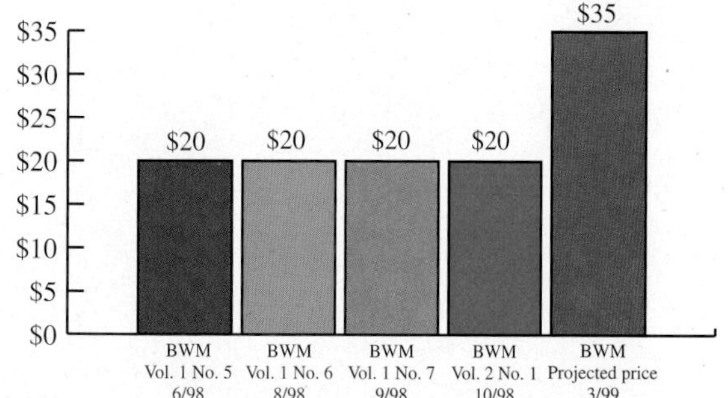

Median U.K. Price: £12.15 Median Canadian Price: $30.07

Hissy the snake

Fast Facts
Style Number: 4185
Introduced: 12-31-97
Status: Current
Birthday: 4-4-97

Collector Trivia
Baseball's Arizona Diamondbacks chose Hissy for their Beanie giveaway day on June 14, 1998.

Median U.S. Prices By Hang Tag

Available Tush Tag Generations: 6th

Median U.S. Prices Over Time

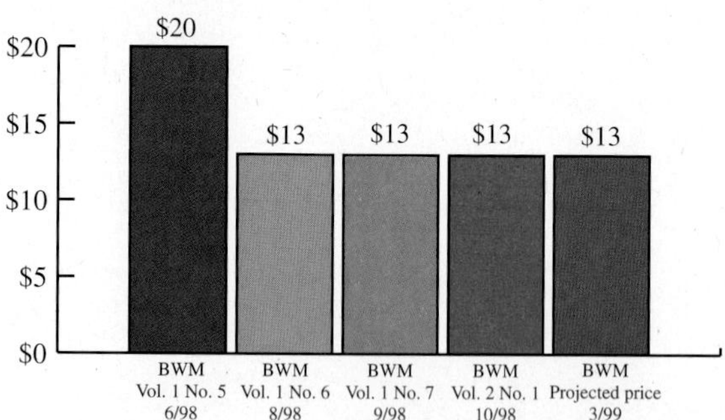

Median U.K. Price: £7.90 Median Canadian Price: $19.54

Hoot the owl

Fast Facts
Style Number: 4073
Introduced: 1996
Status: Retired 10-1-97
Birthday: 8-9-95

Collector Trivia
It came as a big surprise to many collectors when Hoot was retired on October 1, 1997.

Median U.S. Prices By Hang Tag

Available Tush Tag Generations: 2nd, 3rd, 4th

Median U.S. Prices Over Time

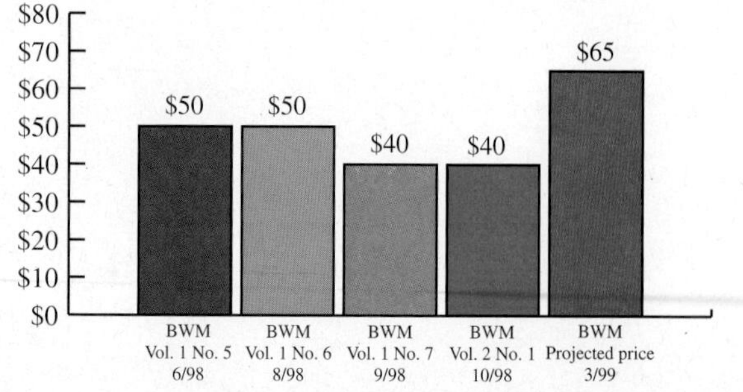

Median U.K. Price: £24.31 Median Canadian Price: $60.14

Hoppity the pink bunny

Fast Facts
Style Number: 4117
Introduced: 1-1-97
Status: Retired 5-1-98
Birthday: 4-3-96

Collector Trivia
Holiday-related Beanies are traditionally more plentiful in stores during the month preceding the holiday they represent.

Median U.S. Prices By Hang Tag

Available Tush Tag Generations: 3rd, 4th, 5th, 6th

Median U.S. Prices Over Time

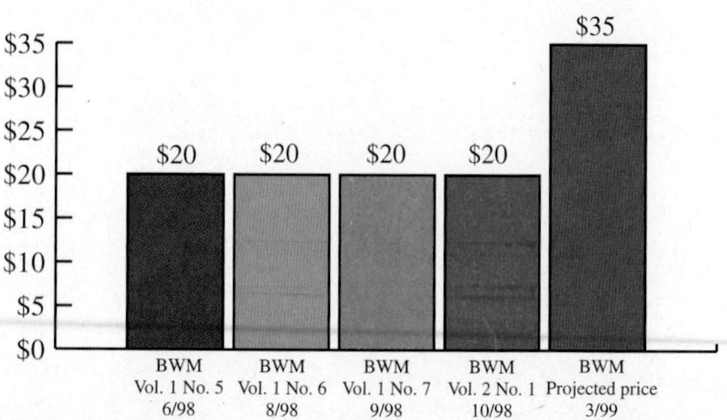

Median U.K. Price: £12.15 Median Canadian Price: $30.07

Humphrey the camel

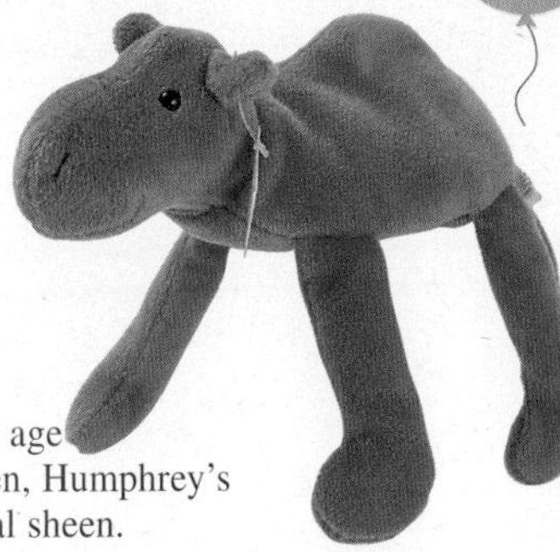

Fast Facts
Style Number: 4060
Introduced: 1994
Status: Retired 1995
Birthday: Unknown

Collector Trivia
Inexplicably, Humphrey seems to age well. Even when played with often, Humphrey's material tends to retain its original sheen.

Median U.S. Prices By Hang Tag

1st	2nd	3rd	4th	5th
$2350-2600	$2100-2400	$1800-2100	N/A	N/A

Available Tush Tag Generations: 1st

Median U.S. Prices Over Time

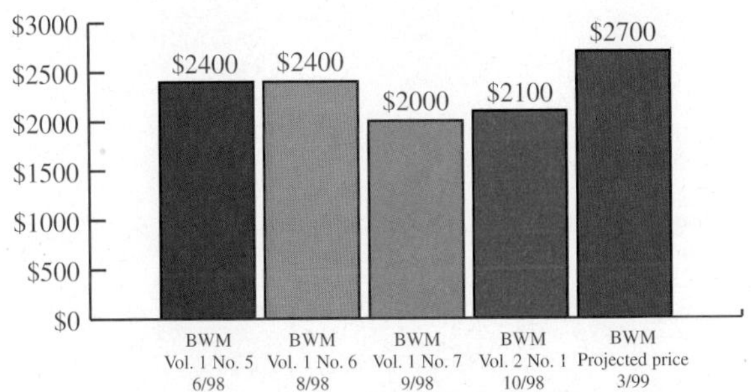

Median U.K. Price: £1276.59 Median Canadian Price: $3157.35

Iggy the iguana

Fast Facts
Style Number: 4038
Introduced: 12-31-97
Status: Current
Birthday: 8-12-97

Collector Trivia
All of the first shipments of Iggy and Rainbow had both their swing tags and tush tags mixed up.

Median U.S. Prices By Hang Tag

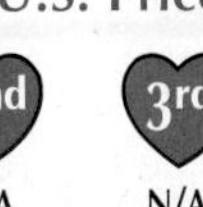

1st	2nd	3rd	4th	5th
N/A	N/A	N/A	N/A	$8-12

Available Tush Tag Generations: 6th

Median U.S. Prices Over Time

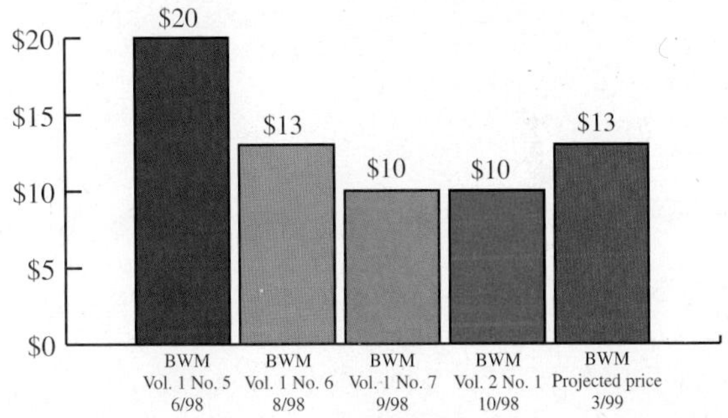

Median U.K. Price: £6.07 Median Canadian Price: $15.03

Inch the inchworm with felt antennas

Fast Facts
Style Number: 4044
Introduced: 1996
Status: Retired 1996
Birthday: Unknown

Collector Trivia
There has been little value distinction between third and fourth generation tags for Inch.

Median U.S. Prices By Hang Tag

1st	2nd	3rd	4th	5th
N/A	N/A	$160-180	$160-180	N/A

Available Tush Tag Generations: 1st, 2nd, 3rd, 4th

Median U.S. Prices Over Time

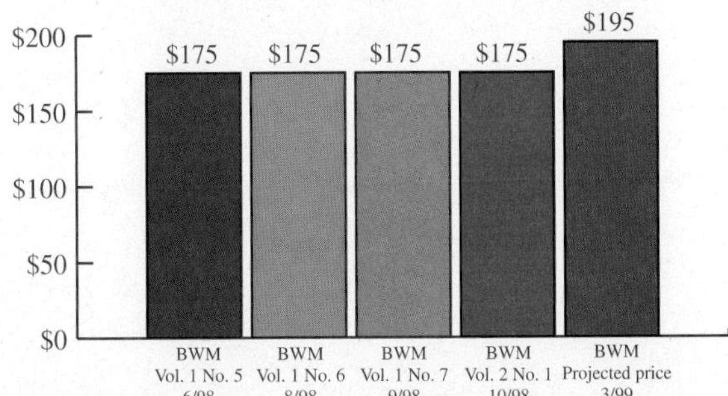

Median U.K. Price: £106.38 Median Canadian Price: $263.11

Inch the inchworm with yarn antennas

Fast Facts
Style Number: 4044
Introduced: 1996
Status: Retired 5-1-98
Birthday: 9-3-95

Collector Trivia
With its intricate color scheme, it surprised many that Inch was able to be made much smaller for the 1998 McDonald's Teenie Beanie Babies promotion.

Median U.S. Prices By Hang Tag

1st	2nd	3rd	4th	5th
N/A	N/A	N/A	$15-20	$15-20

Available Tush Tag Generations: 4th, 5th, 6th

Median U.S. Prices Over Time

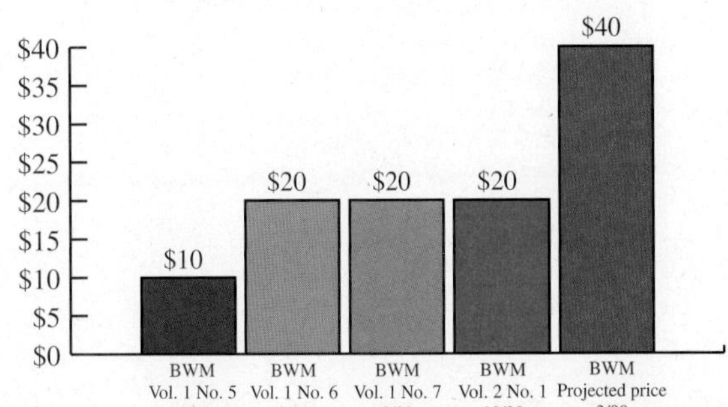

Median U.K. Price: £12.15 Median Canadian Price: $30.07

Inky the pink octopus

Fast Facts
Style Number: 4028
Introduced: 1995
Status: Retired 5-1-98
Birthday: 11-29-94

Collector Trivia
This version of Inky has been seen in versions having seven or nine legs.

Median U.S. Prices By Hang Tag

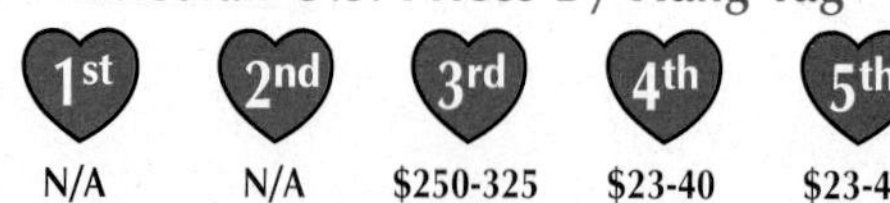

1st	2nd	3rd	4th	5th
N/A	N/A	$250-325	$23-40	$23-40

Available Tush Tag Generations: 1st, 2nd, 3rd, 4th, 5th

Median U.S. Prices Over Time

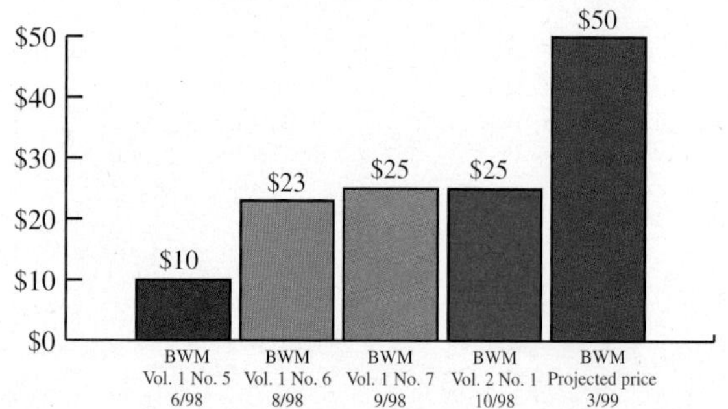

Median U.K. Price: £15.19 Median Canadian Price: $37.58

Inky the tan octopus without a mouth

Fast Facts
Style Number: 4028
Introduced: 1994
Status: Retired 1994
Birthday: Unknown

Collector Trivia
This rare version was produced only with first or second generation heart tags. Look carefully to be sure.

Median U.S. Prices By Hang Tag

1st	2nd	3rd	4th	5th
$1100-1400	$850-1100	N/A	N/A	N/A

Available Tush Tag Generations: 1st

Median U.S. Prices Over Time

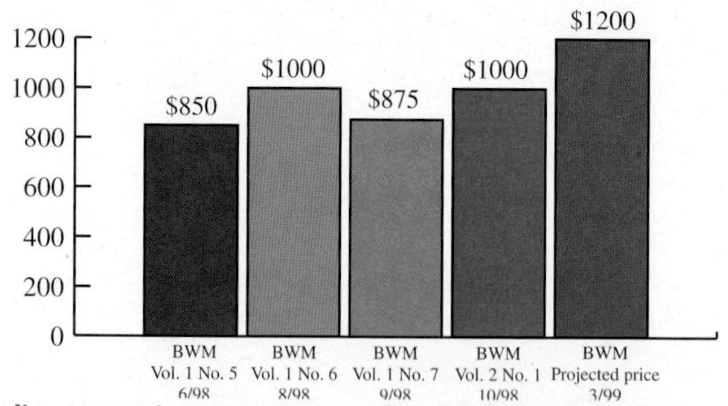

Median U.K. Price: £607.90 Median Canadian Price: $1503.50

Inky the tan octopus with a mouth

Fast Facts
Style Number: 4028
Introduced: 1995
Status: Retired 1995
Birthday: Unknown

Collector Trivia
Collectors were not surprised to see the dull tan fabric of inky changed in favor of the bright pink.

Median U.S. Prices By Hang Tag

1st	2nd	3rd	4th	5th
N/A	$750-800	$620-690	N/A	N/A

Available Tush Tag Generations: 1st

Median U.S. Prices Over Time

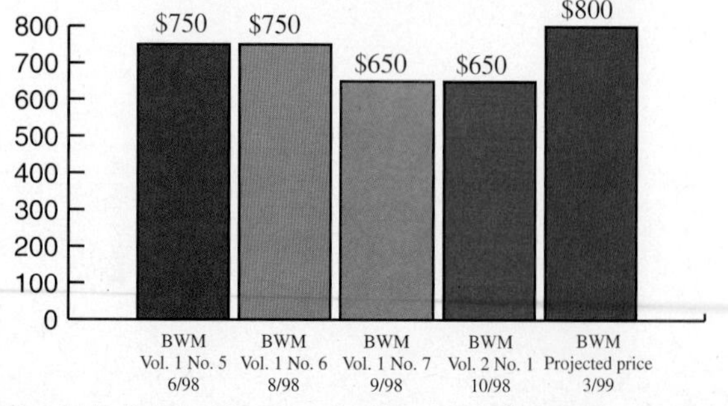

Median U.K. Price: £607.90 Median Canadian Price: $1503.50

Jabber the parrot

Fast Facts
Style Number: 4197
Introduced: 5-30-98
Status: Current
Birthday: 10-10-97

Collector Trivia
Jabber was one of 14 new Beanie Babies announced by Ty Inc. on May 30, 1998.

Median U.S. Prices By Hang Tag

1st	2nd	3rd	4th	5th
N/A	N/A	N/A	N/A	$15-25

Available Tush Tag Generations: 6th

Median U.S. Prices Over Time

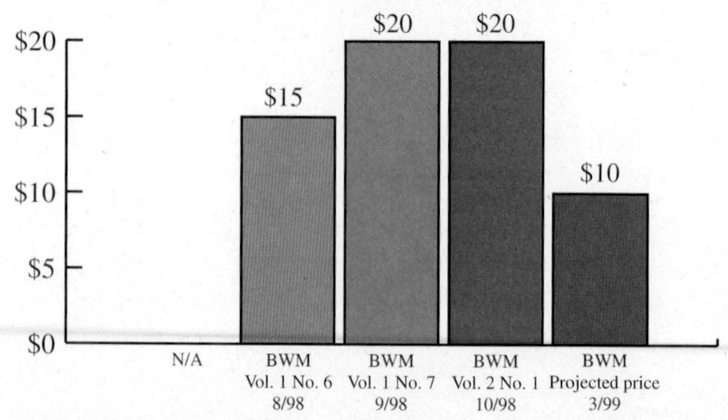

Median U.K. Price: £12.15 Median Canadian Price: $30.07

Jake the mallard duck

Fast Facts

Style Number: 4199
Introduced: 5-30-98
Status: Current
Birthday: 4-16-97

Collector Trivia

Jake was one of 14 new Beanie Babies announced by Ty Inc. on May 30, 1998.

Median U.S. Prices By Hang Tag

Available Tush Tag Generations: 6th

Median U.S. Prices Over Time

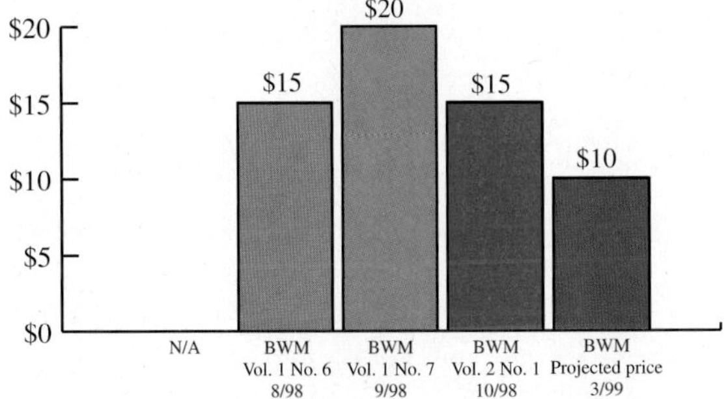

Median U.K. Price: £9.11 **Median Canadian Price: $22.55**

Jolly the walrus

Fast Facts

Style Number: 4082
Introduced: 5-11-97
Status: Retired 5-1-98
Birthday: 12-2-96

Collector Trivia

Jolly was a nice walrus replacement for retired friend Tusk.

Median U.S. Prices By Hang Tag

Available Tush Tag Generations: 3rd, 4th, 5th, 6th

Median U.S. Prices Over Time

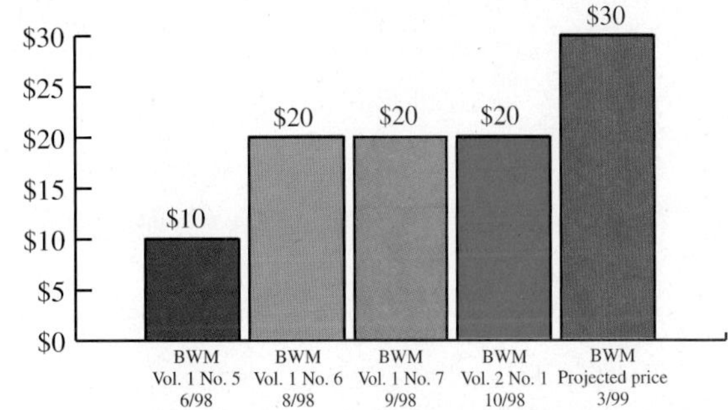

Median U.K. Price: £12.15 **Median Canadian Price: $30.07**

Kiwi the toucan

Retired

Fast Facts

Style Number: 4070
Introduced: 1995
Status: Retired 1-1-97
Birthday: 9-16-95

Collector Trivia

Kiwi and Inch are the only two Beanies to have the same fabric as the rare royal blue version of Peanut.

Median U.S. Prices By Hang Tag

N/A N/A $200-225 $160-185 N/A

Available Tush Tag Generations: 1st, 2nd, 3rd

Median U.S. Prices Over Time

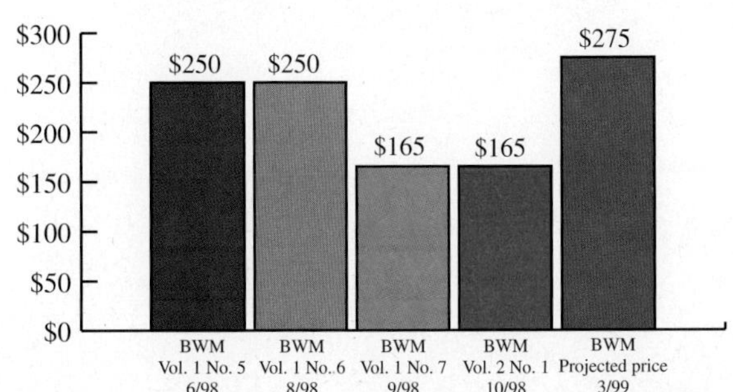

Median U.K. Price: £100.30 **Median Canadian Price: $248.07**

Kuku the cockatoo

Fast Facts

Style Number: 4192
Introduced: 5-30-98
Status: Current
Birthday: 1-15-97

Collector Trivia

Kuku was one of 14 new Beanie Babies announced by Ty Inc. on May 30, 1998.

Median U.S. Prices By Hang Tag

Available Tush Tag Generations: 6th

Median U.S. Prices Over Time

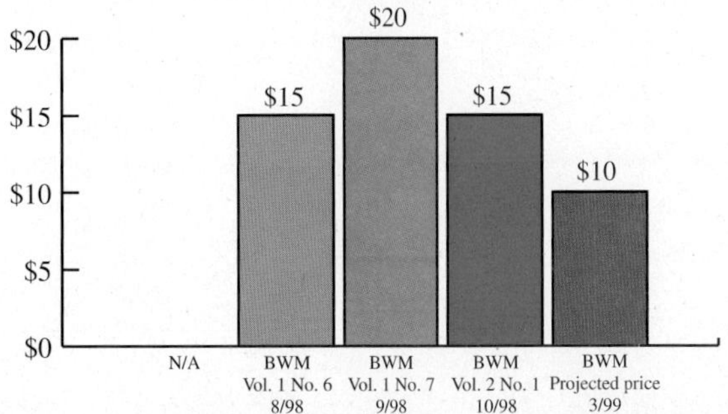

Median U.K. Price: £9.11 **Median Canadian Price: $22.55**

Lefty the American flag donkey

Retired

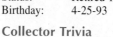

Fast Facts

Style Number: 4057
Introduced: 1996
Status: Retired 1-1-97
Birthday: 7-4-96

Collector Trivia

With the same birthdate and poem as Righty, Lefty was released to represent the Democratic Party in the 1996 U.S. elections.

Median U.S. Prices By Hang Tag

Available Tush Tag Generations: 3rd

Median U.S. Prices Over Time

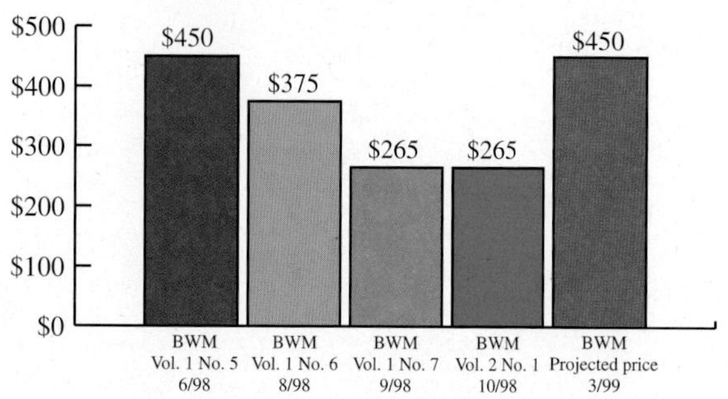

Median U.K. Price: £161.09 Median Canadian Price: $398.42

Legs the frog

Retired

Fast Facts

Style Number: 4020
Introduced: 1994
Status: Retired 10-1-97
Birthday: 4-25-93

Collector Trivia

Legs' value has been slow to increase due to plentiful supply, but a Legs with early tags is quite valuable because it is one of the first nine Beanies.

Median U.S. Prices By Hang Tag

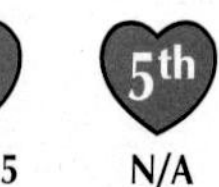

Available Tush Tag Generations: 1st, 2nd, 3rd, 4th, 5th

Median U.S. Prices Over Time

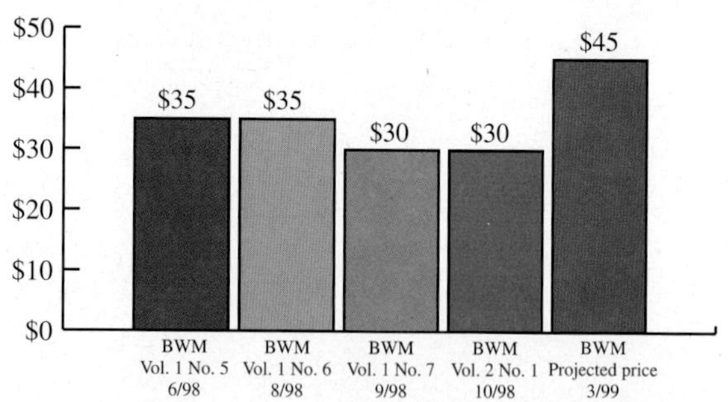

Median U.K. Price: £18.23 Median Canadian Price: $45.10

Libearty the American flag teddy

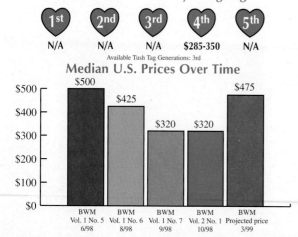

Retired

Fast Facts

Style Number: 4057
Introduced: 1996
Status: Retired 1-1-97
Birthday: Summer 1996

Collector Trivia

Libearty was the first Beanie Baby to display the fourth generation heart hang tag.

Median U.S. Prices By Hang Tag

1st 2nd 3rd 4th 5th

N/A N/A N/A $285-350 N/A

Available Tush Tag Generations: 3rd

Median U.S. Prices Over Time

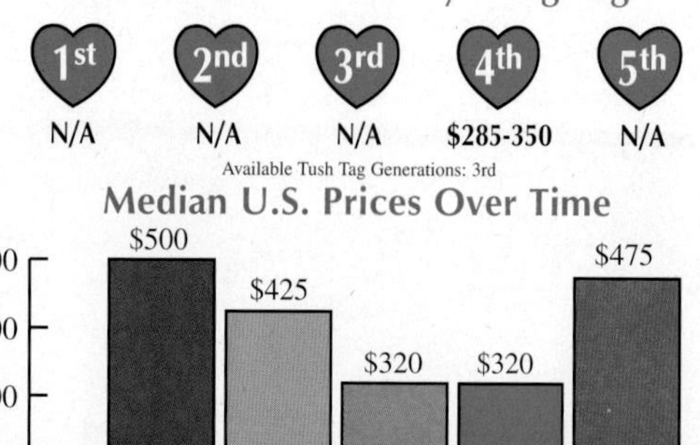

Median U.K. Price: £194.52 Median Canadian Price: $481.12

Lizzy the blue lizard

Retired

Fast Facts

Style Number: 4033
Introduced: 1996
Status: Retired 12-31-97
Birthday: 5-11-95

Collector Trivia

The Teenie Beanie version of Lizzy has a shortened name, Lizz.

Median U.S. Prices By Hang Tag

Available Tush Tag Generations: 1st, 2nd, 3rd, 4th, 5th, 6th

Median U.S. Prices Over Time

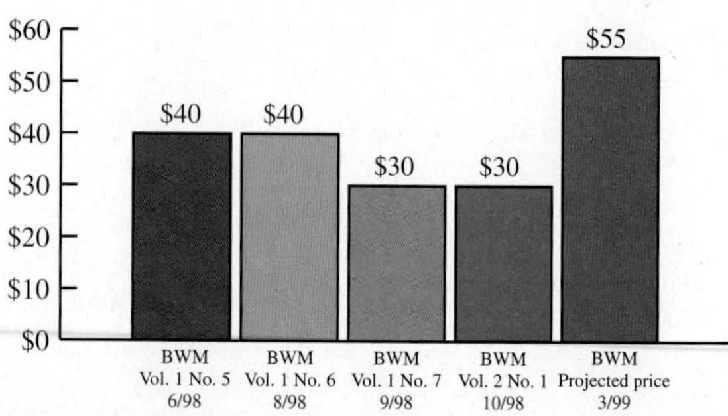

Median U.K. Price: £18.23 Median Canadian Price: $45.10

Lizzy the tie-dyed lizard

Fast Facts
Style Number: 4033
Introduced: 1995
Status: Retired 1995
Birthday: Unknown

Collector Trivia
The market value of tie-dyed Lizzie may fluctuate based on the attractiveness of its coloring.

Median U.S. Prices By Hang Tag

1st	2nd	3rd	4th	5th
N/A	N/A	$875-1100	N/A	N/A

Available Tush Tag Generations: 1st

Median U.S. Prices Over Time

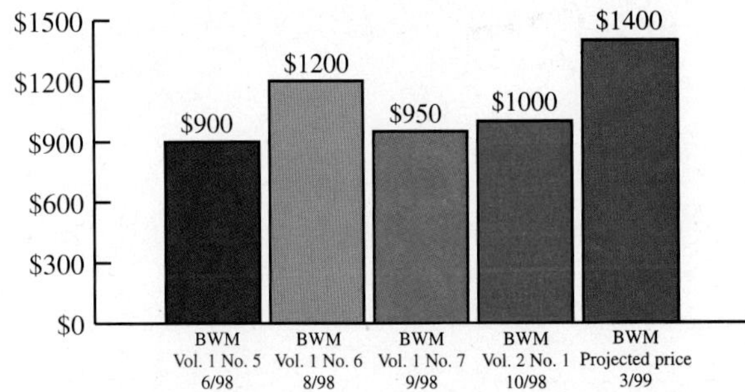

Median U.K. Price: £607.90 **Median Canadian Price: $1503.50**

Lucky the ladybug with approximately 11 spots

Fast Facts
Style Number: 4040
Introduced: 1996
Status: Retired 5-1-98
Birthday: 5-1-95

Collector Trivia
The Beanie referred to as 11-spot Lucky actually may have anywhere from eight to 14 spots.

Median U.S. Prices By Hang Tag

1st	2nd	3rd	4th	5th
N/A	N/A	N/A	$15-20	$15-20

Available Tush Tag Generations: 3rd, 4th, 5th, 6th

Median U.S. Prices Over Time

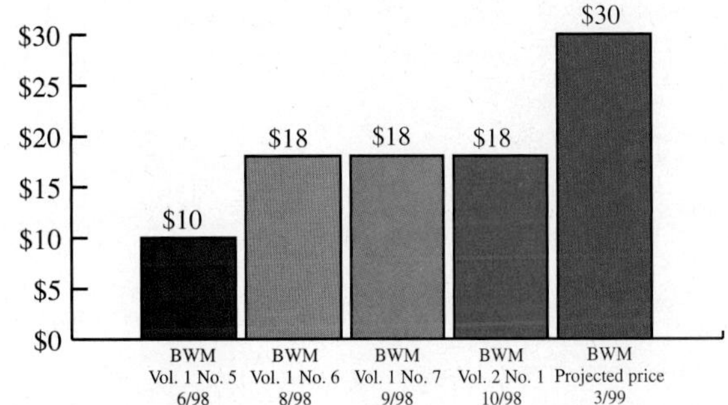

Median U.K. Price: £10.94 **Median Canadian Price: $27.06**

Lucky the ladybug with approximately 21 spots

Fast Facts
Style Number: 4040
Introduced: 1996
Status: Retired 1997
Birthday: 5-1-95

Collector Trivia
When first spotted on the market, the 21-spot Lucky did not sell well. Who could have forecast its value today?

Median U.S. Prices By Hang Tag

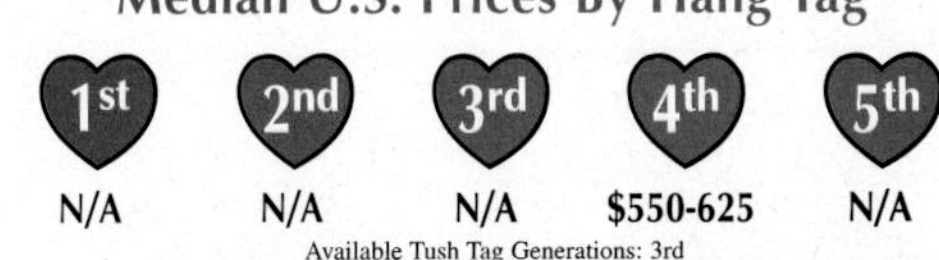

1st	2nd	3rd	4th	5th
N/A	N/A	N/A	$550-625	N/A

Available Tush Tag Generations: 3rd

Median U.S. Prices Over Time

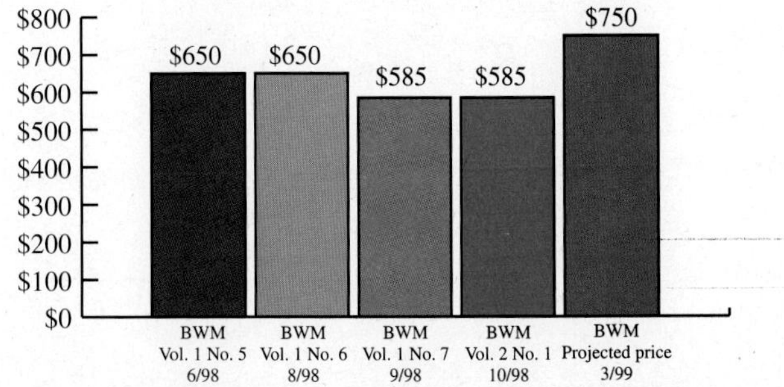

Median U.K. Price: £355.62 **Median Canadian Price: $879.54**

Lucky the ladybug with 7 glued on spots

Fast Facts
Style Number: 4040
Introduced: 1994
Status: Retired 1996
Birthday: Unknown

Collector Trivia
Lucky's seven glued-on spots often fell off. The first and second generation Beanies used a glue that cracked over time.

Median U.S. Prices By Hang Tag

1st	2nd	3rd	4th	5th
$750-850	$450-550	$175-200	N/A	N/A

Available Tush Tag Generations: 1st, 2nd

Median U.S. Prices Over Time

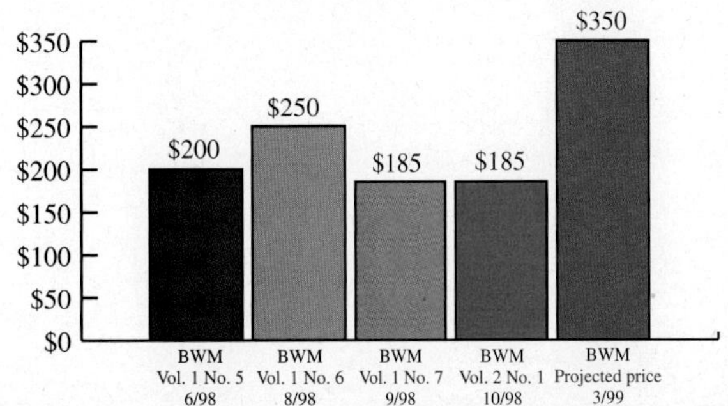

Median U.K. Price: £112.46 **Median Canadian Price: $278.14**

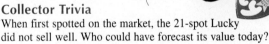

Magic the dragon with the light pink stitching

Fast Facts
Style Number: 4088
Introduced: 1995
Status: Retired 12-31-97
Birthday: 9-5-95

Collector Trivia
Variations in thread color used for the top stitching on Magic's wings include white, light pink, dark pink and hot pink (rarest).

Median U.S. Prices By Hang Tag

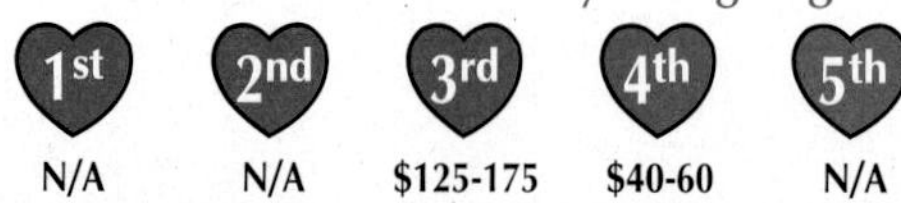

1st	2nd	3rd	4th	5th
N/A	N/A	$125-175	$40-60	N/A

Available Tush Tag Generations: 1st, 2nd, 3rd, 4th, 5th

Median U.S. Prices Over Time

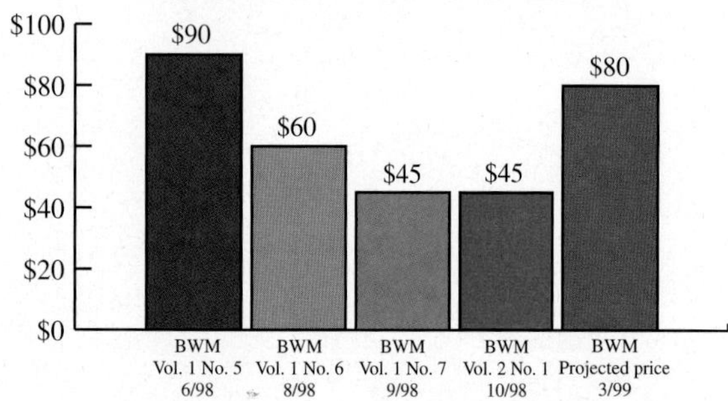

Median U.K. Price: £27.35 Median Canadian Price: $67.65

Manny the manatee

Fast Facts
Style Number: 4081
Introduced: 1996
Status: Retired 5-11-97
Birthday: 6-8-95

Collector Trivia
Manny was one of the slowest sellers when current, but once he retired, he became one of the hardest to find.

Median U.S. Prices By Hang Tag

1st	2nd	3rd	4th	5th
N/A	N/A	$180-225	$145-175	N/A

Available Tush Tag Generations: 2nd, 3rd

Median U.S. Prices Over Time

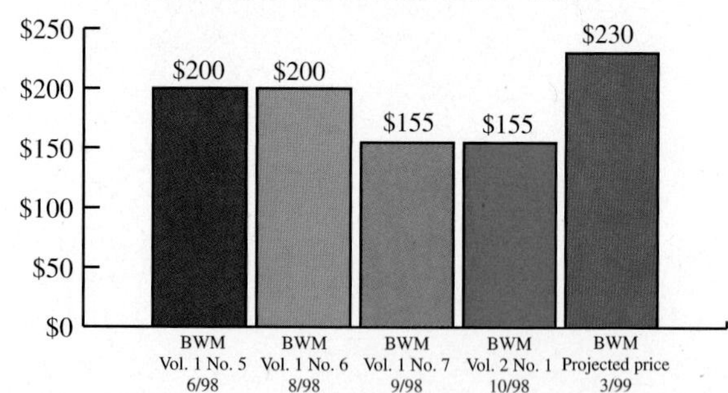

Median U.K. Price: £94.22 Median Canadian Price: $233.04

Maple the Canadian teddy

Fast Facts
Style Number: 4600
Introduced: 2-97
Status: Current
Birthday: 7-1-96

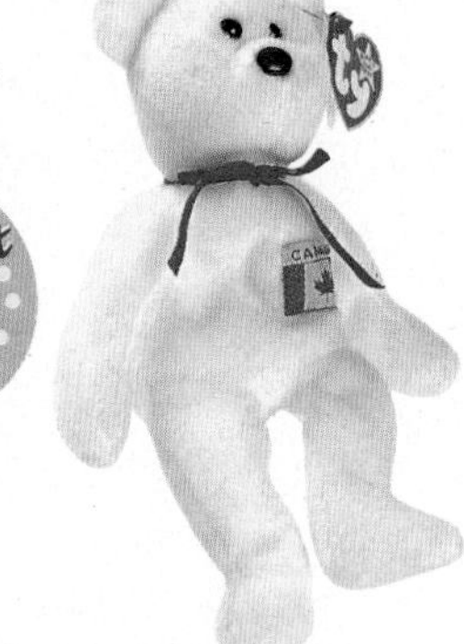

Collector Trivia
The first, limited run of Maple displayed a tush tag showing "PRIDE" while the hang tag read "MAPLE." This Canadian exclusive is considered a hot commodity.

Median U.S. Prices By Hang Tag

1st	2nd	3rd	4th	5th
N/A	N/A	N/A	$225-265	$185-230

Available Tush Tag Generations: 3rd, 4th, 5th

Median U.S. Prices Over Time

	BWM Vol. 1 No. 5 6/98	BWM Vol. 1 No. 6 8/98	BWM Vol. 1 No. 7 9/98	BWM Vol. 2 No. 1 10/98	BWM Projected price 3/99
Price	$250	$285	$225	$225	$325

Median U.K. Price: £136.77 Median Canadian Price: $338.28

Mel the koala bear

Fast Facts
Style Number: 4162
Introduced: 1-1-97
Status: Current
Birthday: 1-15-96

Collector Trivia
Mel is rumored to be named after actor Mel Gibson.

Median U.S. Prices By Hang Tag

1st	2nd	3rd	4th	5th
N/A	N/A	N/A	$8-10	$8-10

Available Tush Tag Generations: 3rd, 4th, 5th, 6th

Median U.S. Prices Over Time

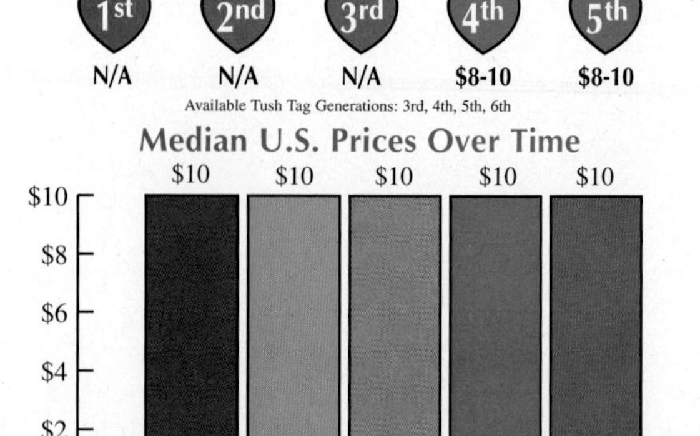

Median U.K. Price: £6.07 Median Canadian Price: $15.03

Mystic the coarse mane unicorn with iridescent horn

Fast Facts
Style Number: 4007
Introduced: 11-97
Status: Current
Birthday: 5-21-94

Collector Trivia
Long rumored to exist, Mystic with an iridescent horn was finally introduced in late 1997.

Median U.S. Prices By Hang Tag

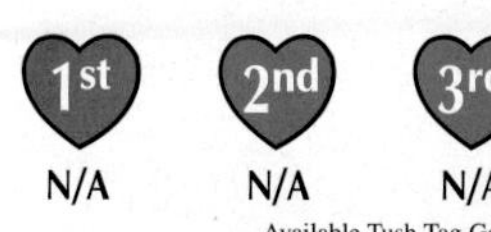

1st	2nd	3rd	4th	5th
N/A	N/A	N/A	$10-20	$10-20

Available Tush Tag Generations: 5th, 6th

Median U.S. Prices Over Time

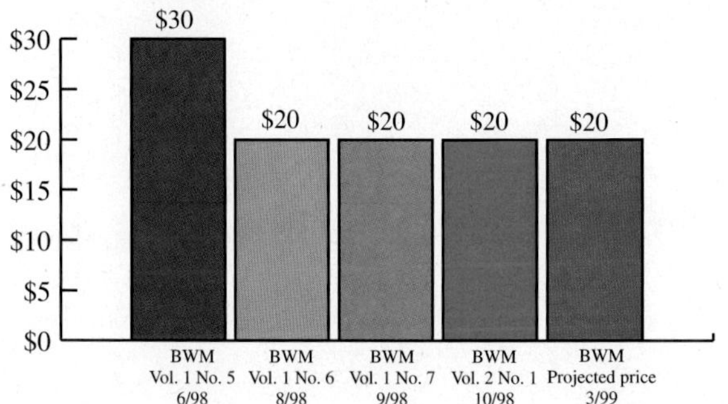

Median U.K. Price: £12.15 Median Canadian Price: $30.07

Mystic the coarse mane unicorn with tan horn

Fast Facts
Style Number: 4007
Introduced: 1996
Status: Retired 1997
Birthday: 5-21-94

Collector Trivia
Though not officially retired, Mystic with a tan horn was widely considered as a retired Beanie when Mystic with an iridescent horn came out.

Median U.S. Prices By Hang Tag

1st	2nd	3rd	4th	5th
N/A	N/A	$125-140	$30-50	N/A

Available Tush Tag Generations: 4th, 5th, 6th

Median U.S. Prices Over Time

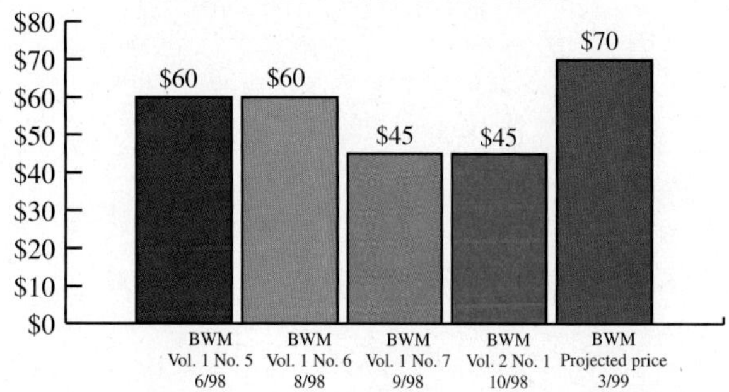

Median U.K. Price: £27.35 Median Canadian Price: $67.65

Mystic the fine mane unicorn

Fast Facts
Style Number: 4007
Introduced: 1994
Status: Retired 1995
Birthday: Unknown

Collector Trivia
The Mystic with baby fine yarn is much more plentiful than the fine mane Derby.

Median U.S. Prices By Hang Tag

1st	2nd	3rd	4th	5th
$600-800	$325-450	$225-300	N/A	N/A

Available Tush Tag Generations: 1st, 2nd

Median U.S. Prices Over Time

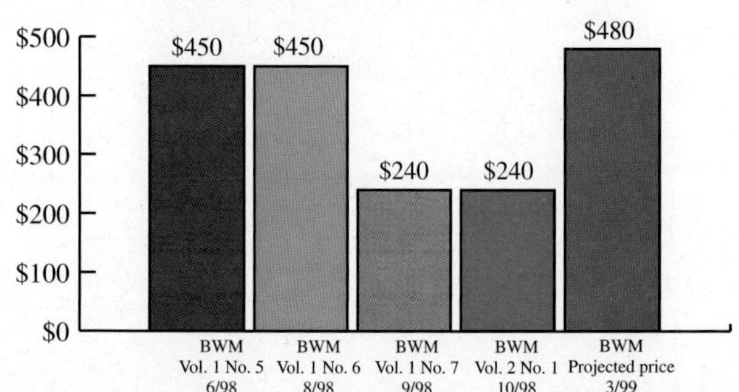

Median U.K. Price: £145.89 Median Canadian Price: $360.84

Nana the brown monkey

Fast Facts
Style Number: 4067
Introduced: 1995
Status: Retired 1995
Birthday: Unknown

Collector Trivia
The earliest Bongos were named Nana. They are identical to the b/w tush, light-tailed Bongo except for the swing tag that says "NANA" or has a sticker over "NANA" that says "BONGO."

Median U.S. Prices By Hang Tag

1st	2nd	3rd	4th	5th
N/A	N/A	$3600-4100	N/A	N/A

Available Tush Tag Generations: 1st

Median U.S. Prices Over Time

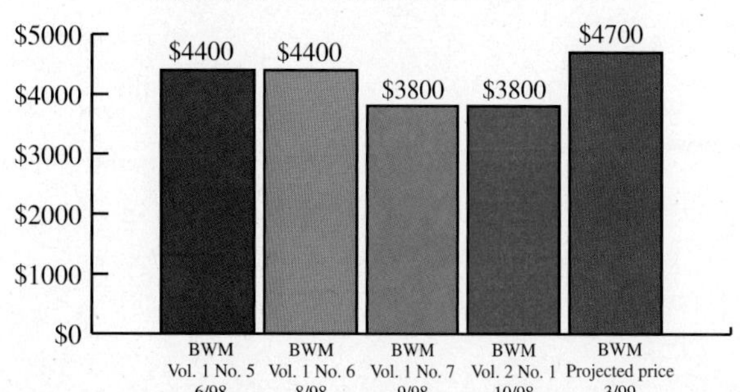

Median U.K. Price: £2310.02 Median Canadian Price: $5713.30

Nanook the husky

Fast Facts
Style Number: 4104
Introduced: 5-11-97
Status: Current
Birthday: 11-21-96

Collector Trivia
This Alaskan husky was a wonderful addition to the growing family of Beanie dogs.

Median U.S. Prices By Hang Tag

1st	2nd	3rd	4th	5th
N/A	N/A	N/A	$10-15	$10-15

Available Tush Tag Generations: 3rd, 4th, 5th, 6th

Median U.S. Prices Over Time

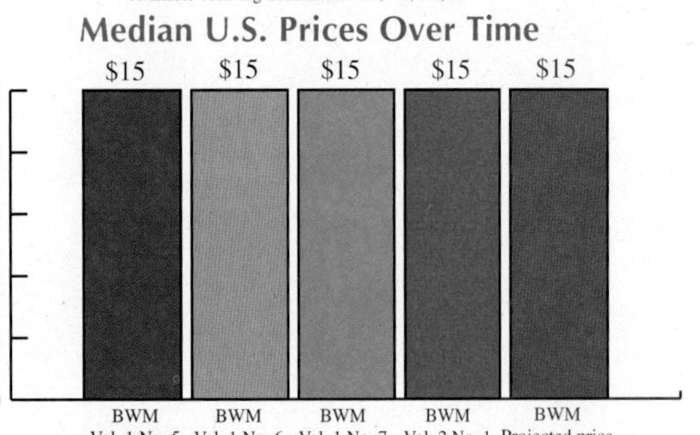

Median U.K. Price: £9.11 Median Canadian Price: $22.55

Nip the all gold cat

Retired

Fast Facts
Style Number: 4003
Introduced: 1995
Status: Retired 1995
Birthday: Unknown

Collector Trivia
This is the middle version of Nip's three variations. It is the most valuable because the fewest of these were manufactured.

Median U.S. Prices By Hang Tag

1st	2nd	3rd	4th	5th
N/A	N/A	$850-1000	N/A	N/A

Available Tush Tag Generations: 1st

Median U.S. Prices Over Time

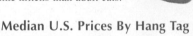

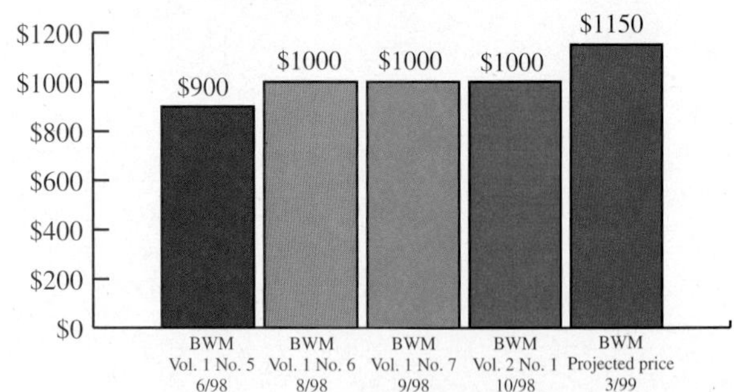

Median U.K. Price: £607.90 Median Canadian Price: $1503.50

Nip the gold cat with white paws

Fast Facts
Style Number: 4003
Introduced: 1996
Status: Retired 12-31-97
Birthday: 3-6-94

Collector Trivia
Nip was the only cat included in the December 31, 1997, retirement announcement.

Median U.S. Prices By Hang Tag

1st	2nd	3rd	4th	5th
N/A	N/A	$300-350	$20-35	$20-35

Available Tush Tag Generations: 2nd, 3rd, 4th, 5th, 6th

Median U.S. Prices Over Time

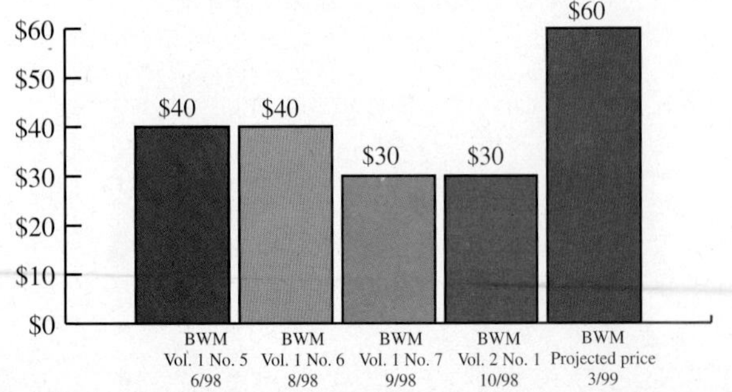

Median U.K. Price: £18.23 Median Canadian Price: $45.10

Nip the gold kitten with the white belly

Retired

Fast Facts
Style Number: 4003
Introduced: 1995
Status: Retired 1995
Birthday: Unknown

Collector Trivia
The white belly versions of Nip and Zip are the oldest versions. To many, they look more like kittens than adult cats.

Median U.S. Prices By Hang Tag

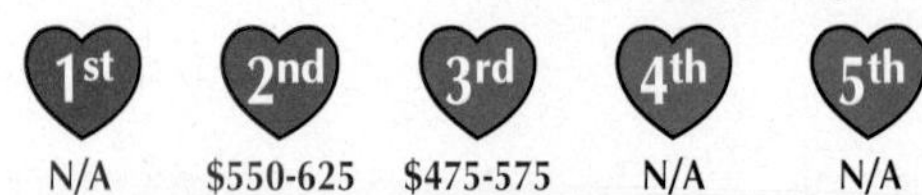

1st	2nd	3rd	4th	5th
N/A	$550-625	$475-575	N/A	N/A

Available Tush Tag Generations: 1st

Median U.S. Prices Over Time

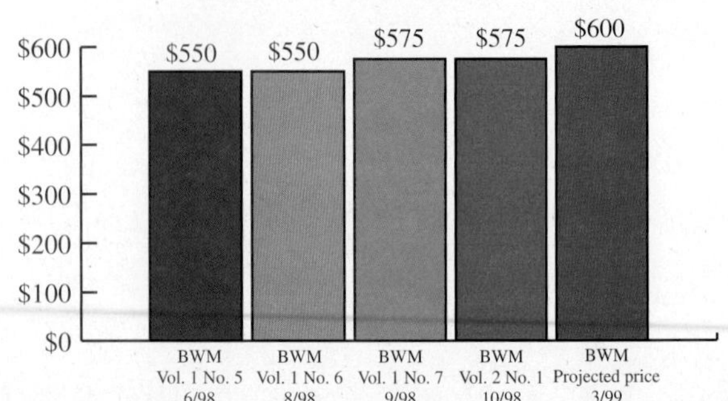

Median U.K. Price: £349.54 Median Canadian Price: $864.51

Nuts the squirrel

Fast Facts

Style Number: 4114
Introduced: 1-1-97
Status: Current
Birthday: 1-21-96

Collector Trivia

Nuts was the first Beanie to use the thick, "fake fur" accent for its tail. Roary and Stretch later used a similar material.

Median U.S. Prices By Hang Tag

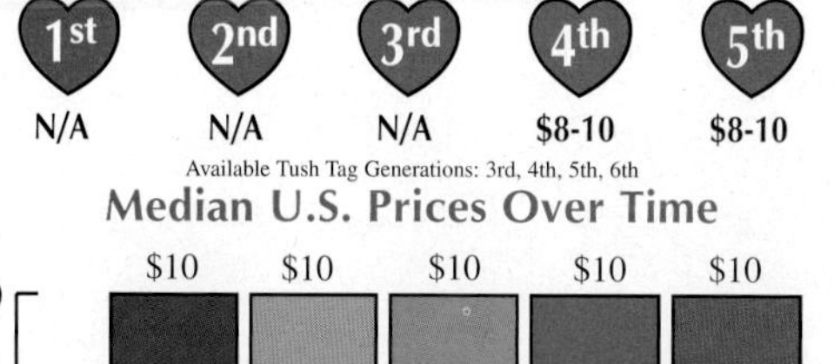

1st	2nd	3rd	4th	5th
N/A	N/A	N/A	$8-10	$8-10

Available Tush Tag Generations: 3rd, 4th, 5th, 6th

Median U.S. Prices Over Time

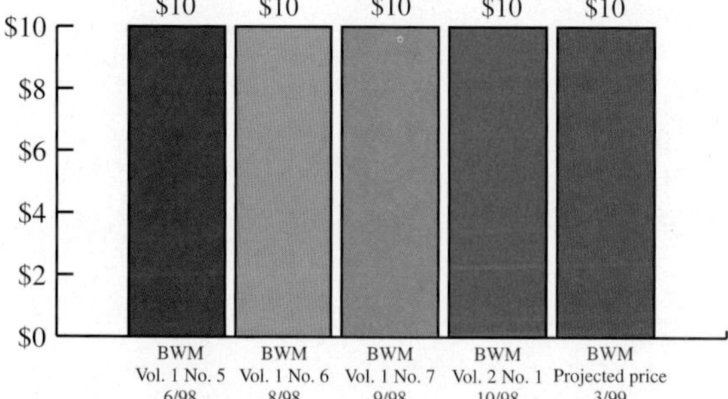

Median U.K. Price: £6.07 Median Canadian Price: $15.03

Patti the deep magenta/ maroon/raspberry platypus

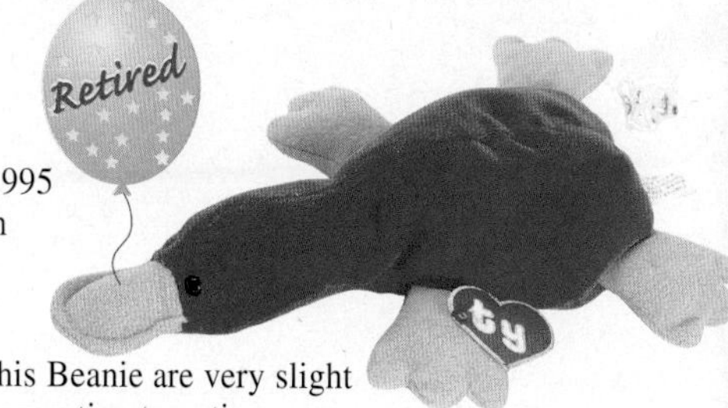

Fast Facts

Style Number: 4025
Introduced: 1993
Status: Retired 1995
Birthday: Unknown

Collector Trivia

The color variations of this Beanie are very slight and often require close inspection to notice.

Median U.S. Prices By Hang Tag

1st	2nd	3rd	4th	5th
$900-1000	$800-950	$650-800	N/A	N/A

Available Tush Tag Generations: 1st, 2nd, 3rd

Median U.S. Prices Over Time

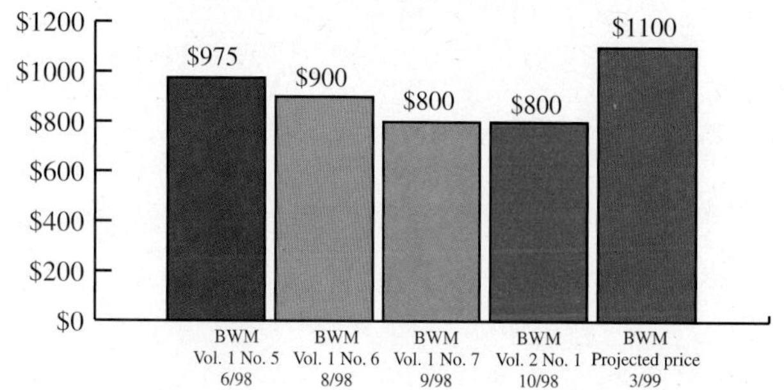

Median U.K. Price: £486.32 Median Canadian Price: $1202.80

Patti the purple platypus

Fast Facts

Style Number: 4025
Introduced: 1993
Status: Retired 5-1-98
Birthday: 1-6-93

Collector Trivia

This version of Patti matches the color of Inch the inchworm's tail.

Median U.S. Prices By Hang Tag

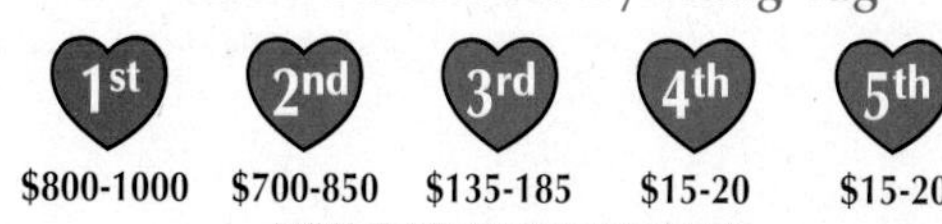

1st	2nd	3rd	4th	5th
$800-1000	$700-850	$135-185	$15-20	$15-20

Available Tush Tag Generations: 4th, 5th, 6th

Median U.S. Prices Over Time

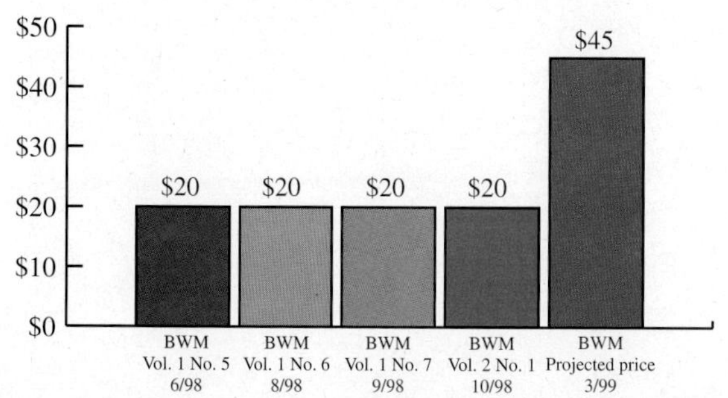

Median U.K. Price: £12.15 Median Canadian Price: $30.07

Peace the tie-dyed teddy

Fast Facts

Style Number: 4053
Introduced: 5-11-97
Status: Current
Birthday: 2-1-96

Collector Trivia

Available in England before the United States, U.S. secondary market prices for Peace started out quite high before leveling off.

Median U.S. Prices By Hang Tag

1st	2nd	3rd	4th	5th
N/A	N/A	N/A	$20-35	$20-35

Available Tush Tag Generations: 3rd, 4th, 5th, 6th

Median U.S. Prices Over Time

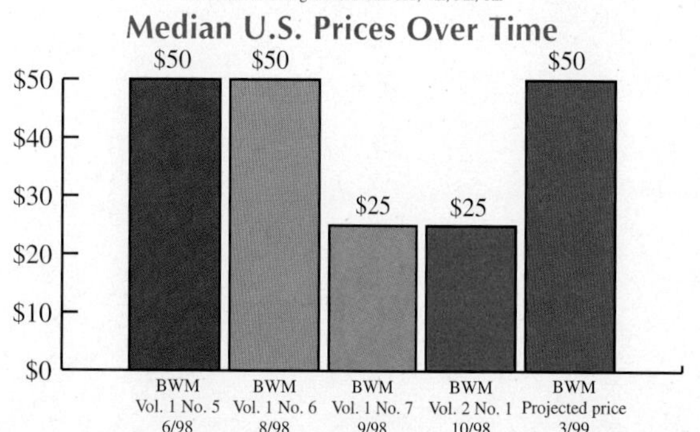

Median U.K. Price: £15.19 Median Canadian Price: $37.58

Peanut the light blue elephant

Retired

Fast Facts

Style Number: 4062
Introduced: 1996
Status: Retired 5-1-98
Birthday: 1-25-95

Collector Trivia

The newly retired Peanut was part of the Oakland Athletics' giveaway on August 1, 1998.

Median U.S. Prices By Hang Tag

1st	2nd	3rd	4th	5th
N/A	N/A	$350-600	$12-23	$12-23

Available Tush Tag Generations: 1st, 2nd, 3rd, 4th, 5th, 6th

Median U.S. Prices Over Time

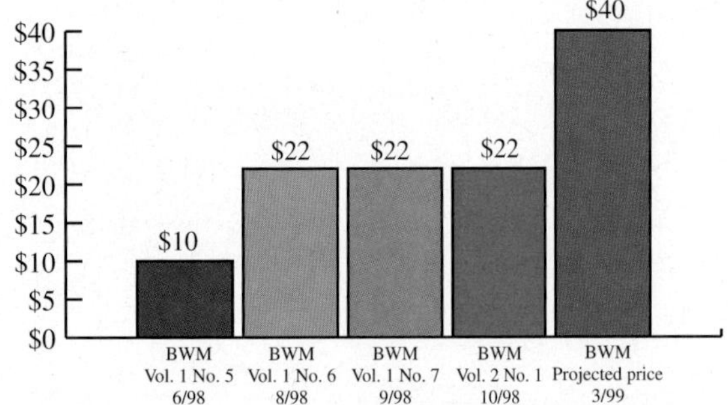

Median U.K. Price: £13.37 **Median Canadian Price: $33.07**

Peanut the royal blue elephant

Retired

Fast Facts

Style Number: 4062
Introduced: 1995
Status: Retired 1995
Birthday: Unknown

Collector Trivia

The jewel of the entire Beanie Babies Collection, Peanut's rich blue color was actually a manufacturing mistake in 1995.

Median U.S. Prices By Hang Tag

1st	2nd	3rd	4th	5th
N/A	N/A	$3800-4700	N/A	N/A

Available Tush Tag Generations: 1st

Median U.S. Prices Over Time

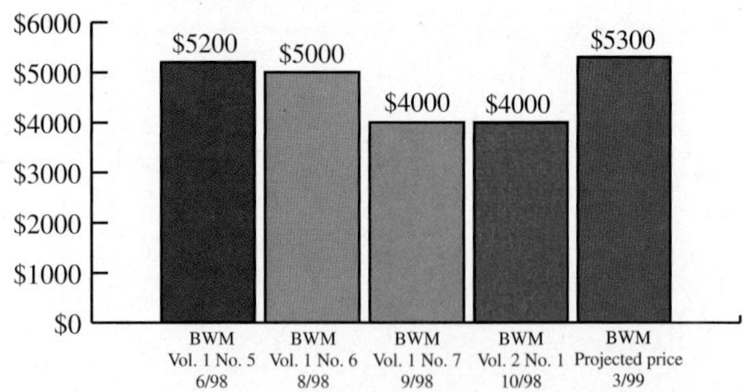

Median U.K. Price: £2431.60 **Median Canadian Price: $6014.00**

Peking the panda

Retired

Fast Facts

Style Number: 4013
Introduced: 1994
Status: Retired 1995
Birthday: Unknown

Collector Trivia

Counterfeit Pekings with a longer snout began surfacing on the market in late 1997.

Median U.S. Prices By Hang Tag

1st	2nd	3rd	4th	5th
$2200-2450	$2100-2300	$1750-2200	N/A	N/A

Available Tush Tag Generations: 1st

Median U.S. Prices Over Time

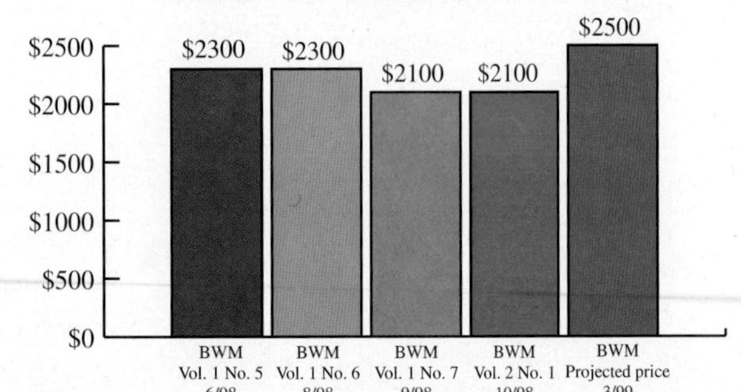

Median U.K. Price: £1276.59 **Median Canadian Price: $3157.35**

Pinchers the lobster

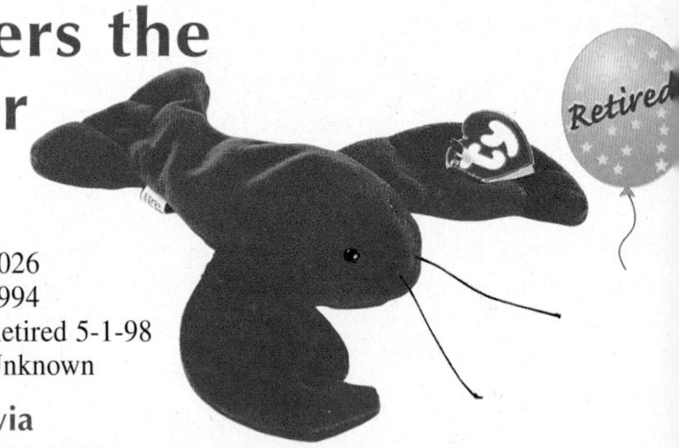

Retired

Fast Facts

Style Number: 4026
Introduced: 1994
Status: Retired 5-1-98
Birthday: Unknown

Collector Trivia

The existence of an orange Pinchers was strongly rumored in the fall of 1996 but never verified.

Median U.S. Prices By Hang Tag

1st	2nd	3rd	4th	5th
$1000-1200	$700-750	$100-125	$12-20	$12-20

Available Tush Tag Generations: 1st, 2nd, 3rd, 4th, 5th, 6th

Median U.S. Prices Over Time

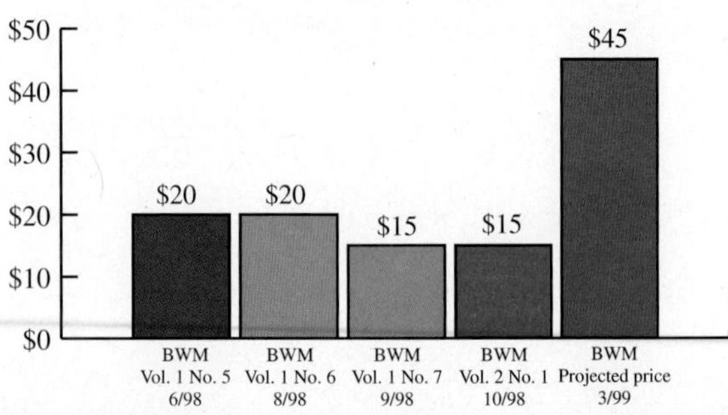

Median U.K. Price: £9.11 **Median Canadian Price: $22.55**

Pinky the flamingo

Current

Fast Facts
Style Number: 4072
Introduced: 1996
Status: Current
Birthday: 2-13-95

Collector Trivia
Teenie Pinky is considered the most valuable of the 1997 Teenie Beanie Baby family.

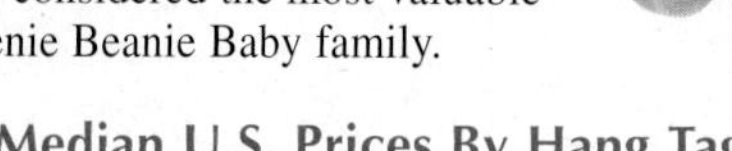

Median U.S. Prices By Hang Tag

1st	2nd	3rd	4th	5th
N/A	N/A	$145-195	$8-10	$8-10

Available Tush Tag Generations: 1st, 2nd, 3rd, 4th, 5th, 6th

Median U.S. Prices Over Time

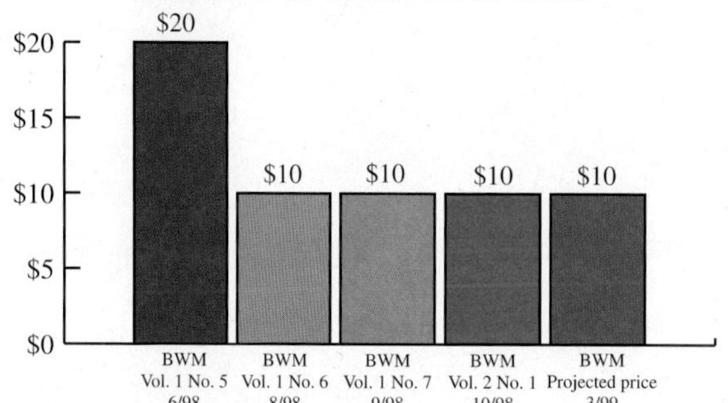

Median U.K. Price: £6.07 **Median Canadian Price: $15.03**

Pouch the kangaroo

Current

Fast Facts
Style Number: 4161
Introduced: 1-1-97
Status: Current
Birthday: 11-6-96

Collector Trivia
Rumors continue to swell concerning the re-design of Pouch's baby, which has only a head at this point!

Median U.S. Prices By Hang Tag

1st	2nd	3rd	4th	5th
N/A	N/A	N/A	$8-10	$8-10

Available Tush Tag Generations: 3rd, 4th, 5th, 6th

Median U.S. Prices Over Time

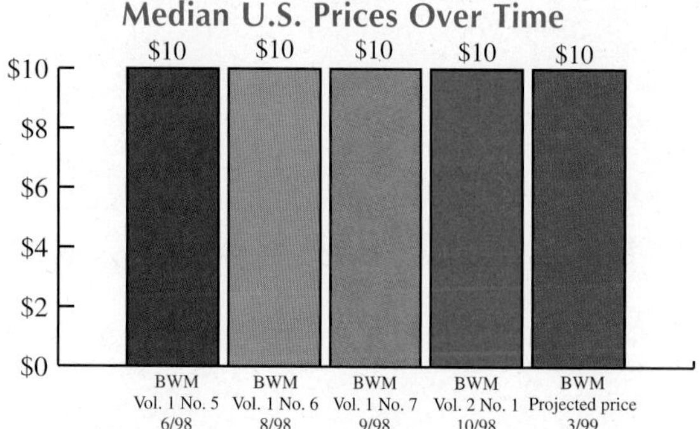

Median U.K. Price: £6.07 **Median Canadian Price: $15.03**

Pounce the brown cat

Current

Fast Facts
Style Number: 4122
Introduced: 12-31-97
Status: Current
Birthday: 8-28-97

Collector Trivia
Pounce and Prance were the first cats without rhyming names.

Median U.S. Prices By Hang Tag

1st	2nd	3rd	4th	5th
N/A	N/A	N/A	N/A	$8-12

Available Tush Tag Generations: 6th

Median U.S. Prices Over Time

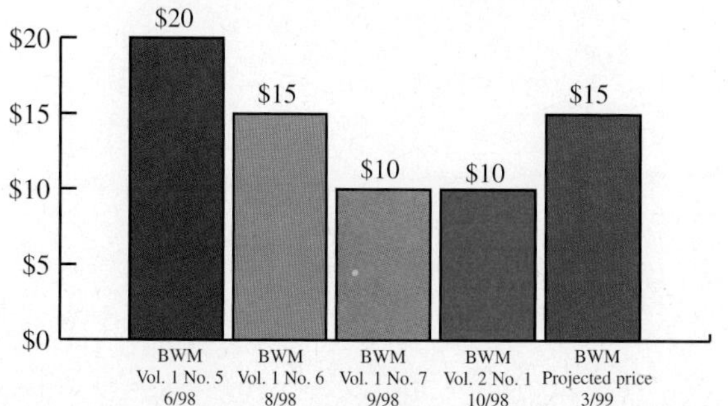

Median U.K. Price: £6.07 **Median Canadian Price: $15.03**

Prance the gray cat

Current

Fast Facts
Style Number: 4123
Introduced: 12-31-97
Status: Current
Birthday: 11-20-97

Collector Trivia
Prance and Snip are the two Beanie cats with blue eyes.

Median U.S. Prices By Hang Tag

1st	2nd	3rd	4th	5th
N/A	N/A	N/A	N/A	$8-12

Available Tush Tag Generations: 6th

Median U.S. Prices Over Time

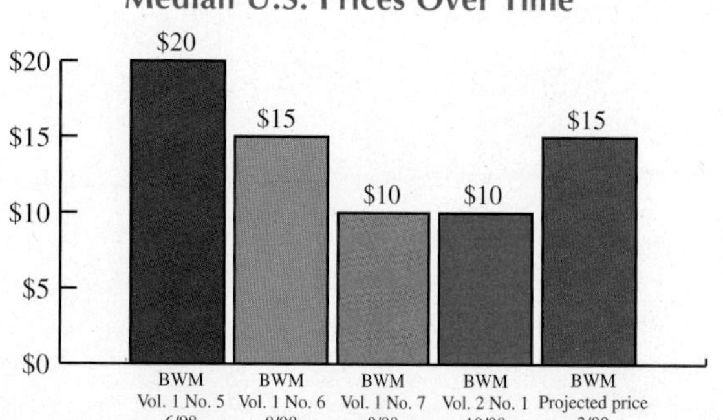

Median U.K. Price: £6.07 **Median Canadian Price: $15.03**

Princess: The Diana, Princess of Wales Bear

Fast Facts
Style Number: 4300
Introduced: 10-29-97
Status: Current
Birthday: Unknown

Collector Trivia
Princess bears can come with PVC or PE pellets. The PVC median market value is about $125, while the PE value is $40 or so. Prices shown in the graph below are for Princess with PE pellets.

Median U.S. Prices By Hang Tag

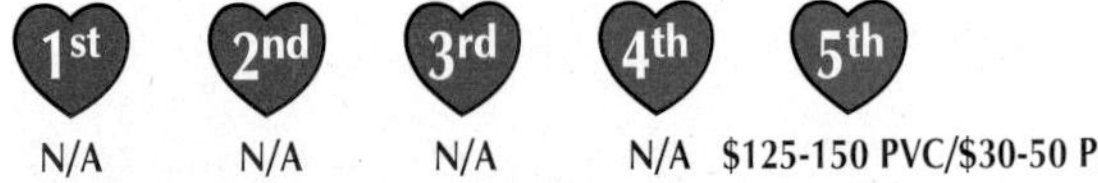

1st	2nd	3rd	4th	5th
N/A	N/A	N/A	N/A	$125-150 PVC/$30-50 PE

Available Tush Tag Generations: 6th

Median U.S. Prices Over Time

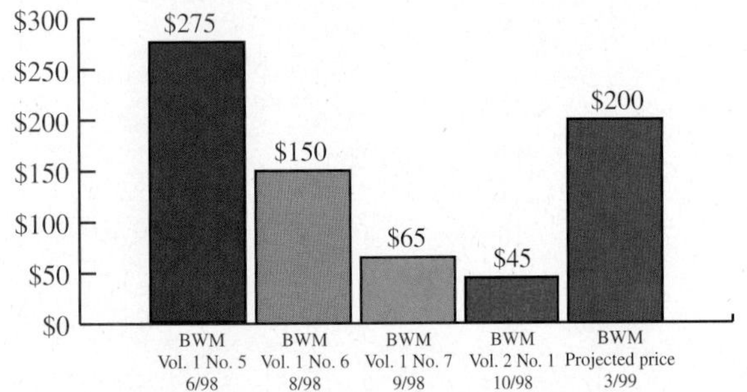

Median U.K. Price: £27.35 **Median Canadian Price: $67.65**

Puffer the puffin

Fast Facts
Style Number: 4181
Introduced: 12-31-97
Status: Current
Birthday: 11-3-97

Collector Trivia
Puffer was one of seven birds until the latest Ty retirement, which left Puffer as one of only three birds in the lineup. Several birds were then added in the May 30 new release announcement.

Median U.S. Prices By Hang Tag

1st	2nd	3rd	4th	5th
N/A	N/A	N/A	N/A	$8-10

Available Tush Tag Generations: 6th

Median U.S. Prices Over Time

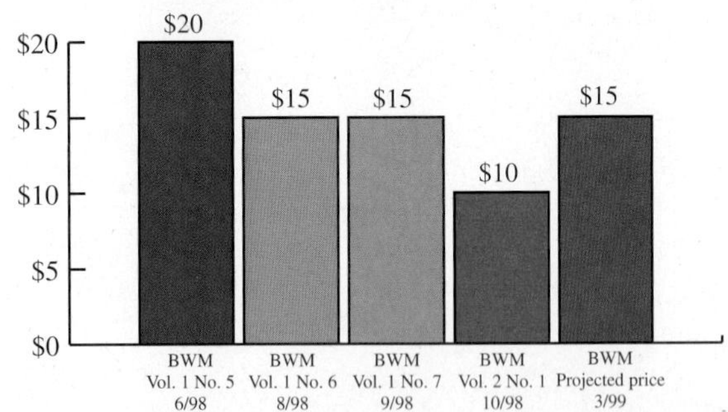

Median U.K. Price: £6.07 **Median Canadian Price: $15.03**

Pugsly the pug dog

Fast Facts
Style Number: 4106
Introduced: 5-11-97
Status: Current
Birthday: 5-2-96

Collector Trivia
Pugsly was part of the Texas Rangers' Beanie Baby giveaway on August 4, 1998, at The Ballpark In Arlington.

Median U.S. Prices By Hang Tag

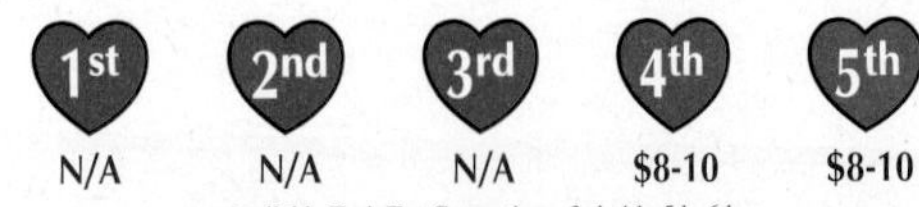

1st	2nd	3rd	4th	5th
N/A	N/A	N/A	$8-10	$8-10

Available Tush Tag Generations: 3rd, 4th, 5th, 6th

Median U.S. Prices Over Time

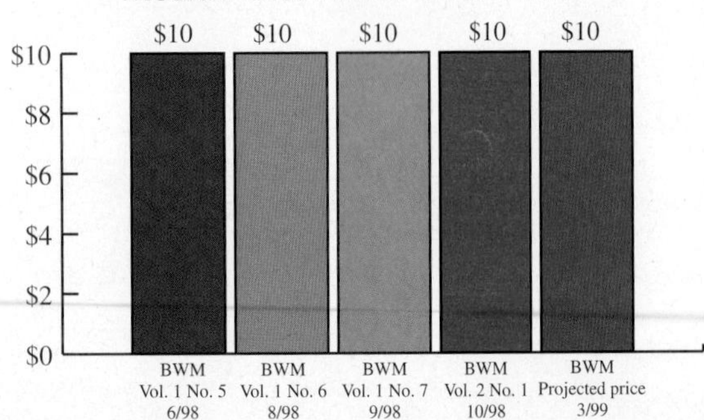

Median U.K. Price: £6.07 **Median Canadian Price: $15.03**

Punchers the lobster

European Retired American

Fast Facts
Style Number: 4026
Introduced: 1993
Status: Retired 1993
Birthday: Unknown

Collector Trivia
The European version of Punchers has long string feelers with knotted ends. The American version has shorter twisted yarn feelers.

Median U.S. Prices By Hang Tag

1st	2nd	3rd	4th	5th
$3600-4000	N/A	N/A	N/A	N/A

Available Tush Tag Generations: 1st

Median U.S. Prices Over Time

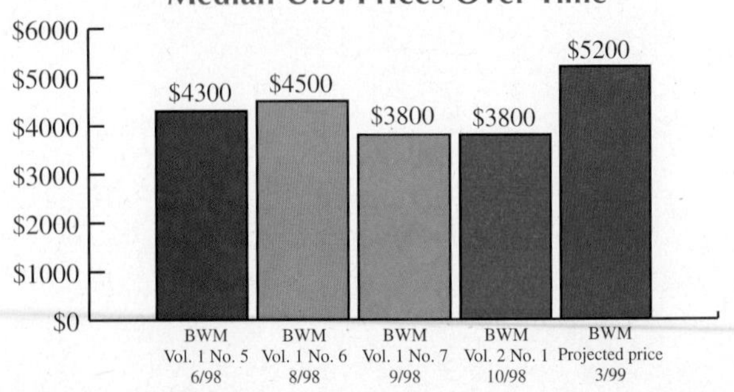

Median U.K. Price: £2310.02 **Median Canadian Price: $5713.30**

Quackers the duck with wings

Fast Facts
Style Number: 4024
Introduced: 1995
Status: Retired 5-1-98
Birthday: 4-19-94

Collector Trivia
Second generation swing tags list this duck's name as QUACKER.

Median U.S. Prices By Hang Tag

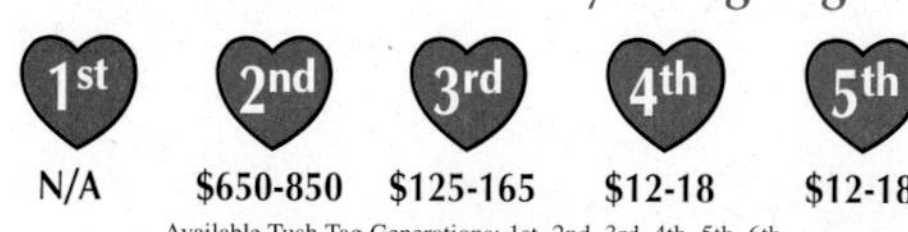

1st	2nd	3rd	4th	5th
N/A	$650-850	$125-165	$12-18	$12-18

Available Tush Tag Generations: 1st, 2nd, 3rd, 4th, 5th, 6th

Median U.S. Prices Over Time

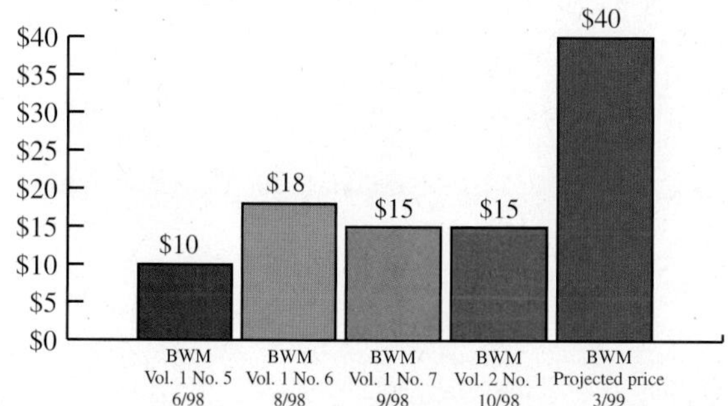

Median U.K. Price: £9.11 **Median Canadian Price: $22.55**

Quacker(s) the wingless duck

Fast Facts
Style Number: 4024
Introduced: 1994
Status: Retired 1995
Birthday: Unknown

Collector Trivia
The first generation duck without wings is named Quackers on the swing tag. The second generation is labeled QUACKER.

Median U.S. Prices By Hang Tag

1st	2nd	3rd	4th	5th
$2000-2400	$1700-2000	N/A	N/A	N/A

Available Tush Tag Generations: 1st

Median U.S. Prices Over Time

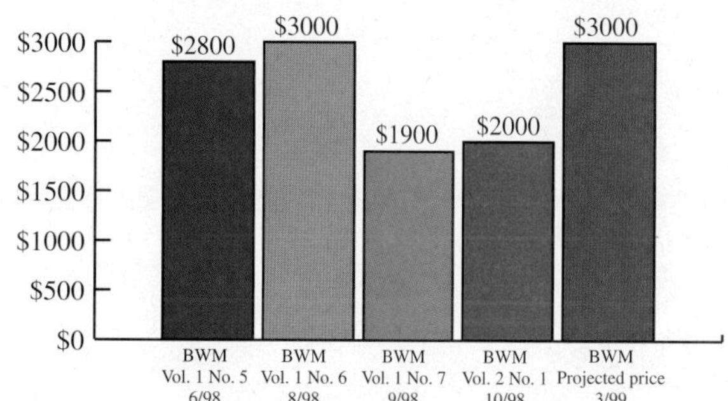

Median U.K. Price: £1215.80 **Median Canadian Price: $3007.00**

Radar the bat

Fast Facts
Style Number: 4091
Introduced: 1996
Status: Retired 5-11-97
Birthday: 10-30-95

Collector Trivia
Radar's replacement, Batty, was introduced four months after Radar was retired.

Median U.S. Prices By Hang Tag

1st	2nd	3rd	4th	5th
N/A	N/A	$225-260	$150-190	N/A

Available Tush Tag Generations: 1st, 2nd, 3rd

Median U.S. Prices Over Time

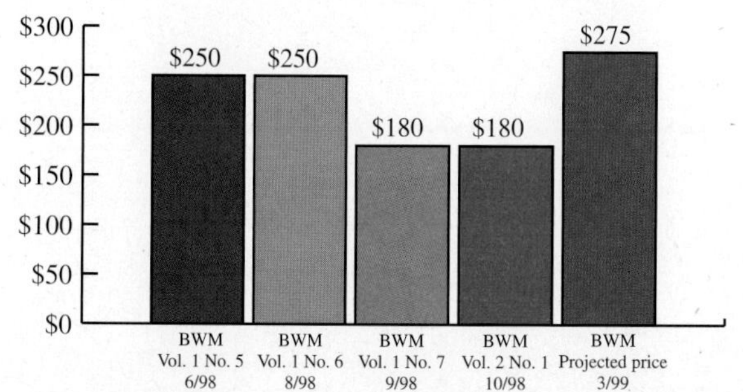

Median U.K. Price: £109.42 **Median Canadian Price: $270.63**

Rainbow the chameleon

Fast Facts
Style Number: 4037
Introduced: 12-31-97
Status: Current
Birthday: 10-14-97

Collector Trivia
Rainbow is a member of the lizard family. In June '98, new shipments of Rainbow revealed a slight design change: a pink tongue that is forked.

Median U.S. Prices By Hang Tag

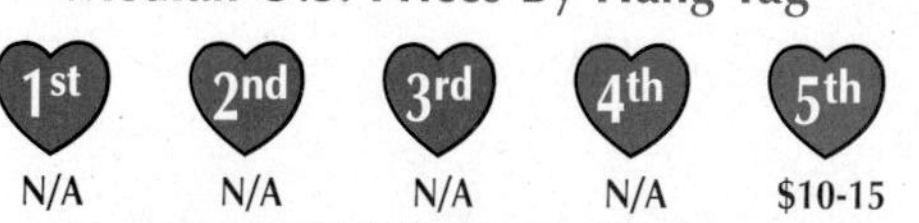

1st	2nd	3rd	4th	5th
N/A	N/A	N/A	N/A	$10-15

Available Tush Tag Generations: 6th

Median U.S. Prices Over Time

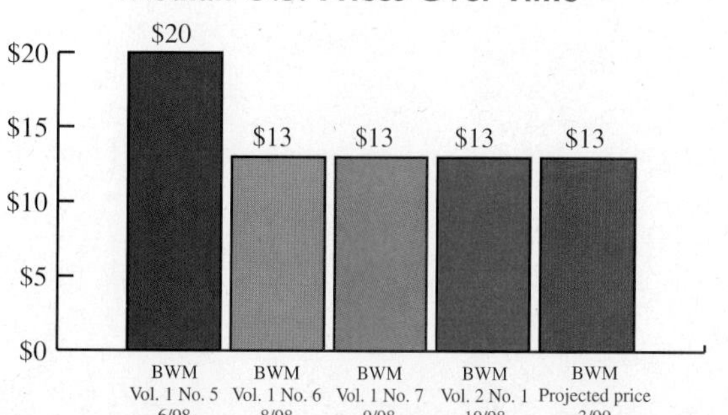

Median U.K. Price: £7.90 **Median Canadian Price: $19.54**

Rex the tyrannosaurus

Fast Facts
Style Number: 4086
Introduced: 1995
Status: Retired 1996
Birthday: Unknown

Collector Trivia
A colorful tie-dyed Beanie, Rex was very plentiful in the United Kingdom up to six months after his retirement.

Median U.S. Prices By Hang Tag

Available Tush Tag Generations: 1st, 2nd

Median U.S. Prices Over Time

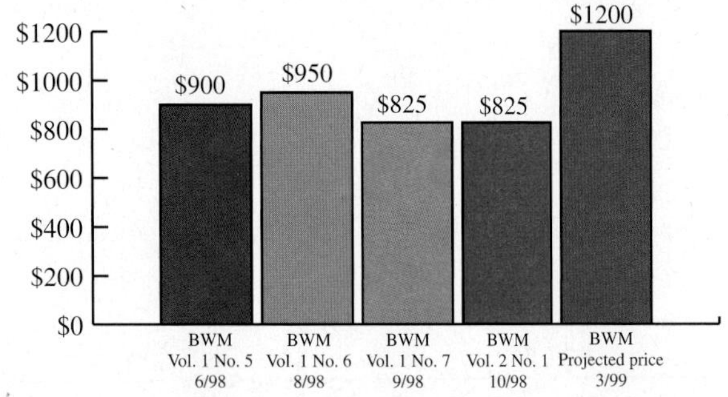

Median U.K. Price: £501.51 **Median Canadian Price: $1240.38**

Righty the American flag elephant

Retired

Fast Facts
Style Number: 4086
Introduced: 1996
Status: Retired 1-1-97
Birthday: 7-4-96

Collector Trivia
With the same birthdate and poem as Lefty, Righty was released to represent the Republican Party in the 1996 U.S. elections.

Median U.S. Prices By Hang Tag

Available Tush Tag Generations: 3rd

Median U.S. Prices Over Time

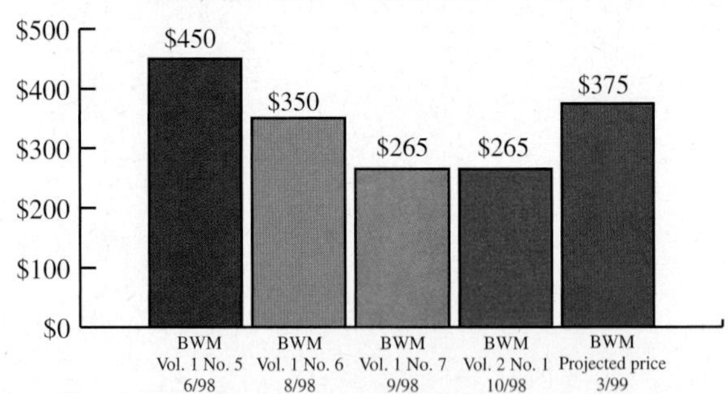

Median U.K. Price: £161.09 **Median Canadian Price: $398.42**

Ringo the raccoon

Fast Facts
Style Number: 4014
Introduced: 1996
Status: Current
Birthday: 7-14-95

Collector Trivia
Ringo, like Peking the panda, has black around his eyes.

Median U.S. Prices By Hang Tag

Available Tush Tag Generations: 2nd, 3rd, 4th, 5th, 6th

Median U.S. Prices Over Time

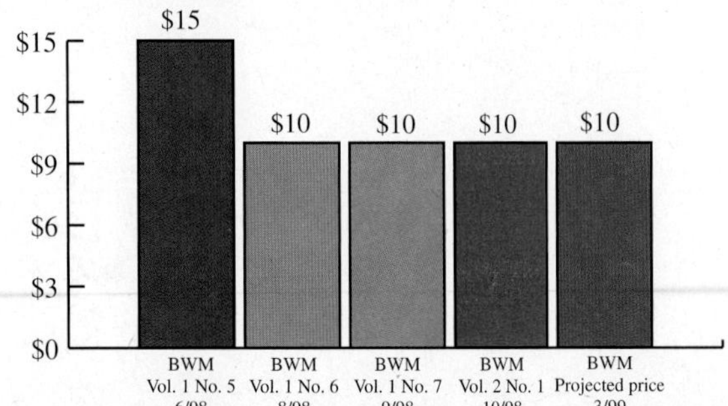

Median U.K. Price: £6.07 **Median Canadian Price: $15.03**

Roary the lion

Fast Facts
Style Number: 4069
Introduced: 5-11-97
Status: Current
Birthday: 2-20-96

Collector Trivia
Roary with a special commemorative card was the official giveaway at the Kansas City Royals baseball game on May 31, 1998.

Median U.S. Prices By Hang Tag

Available Tush Tag Generations: 3rd, 4th, 5th, 6th

Median U.S. Prices Over Time

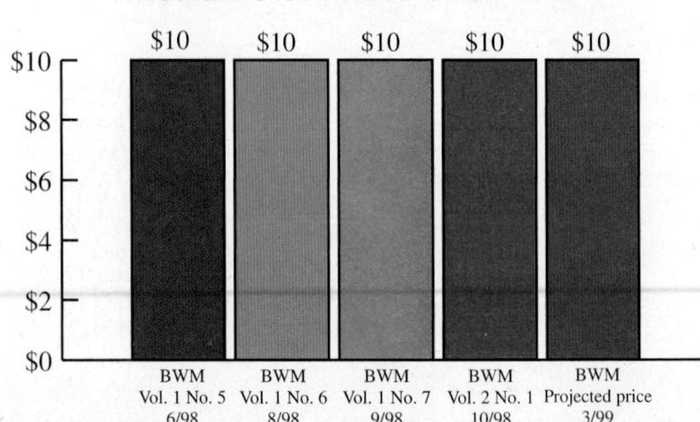

Median U.K. Price: £6.07 **Median Canadian Price: $15.03**

Rocket the bluejay

Fast Facts
Style Number: 4202
Introduced: 5-30-98
Status: Current
Birthday: 3-12-97

Collector Trivia
Some collectors believe Rocket may be named for baseball pitcher Roger "The Rocket" Clemens of the Toronto Blue Jays.

Median U.S. Prices By Hang Tag

Available Tush Tag Generations: 6th

Median U.S. Prices Over Time

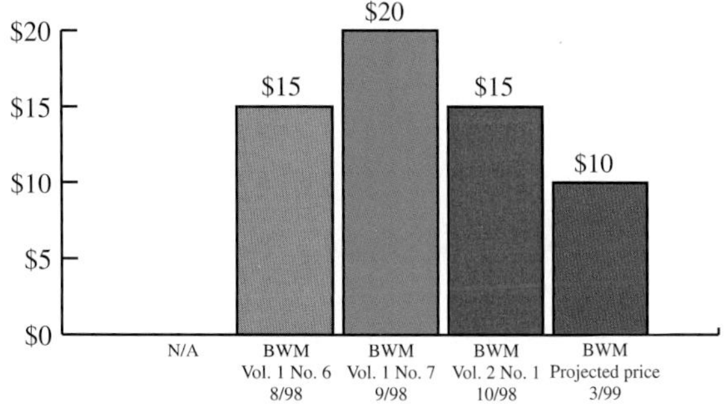

Median U.K. Price: £9.11 Median Canadian Price: $22.55

Rover the red dog

Fast Facts
Style Number: 4101
Introduced: 1996
Status: Retired 5-1-98
Birthday: 5-30-96

Collector Trivia
Rover is a favorite of many preschoolers, who think he resembles the storybook character Clifford the Big Dog.

Median U.S. Prices By Hang Tag

Available Tush Tag Generations: 3rd, 4th, 6th

Median U.S. Prices Over Time

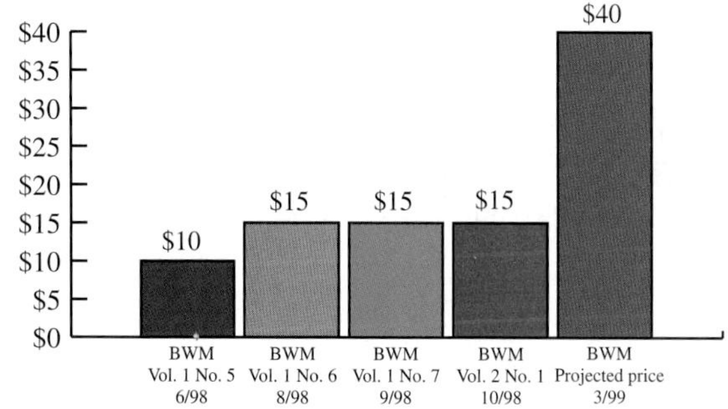

Median U.K. Price: £9.11 Median Canadian Price: $22.55

Scoop the pelican

Fast Facts
Style Number: 4107
Introduced: 1996
Status: Current
Birthday: 7-1-96

Collector Trivia
Scoop shares his fabric with Crunch the shark.

Median U.S. Prices By Hang Tag

Available Tush Tag Generations: 3rd, 4th, 5th, 6th

Median U.S. Prices Over Time

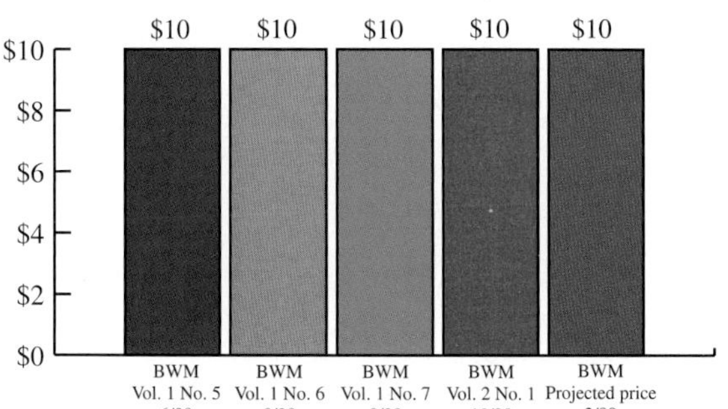

Median U.K. Price: £6.07 Median Canadian Price: $15.03

Scottie the Scottish terrier

Fast Facts
Style Number: 4102
Introduced: 1996
Status: Retired 5-1-98
Birthday: 6-15-96

Collector Trivia
Scottie has been noted with two different birthdates – 6/15/96 and 6/3/96. This does not affect the Beanie's value.

Median U.S. Prices By Hang Tag

Available Tush Tag Generations: 3rd, 4th, 5th

Median U.S. Prices Over Time

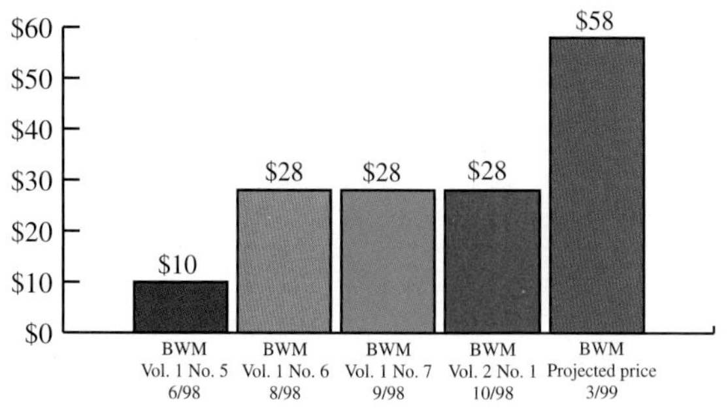

Median U.K. Price: £17.02 Median Canadian Price: $42.09

Seamore the seal

Fast Facts

Style Number: 4029
Introduced: 1994
Status: Retired 10-1-97
Birthday: 12-14-96

Collector Trivia

Seamore continues to have one of the highest market values of all the members of the October 1, 1997, retired family.

Median U.S. Prices By Hang Tag

1st	2nd	3rd	4th	5th
$800-850	$400-450	$175-225	$140-185	N/A

Available Tush Tag Generations: 1st, 2nd, 3rd, 4th

Median U.S. Prices Over Time

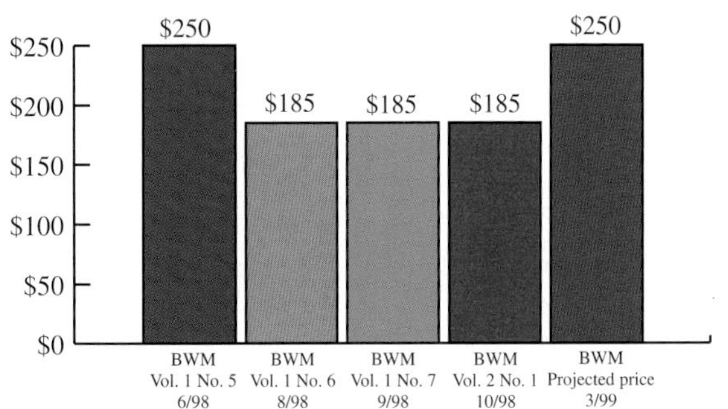

Median U.K. Price: £112.46 **Median Canadian Price: $278.14**

Seaweed the otter

Fast Facts

Style Number: 4080
Introduced: 1996
Status: Current
Birthday: 3-19-96

Collector Trivia

Seaweed is only one of only a few Beanies that uses felt as a decorative accent.

Median U.S. Prices By Hang Tag

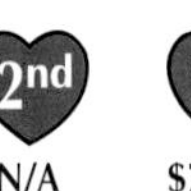

1st	2nd	3rd	4th	5th
N/A	N/A	$70-90	$10-15	$10-15

Available Tush Tag Generations: 2nd, 3rd, 4th, 6th

Median U.S. Prices Over Time

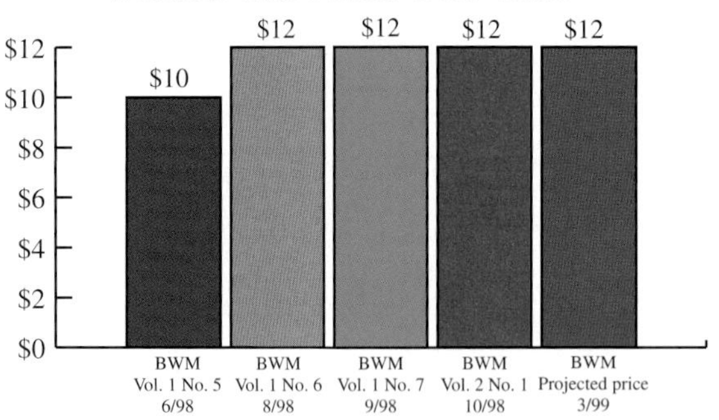

Median U.K. Price: £7.29 **Median Canadian Price: $18.04**

Slither the snake

Retired

Fast Facts

Style Number: 4031
Introduced: 1994
Status: Retired 1995
Birthday: Unknown

Collector Trivia

Slither and Hissy have different head and tongue shapes, but they both measure two feet long.

Median U.S. Prices By Hang Tag

1st	2nd	3rd	4th	5th
$2200-2400	$1800-2100	$1700-1950	N/A	N/A

Available Tush Tag Generations: 1st

Median U.S. Prices Over Time

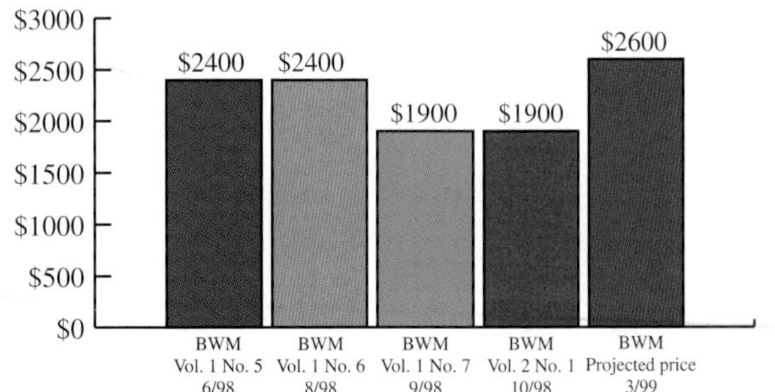

Median U.K. Price: £1155.01 **Median Canadian Price: $2856.65**

Sly the brown bellied fox

Retired

Fast Facts

Style Number: 4115
Introduced: 1996
Status: Retired 1996
Birthday: 9-12-96

Collector Trivia

Sly appeared only for two months with a brown belly when first introduced in spring 1996.

Median U.S. Prices By Hang Tag

1st	2nd	3rd	4th	5th
N/A	N/A	N/A	$160-185	N/A

Available Tush Tag Generations: 3rd

Median U.S. Prices Over Time

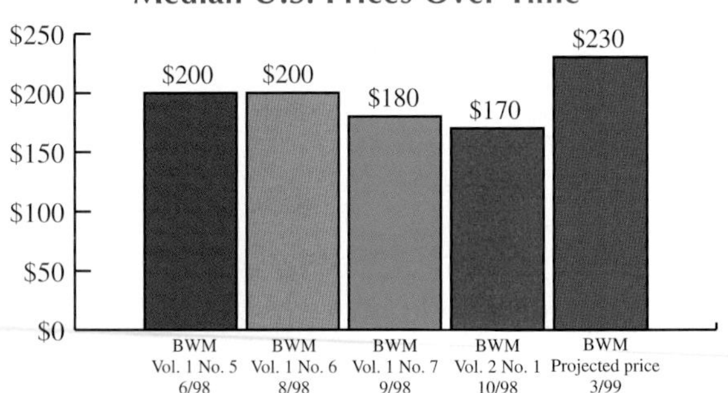

Median U.K. Price: £103.34 **Median Canadian Price: $255.59**

Sly the white bellied fox

Fast Facts
Style Number: 4115
Introduced: 1996
Status: Current
Birthday: 9-12-96

Collector Trivia
Sly's belly color was apparently changed in an effort to make the Beanie look more like a real fox.

Median U.S. Prices By Hang Tag

1st	2nd	3rd	4th	5th
N/A	N/A	N/A	$8-10	$8-10

Available Tush Tag Generations: 3rd, 4th, 5th, 6th

Median U.S. Prices Over Time

BWM Vol. 1 No. 5 6/98	BWM Vol. 1 No. 6 8/98	BWM Vol. 1 No. 7 9/98	BWM Vol. 2 No. 1 10/98	BWM Projected price 3/99
$10	$10	$10	$10	$10

$10 $8 $6 $4 $2 $0

Median U.K. Price: £6.07 Median Canadian Price: $15.03

Smoochy the frog

Current

Fast Facts
Style Number: 4039
Introduced: 12-31-97
Status: Current
Birthday: 10-1-97

Collector Trivia
Smoochy is one of the most popular of the December 31, 1997, new releases.

Median U.S. Prices By Hang Tag

1st	2nd	3rd	4th	5th
N/A	N/A	N/A	N/A	$10-15

Available Tush Tag Generations: 6th

Median U.S. Prices Over Time

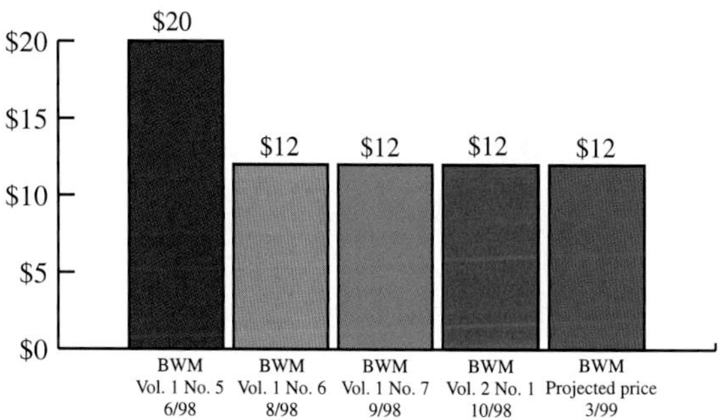

BWM Vol. 1 No. 5 6/98	BWM Vol. 1 No. 6 8/98	BWM Vol. 1 No. 7 9/98	BWM Vol. 2 No. 1 10/98	BWM Projected price 3/99
$20	$12	$12	$12	$12

Median U.K. Price: £7.29 Median Canadian Price: $18.04

Snip the Siamese cat

Current

Fast Facts
Style Number: 4120
Introduced: 1-1-97
Status: Current
Birthday: 10-22-96

Collector Trivia
A Pillow Pal named Meow is modeled after Snip.

Median U.S. Prices By Hang Tag

1st	2nd	3rd	4th	5th
N/A	N/A	N/A	$8-10	$8-10

Available Tush Tag Generations: 3rd, 4th, 5th, 6th

Median U.S. Prices Over Time

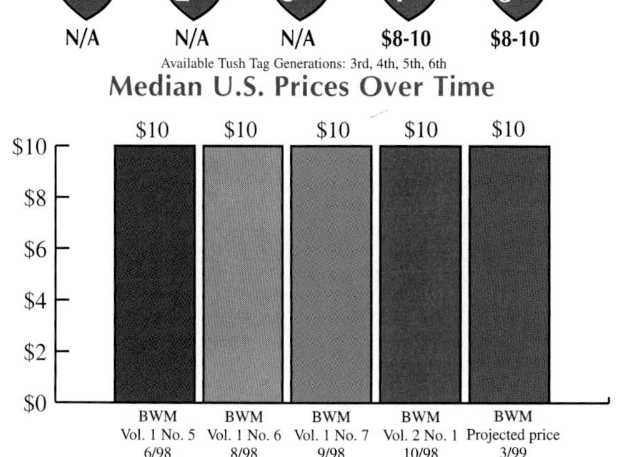

BWM Vol. 1 No. 5 6/98	BWM Vol. 1 No. 6 8/98	BWM Vol. 1 No. 7 9/98	BWM Vol. 2 No. 1 10/98	BWM Projected price 3/99
$10	$10	$10	$10	$10

Median U.K. Price: £6.07 Median Canadian Price: $15.03

Snort the bull with cream paws

Current

Style Number: 4002
Introduced: 1-1-97
Status: Current
Birthday: 5-15-95

Collector Trivia
Some rare versions of Snort have the name "Tabasco" on their hang tags. Also, some Canadian Snorts have been found with "Tabasco" used in the text of the hang tag poem.

Median U.S. Prices By Hang Tag

1st	2nd	3rd	4th	5th
N/A	N/A	N/A	$8-10	$8-10

Available Tush Tag Generations: 3rd, 4th, 5th, 6th

Median U.S. Prices Over Time

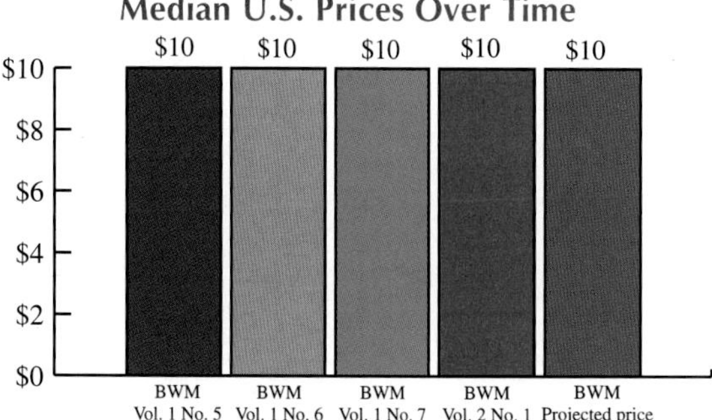

BWM Vol. 1 No. 5 6/98	BWM Vol. 1 No. 6 8/98	BWM Vol. 1 No. 7 9/98	BWM Vol. 2 No. 1 10/98	BWM Projected price 3/99
$10	$10	$10	$10	$10

Median U.K. Price: £6.07 Median Canadian Price: $15.03

Snowball the snowman

Fast Facts
Style Number: 4201
Introduced: 10-1-97
Status: Retired 12-31-97
Birthday: 12-22-96

Collector Trivia
Retired only three months after its release, Snowball remained widely available because Ty kept filling retailers' orders for Snowball for several more months.

Median U.S. Prices By Hang Tag

Available Tush Tag Generations: 5th

Median U.S. Prices Over Time

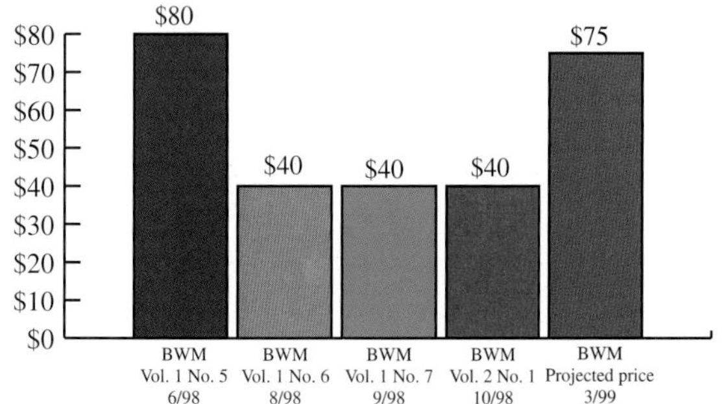

Median U.K. Price: £24.31 **Median Canadian Price: $60.14**

Sparky the Dalmatian

Fast Facts
Style Number: 4100
Introduced: 1996
Status: Retired 5-11-97
Birthday: 2-27-96

Collector Trivia
Sparky was discontinued because its name was already trademarked and used by the mascot for the National Fire Protection Association.

Median U.S. Prices By Hang Tag

Available Tush Tag Generations: 3rd

Median U.S. Prices Over Time

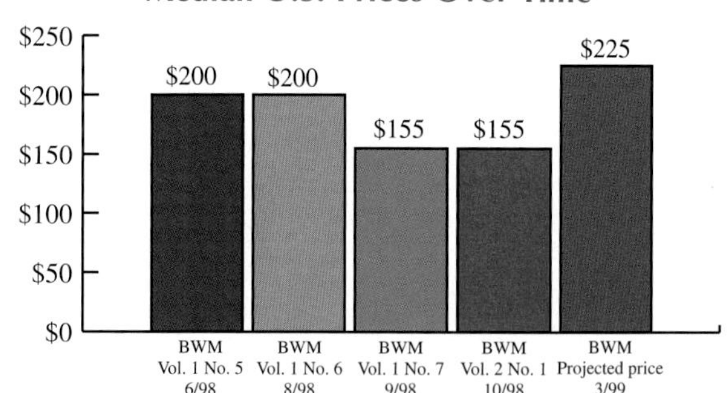

Median U.K. Price: £94.22 **Median Canadian Price: $233.04**

Speedy the turtle

Fast Facts
Style Number: 4030
Introduced: 1994
Status: Retired 10-1-97
Birthday: 8-14-94

Collector Trivia
This Beanie is sure to bring get-well smiles when wishing "A Speedy Recovery!"

Median U.S. Prices By Hang Tag
| $700-900 | $200-250 | $125-150 | $30-35 | N/A |

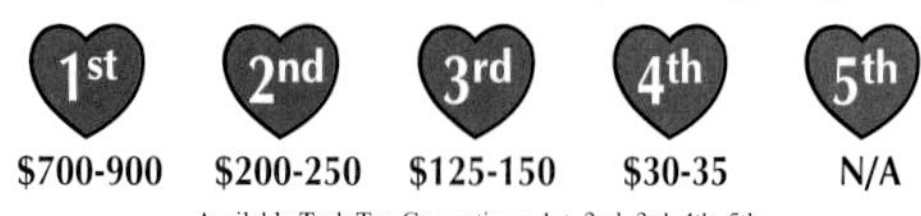

Available Tush Tag Generations: 1st, 2nd, 3rd, 4th, 5th

Median U.S. Prices Over Time

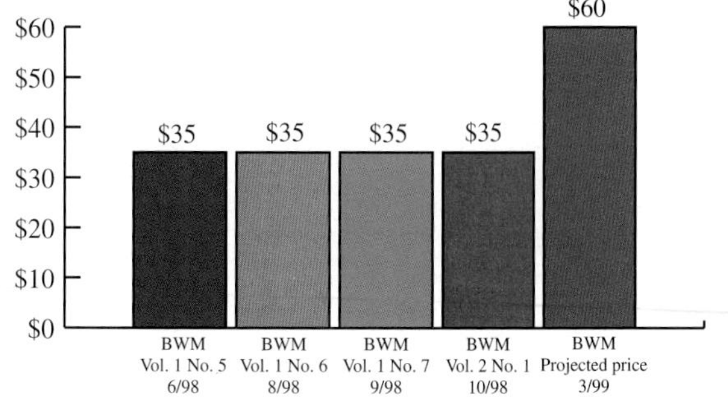

Median U.K. Price: £21.27 **Median Canadian Price: $52.62**

Spike the rhinoceros

Fast Facts
Style Number: 4060
Introduced: 1996
Status: Current
Birthday: 8-13-96

Collector Trivia
Spike has always been a hard-to-find Beanie and continues to fuel rumors of a possible retirement.

Median U.S. Prices By Hang Tag

Available Tush Tag Generations: 3rd, 4th, 5th, 6th

Median U.S. Prices Over Time

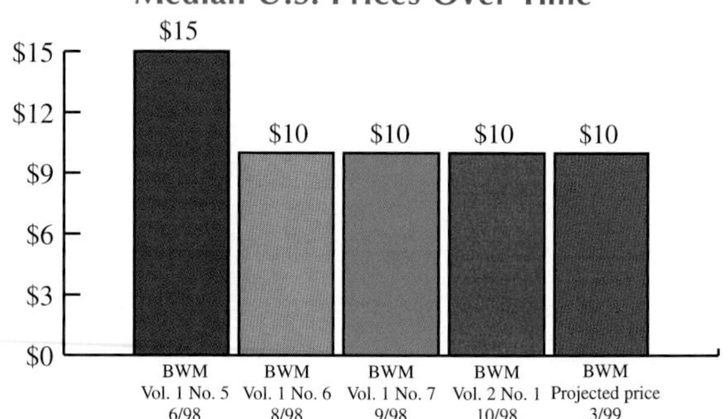

Median U.K. Price: £6.07 **Median Canadian Price: $15.03**

Spinner the spider

Fast Facts

Style Number: 4036
Introduced: 10-1-97
Status: Current
Birthday: 10-28-96

Collector Trivia

The material from the old Stripes, the gold and black tiger, was reinstated for use on this Beanie.

Median U.S. Prices By Hang Tag

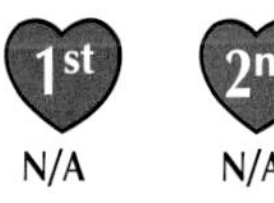

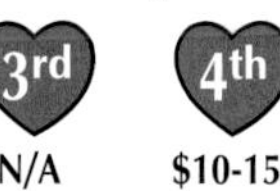

1st	2nd	3rd	4th	5th
N/A	N/A	N/A	$10-15	$10-15

Available Tush Tag Generations: 5th, 6th

Median U.S. Prices Over Time

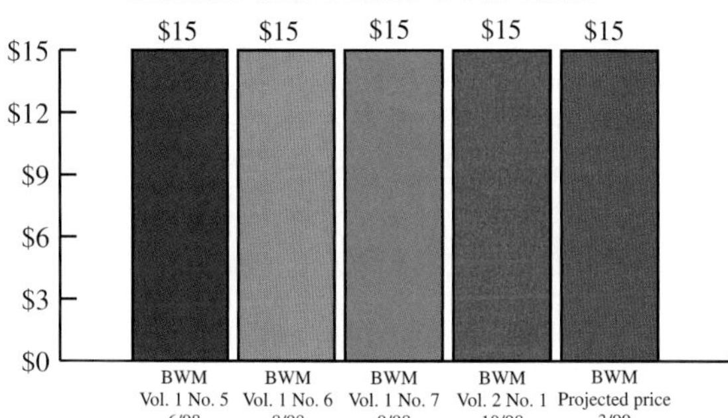

Median U.K. Price: £9.11 **Median Canadian Price: $22.55**

Splash the orca whale

Fast Facts

Style Number: 4022
Introduced: 1994
Status: Retired 5-11-97
Birthday: 7-8-93

Collector Trivia

Splash was retired on Mother's Day 1997 and replaced the same day by the new black Orca whale, Waves.

Median U.S. Prices By Hang Tag

1st	2nd	3rd	4th	5th
$850-1000	$600-700	$150-175	$110-150	N/A

Available Tush Tag Generations: 1st, 2nd, 3rd

Median U.S. Prices Over Time

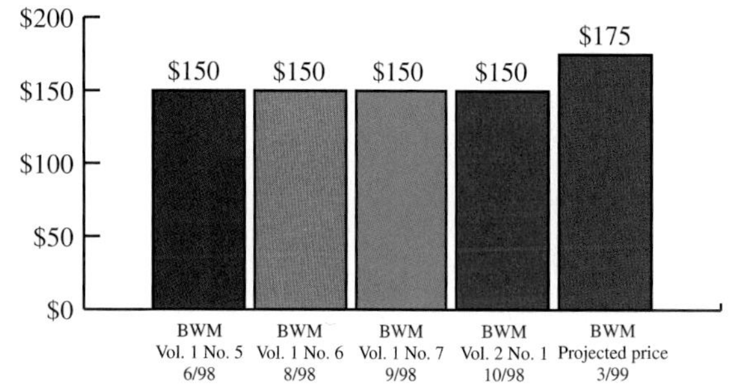

Median U.K. Price: £91.18 **Median Canadian Price: $225.52**

Spook the ghost

Fast Facts

Style Number: 4090
Introduced: 1995
Status: Retired 1995
Birthday: Unknown

Collector Trivia

Spook is the original Spooky. Without this unique hang tag, he is simply a tagless Spooky.

Median U.S. Prices By Hang Tag

1st	2nd	3rd	4th	5th
N/A	N/A	$425-550	N/A	N/A

Available Tush Tag Generations: 1st, 2nd

Median U.S. Prices Over Time

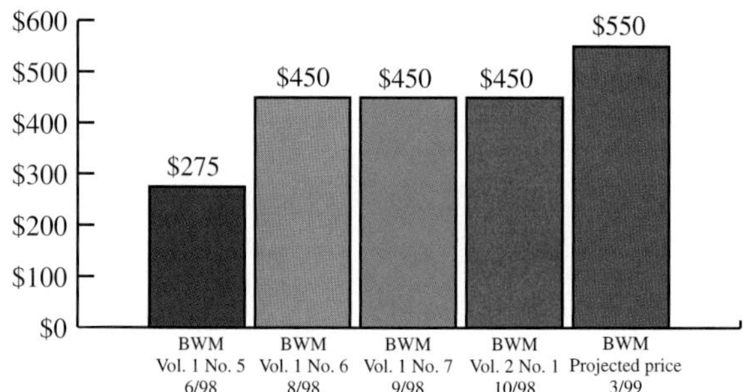

Median U.K. Price: £273.55 **Median Canadian Price: $676.57**

Spooky the ghost

Fast Facts

Style Number: 4090
Introduced: 1996
Status: Retired 12-31-97
Birthday: 10-31-95

Collector Trivia

Spooky has been seen with three different mouth shapes, but this does not affect the value. The third generation tags list "Jenna Boldebuck" as the designer.

Median U.S. Prices By Hang Tag

1st	2nd	3rd	4th	5th
N/A	N/A	$175-225	$25-45	N/A

Available Tush Tag Generations: 1st, 2nd, 3rd, 4th, 5th, 6th

Median U.S. Prices Over Time

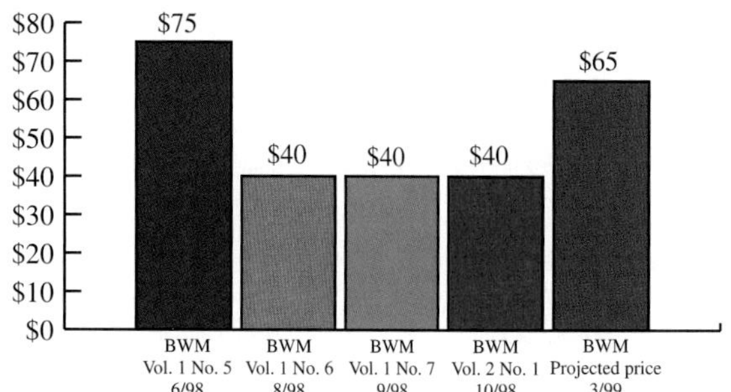

Median U.K. Price: £24.31 **Median Canadian Price: $60.14**

Spot the dog with a spot

Fast Facts
Style Number: 4000
Introduced: 1994
Status: Retired 10-1-97
Birthday: 1-3-93

Collector Trivia
One can only surmise that a black spot was added to this Beanie's back to make his name suit him a little better!

Median U.S. Prices By Hang Tag

1st	2nd	3rd	4th	5th
N/A	$450-550	$150-200	$50-65	N/A

Available Tush Tag Generations: 1st, 2nd, 3rd, 4th, 5th

Median U.S. Prices Over Time

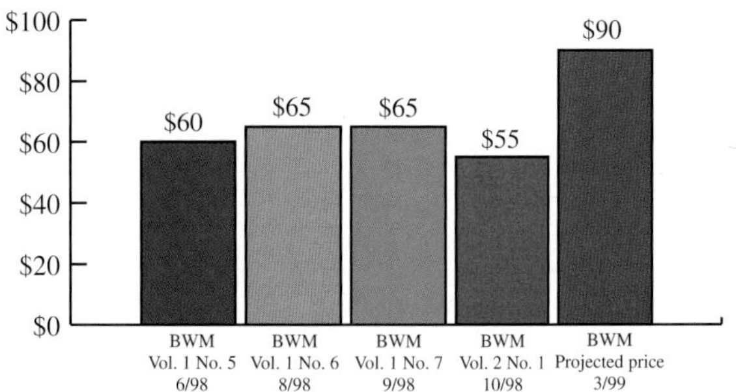

Median U.K. Price: £33.43 **Median Canadian Price: $82.69**

Spot the dog without a spot

Fast Facts
Style Number: 4000
Introduced: 1994
Status: Retired 1994
Birthday: Unknown

Collector Trivia
One of the rarest of all Beanies, Spot without a spot should be kept in a dust-free environment.

Median U.S. Prices By Hang Tag

1st	2nd	3rd	4th	5th
$2000-2200	$1750-1900	N/A	N/A	N/A

Available Tush Tag Generations: 1st

Median U.S. Prices Over Time

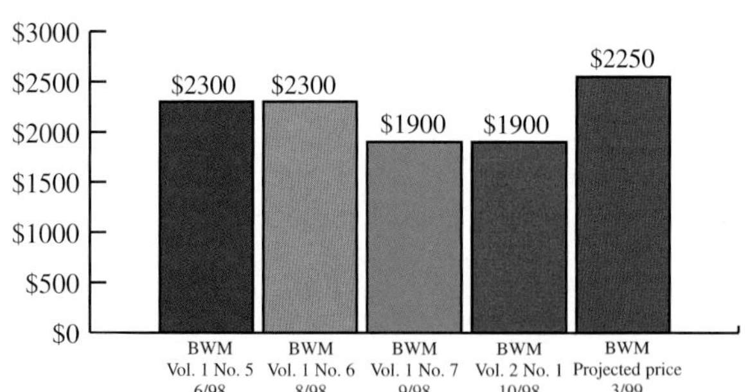

Median U.K. Price: £1155.01 **Median Canadian Price: $2856.65**

Spunky the cocker spaniel

Fast Facts
Style Number: 4184
Introduced: 12-31-97
Status: Current
Birthday: 1-14-97

Collector Trivia
The curly material used on Spunky's ears is unique to this Beanie Baby.

Median U.S. Prices By Hang Tag

1st	2nd	3rd	4th	5th
N/A	N/A	N/A	N/A	$10-15

Available Tush Tag Generations: 6th

Median U.S. Prices Over Time

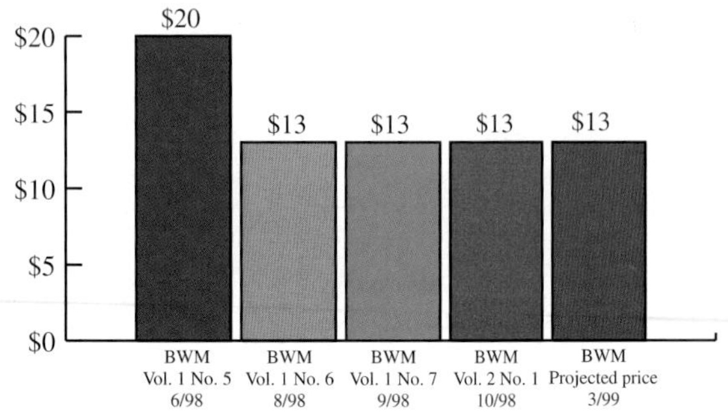

Median U.K. Price: £7.90 **Median Canadian Price: $19.54**

Squealer the pig

Fast Facts
Style Number: 4005
Introduced: 1994
Status: Retired 5-1-98
Birthday: 4-23-93

Collector Trivia
Some collectors have noted an error in the last line of Squealer's poem on some hang tags, but the mistake does not affect the Beanie's value. The error line reads, "He'll will make you smile!"

Median U.S. Prices By Hang Tag

1st	2nd	3rd	4th	5th
$700-900	$275-375	$85-115	$25-40	$25-40

Available Tush Tag Generations: 1st, 2nd, 3rd, 4th, 5th, 6th

Median U.S. Prices Over Time

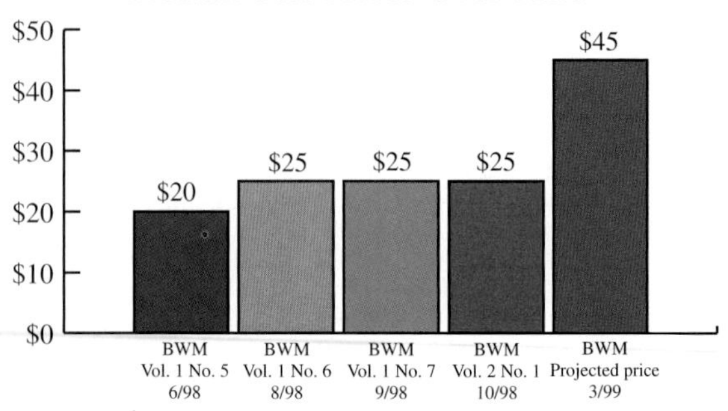

Median U.K. Price: £15.19 **Median Canadian Price: $37.58**

Steg the stegosaurus

Retired

Fast Facts
Style Number: 4087
Introduced: 1995
Status: Retired 1996
Birthday: Unknown

Collector Trivia
Distributed in Canada and the U.S. but never Europe, Steg is far more rare than Rex.

Median U.S. Prices By Hang Tag

Available Tush Tag Generations: 1st, 2nd

Median U.S. Prices Over Time

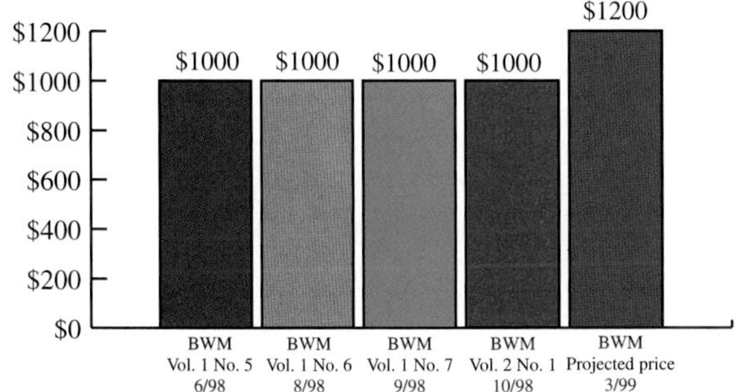

Median U.K. Price: £607.90 Median Canadian Price: $1503.50

Sting the stingray

Retired

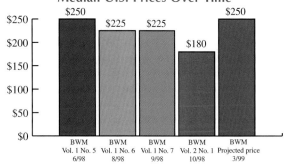

Fast Facts
Style Number: 4077
Introduced: 1995
Status: Retired 1-1-97
Birthday: 8-27-95

Collector Trivia
The prototype of Sting pictured on the spring 1995 New Introduction sheet (sent to retailers) showed him with a white belly.

Median U.S. Prices By Hang Tag

Available Tush Tag Generations: 1st, 2nd, 3rd

Median U.S. Prices Over Time

$250
$200
$150
$100
$50
$0

$250	$225	$225	$180	$250
BWM Vol. 1 No. 5 6/98	BWM Vol. 1 No. 6 8/98	BWM Vol. 1 No. 7 9/98	BWM Vol. 2 No. 1 10/98	BWM Projected price 3/99

Median U.K. Price: £109.42 Median Canadian Price: $270.63

Stinger the scorpion

Current

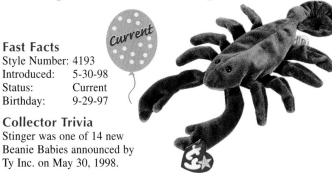

Fast Facts
Style Number: 4193
Introduced: 5-30-98
Status: Current
Birthday: 9-29-97

Collector Trivia
Stinger was one of 14 new Beanie Babies announced by Ty Inc. on May 30, 1998.

Median U.S. Prices By Hang Tag

Available Tush Tag Generations: 6th

Median U.S. Prices Over Time

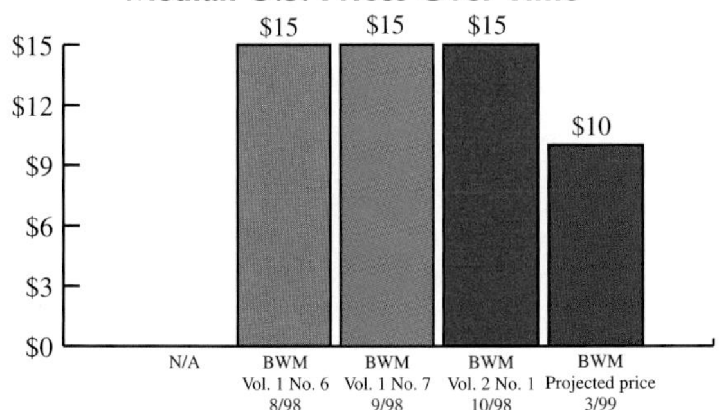

Median U.K. Price: £9.11 Median Canadian Price: $22.55

Stinky the skunk

Current

Fast Facts
Style Number: 4017
Introduced: 1995
Status: Current
Birthday: 2-13-95

Collector Trivia
If you think your collection is complete, try collecting all six versions of Stinky's tush tags!

Median U.S. Prices By Hang Tag

Available Tush Tag Generations: 1st, 2nd, 3rd, 4th, 5th, 6th

Median U.S. Prices Over Time

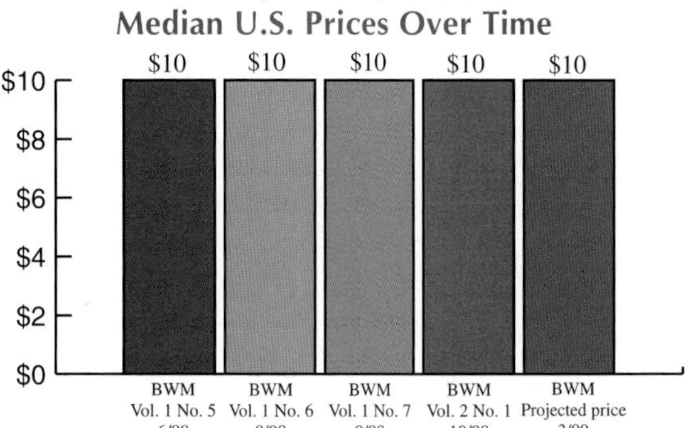

Median U.K. Price: £6.07 Median Canadian Price: $15.03

Stretch the ostrich

Fast Facts
Style Number: 4082
Introduced: 12-31-97
Status: Current
Birthday: 9-21-97

Collector Trivia
A commemorative Stretch was given away at the St. Louis Cardinals baseball game on May 22, 1998.

Median U.S. Prices By Hang Tag

1st	2nd	3rd	4th	5th
N/A	N/A	N/A	N/A	$10-15

Available Tush Tag Generations: 6th

Median U.S. Prices Over Time

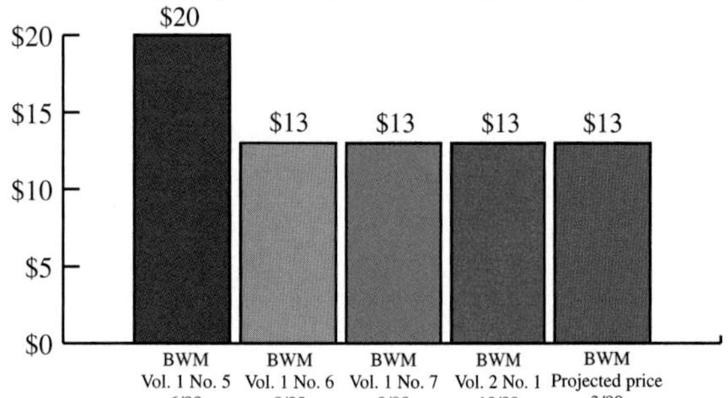

Median U.K. Price: £7.90 Median Canadian Price: $19.54

Stripes the caramel and black tiger

Fast Facts
Style Number: 4065
Introduced: 1996
Status: Retired 5-1-98
Birthday: 6-11-95

Collector Trivia
The Detroit Tigers had, appropriately enough, a Stripes giveaway at their game on May 31, 1998, at historic Tiger Stadium.

Median U.S. Prices By Hang Tag

1st	2nd	3rd	4th	5th
N/A	N/A	N/A	$10-15	$10-15

Available Tush Tag Generations: 3rd, 4th, 5th, 6th

Median U.S. Prices Over Time

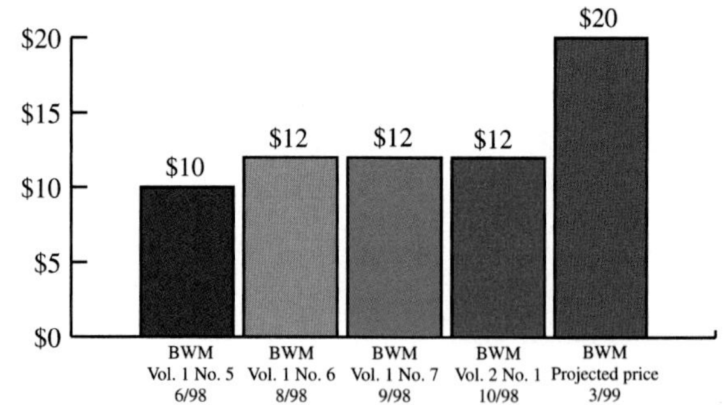

Median U.K. Price: £7.29 Median Canadian Price: $18.04

Stripes the gold and black tiger

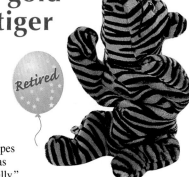

Fast Facts
Style Number: 4065
Introduced: 1995
Status: Retired 1996
Birthday: Unknown

Collector Trivia
A very rare version of this Stripes (often called "Old Stripes") was manufactured with a "fuzzy belly."

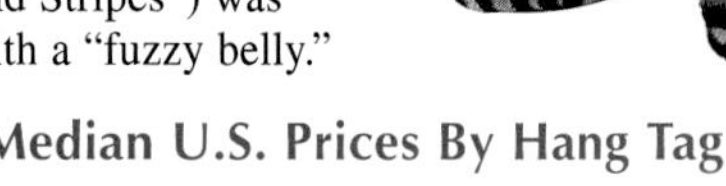
Median U.S. Prices By Hang Tag

1st	2nd	3rd	4th	5th
N/A	N/A	$350-500	N/A	N/A

Available Tush Tag Generations: 1st, 2nd

Median U.S. Prices Over Time

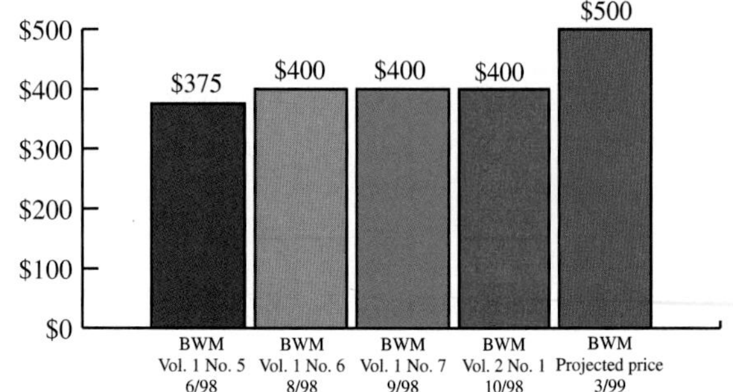

Median U.K. Price: £243.16 Median Canadian Price: $601.40

Strut the rooster

Fast Facts
Style Number: 4171
Introduced: 8-97
Status: Current
Birthday: 3-8-96

Collector Trivia
Struts with a commemorative card were given away at the Indiana Pacers vs. Minnesota Timberwolves game on April 2, 1998.

Median U.S. Prices By Hang Tag

1st	2nd	3rd	4th	5th
N/A	N/A	N/A	$10-15	$10-15

Available Tush Tag Generations: 4th, 5th, 6th

Median U.S. Prices Over Time

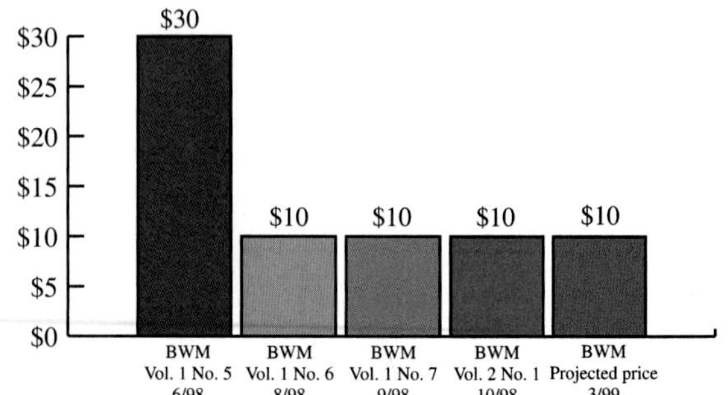

Median U.K. Price: £6.07 Median Canadian Price: $15.03

Tabasco the bull with red feet

Fast Facts
Style Number: 4002
Introduced: 1995
Status: Retired 1-1-97
Birthday: 5-15-95

Collector Trivia
Tabasco was rumored to have been retired because he was too "saucy!"

Median U.S. Prices By Hang Tag

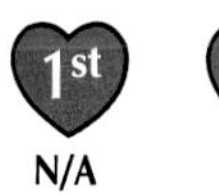

1st	2nd	3rd	4th	5th
N/A	N/A	$250-275	$175-225	N/A

Available Tush Tag Generations: 1st, 2nd, 3rd

Median U.S. Prices Over Time

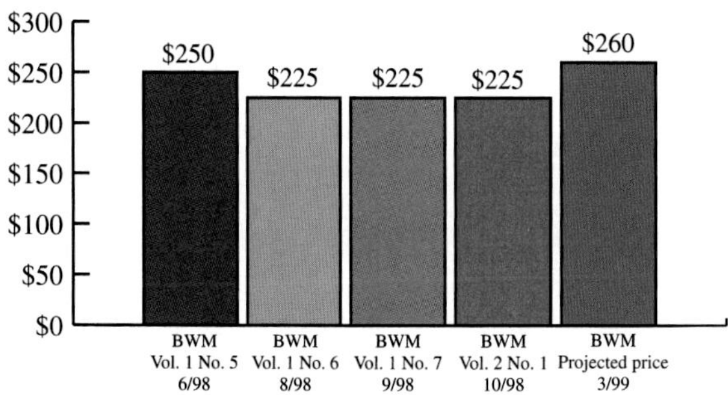

Median U.K. Price: £136.77 Median Canadian Price: $338.28

Tank the short armadillo with shell

Fast Facts
Style Number: 4031
Introduced: 1996
Status: Retired 10-1-97
Birthday: 2-22-95

Collector Trivia
This version of Tank most closely resembles a real armadillo. It has been seen with anywhere from 7 to 11 lines.

Median U.S. Prices By Hang Tag

1st	2nd	3rd	4th	5th
N/A	N/A	N/A	$70-90	N/A

Available Tush Tag Generations: 4th

Median U.S. Prices Over Time

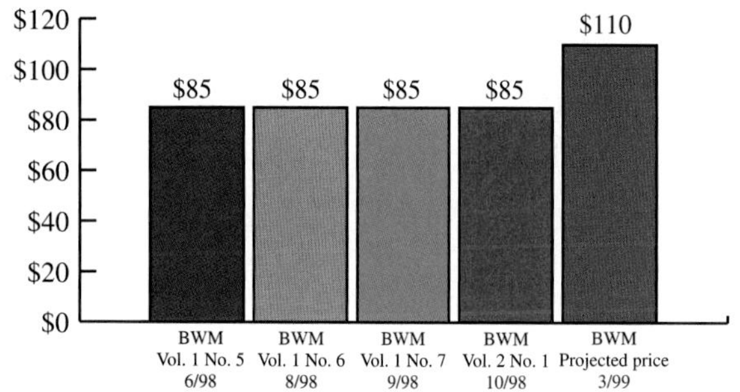

Median U.K. Price: £51.67 Median Canadian Price: $127.79

Tank the long armadillo with 7 lines (no shell)

Fast Facts
Style Number: 4031
Introduced: 1996
Status: Retired 1996
Birthday: Unknown

Collector Trivia
Tank with seven lines was the first to be introduced without the characteristic shell of the armadillo.

Median U.S. Prices By Hang Tag

1st	2nd	3rd	4th	5th
N/A	N/A	$150-200	$150-200	N/A

Available Tush Tag Generations: 1st, 2nd, 3rd

Median U.S. Prices Over Time

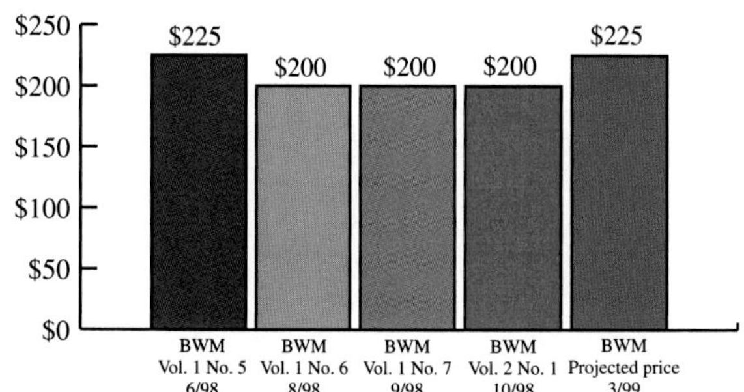

Median U.K. Price: £121.58 Median Canadian Price: $300.70

Tank the long armadillo with 9 lines (no shell)

Fast Facts
Style Number: 4031
Introduced: 1996
Status: Retired 1996
Birthday: 2-22-95

Collector Trivia
While two lines were added to his back and his nose was elongated to appear more authentic, this version of Tank is still missing its shell.

Median U.S. Prices By Hang Tag

1st	2nd	3rd	4th	5th
N/A	N/A	N/A	$125-200	N/A

Available Tush Tag Generations: 3rd

Median U.S. Prices Over Time

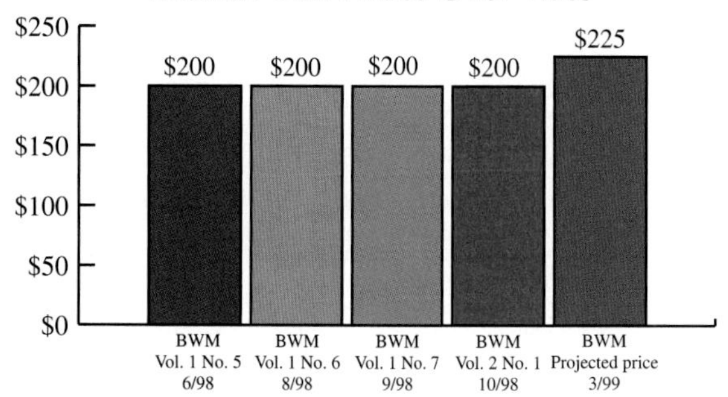

Median U.K. Price: £121.58 Median Canadian Price: $300.70

1997 Teddy the holiday bear

Fast Facts
Style Number: 4200
Introduced: 10-1-97
Status: Retired 12-31-97
Birthday: 12-25-96

Collector Trivia
The 1997 Holiday Teddy has been seen with two different types of fringe on its scarf.

Median U.S. Prices By Hang Tag

1st	2nd	3rd	4th	5th
N/A	N/A	N/A	$35-50	N/A

Available Tush Tag Generations: 3rd

Median U.S. Prices Over Time

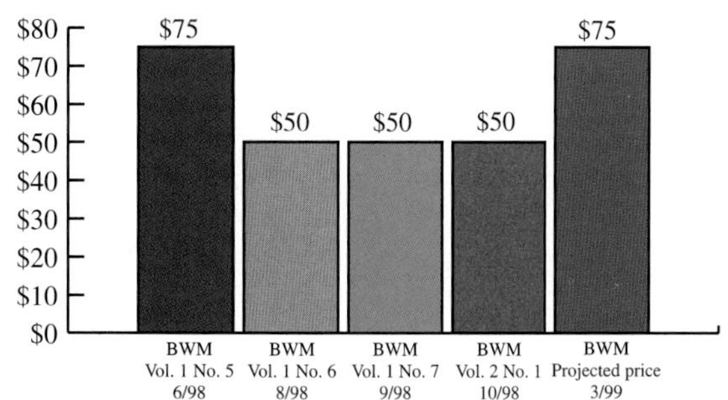

Median U.K. Price: £30.39 Median Canadian Price: $75.17

Teddy New Face Brown

Fast Facts
Style Number: 4050
Introduced: 1995
Status: Retired 10-1-97
Birthday: 11-28-95

Collector Trivia
Teddy New Face Brown was the Teddy that remained on the current list the longest, finally retiring on October 1, 1997.

Median U.S. Prices By Hang Tag

1st	2nd	3rd	4th	5th
N/A	$1000-1300	$300-400	$85-110	N/A

Available Tush Tag Generations: 1st, 2nd, 3rd, 4th

Median U.S. Prices Over Time

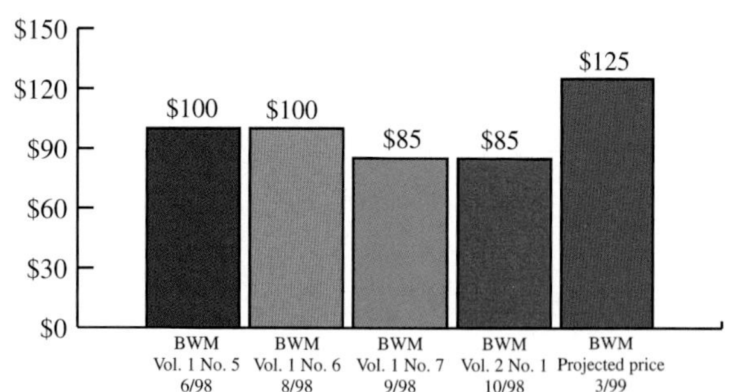

Median U.K. Price: £51.67 Median Canadian Price: $127.79

Teddy New Face Cranberry

Fast Facts
Style Number: 4052
Introduced: 1995
Status: Retired 1995
Birthday: Unknown

Collector Trivia
The family of New Face bears such as this one continues to grow, with Princess and Erin among the most recent additions.

Median U.S. Prices By Hang Tag

1st	2nd	3rd	4th	5th
N/A	$2000-2100	$1850-2000	N/A	N/A

Available Tush Tag Generations: 1st

Median U.S. Prices Over Time

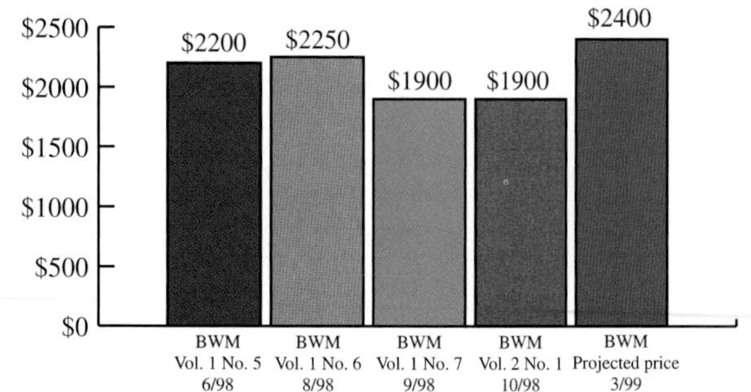

Median U.K. Price: £1155.01 Median Canadian Price: $2856.65

Teddy New Face Jade

Fast Facts
Style Number: 4057
Introduced: 1995
Status: Retired 1995
Birthday: Unknown

Collector Trivia
Teddy New Face Jade rose in popularity in direct relation to "hunter" green becoming the interior design color of choice.

Median U.S. Prices By Hang Tag

1st	2nd	3rd	4th	5th
N/A	$2000-2100	$1850-2000	N/A	N/A

Available Tush Tag Generations: 1st

Median U.S. Prices Over Time

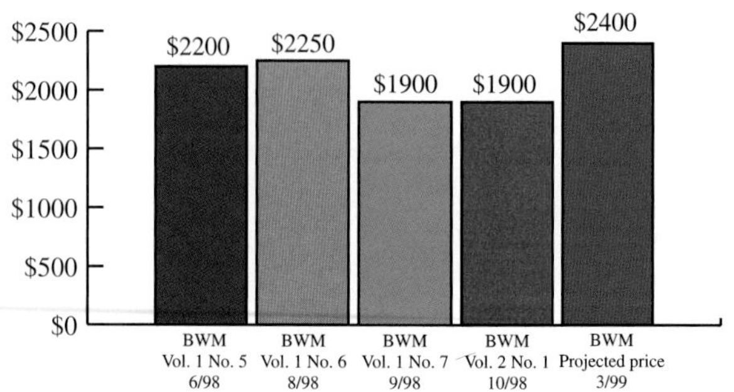

Median U.K. Price: £1155.01 Median Canadian Price: $2856.65

Teddy New Face Magenta

Fast Facts
Style Number: 4056
Introduced: 1995
Status: Retired 1995
Birthday: Unknown

Collector Trivia
This Teddy is the Editor-In-Chief's personal favorite. Teddy Magenta has the same material as one of the oldest Pattis.

Median U.S. Prices By Hang Tag

1st	2nd	3rd	4th	5th
N/A	$2000-2100	$1850-2000	N/A	N/A

Available Tush Tag Generations: 1st

Median U.S. Prices Over Time

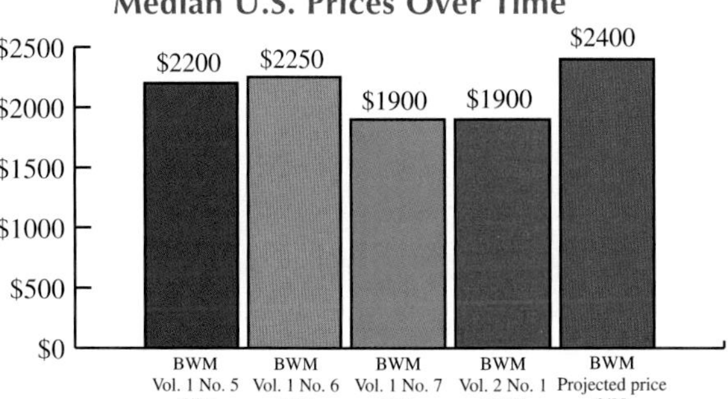

Median U.K. Price: £1155.01 Median Canadian Price: $2856.65

Teddy New Face Teal

Fast Facts
Style Number: 4051
Introduced: 1995
Status: Retired 1995
Birthday: Unknown

Collector Trivia
Sitting together, the five colored bears are a stunning combination of deep, rich jewel tones.\

Median U.S. Prices By Hang Tag

1st	2nd	3rd	4th	5th
N/A	$2000-2100	$1850-2000	N/A	N/A

Available Tush Tag Generations: 1st

Median U.S. Prices Over Time

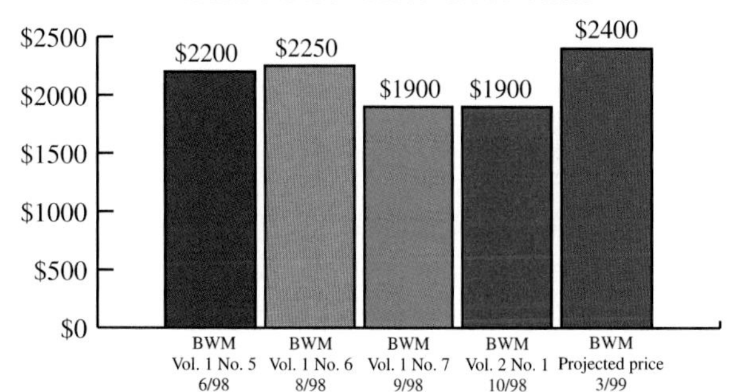

Median U.K. Price: £1155.01 Median Canadian Price: $2856.65

Teddy New Face Violet

Fast Facts
Style Number: 4055
Introduced: 1995
Status: Retired 1995
Birthday: Unknown

Collector Trivia
Teddy New Face Violet was brought back from retirement for a Ty Inc. employee Christmas gift.

Median U.S. Prices By Hang Tag

1st	2nd	3rd	4th	5th
N/A	$2000-2100	$1850-2000	N/A	N/A

Available Tush Tag Generations: 1st

Median U.S. Prices Over Time

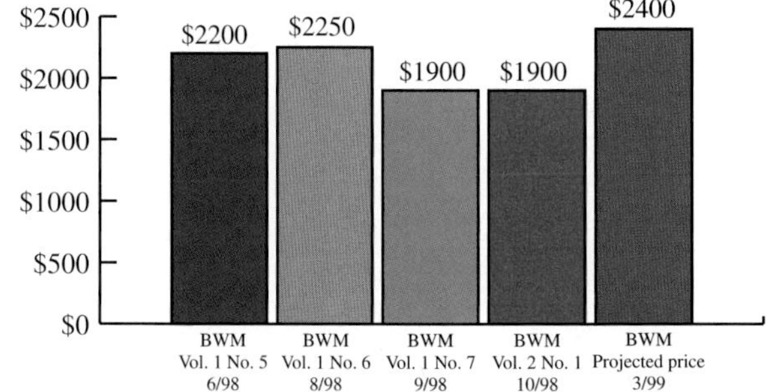

Median U.K. Price: £1155.01 Median Canadian Price: $2856.65

Teddy Old Face Brown

Fast Facts
Style Number: 4050
Introduced: 1994
Status: Retired 1995
Birthday: Unknown

Collector Trivia
One of the most sought-after Beanies for avid collectors, he is often valued at more than $400 over the other Old Face bears.

Median U.S. Prices By Hang Tag

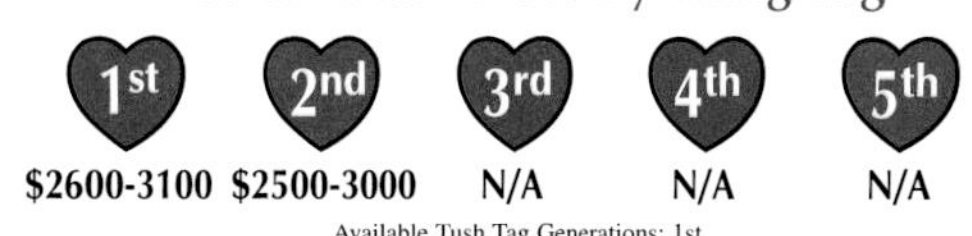

1st	2nd	3rd	4th	5th
$2600-3100	$2500-3000	N/A	N/A	N/A

Available Tush Tag Generations: 1st

Median U.S. Prices Over Time

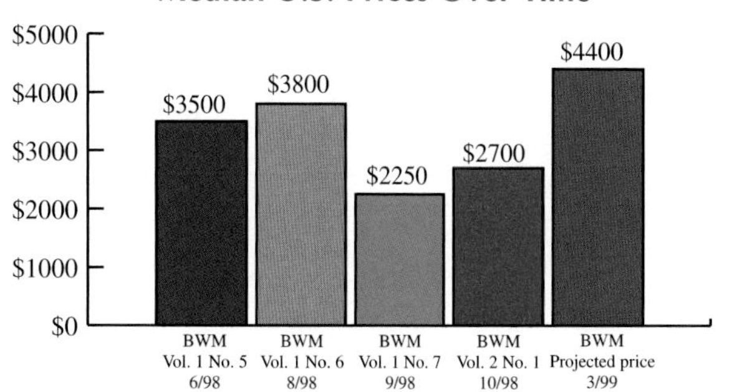

Median U.K. Price: £1641.33 Median Canadian Price: $4059.45

Teddy Old Face Cranberry

Fast Facts
Style Number: 4052
Introduced: 1994
Status: Retired 1995
Birthday: Unknown

Collector Trivia
This Beanie can command a premium over the other jewel-toned Old Face bears due to lesser production quantity.

Median U.S. Prices By Hang Tag

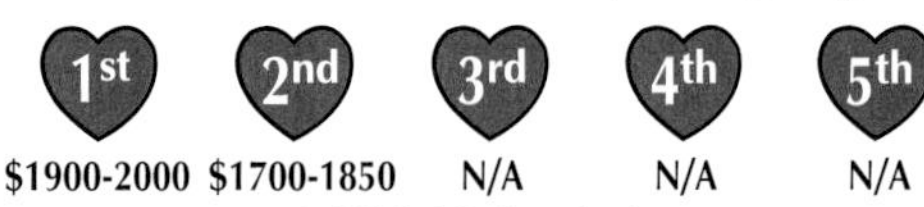

1st	2nd	3rd	4th	5th
$1900-2000	$1700-1850	N/A	N/A	N/A

Available Tush Tag Generations:1st

Median U.S. Prices Over Time

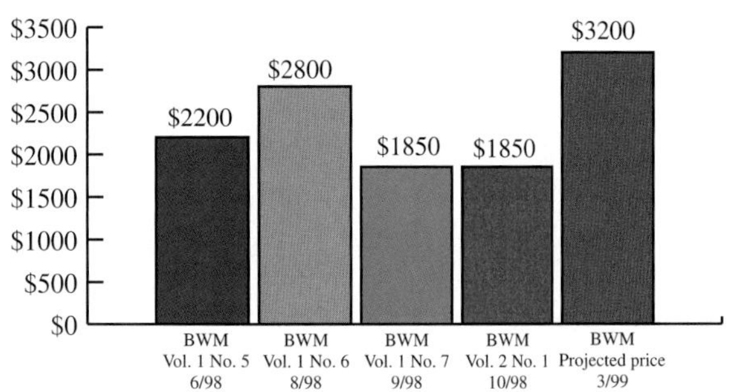

Median U.K. Price: £1124.61   Median Canadian Price: $2781.47

Teddy Old Face Jade

Fast Facts
Style Number: 4057
Introduced: 1994
Status: Retired 1995
Birthday: Unknown

Collector Trivia
Although it's not easy to distinguish Jade from Teal, this shade is actually more like a "hunter" green color.

Median U.S. Prices By Hang Tag

1st	2nd	3rd	4th	5th
$1900-2000	$1700-1850	N/A	N/A	N/A

Available Tush Tag Generations: 1st

Median U.S. Prices Over Time

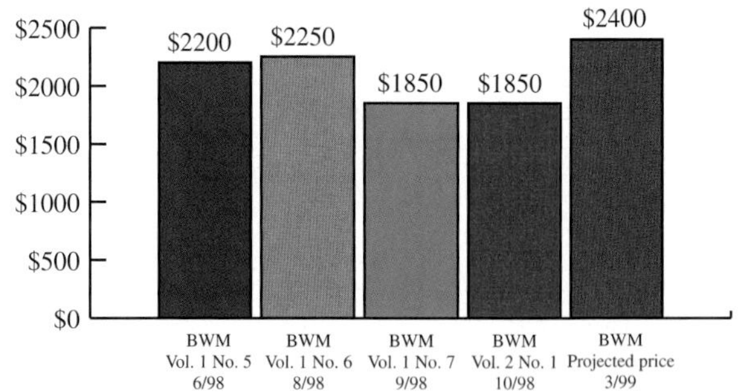

Median U.K. Price: £1124.61   Median Canadian Price: $2781.47

Teddy Old Face Magenta

Fast Facts
Style Number: 4056
Introduced: 1994
Status: Retired 1995
Birthday: Unknown

Collector Trivia
Although some Valentinos, Peaces and Garcias missing a stitch under their chins may look like Old Face bears, only those bears named "Teddy" are actual Old Face bears.

Median U.S. Prices By Hang Tag

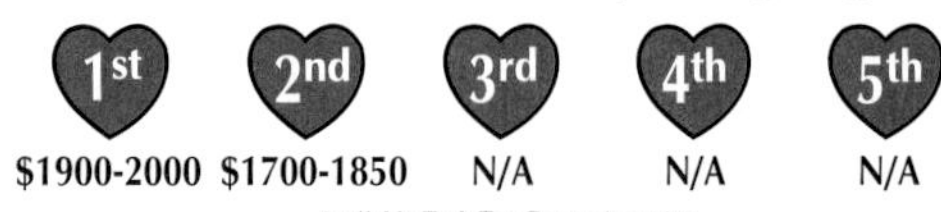

1st	2nd	3rd	4th	5th
$1900-2000	$1700-1850	N/A	N/A	N/A

Available Tush Tag Generations: 1st

Median U.S. Prices Over Time

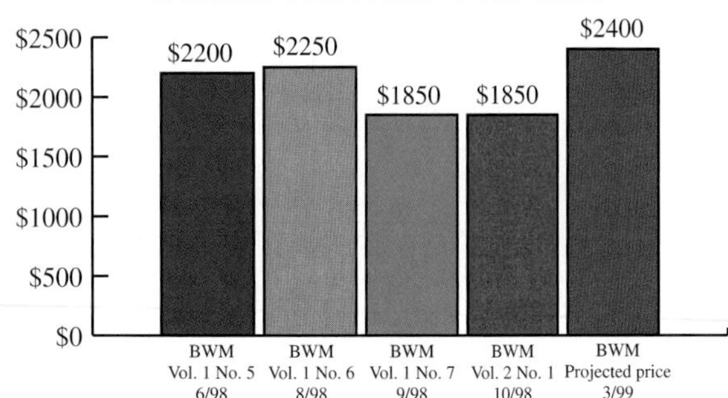

Median U.K. Price: £1124.61   Median Canadian Price: $2781.47

Teddy Old Face Teal

Fast Facts
Style Number: 4051
Introduced: 1994
Status: Retired 1995
Birthday: Unknown

Collector Trivia
Sometimes referred to as a color closer to "kelly" green, Teddy Teal is the lighter and brighter of the two green bears.

Median U.S. Prices By Hang Tag

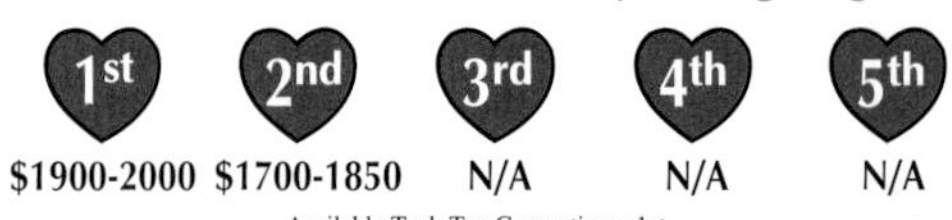

1st	2nd	3rd	4th	5th
$1900-2000	$1700-1850	N/A	N/A	N/A

Available Tush Tag Generations: 1st

Median U.S. Prices Over Time

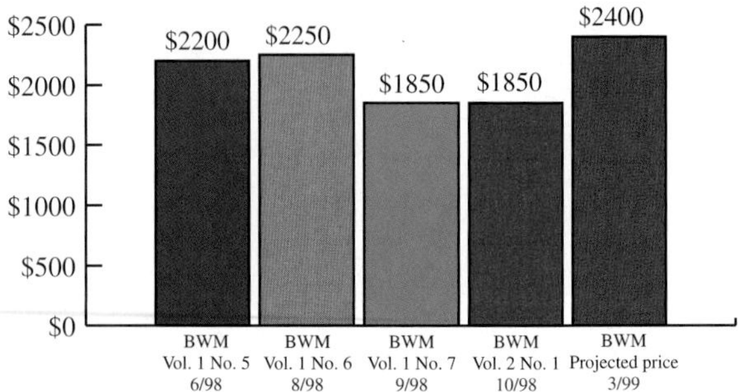

Median U.K. Price: £1124.61   Median Canadian Price: $2781.47

Teddy Old Face Violet

Fast Facts
Style Number: 4055
Introduced: 1994
Status: Retired 1995
Birthday: Unknown

Collector Trivia
In 1996 and 1997, Teddy Violet commanded a higher value over the other jewel tone bears. It has since leveled out in value.

Median U.S. Prices By Hang Tag

1st	2nd	3rd	4th	5th
$1900-2000	$1700-1850	N/A	N/A	N/A

Available Tush Tag Generations: 1st

Median U.S. Prices Over Time

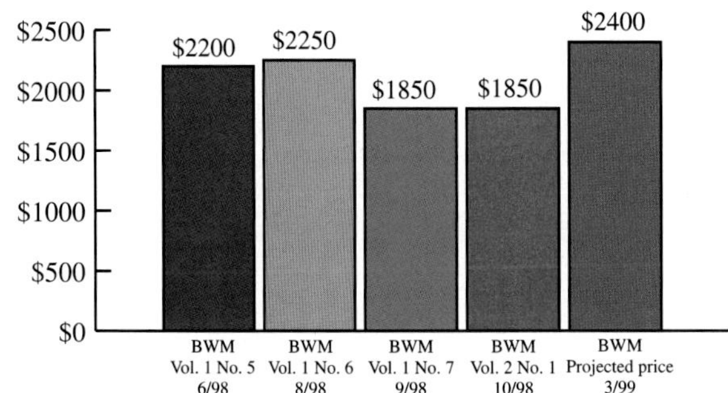

Median U.K. Price: £1124.61 **Median Canadian Price: $2781.47**

Tracker the basset hound

Fast Facts
Style Number: 4198
Introduced: 5-30-98
Status: Current
Birthday: 6-5-97

Collector Trivia
Tracker was one of 14 new Beanie Babies announced by Ty Inc. on May 30, 1998.

Median U.S. Prices By Hang Tag

1st	2nd	3rd	4th	5th
N/A	N/A	N/A	N/A	$15-20

Available Tush Tag Generations: 6th

Median U.S. Prices Over Time

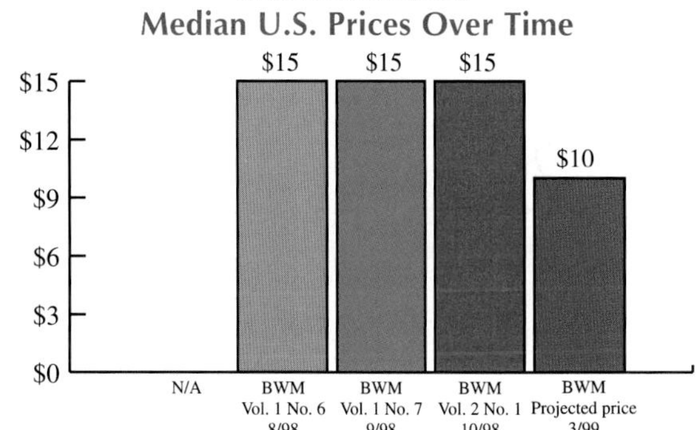

Median U.K. Price: £9.11 **Median Canadian Price: $22.55**

Trap the mouse

Fast Facts
Style Number: 4042
Introduced: 1994
Status: Retired 1995
Birthday: Unknown

Collector Trivia
Trap is the smallest member of Ty's Beanie Baby line.

Median U.S. Prices By Hang Tag

1st	2nd	3rd	4th	5th
$1800-2000	$1650-1850	$1400-1600	N/A	N/A

Available Tush Tag Generations: 1st

Median U.S. Prices Over Time

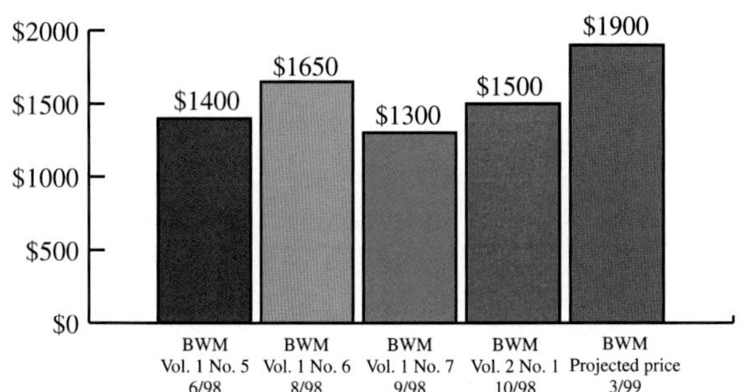

Median U.K. Price: £911.85 **Median Canadian Price: $2255.25**

Tuffy the terrier

Fast Facts
Style Number: 4108
Introduced: 5-11-97
Status: Current
Birthday: 10-12-96

Collector Trivia
Tuffy is one of three Beanie Baby terriers. The others are Scottie and Bruno.

Median U.S. Prices By Hang Tag

1st	2nd	3rd	4th	5th
N/A	N/A	N/A	$8-10	$8-10

Available Tush Tag Generations: 3rd, 4th, 5th, 6th

Median U.S. Prices Over Time

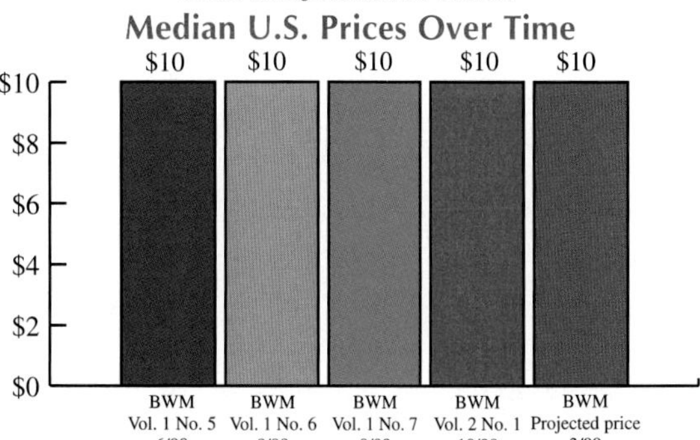

Median U.K. Price: £6.07 **Median Canadian Price: $15.03**

Tusk the walrus

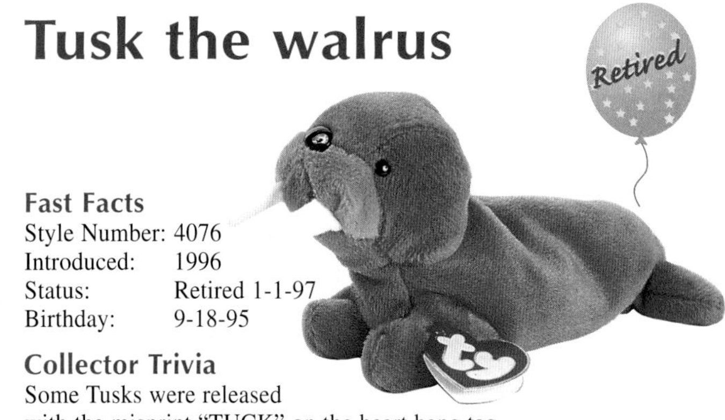

Fast Facts
Style Number: 4076
Introduced: 1996
Status: Retired 1-1-97
Birthday: 9-18-95

Collector Trivia
Some Tusks were released with the misprint "TUCK" on the heart hang tag.

Median U.S. Prices By Hang Tag

Median U.S. Prices Over Time

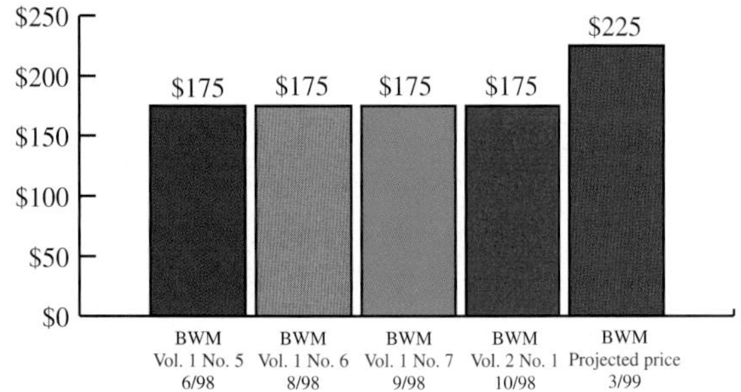

Median U.K. Price: £106.38 Median Canadian Price: $263.11

Twigs the giraffe

Fast Facts
Style Number: 4068
Introduced: 1996
Status: Retired 5-1-98
Birthday: 5-19-95

Collector Trivia
Twigs' poem makes reference to how he "stands tall," but this Beanie is in a sitting position!

Median U.S. Prices By Hang Tag

Median U.S. Prices Over Time

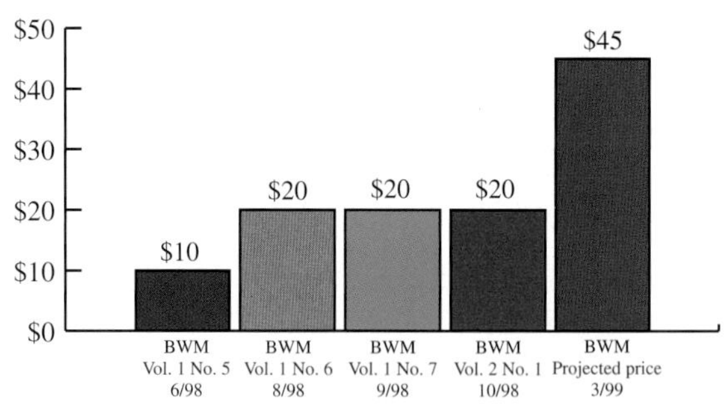

Median U.K. Price: £12.15 Median Canadian Price: $30.07

Valentino the white bear with heart

Fast Facts
Style Number: 4058
Introduced: 1995
Status: Current
Birthday: 2-14-94

Collector Trivia
Thanks to David Wells' recent perfect game for the New York Yankees, a Valentino from the giveaway that day is now in the Baseball Hall of Fame in Cooperstown!

Median U.S. Prices By Hang Tag

Median U.S. Prices Over Time

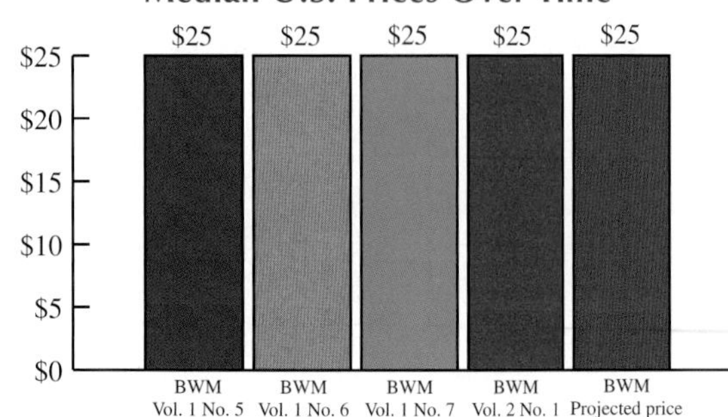

Median U.K. Price: £15.19 Median Canadian Price: $37.58

Velvet the panther

Fast Facts
Style Number: 4064
Introduced: 1995
Status: Retired 10-1-97
Birthday: 12-16-95

Collector Trivia
Velvet's tail was originally flat with the seam showing. Later versions (starting in fall 1996) had a tail with a more rounded look and the seam on the inside.

Median U.S. Prices By Hang Tag

Median U.S. Prices Over Time

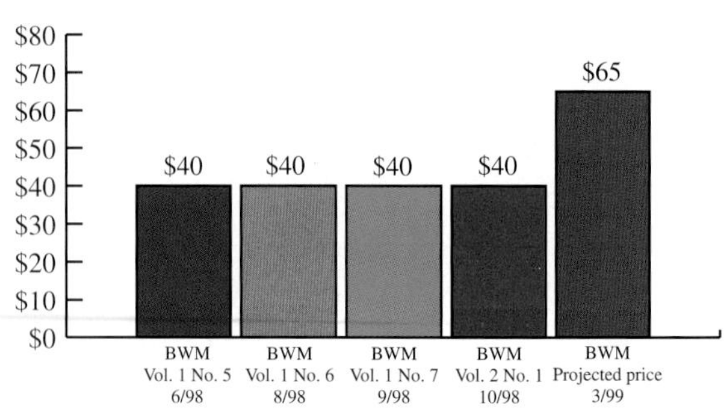

Median U.K. Price: £24.31 Median Canadian Price: $60.14

Waddle the penguin

Fast Facts
Style Number: 4075
Introduced: 1995
Status: Retired 5-1-98
Birthday: 12-19-95

Collector Trivia
The appropriately named Waddle was one of four birds retired in the spring of 1998.

Median U.S. Prices By Hang Tag

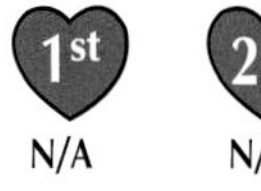
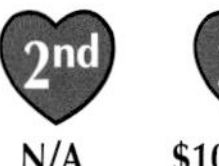

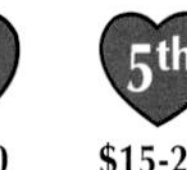

1st	2nd	3rd	4th	5th
N/A	N/A	$100-125	$15-20	$15-20

Available Tush Tag Generations: 1st, 2nd, 3rd, 4th, 5th, 6th

Median U.S. Prices Over Time

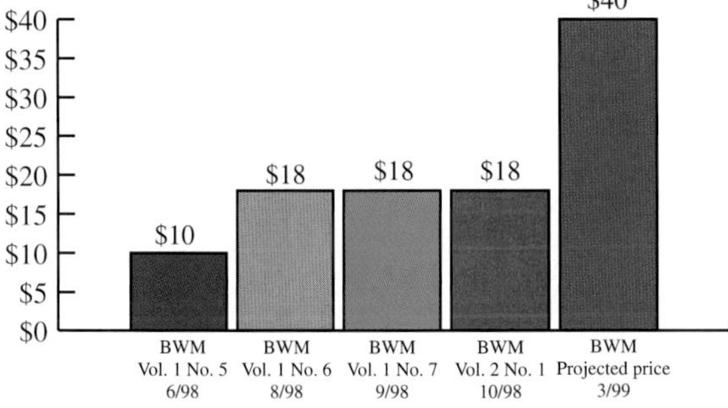

Median U.K. Price: £10.94 Median Canadian Price: $27.06

Waves the whale

Fast Facts
Style Number: 4084
Introduced: 5-11-97
Status: Retired 5-1-98
Birthday: 12-8-96

Collector Trivia
Waves, introduced when his predecessor Splash was retired, was mistagged in the first run.

Median U.S. Prices By Hang Tag

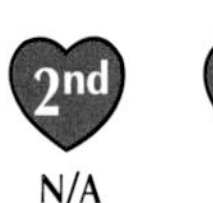

1st	2nd	3rd	4th	5th
N/A	N/A	N/A	$15-25	$15-25

Available Tush Tag Generations: 3rd, 4th, 5th, 6th

Median U.S. Prices Over Time

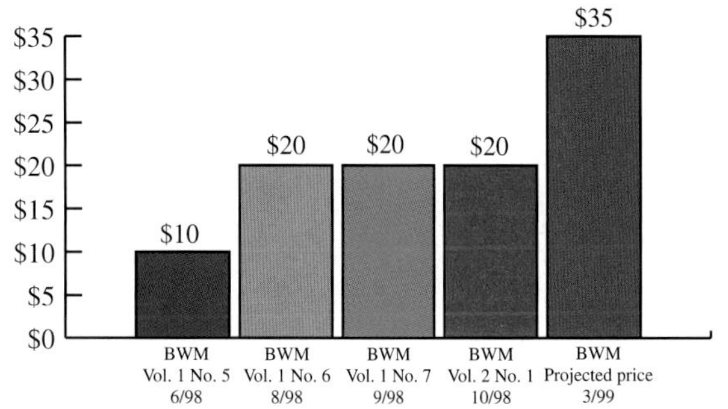

Median U.K. Price: £12.15 Median Canadian Price: $30.07

Web the spider

Fast Facts
Style Number: 4041
Introduced: 1994
Status: Retired 1995
Birthday: Unknown

Collector Trivia
Many "Techies" have purchased Web to sit on their computers, especially those who began their Beanie collections via the Internet.

Median U.S. Prices By Hang Tag

1st	2nd	3rd	4th	5th
$1900-2100	$1700-2000	$1400-1550	N/A	N/A

Available Tush Tag Generations: 1st

Median U.S. Prices Over Time

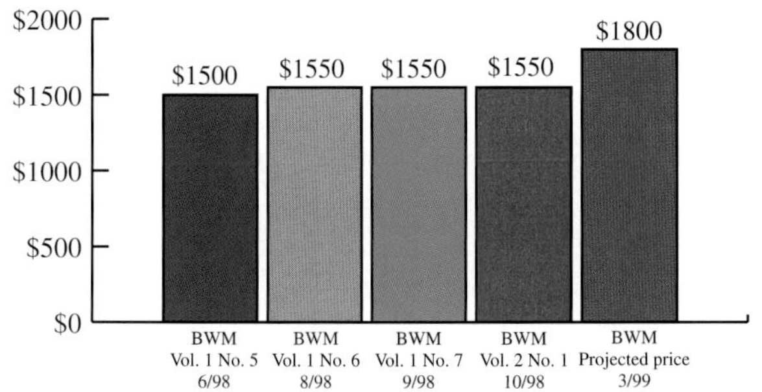

Median U.K. Price: £942.24 Median Canadian Price: $2330.42

Weenie the dachshund

Fast Facts
Style Number: 4013
Introduced: 1996
Status: Retired 5-1-98
Birthday: 7-20-95

Collector Trivia
Baseball's Tampa Bay Devil Rays gave out the newly retired Weenie at their game on July 26, 1998.

Median U.S. Prices By Hang Tag

1st	2nd	3rd	4th	5th
N/A	N/A	$100-125	$20-30	$20-30

Available Tush Tag Generations: 2nd, 3rd, 4th, 5th

Median U.S. Prices Over Time

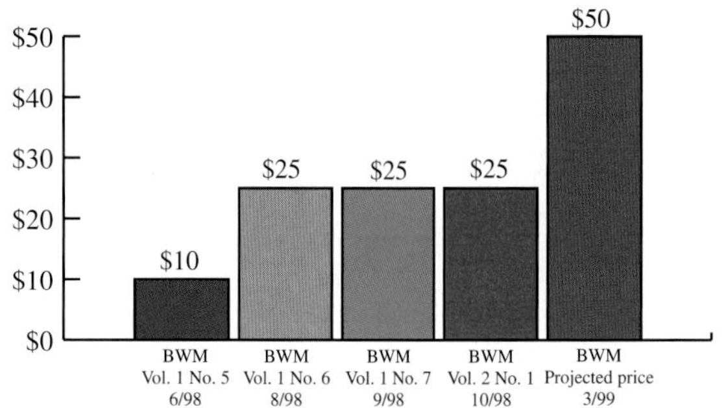

Median U.K. Price: £15.19 Median Canadian Price: $37.58

Whisper the deer

Fast Facts

Style Number: 4187
Introduced: 5-30-98
Status: Current
Birthday: 4-5-97

Collector Trivia

Whisper was one of 14 new Beanie Babies announced by Ty Inc. on May 30, 1998.

Median U.S. Prices By Hang Tag

1st	2nd	3rd	4th	5th
N/A	N/A	N/A	N/A	$10-20

Available Tush Tag Generations: 6th

Median U.S. Prices Over Time

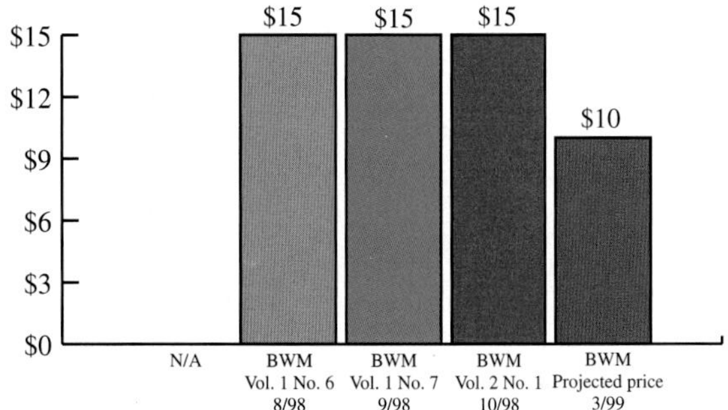

Median U.K. Price: £9.11 **Median Canadian Price: $22.55**

Wise the owl

Fast Facts

Style Number: 4194
Introduced: 5-30-98
Status: Current
Birthday: 5-31-97

Collector Trivia

Wise was one of 14 new Beanie Babies announced by Ty Inc. on May 30, 1998. It is expected to be a big seller among high school graduates because of the mortar board on his head.

Median U.S. Prices By Hang Tag

1st	2nd	3rd	4th	5th
N/A	N/A	N/A	N/A	$15-30

Available Tush Tag Generations: 6th

Median U.S. Prices Over Time

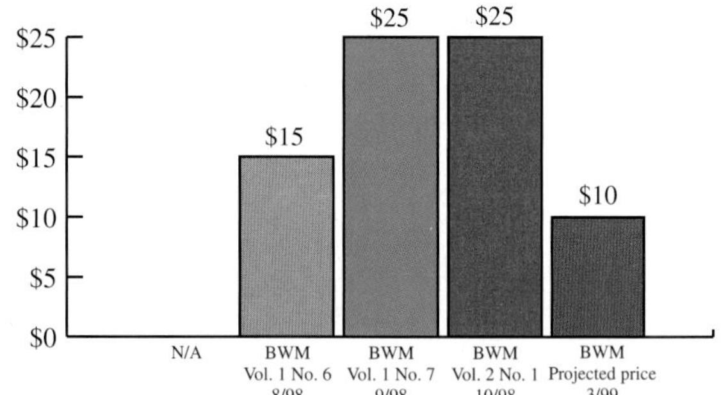

Median U.K. Price: £15.19 **Median Canadian Price: $37.58**

Wrinkles the dog

Current

Fast Facts

Style Number: 4103
Introduced: 1996
Status: Current
Birthday: 5-1-96

Collector Trivia

Wrinkles was the model for the Pillow Pal bulldog named Bruiser.

Median U.S. Prices By Hang Tag

1st	2nd	3rd	4th	5th
N/A	N/A	N/A	$8-10	$8-10

Available Tush Tag Generations: 3rd, 4th, 5th, 6th

Median U.S. Prices Over Time

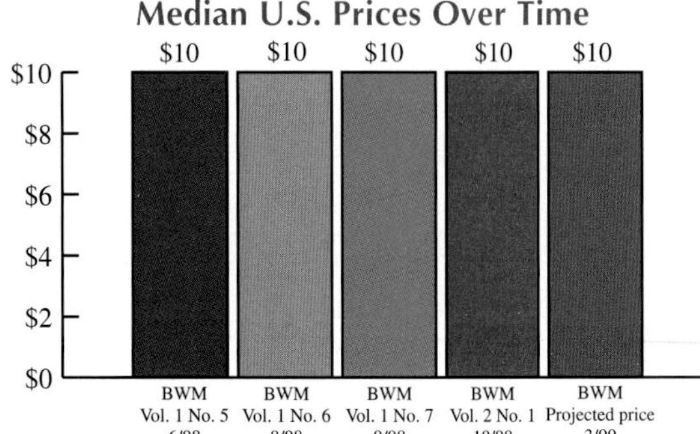

Median U.K. Price: £6.07 **Median Canadian Price: $15.03**

Ziggy the zebra

Retired

Fast Facts

Style Number: 4063
Introduced: 1995
Status: Retired 5-1-98
Birthday: 12-24-95

Collector Trivia

During fall 1997, Ziggy's fabric had a subtle change. The new fabric's stripes are now spaced farther apart (about 3/4 inch).

Median U.S. Prices By Hang Tag

1st	2nd	3rd	4th	5th
N/A	N/A	$90-110	$15-20	$15-20

Available Tush Tag Generations: 1st, 2nd, 3rd, 4th, 5th, 6th

Median U.S. Prices Over Time

$50
$40
$30
$20
$10
$0

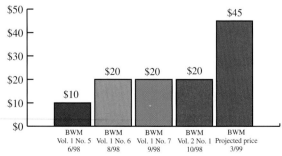

BWM Vol. 1 No. 5 6/98	BWM Vol. 1 No. 6 8/98	BWM Vol. 1 No. 7 9/98	BWM Vol. 2 No. 1 10/98	BWM Projected price 3/99
$10	$20	$20	$20	$45

Median U.K. Price: £12.15 **Median Canadian Price: $30.07**

Zip the all black cat

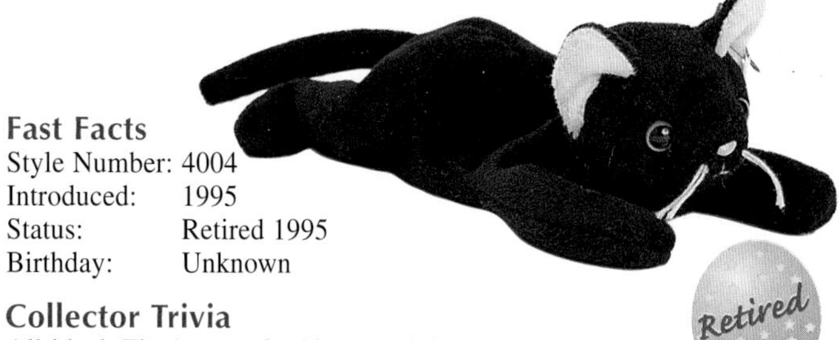

Fast Facts

Style Number: 4004
Introduced: 1995
Status: Retired 1995
Birthday: Unknown

Collector Trivia

All-black Zip (except for his cute pink ears and pink whiskers) is the most valuable of the three Zip variations.

Median U.S. Prices By Hang Tag

1st	2nd	3rd	4th	5th
N/A	N/A	$1700-1850	N/A	N/A

Available Tush Tag Generations: 1st

Median U.S. Prices Over Time

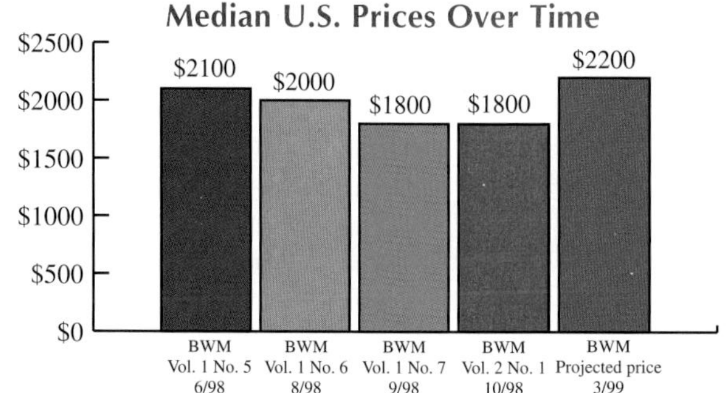

Median U.K. Price: £1094.22 **Median Canadian Price: $2706.30**

Zip the black cat with white paws

Fast Facts

Style Number: 4004
Introduced: 1996
Status: Retired 5-1-98
Birthday: 3-28-94

Collector Trivia

Zip with white paws is one of the most valuable of the May 1, 1998, retireds.

Median U.S. Prices By Hang Tag

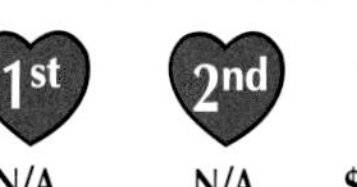

1st	2nd	3rd	4th	5th
N/A	N/A	$400-500	$30-50	$30-50

Available Tush Tag Generations: 2nd, 3rd, 4th, 5th, 6th

Median U.S. Prices Over Time

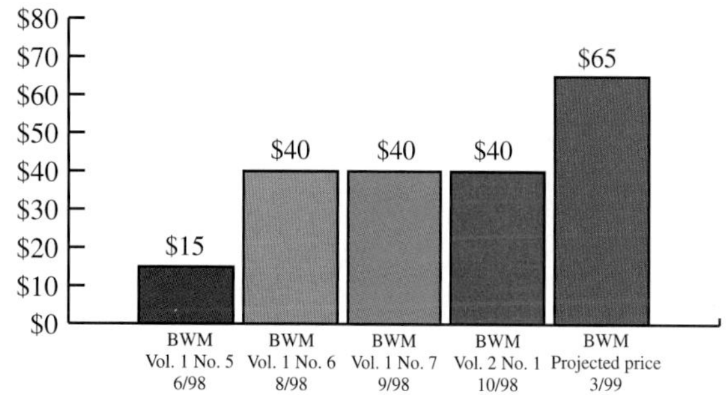

Median U.K. Price: £24.31 **Median Canadian Price: $60.14**

Zip the black kitten with the white belly

Fast Facts

Style Number: 4004
Introduced: 1995
Status: Retired 1995
Birthday: Unknown

Collector Trivia

This first version of Zip resembles a young, playful kitten.

Median U.S. Prices By Hang Tag

1st	2nd	3rd	4th	5th
N/A	$650-750	$450-550	N/A	N/A

Available Tush Tag Generations: 1st

Median U.S. Prices Over Time

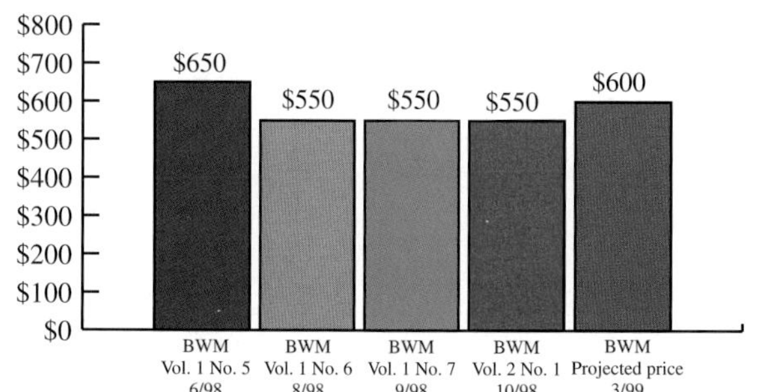

Median U.K. Price: £334.34 **Median Canadian Price: $826.92**

Beanie Babies Quick Reference Guide

NAME	1st	2nd	3rd	4th	5th
Ally the alligator	$300-325	$225-250	$100-120	$40-60	N/A
Ants the anteater	N/A	N/A	N/A	N/A	$15-20
Baldy the eagle	N/A	N/A	N/A	$15-20	$15-20
Batty the bat	N/A	N/A	N/A	$10-15	$10-15
Bernie the St. Bernard	N/A	N/A	N/A	$8-10	$8-10
Bessie the brown & white cow	N/A	N/A	$120-145	$45-65	N/A
Blackie the black bear	$300-325	$200-225	$70-95	$8-10	$8-10
Blizzard the black & white tiger	N/A	N/A	N/A	$15-20	$15-20
Bones the brown dog	$300-325	$200-225	$90-110	$12-20	$10-20
Bongo brown monkey and tail	N/A	N/A	$125-135	$40-50	N/A
Bongo monkey with tan tail	N/A	N/A	$100-150, B&W $75-100, Red Tush	$8-10	$8-10
Britannia the British bear	N/A	N/A	N/A	N/A	$425-550
Bronty the brontosaurus	N/A	N/A	$1000-1200	N/A	N/A
Brownie the brown bear	$3600-4200	N/A	N/A	N/A	N/A
Bruno the terrier	N/A	N/A	N/A	N/A	$8-10
Bubbles the black & yellow fish	N/A	N/A	$175-205	$150-175	N/A
Bucky the beaver	N/A	N/A	$100-125	$30-45	N/A
Bumble the bee	N/A	N/A	$535-560	$600-625	N/A
Caw the crow	N/A	N/A	$600-650	N/A	N/A
Chilly the polar bear	$2200-2400	$2100-2300	$1800-2000	N/A	N/A
Chip the calico cat	N/A	N/A	N/A	$8-10	$8-10
Chocolate the moose	$700-900	$425-500	$165-185	$10-15	$10-15
Chops the lamb	N/A	N/A	$235-260	$150-195	N/A
Claude the tie-dyed crab	N/A	N/A	N/A	$10-15	$10-15
Clubby the bear	N/A	N/A	N/A	N/A	$10
Congo the gorilla	N/A	N/A	N/A	$8-10	$8-10
Coral the tie-dyed fish	N/A	N/A	$250-285	$175-225	N/A
Crunch the shark	N/A	N/A	N/A	$8-10	$8-10
Cubbie the brown bear	$700-750	$450-495	$160-180	$25-40	$25-40
Curly the brown napped teddy	N/A	N/A	N/A	$15-35	$15-35
Daisy the black & white cow	$300-325	$200-225	$75-100	$10-15	$10-15
Derby horse with forehead star	N/A	N/A	N/A	N/A	$10-15
Derby horse w/out forehead star	N/A	N/A	$365-450	$20-35	$20-35
Derby the fine mane horse	N/A	N/A	$3200-3900	N/A	N/A
Digger the orange crab	$800-1100	$800-900	$700-800	N/A	N/A
Digger the red crab	N/A	N/A	$225-250	$110-150	N/A
Doby the doberman	N/A	N/A	N/A	$8-10	$8-10
Doodle the rooster	N/A	N/A	N/A	$40-60	N/A
Dotty the Dalmatian w/black ears	N/A	N/A	N/A	$8-10	$8-10
Early the robin	N/A	N/A	N/A	N/A	$15-25
Ears the brown rabbit	N/A	N/A	$100-125	$15-25	$15-25
Echo the dolphin	N/A	N/A	N/A	$15-25	$15-25
Erin the emerald green bear	N/A	N/A	N/A	N/A	$45-70
Fetch the golden retriever	N/A	N/A	N/A	N/A	$15-20
Flash the dolphin	$800-950	$550-650	$225-250	$110-150	N/A
Fleece the napped lamb	N/A	N/A	N/A	$8-10	$8-10
Flip the white cat	N/A	N/A	$100-125	$25-40	N/A
Floppity the lavender bunny	N/A	N/A	N/A	$15-25	$15-25
Flutter the butterfly	N/A	N/A	$1000-1200	N/A	N/A
Fortune the panda	N/A	N/A	N/A	N/A	$40-65
Freckles the leopard	N/A	N/A	N/A	$8-10	$8-10
Garcia the tie-dyed teddy	N/A	N/A	$250-300	$170-200	N/A
Gigi the poodle	N/A	N/A	N/A	N/A	$15-20
Glory the bear	N/A	N/A	N/A	N/A	$100-150
Gobbles the turkey	N/A	N/A	N/A	$10-20	$10-20
Goldie the goldfish	$500-700	$250-350	$125-150	$35-45	$35-45
Gracie the swan	N/A	N/A	N/A	$12-18	$12-18
Grunt the red razorback	N/A	N/A	$235-260	$160-195	N/A
Happy the gray hippo	$1100-1200	$850-950	$700-800	N/A	N/A
Happy the lavender hippo	N/A	N/A	$250-325	$15-25	$15-25
Hippity the mint green bunny	N/A	N/A	N/A	$15-25	$15-25
Hissy the snake	N/A	N/A	N/A	N/A	$10-15
Hoot the owl	N/A	N/A	$100-125	$30-50	N/A

Beanie Babies Quick Reference Guide

NAME	1st	2nd	3rd	4th	5th
Hoppity the pink bunny	N/A	N/A	N/A	$15-25	$15-25
Humphrey the camel	$2220-2450	$2000-2200	$1700-1900	N/A	N/A
Iggy the iguana	N/A	N/A	N/A	N/A	$8-12
Inch the inchworm felt antennas	N/A	N/A	$160-180	$160-180	N/A
Inch the inchworm yarn antennas	N/A	N/A	N/A	$15-20	$15-20
Inky the pink octopus	N/A	N/A	$250-325	$23-40	$23-40
Inky tan octopus w/out mouth	$1100-1400	$850-975	N/A	N/A	N/A
Inky tan octopus with mouth	N/A	$750-800	$620-690	N/A	N/A
Jabber the parrot	N/A	N/A	N/A	N/A	$20-25
Jake the mallard duck	N/A	N/A	N/A	N/A	$15-25
Jolly the walrus	N/A	N/A	N/A	$15-20	$15-20
Kiwi the toucan	N/A	N/A	$200-225	$160-185	N/A
Kuku the cockatoo	N/A	N/A	N/A	N/A	$15-25
Lefty the American flag donkey	N/A	N/A	N/A	$250-300	N/A
Legs the frog	$850-900	$600-650	$125-150	$20-35	N/A
Libearty the American flag teddy	N/A	N/A	N/A	$285-350	N/A
Lizzy the blue lizard	N/A	N/A	$225-275	$25-40	$15-25
Lizzy the tie-dyed lizard	N/A	N/A	$875-1000	N/A	N/A
Lucky the ladybug w/11 spots	N/A	N/A	N/A	$15-20	$15-20
Lucky the ladybug w/21 spots	N/A	N/A	N/A	$550-625	N/A
Lucky the ladybug w/7 spots	$750-850	$450-550	$175-200	N/A	N/A
Magic dragon w/light pink stitch	N/A	N/A	$125-175	$40-60	N/A
Manny the manatee	N/A	N/A	$180-225	$145-175	N/A
Maple the Canadian teddy	N/A	N/A	N/A	$225-265	$185-230
Mel the koala bear	N/A	N/A	N/A	$8-10	$8-10
Mystic unicorn w/iridescent horn	N/A	N/A	N/A	$10-20	$10-20
Mystic unicorn w/tan horn	N/A	N/A	$125-140	$30-50	N/A
Mystic the fine mane unicorn	$600-800	$325-450	$225-300	N/A	N/A
Nana the brown monkey	N/A	N/A	$3600-4100	N/A	N/A
Nanook the husky	N/A	N/A	N/A	$10-15	$10-15
Nip the all gold cat	N/A	N/A	$850-1000	N/A	N/A
Nip the gold cat w/white paws	N/A	N/A	$300-350	$20-35	$20-35
Nip the gold kitten w/white belly	N/A	$550-625	$475-575	N/A	N/A
Nuts the squirrel	N/A	N/A	N/A	$8-10	$8-10
Patti mag/mar/rasp/platypus	$900-1000	$800-950	$650-800	N/A	N/A
Patti the purple platypus	$800-1000	$700-850	$135-185	$15-20	$15-20
Peace the tie-dyed teddy	N/A	N/A	N/A	$20-35	$20-35
Peanut the light blue elephant	N/A	N/A	$450-700	$12-23	$12-23
Peanut the royal blue elephant	N/A	N/A	$3800-4700	N/A	N/A
Peking the panda	$2200-2450	$2100-2300	$1750-2200	N/A	N/A
Pinchers the lobster	$1000-1200	$700-750	$100-125	$12-20	$12-20
Pinky the flamingo	N/A	N/A	$145-195	$8-10	$8-10
Pouch the kangaroo	N/A	N/A	N/A	$8-10	$8-10
Pounce the brown cat	N/A	N/A	N/A	N/A	$8-12
Prance the gray cat	N/A	N/A	N/A	N/A	$8-12
Princess Diana of Wales bear	N/A	N/A	N/A	N/A	$125-150 PVC/ $45-80 PE
Puffer the puffin	N/A	N/A	N/A	N/A	$10-15
Pugsly the pug dog	N/A	N/A	N/A	$8-10	$8-10
Punchers the lobster	$3600-3900	N/A	N/A	N/A	N/A
Quackers the duck with wings	N/A	$650-850	$125-165	$12-18	$12-18
Quackers the wingless duck	$2000-2300	$1700-1900	N/A	N/A	N/A
Radar the bat	N/A	N/A	$225-260	$150-190	N/A
Rainbow the chameleon	N/A	N/A	N/A	N/A	$10-15
Rex the tyrannosaurus	N/A	N/A	$700-850	N/A	N/A
Righty the American flag elephant	N/A	N/A	N/A	$250-300	N/A
Ringo the raccoon	N/A	N/A	$75-85	$8-10	$8-10
Roary the lion	N/A	N/A	N/A	$8-10	$8-10
Rocket the bluejay	N/A	N/A	N/A	N/A	$15-25
Rover the red dog	N/A	N/A	N/A	$12-18	$12-18
Scoop the pelican	N/A	N/A	N/A	$8-10	$8-10
Scottie the Scottish terrier	N/A	N/A	N/A	$25-30	$25-30
Seamore the seal	$800-850	$400-450	$175-225	$140-185	N/A

Beanie Babies Quick Reference Guide

NAME	1st	2nd	3rd	4th	5th
Seaweed the otter	N/A	N/A	$70-90	$10-15	$10-15
Slither the snake	$2200-2400	$1800-2100	$1700-1950	N/A	N/A
Sly the brown bellied fox	N/A	N/A	N/A	$175-195	N/A
Sly the white bellied fox	N/A	N/A	N/A	$8-10	$8-10
Smoochy the frog	N/A	N/A	N/A	N/A	$10-15
Snip the Siamese cat	N/A	N/A	N/A	$8-10	$8-10
Snort the bull with cream paws	N/A	N/A	N/A	$8-10	$8-10
Snowball the snowman	N/A	N/A	N/A	$30-50	N/A
Sparky the Dalmatian	N/A	N/A	N/A	$135-165	N/A
Speedy the turtle	$700-900	$200-250	$125-150	$30-35	N/A
Spike the rhinoceros	N/A	N/A	N/A	$10-15	$10-15
Spinner the spider	N/A	N/A	N/A	$10-15	$10-15
Splash the orca whale	$850-1000	$600-700	$150-175	$110-150	N/A
Spook the ghost	N/A	N/A	$425-550	N/A	N/A
Spooky the ghost	N/A	N/A	$175-225	$25-45	N/A
Spot the dog with a spot	N/A	$450-550	$150-200	$50-65	N/A
Spot the dog w/out a spot	$2000-2200	$1750-1900	N/A	N/A	N/A
Spunky the cocker spaniel	N/A	N/A	N/A	N/A	$10-15
Squealer the pig	$700-900	$275-375	$85-115	$25-40	$25-40
Steg the stegosaurus	N/A	N/A	$950-1100	N/A	N/A
Sting the stingray	N/A	N/A	$250-300	$175-225	N/A
Stinger the scorpion	N/A	N/A	N/A	N/A	$15-20
Stinky the skunk	N/A	N/A	$80-90	$8-10	$8-10
Stretch the ostrich	N/A	N/A	N/A	N/A	$10-15
Stripes the caramel & black tiger	N/A	N/A	N/A	$10-15	$10-15
Stripes the gold & black tiger	N/A	N/A	$350-500	N/A	N/A
Strut the rooster	N/A	N/A	N/A	$10-15	$10-15
Tabasco the bull with red feet	N/A	N/A	$250-275	$175-225	N/A
Tank the short armadillo w/shell	N/A	N/A	N/A	$70-90	N/A
Tank the long armadillo w/7 lines	N/A	N/A	$150-200	$150-200	N/A
Tank the armadillo with 9 lines	N/A	N/A	N/A	$125-200	N/A
1997 Teddy the holiday bear	N/A	N/A	N/A	$35-50	N/A
Teddy New Face Brown	N/A	$1000-1300	$300-400	$85-110	N/A
Teddy New Face Cranberry	N/A	$2000-2100	$1850-2000	N/A	N/A
Teddy New Face Jade	N/A	$2000-2100	$1850-2000	N/A	N/A
Teddy New Face Magenta	N/A	$2000-2100	$1850-2000	N/A	N/A
Teddy New Face Teal	N/A	$2000-2100	$1850-2000	N/A	N/A
Teddy New Face Violet	N/A	$2000-2100	$1850-2000	N/A	N/A
Teddy Old Face Brown	$2300-2500	$2200-2400	N/A	N/A	N/A
Teddy Old Face Cranberry	$1900-2000	$1700-1850	N/A	N/A	N/A
Teddy Old Face Jade	$1900-2000	$1700-1850	N/A	N/A	N/A
Teddy Old Face Magenta	$1900-2000	$1700-1850	N/A	N/A	N/A
Teddy Old Face Teal	$1900-2000	$1700-1850	N/A	N/A	N/A
Teddy Old Face Violet	$1900-2000	$1700-1850	N/A	N/A	N/A
Tracker the basset hound	N/A	N/A	N/A	N/A	$15-20
Trap the mouse	$1800-2000	$1650-1850	$1200-1350	N/A	N/A
Tuffy the terrier	N/A	N/A	N/A	$8-10	$8-10
Tusk the walrus	N/A	N/A	$250-275	$130-175	N/A
Twigs the giraffe	N/A	N/A	$100-125	$15-20	$15-20
Valentino the bear	N/A	$250-350	$175-200	$18-30	$18-30
Velvet the panther	N/A	N/A	$100-125	$25-40	N/A
Waddle the penguin	N/A	N/A	$100-125	$15-20	$15-20
Waves the whale	N/A	N/A	N/A	$15-25	$15-25
Web the spider	$1900-2100	$1700-2000	$1400-1550	N/A	N/A
Weenie the dachshund	N/A	N/A	$100-125	$20-30	$20-30
Whisper the deer	N/A	N/A	N/A	N/A	$15-20
Wise the owl	N/A	N/A	N/A	N/A	$15-30
Wrinkles the dog	N/A	N/A	N/A	$8-10	$8-10
Ziggy the zebra	N/A	N/A	$90-110	$15-20	$15-20
Zip the all black cat	N/A	N/A	$1700-1850	N/A	N/A
Zip the black cat w/white paws	N/A	N/A	$400-500	$30-50	$30-50
Zip the black kitten w/white belly	N/A	$650-750	$450-550	N/A	N/A

Quick Guide To Current/Retired Beanies

CURRENT BEANIES

Ants the anteater
Batty the bat
Bernie the St. Bernard
Blackie the black bear
Bongo the monkey with tan tail (Version 3)
Britannia the British bear
Bruno the terrier
Chip the calico cat
Chocolate the moose
Claude the tie-dyed crab
Clubby the bear
Congo the gorilla
Crunch the shark
Curly the brown napped teddy
Daisy the black and white cow
Derby the coarse mane horse with a forehead star
Doby the doberman
Dotty the Dalmatian with black ears
Early the robin
Erin the emerald green bear
Fetch the golden retriever
Fleece the napped lamb
Fortune the panda
Freckles the leopard
Gigi the poodle
Glory the bear
Gobbles the turkey
Hissy the snake
Iggy the iguana
Jabber the parrot
Jake the mallard duck
Kuku the cockatoo
Maple the Canadian teddy
Mel the koala bear
Mystic the coarse mane unicorn with iridescent horn
Nanook the husky
Nuts the squirrel
Peace the tie-dyed teddy
Pinky the flamingo
Pouch the kangaroo
Pounce the brown cat
Prance the gray cat
Princess: The Diana, Princess of Wales bear
Puffer the puffin
Pugsly the pug dog
Rainbow the chameleon
Ringo the raccoon
Roary the lion
Rocket the bluejay
Scoop the pelican
Seaweed the otter
Sly the white bellied fox
Smoochy the frog
Snip the siamese cat
Snort the bull with cream paws
Spike the rhinocerous
Spinner the spider
Spunky the cocker spaniel
Stinger the scorpion
Stinky the skunk
Stretch the ostrich
Strut the rooster
Tracker the basset hound
Tuffy the terrier
Valentino the bear
Whisper the deer
Wise the owl
Wrinkles the dog

RETIRED BEANIES

Derby the coarse mane horse without a forehead star (NO DATE GIVEN)

1993

Brownie the brown bear
Punchers the lobster

1994

Inky the tan octopus without a mouth
Spot the dog without a spot

1995

Bongo the monkey with the tan tail (version #1)
Chilly the polar bear
Derby the fine mane horse
Digger the orange crab
Happy the gray hippo
Humphrey the camel
Inky the tan octopus with a mouth
Lizzy the tie-dyed lizard
Mystic the fine mane unicorn
Nana the brown monkey
Nip the all gold cat
Nip the gold kitten with the white belly
Patti the deep magenta/maroon/raspberry platypus
Peanut the royal blue elephant
Peking the panda
Quacker(s) the wingless duck
Slither the snake
Spook the ghost
Teddy New Face Cranberry
Teddy New Face Jade
Teddy New Face Magenta
Teddy New Face Teal
Teddy New Face Violet
Teddy Old Face Brown
Teddy Old Face Cranberry
Teddy Old Face Jade
Teddy Old Face Magenta
Teddy Old Face Teal
Teddy Old Face Violet
Trap the mouse
Web the spider
Zip the all black cat
Zip the black kitten with the white belly

1996

Bongo the brown monkey w/ the brown tail (#1)
Bongo the monkey with the tan tail(version #2)
Bronty the brontosaurus
Bumble the bee
Caw the crow
Flutter the butterfly
Inch the inchworm with felt antennas
Lucky the ladybug with 7 glued on spots
Rex the tyrannosaurus
Sly the brown bellied fox
Steg the stegosaurus
Stripes the gold and black tiger
Tank the long armadillo with 7 lines
Tank the long armadillo with 9 lines

1997 (no specified date)

Bongo the brown monkey w/ brown tail (ver. 2)
Doodle the rooster
Lucky the ladybug with 21 spots
Mystic the coarse mane unicorn with tan horn

1-1-97

Chops the lamb
Coral the tie-dyed fish
Kiwi the toucan
Lefty the American donkey
Libearty the American flag teddy
Righty the American flag elephant
Sting the stingray
Tabasco the bull with red feet
Tusk the walrus

5-11-97

Bubbles the black and yellow fish
Digger the red crab
Flash the dolphin
Garcia the tie-dyed teddy
Grunt the red razorback
Manny the manatee
Radar the bat
Sparky the dalmatian
Splash the orca whale

10-1-97

Ally the alligator
Bessie the brown and white cow
Flip the white cat
Hoot the owl
Legs the frog
Seamore the seal
Speedy the turtle
Spot the dog with a spot
Tank the short armadillo with shell
Teddy New Face Brown
Velvet the panther

12-31-97

Bucky the beaver
Cubbie the brown bear
Goldie the goldfish
Lizzy the blue lizard
Magic the dragon with light pink stitching
Nip the all gold cat with white paws
Snowball the snowman
Spooky the ghost
1997 Teddy the holiday bear

1998
5-1-98

Baldy the eagle
Blizzard the black and white tiger
Bones the brown dog
Ears the brown rabbit
Echo the dolphin
Floppity the lavender bunny
Gracie the swan
Happy the lavender hippo
Hippity the mint green bunny
Hoppity the pink bunny
Inch the inchworm with yarn antennas
Inky the pink octopus
Jolly the walrus
Lucky the ladybug with 11 spots
Patti the purple platypus
Peanut the light blue elephant
Pinchers the lobster
Quackers the duck with wings
Rover the red dog
Scottie the Scottish terrier
Squealer the pig
Stripes the caramel tiger
Twigs the giraffe
Waddle the penguin
Waves the whale
Weenie the dachshund
Ziggy the zebra
Zip the black cat with white paws

KNOW YOUR HANG TAGS

HANG TAG – FIRST GENERATION

The first generation heart hang tag, or swing tag, is very simple. Introduced in early 1994, it is a single heart tag (it does not open) with a small "ty" on the front. The type on the reverse side includes "The Beanie Babies Collection," the name of the Beanie Baby and its style number. Also, note that some were produced in Korea and others in China. For those distributed in Europe, "CE" was added to the bottom of the tag. First generation swing tags came on only those Beanies with a first generation tush tag dated 1993.

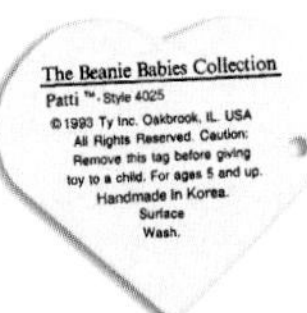

SWING TAG – SECOND GENERATION

The second generation swing tag (introduced in spring 1994) has the same small "ty" on the front of the heart, but instead of being a single two-sided heart, it opens like a locket and has four sides. Three different tags are available in this generation. The inside left of the tag designates where it was meant to be distributed (North America, United Kingdom, or Germany). The inside right of the tag gives the Beanie's name followed by the ™ symbol and its style number. The back of the heart has a large bar code and the sentence "Retain this tag for reference." Second generation swing tags came on Beanies with first generation tush tags dated 1993 or 1995.

SWING TAG – THIRD GENERATION

The third generation swing tag (introduced in spring 1995) has the "Ty" on the front printed in a balloon-style font enlarged to almost the full size of the heart. On the inside left, the type reads: "The Beanie Babies™ Collection" followed by a list containing "Ty Inc. Oakbrook IL, U.S.A." "Ty UK Ltd. Waterlooville, Hants," "Ty Deutschland 90008 Nurnberg," and the phrase "Handmade in Korea" or "Handmade in China." On the inside right of the tag, you have the Beanie's name followed by a ™ and its style number. Below that is, "to____ from____ with love." On the back side of the heart tag is a bar code with a CE printed to the left of the bar. Above the bar is a warning to remove the tag before a child plays with the toy, and below the bar is a line suggesting you keep the tag for reference, followed by "Surface Wash." Third generation swing tags came on Beanies with first generation tush tags dated 1995 and second generation tush tags dated 1993 and 1995.

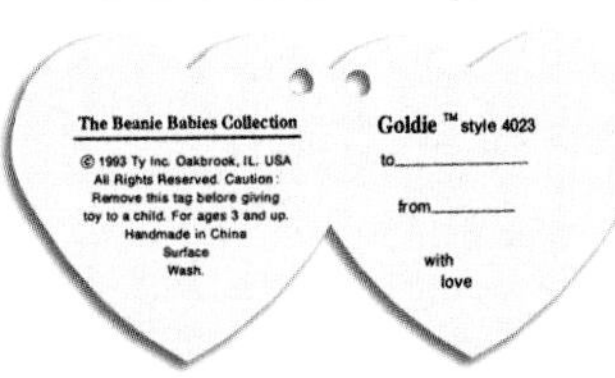

SWING TAG – FOURTH GENERATION

The fourth generation swing tag (introduced in spring 1996) features many important changes. The "Ty" on the front of the heart is moved so the "y" is a bit lower than the "t," and a yellow star is added to the front, upper right, with the words "Original Beanie Baby." The inside right of the tag has the Beanie's name and style number with a birthdate underneath it, followed by a poem. It also includes an invitation to visit Ty Inc.'s Web page at http://www.ty.com. The heart's back side has new type that says, "For ages 3 and up," followed by "Surface Wash." Fourth generation swing tags came on Beanies with third generation tush tags dated 1993, 1995 and 1996, as well as the fourth generation tush tag in red and white with the star added to the upper left of the Ty heart.

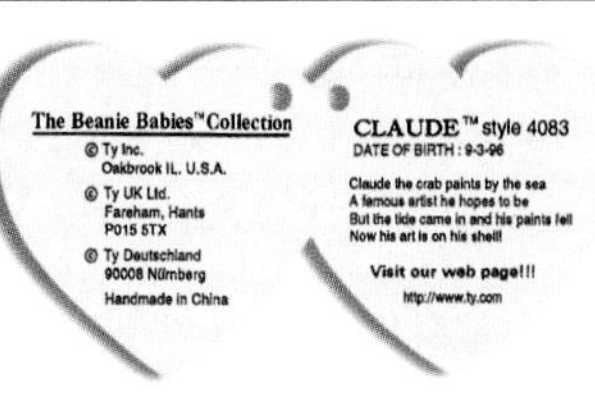

SWING TAG – FIFTH GENERATION

The fifth generation swing tag (introduced in early 1998) sports a new typeface. The yellow heart on the front features a different font, as does the type on the inside of the heart. On the inside left of the tag, "The Beanie Babies Collection" was simply marked as ®. The ™ was deleted. Another change involves the Ty locations. Instead of it mentioning Ty Inc. Oakbrook, UK and Deutschland, the type refers to Ty Inc. Oakbrook, Ty Europe Ltd. and Ty Canada. On the inside right of the tag, the name of the Beanie Baby is listed with a ™ but no style number. "Date of Birth" is now spelled out instead of cited numerically, and "visit our Web page" is deleted, with only "www.ty.com" shown. The back of the tag is unchanged except for the font change. Fifth generation swing tags come on Beanies with fifth and sixth generation tush tags.

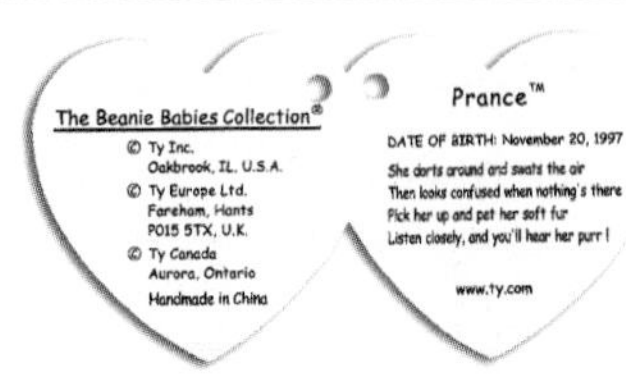

SWING TAG – POSSIBLE SIXTH GENERATION

Rumors began circulating in mid-June 1998 that a sixth generation swing tag had surfaced, and this could be the tag collectors have referred to. This one has the same Comic Sans font as the fifth generation, but the printing appears larger and bolder. The poem seems to be the only thing that stayed the same size. The fifth generation tag's printing is light and smaller by comparison. So, is this a sixth generation tag? It may just be "improved printing" on a fifth generation tag.

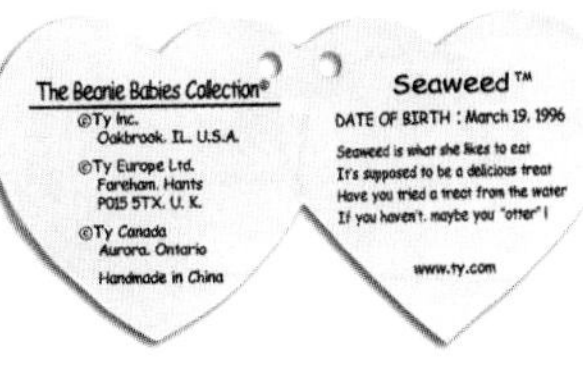

KNOW YOUR TUSH TAGS

"Tush tags" is the term used to describe the sewn-in cloth tags on the bottoms of Ty Beanie Babies. Much like the heart hang tags, tush tags are an important indicator of when a Beanie Baby was produced.

TUSH TAG – FIRST GENERATION

The original Ty Beanie Babies came with a black and white tush tag. Some of these black and white tush tags will have a copyright date of 1993, while others will show 1995. All Beanies with a first or second generation swing tag will have a black and white tush tag. There are no exceptions to this rule. Also, the black and white tush tags may or may not have had a CE on them, and some had "for ages 3 and up" written on them, while others did not.

TUSH TAG – SECOND GENERATION

This tush tag has a large red heart with "ty" inside it and a ® mark to the lower right of the heart. There are no individual Beanie names on the first or second generation tush tags. A copyright date of 1993, 1995, or 1996 will be found on second generation tags.

TUSH TAG – THIRD GENERATION

The third generation tush tag features substantial differences from the prior two generations. "The Beanie Babies Collection" is added to the top of the tush tag with a ™ at the end of the phrase. The Ty heart is considerably smaller, but it retains the ® on its lower right. Also, the name of the individual Beanie is on the third generation tush tag. Copyright dates on this tush tag range from 1993 to 1996.

TUSH TAG – FOURTH GENERATION

When Ty decided to change the Beanie Babies tush tag again, the company must have had an excess of the third generation tags. Initially, Ty attached a transparent sticker over the "ty" heart, which added a small star to the upper left of the heart on the tush tag. This occurred before a new tush tag was printed. When the fourth generation tags were finally printed, the star to the upper left of the red "ty" heart as was the only change.

TUSH TAG – FIFTH GENERATION

The fifth generation tush tag (introduced in October 1997) has many changes from previous generations. "The Beanie Babies Collection" at the top of the tag has ® after Beanie Babies and ™ after the word Collection. The star to the upper left of the ty heart and the ® to the lower right remain, but there is an additional ™ after the name of the Beanie Baby. These tags can have copyright dates from 1993 through 1997.

TUSH TAG – SIXTH GENERATION

The sixth generation tush tag (introduced in January 1998) has the words "The Beanie Babies Collection" with ® after the word Collection (as opposed to the ® after Beanie Babies and ™ after Collection). The "ty" heart remains the same, with a star on the left and ® on the right, and the Beanie's name kept its ™ symbol.

CANADIAN TUSH TAG

Beanie Babies destined for distribution in Canada will sport a double tush tag. The first is one of the aforementioned tags, and the second is one that conforms to Canadian toy import regulations. All information on this tag is printed in English on one side and in French on the other.

EMBROIDERED TUSH TAG

There is also a very rare embroidered tush tag on the market. It is found on very few Beanies of limited styles. All Beanies with this tag have a second generation swing tag and the standard Canadian tush tag. Note also that this tag has a date of 1994, and no Beanie Babies tush tags have a 1994 copyright date. These embroidered tags are thought to have been attached in error, as they are usually used for the larger Ty Plush animals. To date only these styles have been found with these exclusive tush tags: Chocolate, Quacker (no "s"), Spot, Goldie, Cubbie and Pinchers.

MINOR CHANGES WORTH NOTING

Other changes on Beanie Babies tush tags include the placement and font of the CE. Also, some Beanies have "PVC" pellets, while others have "PE" pellets. Finally, the newer Beanie Babies are showing up with a Chinese stamp on the inside of the tush tag.

FIRST GENERATION

© 1993 TY INC., OAKBROOK IL. U.S.A. ALL RIGHTS RESERVED HANDMADE IN CHINA SURFACE WASHABLE	ALL NEW MATERIAL POLYESTER FIBER & P.V.C. PELLETS PA. REG #1965 FOR AGES 3AND UP

SECOND GENERATION

ty
HAND MADE IN CHINA
© 1995 TY INC.,
OAKBROOK IL. U. S. A.
SURFACE WASHABLE
ALL NEW MATERIAL
POLYESTER FIBER &
P. V. C. PELLETS
REG. NO PA-1965(KR)

THIRD GENERATION

FOURTH GENERATION

FIFTH GENERATION

SIXTH GENERATION

EMBROIDERED TUSH TAG

TY, INC. ©1994
OAKBROOK, IL.
REG.NO.PA-1965(KR)
ALL NEW MATERIAL
CONTENTS: POLYESTER
HAND MADE IN CHINA
FOR ALL AGES

CANADIAN TUSH TAG

Not to be removed until delivered to the consumer	Ne pas enlever avant livraison au consommateur
This label is affixed in compliance with the Upholstered and Stuffed Articles Act	Cette étiquette est apposée conformément à loi sur les articles rembourrés
This article contains NEW MATERIAL ONLY	Cet article contient MATÉRIAU NEUF SEULEMENT
Made by Ont. Reg. No. 20B6484	Fabriqué par No d'enrg. Ont. 20B6484
Content: Plastic Pellets Polyester Fibers Made in China	Contenu: Boulette de plastique Fibres de Polyester Fabriqué en Chine

Other Ty Products Secondary Market Prices
Ty Oddities and Promotional Beanies

MISTAGS / VARIATIONS

ITEM	MARKET PRICE
Echo with Waves tags	$20-25
Libearty with Beanine tush tag	$350-400
Maple with Pride tush tag	$650-800
Snort with Tabasco swing tag	$50-75
Snort with Tabasco name within poem of swing tag	$45-65
Sparky with Dotty tush tag	$100-125
Spinner with Creepy tag	$60-75
Tusk with Tuck swing tag	$125-175
Waves with Echo tags	$20-25

Inky wtih 7 legs

Inky with 9 legs

ODDS 'N ENDS

ITEM	MARKET PRICE
Britannia without flag	$750-1850
Britannia with sewn-on flag instead of embroidered flag	$500-700
Erin without shamrock	$200-250
Inky (pink) with 7 legs	$250-325
Inky (pink) with 9 legs	$275-350
Lefty without flag	$400-450
Lefty with upside down flag	$400-450
Libearty without flag	$425-500
Libearty with upside down flag	$425-500
Magic w/ hot pink stitching on wings	$75-100
Maple without flag	$350-425
Maple with upside down flag	$350-425
Princess without rose	$500-575
Righty without flag	$400-450
Righty with upside down flag	$400-450
Stripes black and gold w/fuzzy belly	$900-1500
Valentino without heart	$300-700

SPORTS PROMOTIONS

The following information on sports Beanie Babies giveaways was compiled exclusively for "Mary Beth's Beanie World Monthly." Copying and/or redistribution of this information in any form is strictly prohibited. *For a closer look at several recent, sports promotions please see pages 88-89.*

BASEBALL PROMOTIONS

HOST TEAM	Opponent	DATE	GIVEAWAY	QUANTITY	PRICE
Chicago Cubs	San Francisco Giants	May 18, 1997	Cubbie the bear	10,000 kids 13 & under	$200-225
Chicago Cubs	New York Mets	September 6, 1997	Cubbie the bear	10,000 kids 13 & under	$175-200
Chicago Cubs	Convention	January 16-18, 1998	Cubbie the bear	100 (raffle)	$425-500
	Web Site: http://www.cubs.com/index2.htm				
New York Yankees	Toronto Blue Jays	March 10th, 1998	Bones the dog	5,000 kids 14 & under	$225-275
(Spring Training Game)	*Web Site: http://www.yankees.com/web/home/main.html*				
Oakland A's	Anaheim Angels	March 15, 1998	Ears the rabbit	500 kids 14 & under	$200-250
(Spring Training Game)	*Web Site: http://www.oaklandathletics.com*				
Chicago Cubs	St. Louis Cardinals	May 3, 1998	Daisy the cow	15,000 kids 12 & under	$400-450
	Web Site: http://www.cubs.com/index2.htm				
New York Yankees	Minnesota Twins	May 17, 1998	Valentino the bear	20,000 kids 14 & under	$250-275
	Web Site: http://www.yankees.com/web/home/main.html				
St. Louis Cardinals	San Francisco Giants	May 22, 1998	Stretch the ostrich	20,000 kids 15 & under	$150-200
	Web Page: http://www.stlcardinals.com/				
Detroit Tigers	Chicago White Sox	May 31, 1998	Stripes the tiger	10,000 kids 12 & under	$150-200
	Web Site: http://www.detroittigers.com/				
Kansas City Royals	Oakland Athletics	May 31, 1998	Roary the lion	13,000 kids 14 & under	$150-200
	Web Site: http://www.kcroyals.com				
Milwaukee Brewers	Florida Marlins	May, 31, 1998	Batty the bat	12,000 kids 12 & under	$150-200
	Web Page: http://www.milwaukeebrewers.com				
Arizona Diamondbacks	St. Louis Cardinals	June 14, 1998	Hissy the snake	6,500 kids 15 & under	$100-150
	Web Site: http://azdiamondbacks.com/				
1998 Major League Baseball All-Star Game		July 7, 1998	Glory the bear	All fans (about 51,000)	$250-425
	Web Site: http://www.majorleaguebaseball.com				
Chicago White Sox	Kansas City Royals	July 12, 1998	Blizzard the tiger	25,000 kids 14 & under	$150-175
	Web Site: http://www.chisox.com/				
New York Mets	Montreal Expos	July 12, 1998	Batty the bat	All fans 14 & under (about 30,000)	$150-200
	Web Page: http://www.mets.com/homepage/middle.asp				

BASEBALL PROMOTIONS continued

HOST TEAM	OPPONENT	DATE	GIVEAWAY	QUANTITY	PRICE
Tampa Bay Devil Rays	Oakland A's *Web Page: http://www.devilray.com/home.html*	July 26, 1998	Weenie the dachshund	15,000 kids 14 & under	$150-200
Minnesota Twins	Toronto Blue Jays *Web Page: http://www.wcco.com/sports/twins*	July 31, 1998	Lucky the ladybug	10,000 kids 14 & under	$150-200
Oakland A's	Cleveland Indians *Web Page: http://www.oaklandathletics.com/home.htm*	August 1, 1998	Peanut the elephant	15,000 kids 14 & under	$150-200
Texas Rangers	Toronto Blue Jays *Web Page: http://www.texasrangers.com*	August 4, 1998	Pugsly the pug dog	10,000 kids	$175-200
Detroit Tigers	Seattle Mariners *Web Site: http://www.detroittigers.com/*	August 8, 1998	Stripes the tiger	10,000 kids 14 & under	TBA
New York Yankees	Kansas City Royals *Web Site: http://www.yankees.com/web/home/main.html*	August 9, 1998	Stretch the ostrich	All fans 14 & under	TBA
St. Louis Cardinals	Pittsburgh Pirates *Web Page: http://www.stlcardinals.com/*	August 14,1998	Smoochy the frog	20,000 15 & under	TBA
Cincinnati Reds	Montreal Expos *Web Site: http://www.cincinnatireds.com/home.html*	August 16, 1998	Rover the dog	15,000 kids 14 & under	TBA
Houston Astros	Chicago Cubs *Web Site: http://www.astros.com/welcome.htm*	August 16, 1998	Derby the horse	15,000 kids 14 & under	TBA
Atlanta Braves	San Francisco Giants *Web Site: http://www.atlantabraves.com/*	August 19, 1998	Chip the cat	12,000 kids 14 & under	TBA
New York Mets	Arizona Diamondbacks *Web Page: http://www.mets.com/homepage/middle.asp*	August 22, 1998	Curly the bear	All fans 14 & under (about 30,000)	TBA
Tampa Bay Devil Rays	Kansas City Royals *Web Page: http://www.devilray.com/home.html*	August 23, 1998	Pinky the flamingo	10,000 kids 14 & under	TBA
San Francisco Giants	Milwaukee Brewers *Web Site: http://www.sfgiants.com*	August 30, 1998	Tuffy the terrier	10,000 kids 10 & under	TBA
Oakland A's	Tampa Bay Devil Rays *Web Page: http://www.oaklandathletics.com/home.htm*	September 6, 1998	Peanut the elephant	15,000 kids 14 & under	TBA
Chicago Cubs	Milwaukee Brewers *Web Site: http://www.cubs.com/index2.htm*	September 13, 1998	Gracie the swan	10,000 kids 13 & under	TBA

NBA PROMOTIONS

HOST TEAM	OPPONENT	DATE	GIVEAWAY	QUANTITY	PRICE
Philadelphia 76ers	Golden State Warriors *Web Site: http://www.nba.com/sixers/*	January, 17,1998	Baldy the eagle	5,000 kids 12 and under	$200-250
Indiana Pacers	Minnesota T'Wolves *Web Site: http://www.nba.com/pacers/*	April 2, 1998	Strut the rooster	5,000 kids	$200-250
Cleveland Cavs	Los Angeles Clippers *Web Site: http://www.nba.com/cavs/*	April 5, 1998	Bongo the monkey	5,000 kids 14 & under	$200-250
Denver Nuggets	Portland Trail Blazers *Web Site: http://www.nba.com/nuggets/*	April 17, 1998	Chocolate the moose	5,000 kids 12 & under	$200-250
San Antonio Spurs	Phoenix Suns *Web Site: http://www.nba.com/spurs/*	April 27, 1998	Curly the bear	2,500 kids 14 & under	$200-250
San Antonio Spurs	Phoenix Suns *Web Site: http://www.nba.com/spurs/*	April 29, 1998	Pinky the flamingo	2,500 kids 14 & under	$200-250

Baldy

WNBA PROMOTIONS

HOST TEAM	OPPONENT	DATE	GIVEAWAY	QUANTITY	PRICE
Charlotte Sting	Houston Comets *Web site: http://www.wnba.com/sting/index.html*	June 15, 1998	Curly the bear	5,000 kids 12 & under	$200-250
Washington Mystics	Detroit Shock *Web site: http://www.wnba.com/shock/index.html*	July 11, 1998	Mystic the unicorn	5,000 kids 17 & under	$200-250
Charlotte Sting	Washington Mystics *Web site: http://www.wnba.com/sting/index.html*	July 17, 1998	Bongo the Monkey	3,000 kids 14 & under	$200-250
Detroit Shock	Los Angeles Sparks *Web site: http://www.wnba.com/sparks/index.html*	July 25, 1998	Mel the koala bear	5,000 kids 15 & under	$100-185
Houston Comets	Phoenix Mercury *Web site: http://www.wnba.com/comets/index.html*	August 6, 1998	Scoop the pelican	5,000 kids 14 & under	$200-250

ARENA FOOTBALL

HOST TEAM	OPPONENT	DATE	GIVEAWAY	QUANTITY	PRICE
Orlando Predators	Nashville Kats	August 7, 1998	Crunch the shark	3,000 kids 14 & under	$150-200

BEANIES ON BROADWAY

ITEM	PROMOTION DATE/YEAR	U.S. MARKET PRICE
"Candide" Fleece and Roary with light blue ribbons	1997	$75-125
"Joseph and the Amazing Color Dreamcoat" Garcia with multi-colored ribbon (no embossing)	1997	$225-250
"Joseph and the Amazing Color Dreamcoat"" Peace with multi-colored ribbon (no embossing)	1997	$75-150
"Joseph and the Amazing Color Dreamcoat" Fleece and Inch with multi-colored ribbon (no embossing)	1997	$45-90
"Phantom of the Opera" Maple with embossed red ribbon	1997	$250-500
"Phantom of the Opera" Velvet with embossed red ribbon	1997	$50-100
"Ragtime" Curly with embossed maroon, cream, or navy ribbons	1997-1998	$150-200/set of 3
"Ragtime" Nanook with embossed maroon, navy and cream ribbons	1998	$175-250/set
"Showboat" Goldie with embossed light blue ribbon	1997	$50-100
"Phantom of the Opera" Bongo with embossed red ribbon	1998	$65-75
"Phantom of the Opera" Peanut with embossed red ribbon	1998	$75-90
"Showboat" Scoop with embossed light blue ribbon	1997	$30-50
"Livent" Nanook with embossed black ribon	1998	$50-90
"Showboat" Valentino with embossed light blue ribbon	1998	$75-100
"Ragtime" NF brown teddy w/ maroon, navy and cream ribbon	1997	$275-400/set
"Fosse" Strut with red embossed ribbon	1998	$125-225
"Livent" Blackie with embossed black ribbon	1998	$50-90
"Livent" Rocket with embossed black ribbon	1998	$50-90

McDONALD'S TEENIE BEANIE BABIES – 1998 & 1997

1998 ITEM	U.S. MARKET PRICE
Doby	$10-15
Bongo	$10-15
Twigs	$5-10
Inch	$5-7
Pinchers	$5-7
Happy	$5-7
Mel	$5-7
Scoop	$5-7
Bones	$5-8
Zip	$5-8
Waddle	$5-8
Peanut	$5-8

1998 ITEM	U.S. MARKET PRICE
Complete set of 12 1998 Teenie Beanies (unopened)	$50-80
Set of 12 1998 Teenie Beanie Pins	$100-150
20' vinyl banner	$150-175
Employee Hat	$15-30
Employee T-Shirt	$20-25
McDonald's 1998 Restaurant Display incl. 12 new Teenie Beanies	$225-300
McDonald's 1998 Teenie Beanie Babies Media Kit	$300-400
Unused 1998 Teenie Beanie Babies Happy Meal bags	$1-1.50
Unused 1998 Teenie Beanie Babies Happy Meal bags with special "A Parents Guide to Safeand Sane Road Trips" attachment	$1.50-2

Inch 1998

1997 ITEM	U.S. MARKET PRICE
Patti	$35-45
Pinky	$35-45
Chops	$25-35
Chocolate	$25-35
Goldie	$20-25
Speedy	$20-25
Seamore	$20-30
Lizz	$15-20
Snort	$10-20
Quacks	$10-20

Chocolate 1997

1997 ITEM	U.S. MARKET PRICE
Complete set of 10 1997 Teenie Beanies (unopened)	$175-225
McDonald's 1997 Restaurant Display featuring boy holding 10 Teenies	$450-550
McDonald's 1997 Teenie Beanie Babies Media Kit	$800-1500
Unused 1997 Teenie Beanie Babies Happy Meal bags	$3-6
Unused 1997 Teenie Beanie Babies Happy Meal bags w/ special "A Parents Guide to Safe and Sane Road Trips" attachment	$6-8

OTHER PROMOTIONS

ITEM	# ISSUED	PROMOTION DATE	U.S. MARKET PRICE
Teddy New Face Violet Employee Christmas Bear	300--400	Dec. 1997	$3500-4200
Alexander Doll Company "Playdate With Spot"	unknown	unknown	$1000-1200
Special Olympics Maple with second tag	20,000	August 1997	$500-600
Toys for Tots Valentino with second tag and card	5,500	March 1998	$165-200
Special Olympics Valentino w/ certificate of authenticity		1998	$150-300

Maple the Special Olympics Teddy

OTHER PROMOTIONS CONTINUED

NAME	CELEBRITY	DATE	MARKET PRICE
Heart to Heart Valentino with second tag signed by:	Michael Bolton	June 26, 1998	$300-500
	Steve Kerr	June 26, 1998	$175-300
	Mike Singletary	June 26, 1998	$250-500
	Richard Marx	June 26, 1998	$150-275

TY PLUSH

Peggy Gallagher and Paula Abrinko have compiled the following information on Ty Plush, Attic Treasures and Pillow Pals exclusively for "Mary Beth's Beanie World Monthly." Copying and/or redistribution of this information in any form is strictly prohibited. Retired Plush are in red type.

FIRST GENERATION

Version 1
A plain red heart with tiny "ty."

Version 2
Has yellow banner with "BEAN BAG"

SECOND GENERATION

Version 1
Ty printed vertical with "to you with love" in script

Version 2
Ty printed vertical without yellow "BEAN BAG" banner

THIRD GENERATION

This third generation hang tag has the addition of bold black outline that defines the "ty."

FOURTH GENERATION

This fourth generation hang tag features the word "ty" in a larger, balloon-style typeface. The tag comes in two sizes that are otherwise identical.

Ace	Dalmatian	12 inch	2027		Current
Al E. Cat	striped w/white paws	23 inch	1111	$800	Retired
Al E. Cat gold	gold cat	20 inch	1111	flat: $100	*
variations:curled and lying flat -- curled is current; flat is retired					
Al E. Cat gray	gray cat	20 inch	1112	flat: $100	*
variations:curled and lying flat- - curled is current; flat is retired					
Angel	White cat	17 inch	1122	------------	Current
Angel	White cat	20 inch	1001	$70	Retired
Angel Himalaya	White cat	20 inch	1001H	$1800	Retired
Angora	White rabbit	14 inch	8004	$120	Retired
Angora	White rabbit	20 inch	8005	$350	Retired
Arctic	Polar bear	12 inch	7419	$50	Retired
variations: black thread in paws (95) and no black thread in paws (97)					
Arnold	Pig		6001W	$1000	Retired
Arnold	Pig	20 inch	6001	$1000	Retired
Arnold	Pig		6002	$600	Retired
Ashes	Black dog	8 inch	2018	$50	Retired
Aurora	Polar bear	13 inch	5103	$40	Retired
Baby Buddy	Brown bear	20 inch	5011	$500	Retired
Baby Butterball	Cat			$500	Retired
Baby Cinnamon	Teddy bear	13 inch	5105	$40	Retired
Baby Clover	Cow	12 inch	8023	$80	Retired
Baby Curly Bunny beige	Rabbit	12 inch	8025	$30	Retired
Baby Curly Bunny white	Rabbit	12 inch	8024	$30	Retired
Baby Curly gold	Teddy bear	12 inch	5018	------------	Current
Baby Curly tan	Teddy bear	12 inch	5017	$30	Retired
Baby George	Gorilla	12 inch	7300	------------	Current
Baby Ginger	Teddy bear	14 inch	5108	------------	Current
Baby Lovie	Lamb	12 inch	8020	$80	Retired
Baby Paws black	Black bear	12 inch	5111	------------	Current
Baby Paws sable	Sable bear	12 inch	5110	------------	Current
Baby Paws white	White bear	12 inch	5112	------------	Current
Baby Petunia	Pig	12 inch	8021	$100	Retired
variations: blue gingham bow (93) or red gingham bow (94)					
Baby PJ sable	Sable teddy bear	12 inch	5016	------------	Current
Baby PJ white	White teddy bear	12 inch	5100	$100	Retired
Baby Pokey	Rabbit	13 inch	8022	$30	Retired
Baby Powder	Cream teddy bear	14 inch	5109	------------	Current
Baby Smokey	Rabbit	13 inch	8023	$30	Retired

Romeo

TY PLUSH continued

NAME	TYPE	SIZE	STYLE NO.	RETIREDS' MARKET PRICE	STATUS
Baby Sparky	Dalmatian	20 inch	2102	$120	Retired
Baby Spice	Teddy bear	13 inch	5104	$30	Retired
**tag variation states name: ByBy Spice*					
Bailey	Teddy bear	19 inch	5502	$40	Retired
Bamboo	Panda	13 inch	5106	$40	Retired
Bamboo	Panda	12 inch	5113	------------	Current
Bandit	Brown racooon	20 inch	8009	$75	Retired
Bandit	Gray raccoon		1119	$550	Retired
Barney	Black lab	20 inch	2003	$800	Retired
Baron	Brown teddy bear with black ribbon	18 inch	5200	$100	Retired
Beanie Bear	Teddy bear	12 inch	5100	$800	Retired
Beanie Bear	Teddy bear	12 inch	5000	$800	Retired
Beanie Bunny white	Rabbit	12 inch	8001	$650	Retired
Beanie Bunny beige	Rabbit	12 inch	8000	$650	Retired
Bengal	Tiger no white on chest	12 inch	7423	$50	Retired
Bengal	Tiger	12 inch	7423	------------	Current
Big Beanie Bear	Dark brown teddy bear		5200	$850	Retired
Big Beanie Bear	Beige teddy bear		5011	$850	Retired
Big Beanie Bear	Dark brown teddy bear		5202	$1000	Retired
Big Beanie Bear	Multi brown colored teddy bear		5200	$850	Retired
Big Beanie Bear	Dark brown teddy bear		5011	$1500	Retired
Big Beanie Bunny white	Rabbit	15 inch	8012	$650	Retired
Big Beanie Bunny beige	Rabbit	15 inch	8011	$650	Retired
Big Beanie Bunny Gold	Rabbit	15 inch	8011	$650	Retired
Big George	Gorilla	27 inch	7302	------------	Current
Big Jake auburn	Monkey		7201	$350	Retired
Big Jake auburn	Monkey	16 inch	7002A	$400	Retired
Big Jake chocolate	Monkey	16 inch	7002C	$400	Retired
Big Jake white	Monkey	16 inch	7002	$350	Retired
Big Pudgy	Teddy bear	28 inch	9006	$200	Retired
Big Shaggy brown	Teddy bear	26 inch	9015	$300	Retired
Biscuit	Beige dog	17 inch	2026	$35	Retired
Blackie	Black teddy bear	13 inch	5003	$600	Retired
Blossom	Rabbit	18 inch	8013	$100	Retired
Bo	Hound dog	20 inch	2009	$400	Retired
Boots	Cat	16 inch	1123	------------	Current
Bows	Rabbit	11 inch	8030	------------	Current
Brownie	Brown bear	13 inch	5100	$60	Retired
Buckshot	Beagle	20 inch	2009	$800	Retired
Buddy	Brown bear	20 inch	5019	$50	Retired
Buddy	Bear		5007	$800	Retired
Buster	Gold dog		2005	$900	Retired
Butterball	Cat			$500	Retired
Buttercup	Rabbit	18 inch	8012	$100	Retired
Buttons	Rabbit	11 inch	8031	------------	Current
Candy	White rabbit		8011	$60	Retired
Cha Cha	Monkey	12 inch	7005	------------	Current
Charlie	Cocker spaniel	20 inch	2001	$800	Retired
Charlie sitting	Cocker spaniel	20 inch	2005	$60	Retired
**variations: laying down*				$35	Retired
Chestnut	Squirrel	12 inch	8022	$150	Retired
Chi-Chi	Cheetah	20 inch	1114	$900	Retired
Chi-Chi	Cheetah	20 inch	7414	$600	Retired
Chips	Brown dog	12 inch	2025	----------	Current
Chuckles	Chimp	15 inch	7303	$75	Retired
Churchill	Bulldog	12 inch	2017	------------	Current

Prayer Pal

Baby Paws

NAME	TYPE	SIZE	STYLE NO.	RETIREDS' MARKET PRICE	STATUS
Cinders	Black dog	20 inch	2008	$40	Retired
Cinnamon	Teddy bear	18 inch	5021	$45	Retired
Cinnamon	Gold teddy bear	13inch	5004	$800	Retired
Clover	Cow	20 inch	8007	$75	Retired
Coal	Cat	16 inch	1119	$40	Retired
Cocoa	**Bear**	**12 inch**	**5107**	------------	**Current**
Corky	**Brown dog**	**12 inch**	**2023**	------------	**Current**
Cotton	Rabbit	14 inch	8003	$45	Retired
Crystal	**Cat**	**16 inch**	**1120**	------------	**Current**
Curly Bunny beige	**Rabbit**	**22 inch**	**8017**	------------	**Current**
Curly Bunny white	**Rabbit**	**22 inch**	**8018**	------------	**Current**
Curly gold	**Teddy bear**	**18 inch**	**5302**	------------	**Current**
Curly tan	Teddy bear	18 inch	5300	$35	Retired
Cuzzy	Teddy bear	13 inch	5203	$100	Retired
Dakota sitting	Husky dog	12 inch	7418	$40	Retired
Dakota floppy legs	**Husky dog**	**12 inch**	**7418**	------------	**Current**
Domino	White and black rabbit	20 inch	8006	$550	Retired
Dopey	Dog	17 inch	2022	$100	Retired
Droopy	Dog	15 inch	2009	$60	Retired
Dumpling brown	Teddy bear	12 inch	5022	$60	Retired
Dumpling white	Teddy bear	12 inch	5023	$60	Retired
Edmond	Gold teddy bear	21 inch		$325	Retired
**numberless 92 collectors bear*					
Eleanor	Teddy bear	19 inch	5500	$45	Retired
Elmer	Elephant	20 inch	1116	$900	Retired
Elmer long trunk	Elephant	20 inch	7416	$100	Retired
**variations: short trunk*				$280	Retired
Elvis	**Dog**	**20 inch**	**2010**	------------	**Current**
Faith	**White teddy bear**	**10 inch**	**5600**	------------	**Current**
Fido	White dog	8 inch	2019	$60	Retired
Fluffy	White cat	15 inch	1002	$50	Retired
Forest	**Brown bear**	**12 inch**	**5114**	------------	**Current**
Freddie	**Frog**	**16 inch**	**8010**	------------	**Current**
Freddie	Frog	10 inch	1117	$700	Retired
Frisky	Black cat	17 inch	1007	$100	Retired
Fritz	Dalmatian	20 inch	2002	$500	Retired
Fuzzy	Teddy bear	13 inch	5204	$100	Retired
George	**Gorilla**	**20 inch**	**7301**	------------	**Current**
Ginger	Cat	20 inch	1007	$400	Retired
Ginger	Teddy bear	18 inch	5306	$40	Retired
Ginger Himalaya	Cat	20 inch	1007H	$1800	Retired
Harris	Lion	20 inch	1115	$600	Retired
Harris	Lion	20 inch	7415	$75	Retired
Honey	**Dog**	**20 inch**	**2001**	------------	**Current**
Honey	Teddy bear	14 inch	5004	$225	Retired
Hooters	Owl	9 inch	8016	$375	Retired
Hope	**Gold teddy bear**	**10 inch**	**5601**	------------	**Current**
Jake	Brown monkey		7001B	$600	Retired
Jake auburn	Orangutan	24 inch	7101	$300	Retired
Jake auburn	Monkey	12 inch	7001A	$600	Retired
Jake chocolate	Monkey	12 inch	7001C	$600	Retired
Jake white	Monkey	12inch	7001	$600	Retired
Jake white	Orangutang	24 inch	7100	$300	Retired
Jersey	Cow beige and white	20 inch	8026	$40	Retired
Jersey	**Cow black and white**	**20 inch**	**8026**	------------	**Current**
Josh	Orangutan	24 inch	7101	$100	Retired
Jumbo George	**Gorilla**	**48 inch**	**9008**	------------	**Current**

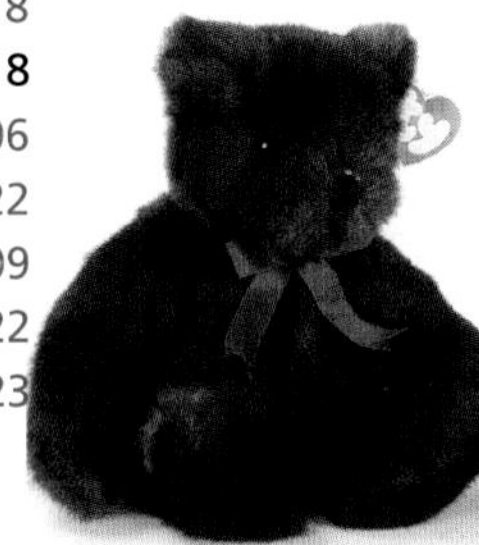

Baby PJ

Curly Bunny

TY PLUSH continued

NAME	TYPE	SIZE	STYLE NO.	RETIREDS' MARKET PRICE	STATUS
Jumbo PJ sable	Sable teddy bear	40 inch	9020	------------	Current
Jumbo PJ	White teddy bear	40 inch	9016	$600	Retired
Jumbo Pumpkin	Teddy bear	40 inch	9017	$750	Retired
Jumbo Rumples beige	Teddy bear	40 inch	9016	$200	Retired
Jumbo Shaggy beige	Teddy bear	40 inch	9026	$475	Retired
Jumbo Shaggy brown	Teddy bear	40 inch	9017	$500	Retired
Jumbo Shaggy gold	Teddy bear	40 inch	9016	$500	Retired
Kasey brown	Koala bear	13 inch	5006	$800	Retired
Kasey gray	Koala bear		5006	$750	Retired
Large Curly Bunny beige	Rabbit	24 inch	9003	$70	Retired
Large Curly Bunny white	Rabbit	24 inch	9007	$70	Retired
Large Curly Gold	Teddy bear	26 inch	9019	------------	Current
Large Curly tan	Teddy bear	26 inch	9018	$80	Retired
Large Ginger	Teddy bear	22 inch	9027	$75	Retired
Large Honey	Teddy bear	26 inch	9021	$400	Retired
Large McGee	Teddy bear	26 inch	9005	$80	Retired
Large Moonbeam	Teddy bear	20 inch	9009	$200	Retired
Large Paws black	Bear	28 inch	9030	------------	Current
Large Paws sable	Bear	28 inch	9029	------------	Current
Large Paws white	Bear	28 inch	9031	------------	Current
Large Petunia	Pig	26 inch	9003	$500	Retired
Large Ping Pong	Panda	26 inch	9010	$600	Retired
Large PJ sable	Sable teddy bear	26 inch	9012	------------	Current
Large PJ	White teddy bear	26 inch	9014	$275	Retired
Large Powder	Teddy bear	22 inch	9028	$80	Retired
Large Pudgy	Teddy Bear	28 inch	9006	$500	Retired
Large Pumpkin	Teddy bear	26 inch	9015	$300	Retired
Large Rumples beige	Teddy bear	26 inch	9002	$100	Retired
Large Rumples gold	Teddy bear	26 inch	9000	$175	Retired
Large Rusty	Dog	26 inch	9011	$125	Retired
Large Scruffy	Gold teddy bear	28 inch	9000	$200	Retired
Large Scruffy	Gold teddy bear	26 inch	9008	$300	Retired
Large Scruffy	Cream teddy bear	26 inch	9013	$300	Retired
Large Scruffy	Gold dog	26 inch	9011	$200	Retired
Large Shaggy beige	Teddy bear	26 inch	9025	$175	Retired
Large Shaggy brown	Teddy bear	26 inch	9015	$325	Retired
Large Shaggy gold	Teddy bear	26 inch	9014	$325	Retired
Large Snowball	Teddy bear	26 inch	9009	$250	Retired
Large Sparky	Dalmatian	26 inch	9002	$250	Retired
Lazy	Bear	20 inch	5008	$50	Retired
Leo	Lion	22 inch	7427	-----------	Current
Licorice	Cat	17 inch	1125	------------	Current
Licorice	Cat	20 inch	1009	$100	Retired
Lilly	Lamb		8004	$500	Retired
Lovie	Beige lamb	10 inch	8027	$30	Retired
Lovie	Lamb	20 inch	8019	$175	Retired
Lovie	Lamb	18 inch	8001	$800	Retired
Lovie	Lamb standing	20 inch	8004	$450	Retired
Magee	Brown bear	10 inch	5027	------------	Current
Maggie	Cat	20 inch	1115	flat: $75	Retired
**variations: curled and laying flat*				-----------	Current
Mandarin	Panda	13 inch	5201	$100	Retired
Mango	Orange orangutan	20 inch	7102	------------	Current
Mango	White orangutan	20 inch	7100	------------	Current
Max	White sheep dog	20 inch	3001	$1000	Retired
Max	White sheep dog	20 inch	2008	$300	Retired
McGee	Teddy bear	14 inch	5001	$60	Retired

Muffin

Baby George

TY PLUSH continued

NAME	TYPE	SIZE	STYLE NO.	RETIREDS' MARKET PRICE	STATUS
McGee	Teddy bear	13 inch	5001	$800	Retired
Midnight	Standing black bear	20 inch	5009	$350	Retired
Midnight	Black bear lying down	13 inch	5101	$60	Retired
Mischief	Monkey	21 inch	7414	$100	Retired
Mischief	Brown monkey		7000B	$400	Retired
Mischief auburn	Monkey	18 inch	7001	$300	Retired
Mischief auburn	Monkey	18 inch	7000A	$400	Retired
Mischief chocolate	Monkey		7002	$600	Retired
Mischief chocolate	Monkey	18 inch	7000C	$400	Retired
Mischief white	Monkey	18 inch	7000	$300	Retired
Mischief white	Monkey	18 inch	7000	$300	Retired
Misty	White seal	14 inch	7400	$200	Retired
Misty	White seal	11 inch	7431	------------	Current
Mittens Gold	Cat	12 inch	1117	$200	Retired
Mittens Grey	Cat	12 inch	1118	$200	Retired
Moonbeam	Teddy bear	14 inch	5009	$150	Retired
Mortimer	Moose	18 inch	7417	------------	Current
Muffin	Dog	13 inch	2020	------------	Current
Nibbles	Brown rabbit	9 inch	8000	------------	Current
Nibbles	White rabbit	9 inch	8001	------------	Current
Nutmeg	Teddy bear	18 inch	5013	$50	Retired
Oreo	Panda laying down	20 inch	5005	$75	Retired
Oreo	Panda		5010	$300	Retired
Otto	Otter	20 inch	7417	$200	Retired
Papa PJ sable	Sable teddy bear	50 inch	9021	------------	Current
Papa Pumpkin	Teddy bear	50 inch	9023	$1500	Retired
Papa Rumples beige	Teddy bear	50 inch	9022	$1000	Retired
Papa Shaggy beige	Teddy bear	50 inch	9024	$1600	Retired
Papa Shaggy gold	Teddy bear	50 inch	9022	$2000	Retired
Patches	Cat	20 inch	1114	$150	Retired
Patches	Dog	18 inch	2003	------------	Current
Patti	Black panther	20 inch	1118	$1000	Retired
Paws black	Black bear	18 inch	5025	------------	Current
Paws sable	Sable bear	18 inch	5024	------------	Current
Paws white	White bear	18 inch	5026	------------	Current
Peaches	Cat	20 inch	1003	$400	Retired
Peaches Himalaya	Cat	20 inch	1003H	$1800	Retired
Peepers	Chick	9 inch	8015	$150	Retired
Pepper	Black dog	12 inch	2024	------------	Current
Peter	Rabbit lying flat	20 inch	3002	$350	Retired
Peter	Realistic rabbit	14 inch	8002	$50	Retired
Petunia w/ pink ribbon	Pig	20 inch	8008	$150	Retired
Petunia w/ blue ribbon	Pig	20 inch	8008	$125	Retired
Petunia w/ red gingham ribbon	Pig	20 inch	8008	$150	Retired
Petunia	Pig	20 inch	6001	$500	Retired
Pierre	White poodle	10 inch	2004	$60	Retired
Ping Pong	Panda	13 inch	5005	$800	Retired
Ping Pong	Panda	14 inch	5005	$300	Retired
PJ Sable	Sable teddy bear	18 inch	5400	------------	Current
PJ	White teddy bear	18 inch	5200	$125	Retired
Pokey	Rabbit	19 inch	8015	$60	Retired
Powder	Teddy bear	18 inch	5307	$50	Retired
Prayer Bear	Gold teddy bear	14 inch	5601	$300	Retired
Prayer Bear	White teddy bear	14 inch	5600	$250	Retired
Pudgy	Teddy bear	14 inch	5006	$120	Retired
Puffy	Grey cat	15 inch	1003	$40	Retired

Curly Bear

Jersey

TY PLUSH continued

NAME	TYPE	SIZE	STYLE NO.	RETIREDS' MARKET PRICE	STATUS
Pumpkin	Teddy bear	18 inch	5304	$180	Retired
Rags	Teddy bear	12 inch	5102	$75	Retired
Rascal	Monkey	16 inch	7001	$40	Retired
Romeo	**Teddy bear**	**14 inch**	**5310**	------------	**Current**
Romeo Gold Ribbon	**Teddy bear**	**14 inch**	**5310**	------------	**Current**
Romeo Mother's Day	**Teddy bear**	**14 inch**	**5310**	------------	**Current**
Rosie	Rabbit	20 inch	8003	$425	Retired
Ruffles	Teddy bear	12 inch	5014	$100	Retired
Rufus	Teddy bear	18 inch	5015	$40	Retired
Rumples beige	Teddy bear	18 inch	5002	$70	Retired
Rumples gold -	Teddy bear	18 inch	5003	$150	Retired
**variations: black nose w/green ribbon or pink nose w/mauve ribbon*					
Rusty	Dog	20 inch	2011	$45	Retired
Sahara	Lion	12 inch	7421	$40	Retired
Sahara	**Lion**	**12 inch**	**7421**	------------	**Current**
Sam	Teddy bear	18 inch	5010	$200	Retired
Sarge	German shepherd	20 inch	2003	$400	Retired
Scratch	Black cat	15 inch	1117	$75	Retired
**variations: shiny black and dull black*					
Screech	Brown cat	15 inch	1116	$75	Retired
Scruffy	Cream teddy bear	18 inch	5013	$225	Retired
Scruffy light gold	Teddy bear	18 inch	5013	$125	Retired
Scruffy darker gold	Teddy bear		5012	$140	Retired
Scruffy	Cream dog	20 inch	2000	$175	Retired
Scruffy	Gold dog	20 inch	2001	$150	Retired
Scruffy	White dog	20 inch	2000	$60	Retired
Shadow	Black cat white paws	23 inch	1112	$1000	Retired
Shadow	Black bear	20 inch	5011	$50	Retired
Shaggy beige	Teddy bear	18 inch	5305	$120	Retired
Shaggy brown	Teddy bear	18 inch	5304	$300	Retired
Shaggy gold	Teddy bear	18 inch	5303	$250	Retired
Sherlock	Cat	20 inch	1110	$325	Retired
Sherlock	**Basset hound**	**12 inch**	**2029**	------------	**Current**
Shivers	Penguin	9 inch	7419	$375	Retired
Silky	Black cat	15 inch	1004	$50	Retired
Smokey	Cat	20 inch	1005	$275	Retired
Smokey Himalaya	Cat	18 inch	1005H	$1800	Retired
Smokey	Rabbit	19 inch	8016	$60	Retired
Sniffles	Dog	18 inch	2021	$175	Retired
Snowball	Teddy bear	14 inch	5002	$200	Retired
Snowball	Teddy bear	13 inch	5002	$800	Retired
Socks	Cat	12 inch	1116	$200	Retired
Spanky	St. Bernard	20 inch	2010	$500	Retired
Spanky	Cocker spaniel	8 inch	2015	$60	Retired
Sparkles	**Unicorn**	**20 inch**	**8100**	------------	**Current**
Sparky	Dalmatian sitting	20 inch	2004	$175	Retired
Sparky	Dalmatian lying	20 inch	2012	$120	Retired
Spice	Teddy bear	18 inch	5020	$40	Retired
Spice	**Cat**	**17 inch**	**1121**	------------	**Current**
Spout	Elephant	9 inch	7426	$30	Retired
Spout	**Elephant**	**9 inch**	**7426**	------------	**Current**
Sugar	Teddy bear	14 inch	5007	$125	Retired
Sugar	Polar bear standing		5008	$225	Retired
Sunny	**Dog**	**14 inch**	**2028**	------------	**Current**
Super Arnold	Pig		9003	$1000	Retired
Super Buddy	Bear			$1000	Retired
Super Chi-Chi	Cheetah	52 inch	9004	$1000	Retired

Baby Powder

Cocoa

TY PLUSH continued

NAME	TYPE	SIZE	STYLE NO.	RETIREDS' MARKET PRICE	STATUS
Super Fritz	Dalmatian	36 inch	9002	$1000	Retired
Super George	Gorilla		9007	$600	Retired
Super Jake	White monkey	16 inch	7002	$1000	Retired
Super Jake	Brown monkey	55 inch	9001	$1000	Retired
Super Max	White dog	26 inch	9001	$800	Retired
Super Max	White dog	32 inch	3002	$800	Retired
Super Scruffy	Teddy bear		9000	$500	Retired
Super Sparky	Dalmatian		9002	$500	Retired
Taffy	Dog	8 inch	2014	$40	Retired
Taffy	Dog	12 inch	2014	------------	Current
Tango	Orange orangutan	12 inch	7002	------------	Current
Tango	White orangutan	12 inch	7000	------------	Current
Theodore	Teddy bear	19 inch	5501	$45	Retired
Timber	Husky dog	20 inch	2002	------------	Current
Toffee	Dog	20 inch	2013	$30	Retired
Tulip	Pig	18 inch	8008	------------	Current
Tumbles	Cat	17 inch	1008	$100	Retired
Twiggy - rust & brown	Giraffe	23 inch	7422	$120	Retired
Tygger	Tiger	20 inch	7420	------------	Current
Tygger	Tiger standing	20 inch	7420	$275	Retired
Tygger	White tiger	20 inch	7421	$500	Retired
Vanilla	Teddy bear	18 inch	5012	$70	Retired
Wally	Walrus	12 inch	7423	$175	Retired
Whinnie	Horse	20 inch	8006	$300	Retired
Winston	Bull dog	20 inch	2007	------------	Current
Woolly	Lamb	9 inch	8005	------------	Current
Wuzzy	Teddy bear	13 inch	5202	$100	Retired
Yappy	Yorkie	8 inch	2016	$40	Retired
Yappy	Yorkie	12 inch	2016	------------	Current
Yorkie	Yorkie	20 inch	2006	$80	Retired
Yukon	Bear		7424	$125	Retired
Zulu	Zebra	20 inch	7421	$350	Retired
1991 Collectors Bear	Teddy bear		5500	$1500	Retired
1992 Collectors Bear	Teddy bear	21 inch	5500	$800	Retired
1997 Holiday Bear	Teddy bear		5700	$40	Retired

TY ATTIC TREASURES COLLECTION

Attic Treasures tags are described above in a way that best facilitates understanding for Beanie Babies collectors. Tag styles correspond to Beanie Babies swing tag generations. Retired Attic Treasures are in red type.

FIRST GENERATION

The front of this tag looks exactly like the first generation Beanie Babies hang tag with the skinny "ty."

SECOND GENERATION

The outside of this tag looks just like the second generation Beanie Babies hang tag. It opens like a book.

THIRD GENERATION

VERSION A

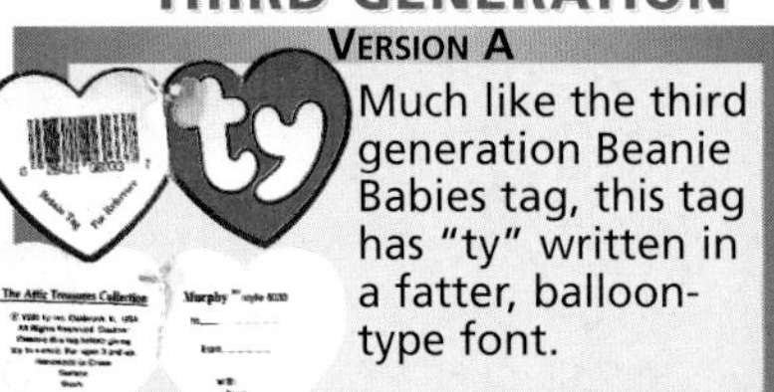

Much like the third generation Beanie Babies tag, this tag has "ty" written in a fatter, balloon-type font.

VERSION B

This tag has an added green banner across the upper right of the tag reading "collectible."

FOURTH GENERATION

VERSION A

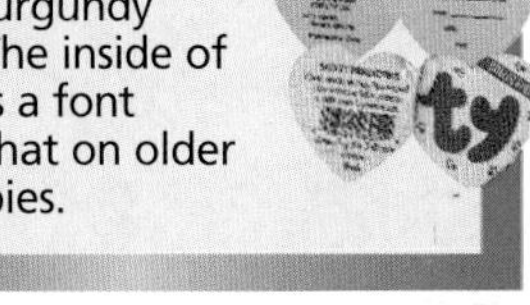

This is a beige paper tag with burgundy lettering. The inside of the tag has a font similar to that on older Beanie Babies.

VERSION B

This is also a beige paper tag with burgundy lettering. The inside of the tag, however, has a font similar to that on the tags for newer Beanie Babies.

NAME	SIZE & TYPE	STATUS	STYLE NO.	1ST	2ND	3RD A	3RD B	4TH A	4TH B	NOTES
Abby	8" Teddy Bear	Retired	6027		$90	$75	$75	$20	$15	
Amethyst	13" Cat	Retired	6131						$15	
Barry	11" Teddy Bear	Retired	6073					$90		
Bearington	14"Teddy Bear	Current	6102						retail	

TY ATTIC TREASURES continued

NAME	SIZE & TYPE	STATUS	STYLE NO.	1ST	2ND	3RD A	3RD B	4TH A	4TH B	NOTES
Benjamin	9″ Rabbit	Retired	6023		$90	$90	$90	$70		
Bloom	16″ Rabbit	Retired	6122					$20		
Bluebeary	8″ Teddy Bear	Current	6080						retail	
Bonnie	9″ Chick	Current	6075						retail	
Boris	12″ Teddy Bear	Retired	6041					$50		
Brewster	12″ Dog	Retired	6034		$90	$60	$60	$50		
Carlton	16″ Teddy Bear	Retired	6064					$40		
Casanova	8″ Teddy Bear	Current	6073						retail	
Cassie	8″ Teddy Bear	Retired	6028		$200	$175	$175	$150		
Charles	12″ Teddy Bear	Retired	6039					$40		
Checkers	8″ Panda	Current	6031		$80	$60	$60	$20	retail	
Chelsea	8″ Teddy Bear	Current	6070					$10	retail	
Christopher	8″ Teddy Bear	Retired	6071					$15	$15	
Clifford w/ Hump	12″ w/Teddy	Retired	6003	$400						
Clifford w/out Hump	12″ w/Teddy	Retired	6003	$300						
Clyde	12″ Teddy Bear	Retired	6040					$40		
Cody	8″ Teddy Bear	Current	6030		$75	$50	$50	$10	retail	
Colby	11″ Mouse	Retired	6043					$50		
Copperfield	16″ Teddy Bear	Retired	6060					$40		
Dexter	9″ Teddy Bear	Retired	6009	$150	$100		$75	$40		
Dickens	8″ Teddy Bear	Retired	6038				$30	$20	$15	
Digby with hump	12″ Teddy Bear	Retired	6013	$400						
Digby- no hump	12″ Teddy Bear	Retired	6013	$250	$100	$75	$75	$40		
Domino	12″ Panda	Retired	6042					$40		
Ebony	15″ Cat	Retired	6063					$40		
Ebony	13″ Cat	Retired	6130						$15	
Emily	12″ Teddy Bear	Retired	6016	$225						no head bow
Emily	12″ Teddy Bear	Retired	6016			$100	$75			w/ head bow
Emily	12″ Teddy Bear	Retired	6016					$50		w/ hat & dress
Eve	12″ Teddy Bear	Current	6106						retail	
Fraser	8″ Teddy Bear	Retired	6010	$150	$100		$50	$20	$15	
Frederick	8″ Teddy Bear	Retired	6072				$40			
Gilbert Gold	8″ Teddy Bear	Retired	6006	$150	$100	$100	$100	$40		
Gilbert White	8″ Teddy Bear	Retired	6015	$400						
Gloria	12″ Rabbit	Retired	6123						$25	
Grace	12″ Hippo	Current	6142						retail	
Grady	16″ Teddy Bear	Retired	6051				$40	$50		
Grant	13″ Teddy Bear	Current	6101						retail	
Grover	16″ Teddy Bear	Retired	6050		$100	$70	$70	$40		
Grover	13″ Teddy Bear	Retired	6100						$25	
Grover Gold	16″ Teddy Bear	Retired	6051					$50		
Heather	20″ Rabbit	Retired	6061					$40		
Henry Brown	8″ Teddy Bear	Retired	6005	$200	$125	$125	$125	$40		
Henry Gold	8″ Teddy Bear	Retired	6005	$1000						
Iris	10″ Rabbit	Current	6077						retail	
Ivan	8″ Teddy Bear	Current	6029		$100	$60	$60	$20	retail	
Ivory	15″ Cat	Retired	6062					$40		
Ivy	10″ Rabbit	Current	6076						retail	
Jeremy	12″ Rabbit	Retired	6008	$200	$100		$60	$40		
Justin	14″ Monkey	Retired	6044					$40		
King	9″ Frog	Retired	6049					$60		
King	11″ Frog	Retired	6140						$30	
Lilly	9″ Lamb	Retired	6037		$100	$50	$50	$40	$25	
Madison	10″ Cow	Retired	6035		$100	$60	$60	$40	$20	
Malcolm	12″ Teddy Bear	Retired	6026		$100	$60	$60	$40		
Mason	8″ Teddy Bear	Retired	6020		$100		$60	$40	$20	
Montgomery	15″ Moose	Current	6143						retail	
Morgan	8″ Monkey	Retired	6018	$250		$100	$100	$40	$15	
Murphy	9″ Dog	Retired	6033		$100	$50	$50	$40		
Nicholas	8″ Teddy Bear	Retired	6015	$200	$200	$60	$60	$40	$15	
Nola	12″ Teddy Bear	Retired	6014	$250						no head bow
Nola	12″ Teddy Bear	Retired	6014		$200	$100	$100			w/ head bow
Nola	12″ Teddy Bear	Retired	6014					$60		w/ hat & dress
Oscar	12″ Teddy Bear	Retired	6025		$100	$50	$50	$40	$20	
Penelope	9″ Pig	Retired	6036		$100	$75	$75	$40		
Peppermint	8″ Teddy Bear	Current	6074						retail	

Chelsea

Grover

Mason

TY ATTIC TREASURES continued

NAME	SIZE & TYPE	STATUS	STYLE NO.	1ST	2ND	3RD A	3RD B	4TH A	4TH B	NOTES
Pouncer	8″ Cat	Retired	6011	$300						identical ears
Pouncer	8″ Cat	Current	6011		$200	$75	$75	$40	retail	
Precious	2″ Teddy Bear	Current	6104						retail	
Prince	7″ Frog	Current	6048					$30	retail	
Priscilla	12″ Pig	Retired	6045					$40		
Purrcy	8″ Cat	Current	6022		$200	$60	$60	$30	retail	
Rebecca	12″ Teddy Bear	Retired	6019		$175	$100	$100			w/ head bow
Rebecca	12″ Teddy Bear	Retired	6019					$50		with clothes
Reggie w/ Red Ribbon	8″ Teddy Bear	Retired	6004	$1000						
Reggie w/ Navy Ribbon	8″ Teddy Bear	Retired	6004	$350						
Rose	10″ Rabbit	Current	6078						retail	
Samuel	13″ Teddy Bear	Current	6105						retail	
Sara	12″ Rabbit	Retired	6007	$300	$200	$80	$80	$55		
Sara	15″ Rabbit	Current	6120						retail	
Scooter	Dog	Retired	6032		$100	$60	$60	$40		
Scotch	14″ Teddy Bear	Retired	6103						$15	
Scruffy	9″ Dog	Current	6085						retail	
Shelby	9″ Rabbit	Retired	6024		$150			$40	$20	
Sidney	15″ Rabbit	Retired	6121						$15	
Sire	13″ Lion	Current	6141						retail	
Spencer	15″ Dog	Retired	6046				$40			
Squeaky	8″ Mouse	Retired	6017	$200						blk nose/whiskers
Squeaky	8″ Mouse	Current	6017		$175	$75	$75	$40	retail	
Strawbunny	10″ Rabbit	Current	6079						retail	
Tiny Tim	8″ Teddy Bear	Retired	6001	$200	$100	$60	$60	$40		
Tracey	15″ Dog	Retired	6047					$40		
Tulip	10″ Rabbit	Retired	6024							
Tyler	12″ Teddy Bear	Retired	6002	$200						with hump
Tyler	12″ Teddy Bear	Retired	6002	$175	$100		$60	$40		w/out hump
Watson	14″ Teddy Bear	Retired	6065					$40		
Wee Willie	8″ Teddy Bear	Retired	6021		$100		$50	$40		
Whiskers	8″ Cat	Retired	6012	$300	$200			$30		retail
Woolie Gold	6″ Teddy Bear	Retired	6011	$1200						rare - no price
Woolie Brown	6″ Teddy Bear	Retired	6012							

Purrcy

TY PILLOW PALS

NAME	INTRODUCED	STATUS	RETIREDS' MARKET PRICE
BaBa the lamb #3008	January 1997	Current	
Bruiser the bulldog #3018	September 1997	Current	
Carrots the pink rabbit #3010	January 1997	Current	
Clover the white rabbit #3020	January 1998	Current	
Foxy the fox #3022	January 1998	Current	
Glide the dolphin #3025	January 1998	Current	
Huggy the blue bear #3002	January 1995	Retired January 1, 1998	$25
Meow the Siamese cat #3011	May 1997	Current	
Meow the gray cat #3011	January 1997	Retired May 1997	$150
Moo the cow #3004	January 1995	Current	
Oink the pig #3005	January 1995	Current	
Paddles the platypus #3026	May 30, 1998	Current	
Purr the tiger #3016	January 1997	Retired May 1, 1998	$20
Red the bull #3021	January 1998	Current	
Ribbit the yellow and green frog #3009	January 1997	Current	
Ribbit the green frog #3006	January 1995	Retired Summer 1996	$400
Sherbet the tie-dyed teddy bear #3027	May 30, 1998	Current	
Snap the green and yellow turtle #3015	January 1997	Retired January 1, 1998	$25
Snap the yellow turtle #3007	January 1995	Retired Summer 1996	$400
Snuggy the pink bear #3001	January 1995	Retired January 1, 1998	$25
Speckles the leopard #3017	May 1997	Current	
Spotty the Dalmatian #3019	January 1998	Current	
Squirt the elephant #3013	January 1997	Current	
Swinger the monkey #3023	January 1998	Current	
Tide the whale #3024	January 1998	Current	
Tubby the hippo #3012	January 1997	Current	
Woof the dog #3003	January 1995	Current	
Zulu the thin-striped zebra #3014	January 1997	Retired Spring 1997	$75
Zulu the six-striped zebra #3014	Spring 1997	Retired January 1, 1998	$20

Bean Bag Toys Secondary Market Prices

This section of the "Mary Beth's Beanie World Monthly" Bean Bag Toy Buyer's Guide is designed to give you a composite look at a variety of toys on the market made by companies other than Ty Inc. Every month, we will update information and add to this guide as new products are released. You can take an in-depth look at many of these products in our monthly Bean Bag Bonanza section, which begins on page 191 of this issue.

All retired products are in red type.

ADVERTISING

The following bean bag toys are promotional items offered by various companies. The list of so-called "advertising Beanies" often changes as more companies release such toys. Products are listed alphabetically by company name with secondary market prices for each.

BELLY BEANS
Girl Scouts INTRODUCED MARCH '98

Brownie Girl Scout Bear	$7
Cadette Girl Scout Cat	$7
Daisy Girl Scout Cow	$7
Girl Scout Dog	$7

ENERGIZER

Bunny	$35

ENTEMANN'S

Entemann's Chip Cookie	$8
Entemann's Richie Donut	$8
Entemann's Sprinkles Cupcake	$8

GENERAL MILLS

General Mills Trix	$15
General Mills Rabbit	$15
General Mills Sonny	$15
General Mills Cuckoo Bird	$15
General Mills Lucky Leprechaun	$15
General Mills Wendell Baker	$15
General Mills Honey Nut Cheerios Bee	$15
General Mills Chip Cookie Hound	$15
General Mills Set of 7	$125

KELLOGG'S

Kellogg's Set of 3 Snap, Crackle & Pop	$55
Kellogg's Tony the Tiger	$15
Kellogg's Toucan Sam	$15
Kellogg's Frog	$15

KRAFT

Kraft Dairy Fairy	$10

M & M

M & M Set of 4 Round with legs and arms	$50
M & M Set of 4 Round	$20

NBC

NBC White Peacock	$30

OSCAR MAYER

Weiner Mobile and Whistle	$15

PILLSBURY

Pillsbury Doughboy Hard hat	$30
Pillsbury Doughboy Soft hat	$15

QUAKER OATS

Waldo and Woof	$20

APPLAUSE

Applause specializes in plush toys, figurines and other collectibles, and the company's bean bag toys are among the most popular in the business. All have large square hang tags and large tush tags. The company is licensed to produce some very popular toys as seen in this list. The list is broken down by product line.

PEANUTS

Charlie Brown	$5
Snoopy	$5
Woodstock	$5

RUGRATS

Angelica	$8
Chuckie	$5
Reptar	$5
Spike	$5
Tommy	$6

SESAME STREET

Big Bird	$5
Cookie Monster	$5
Elmo	$5
Ernie	$5
Grover	$5

WARNER BROTHERS

Bugs Bunny	$5
Michigan J. Frog	$5
Sylvester	$5
Taz	$5
Tweety Bird	$5

BABY BOYDS

The BabyBoyds are a new addition to the popular Boyds Plush line. These bean bag toys are listed alphabetically by name along with the type of animal it is and the product's estimated secondary market price. BabyBoyds designated with "QVC" are available only through that television shopping network and not at retail stores.

Allie Fuzzbucket - Cat	$10
Daffodil de la Hoppsack - Bunny	$10
Dickie the Lionhart - Lion	$6
Iris de la Hoppsack - Bunny QVC	$10
Lance - Large Lion	$7
Millie LaMoose - Moose	$12
Orchid de la Hoppsack - Bunny	$10
Paddy McDoodle - Bear	$12
Petunia de la Hoppsack Bunny - QVC	$10

SALVINO'S BAMM BEANO'S

The first series of Bamm Beano's were officially "sold out" before even one bear was shipped to stores!

Series 1

Dante Bichette	$15
Ken Griffey Jr.	$30

Juan Gonzalez $15
Tony Gwynn $15
Derek Jetter $15
Greg Maddux $15
Mark McGwire $35
Mike Piazza $15
Cal Ripken Jr. $25
Gary Sheffield $15
Frank Thomas $15
Kerry Wood $15

Series 1 - Denver, CO.
Dante Bichette $15
Vinny Castillo $15
Larry Walker $15

Series 2
Barry Bonds $10
Roger Clements $10
Jim Edmonds $10
Ken Griffey Jr. $15
Chipper Jones $10
David Justice $10
Tino Martinez $10
Mark McGwire $15
Cal Ripken Jr. $10
Alex Rodriquez $10
Ivan Rodriquez $10
Sammy Sosa $10

BEANY BEETLES

Only 50,000 of each type will be made by Starr Marketing.

Bear $10
Dream $10
Junior $10
Ken $10
Larry $10
Ray $10
Rollsbug $10
Route 66
White's Guide $20

COCA-COLA

Coca-Cola bean bags have long been among the most popular toys produced by Cavanagh Group International. The list is categorized by date of the toys' release, with the oldest products listed first. Each toy has a brief description, item number and median secondary market price.

MAY 1997 RELEASES

Seal in Baseball Cap (107) $30
Penquin in Delivery Cap (108) $20
Polar Bear with bottle (109) $20
Polar Bear in Pink Bow (110) $20

Coca Cola can

Polar Bear in T-shirt (112) $20
Polar bear in baseball cap (111) $35

SEPTEMBER 1997 RELEASES

Seal in Scarf (101) $15
Seal in Snowflake Cap (102) $15
Penquin in Snowflake Cap (103) $15
Polar Bear in Snowflake Cap (104) $15
Polar Bear in Plaid Bow Tie (105) $15
Polar Bear in Red Bow (106) $15

JANUARY 1998 SPECIALTY STORE

Coca-Cola Seal in ski cap (114) $20
Coca-Cola Polar Bear in sweater (116) $20
Walrus with Coca Cola bottle and logo scarf (124) $20
Coca-Cola Can in shades (132) $20
Reindeer in shirt (133) $20
Coca-Cola Polar Bear in Driver's Cap and bow tie (140) $20

Coca-Cola reindeer

JANUARY 1998 MASS MARKET

Husky with Bottle (136) $10
Polar Bear w/ argyle shirt (131) $10
Penquin in chef's hat (127) $10
Whale with bottle (137) $10
Walrus with bottle (135) $10
Reindeer with bottle (152) $10

WINTER 98 MASS MARKET

Polar Bear in Coca Cola Cap $8
Walrus in Coca Cola Cap $8
Seal in green scarf $8
Reindeer in Coca Cola Scarf $8
Polar Bear in Red scarf with Coca Cola $8
Penquin in Coca Cola scarf $8

NOVEMBER 1997 BLOCKBUSTER

Polar Bear w/ green bow on head (144) $35
Seal in green strip scarf (145) $35
Polar Bear in driver's cap (146) $35
Seal in Coca-Cola Snowflake Cap (147) $35
Kissing Bears - first edition White's Guide LE 15,000 $35
Bear in snowflake cap Media Play and Musicland LE 5,000 $45
Penguin in snowflake cap (148) $35
Polar bear in red vest (149) $35
McDonald's owner-operator worldwide convention LE 20,000 $45
Kissing bears - 2nd edition White's Guide $20

COSMO CRITTERS Zinc, Inc.

Cosmo Critters – an alien creature bean bag line by Zinc, Inc. – are listed here alphabetically by name. The list contains the limited edition (LE) quantity released for each, descriptions if needed for distinction, and median market prices.

Annie - LE 225,000 $10
Apollo - LE 300,000 $15
Boz LE 80,000 $15
Chilly - LE 400,000 $10
Cosmo - LE 3,000 $100-150
Darker lime green with frosted tint, Explorer
Cosmo - LE 2,000 $150-200
Light lime green
Groovey - LE 500,000 $10
Hootie - LE 300,000 $10
Jeepy - LE 400,000 $10
Jolly - LE 500,000 $10
Mattie - LE 20,000 $15
Wally - LE 450,000 $10
Zet - LE 2,000 $30
Light blue with tusks
NO police badge
Zet - LE 38,000 $10
Light blue with tusks
Police badge

CUSHY CRITTERS

Cushy Critters – released by Purr-fection by MJC – are increasingly popular among bean bag toy collectors. This list is broken down into three categories: Cushy Critters, Cushy Kids and the new Cushy Pals. With each character name comes the type of animal it is and the product's median secondary market price.

Adrienne - Bunny $6
Arnold - Pig $6
Avalanche - Snowman LE Dec 1998 $10
Bandit - Cardinal $6
Bat $6
Benny - Beaver $6
Boomer - Mouse $6
Boulder - Ram $6
Brandi - Bunny $6
Bubba - Buffalo $6

Bud - Frog	$6
Buttermilk - Cow	$6
Charlie - Monkey	$6
Chee Chee - Monkey	$6
Dimples - Elephant	$6
Dudley - Platypus	$6
Fiesta - Red Bull	$6
Flame - Flamingo	$6
Freedom - Eagle	$6
Ginger - Giraffe	$6
Ginger - Giraffe Incorrect birthdate of 2-29-98	$15
Hazel - Squirrel	$6
Hunny Jr. - Bear	$6
Ice Cube - Penquin	$6
Ivory - Walrus Fabric is dark brown and uniform in length	$15
Ivory - Walrus shorter gray fur with longer fur around face	$6
Jazz - Ladybug	$6
Kayla - Koala Caramel nose	$6
Kayla - Koala Dark brown nose	$15
Lacey - Unicorn	$6
Leon - Lion	$6
Leopard	$6
Mick - Kangaroo	$6
Minky Jr. - Bear	$6
Missy - Cat	$15
Molly - Moose	$6
Newport - Seal	$6
Nicolas - Santa LE Dec. 1998	$8
Nutmeg - Tabby Cat	$6
Orangutan	$6
Patches - Panda	$6
Patty - Tan Bear	$6
Pumpkin - Dog	$6
Q-Ball - Turtle	$6
Quincy - Porcupine	$6
Racer - Reindeer LE Dec. 1998	$8
Randy - Black Bear	$6
Rico - Raccoon	$6
Riley - Horse	$6
Rosie - Hippo	$6
Roy - Rhino	$6
Ruby - Red Fox	$6
Sammy - White Tiger Eye color: bright blue	$6
Sammy - White Tiger Eye color: dark brown	$15
Samson - Gorilla	$8
Sea Breeze - Whale	$6
Seymour - Dinosaur	$6
Sly - Fox	$6
Spike - Bulldog	$6
Spooky - Owl	$6
Squiggy - Octopus	$6
Stalker - Black cat	$6
Stinky - Skunk	$6
Stricker - Alligator	$6
Stripes - Toucan	$6
Timmy - Tiger Eye color: dark brown	$15
Timmy - Tiger Eye color: yellowish green	$6
Torch - Dragon	$12
Tubs - chick	$6
Virgil - Lamb	$6
Zack - Dalmatian	$6
Zellie - Zebra	$6

CUSHY KIDS

Beaver	$4
Black Bear	$4
Bunnie	$4
Dog	$4
Frog	$4
Koala	$4
Moose	$4
Panda	$4
Raccoon	$4
Squirrel	$4
Tan Bear	$4
Turtle	$4

CUSHY PALS

Hayley Hippo	$10
Jade Frog	$10
Morris Cow	$10
Paige Pig	$10
Skip Dog	$10

CUSTOM EDGE

Custom Edge, Inc., introduced the National Football League Coolbeans in September 1997 and followed up with Major League Baseball Coolbeans in July 1998. For each line of bean bag toys, a list of available animals is provided along with a complete team/jersey list and median secondary market price.

SERIES 1 INTRODUCED SEPTEMBER 1997

SIX TYPES OF ANIMALS

Cheers the Frog
Cleats the Cow
Pigskin the Pig
Rah Rah the Rhino
Tackle the Elephant
Touchdown the Lion

TEAMS AVAILABLE

Arizona Cardinals	$15
Atlanta Falcons	$25
Baltimore Ravens	$15
Buffalo Bills	$15
Carolina Panthers	$15
Chicago Bears	$15
Cincinnati Bengals	$15
Cleveland Browns	$15
Dallas Cowboys	$15
Denver Broncos	$15
Detroit Lions	$15
Green Bay Packers	$10
Indianapolis Colts	$15
Jacksonville Jaguars	$15
Kansas City Chiefs	$15
Miami Dolphins	$15
Minnesota Vikings	$15
New England Patriots	$15
New Orleans Saints	$25
New York Giants	$15
New York Jets	$15
Oakland Raiders	$15
Philadelphia Eagles	$15
Pittsburgh Steelers	$15
San Diego Chargers	$15
San Francisco 49ers	$15
Seattle Seahawks	$15
St. Louis Rams	$15
Tampa Bay Buccaneers	$15
Tennessee Oilers	$15
Washington Redskins	$15

SERIES 1 MLB INTRODUCED JULY 1998

SIX TYPES OF ANIMALS

Bones the Dinosaur
Homer the Horse
Joey the Kangaroo
Scoop the Leopard
Sparky the Dragon
Slider the Fox

TEAMS AVAILABLE

Anaheim Angels	$9
Arizona Diamondbacks	$9
Atlanta Braves	$9
Baltimore Orioles	$9
Boston Red Sox	$9
Chicago White sox	$9
Cincinnati Reds	$9
Cleveland Indians	$9
Colorado Rockies	$9
Detroit Tigers	$9
Florida Marlins	$9
Houston Astros	$9
Kansas City Royals	$9
Los Angelas Dodgers	$9
Milwaukee Brewers	$9

Minnesota Twins	$9
Montreal Expos	$9
New York Mets	$9
New York Yankees	$9
Oakland Athletics	$9
Philadelphia Phillies	$9
Pittsburgh Pirates	$9
San Diego Padres	$9
San Francisco Giants	$9
Seattle Mariners	$9
St. Louis Cardinals	$9
Tampa Bay Devil Rays	$9
Texas Rangers	$9
Toronto Blue Jays	$9

DISNEY

The Disney list is alphabetized by character name and includes the type of tag (see key provided), description if needed, and secondary market price for each. For more on the Disney line, see page 162 in this issue. The tag acronyms are as follows: DST = Disney Store, WDW = Walt Disney World, ED = EuroDisney, CD = Club Disney, MKT = Mouseketoy, JAP= Japan, INT-International. HTF = Hard to Find, CAT = Catalog, CDN = Canadian.

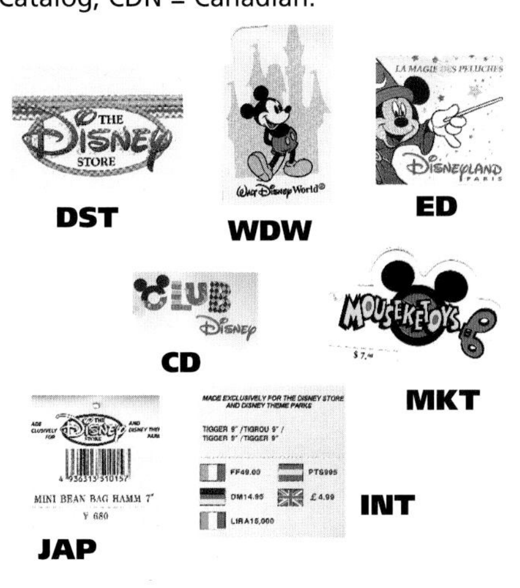

Abu (WDW/CD)	$20-35
NO "V" on forehead	
Abu (DST)	$10-15
"V" sewn in forehead	
Alien (DST/CD)	$10-15
Stitched eyes	
Alien (DST-JAP)	$40-75
Sticker eyes	
Bagheera (DST)	$25-35
2 tush tags, TTT "Bagherra"	
Bagheera (DST)	$15-25
1 tush tag, shinny fabric	
Bagheera (DST)	$15-25
1 tush tag, dull fabric	
Bagheera (DST)	$10-15
2 tush tags, TTT " Bagheera"	
Baloo (INT)	$40-50
Baloo (DST/CD)	$10-15
Bambi (DST/CD)	$25-40
Retired June '98	
Bambi (INT/JAP)	$50-75
Retired June '98	
Bashful (DST/WDW/CD)	$20-35
Retired June '98	
Ben Ali (DST/CD)	$20-30
Tiny Tush Tag says"Croc"	
Swing tag says "Aligator"	
Black Card (DST)	$15-25
Brer Bear (WDW)	$15-25
Brer Fox (WDW)	$15-25
Brer Rabbit (WDW)	$15-25
Brontosaurus (MKT/WDW)	$35-55
Animal Kingdom exclusive	
Buzz (DST/WDW)	$20-30
Knee pads, upward "V" on green shirt	
Buzz (DST/CD)	$10-15
NO knee pads	
Captain Hook (DST/CD)	$10-15
Cheshire (DST)	$20-35
Chip (DST/CD)	$10-15
Chip (MKT)	$20-30
Short fur on chest	
Christopher Robin (DST/CD)	$20-30
Classic Piglet (DST/WDW/CD)	$15-25
Classic Eeyore (DST/WDW/CD)	$10-15
Classic Pooh (DST/WDW/CD)	$10-15
Classic Tigger (DST/WDW/CD)	$15-25
Cricket (DST/CD)	$10-15
Crock (DST/CD)	$15-25
Daisy (DST)	$10-15
Daisy (MKT)	$10-15
Plush fabric, plastic eyes	
Dale (DST/CD)	$10-15
Dale (MKT)	$20-30
Short fur on chest	
Dewey (DST/CAT)	$35-50
Green shirt	
Dewey (WDW)	$25-45
Green shirt, plush fabric	
Dewey (DST/CD)	$10-15
Blue shirt	
Dewey(WDW)	$15-20
Blue shirt, plush fabric	
Doc (DST/WDW/CD)	$20-40
Retired June '98	
Donald (DST/CD)	$10-15
Donald (MKT)	$30-50
yellow ribbon goes around neck	
black ribbon sticks out front	
Donald (MKT)	$15-20
Plastic eyes, plush fabric	
Donald Soccer (INT)	$100-150
Europe Exclusive HTF	
Donald - Space Suit (MKT)	$30-40
Tomorrowland	
Dopey (DST)	$50-75
TEST version CDN	
Swing tag says "BEANBAG"	
Retired June '98	
Dopey (DST/MKT/CD)	$20-35
Swing tag says "BEAN BAG"	
Retired June '98	
Dumbo (DST)	$20-30
Foam ears, blue and pink collar	
Dumbo (DST)	$15-25
NO foam ears, blue and pink collar	
Dumbo (CAT)	$25-35
Trunk holds feather, blue and pink collar	
Dumbo (WDW)	$20-35
Trunk holds feather, yellow and pink collar	
Dumbo	$10-15
Foam ears, 2 tush tags	
Dumbo (INT)	$40-50
NO foam in ears, blue collar	
Duchess (CAT)	$35-50
Whiskers, Hard button nose	
Duchess (DST)	$35-45
Whiskers, stitched nose	
Duchess (DST/CD)	$10-15
NO whiskers, stitched nose	
Eeyore (DST)	$45-65
TEST CDN $10	
Tush tag attached at top of leg	
Eeyore (MKT/CD)	$15-25
Eeyore (INT)	$45-65
Eeyore (DST)	$10-15
Tush tag attached to bottom	
Eeyore (WDW)	$25-35
Gray Eeyore	
Eeyore-Reindeer (DST/MKT)	$35-45
Seasonal Product '98	
Fairfolk (DST)	$10-15
Figaro (DST/CD)	$10-15
Figment (WDW)	$35-45
Exclusive to Walt Disney World	
Flounder (DST)	$40-55
TEST CDN $10	
Separate pieces of fabric make up fin	
Retired Dec. '97	
Flounder (MKT/INT)	$35-45
Separate pieces of fabric make up fin	
Retired Dec. '97	
Flounder (DST/MKT)	$25-35
Striped fabric makes fin	
Retired Dec. '97	
Flower (DST/CD)	$25-40
Retired June '98	
Flubber (DST/JAP)	$75-95
Retired Dec. '97	
Flubber Sound (DST)	$50-65
Genie (WDW/CD)	$15-20
Genie (DST/CD)	$10-15
Small seam at top of shoulder	

Alien

DISNEY continued

Geppetto (DST)	$10-15
Gopher (DST)	$10-15
Goofy (DST)	$45-65
TEST CDN $10	
Goofy (DST)	$10-15
Goofy (WDW)	$15-25
Plush fabric, plastic eyes	
Goofy - Space Suit (MKT)	$15-25
Tomorrowland	
Grumpy (DST)	$50-75
TEST version	
Swing tag says "BEANBAG"	
Retired June '98	
Grumpy (DST/WDW)	$20-35
Swing tag says "BEAN BAG"	
Retired June '98	
Gugi (DST)	$10-15
Gus (DST)	$10-20
Happy (DST/WDW/CD)	$20-35
Retired June '98	
Hamm (JAP/DST)	$75-95
Hamm (DST/CD)	$10-15
US version	
Hen Wen (DST)	$10-15
Herbie (DST/MKT)	$15-25
Hippo (DST)	$10-15
Huey (DST)	$35-50
Swing tag says "Huwey," blue shirt	
Huey (CAT)	$25-45
Swing tag says "Huey," blue shirt	
Huey (WDW)	$25-35
Blue shirt, plush fabric	
Huey (DST)	$10-15
Red shirt	
Huey (WDW)	$15-20
Red shirt, plush Fabric	
Iago (DST)	$25-45
Jaq (DST)	$10-15
Jewel (DST)	$25-45
Retired Dec. '97	
Jiminy Cricket (DST)	$10-15
Jock (DST)	$10-15
Kiara (DST)	$10-15
Kanga (DST/WDW)	$10-15
Swing tag 7"	
Kanga (DST/WDW)	$10-15
Swing tag 8"	
King Louie (DST)	$10-15
1 Tush Tag	
King Louie (DST)	$10-15
Two tush tags	
Kova (DST)	$10-15
Lady (DST/CD)	$10-15
Lady (INT)	$40-50
Lady Kluck (DST)	$10-15
Little Brother (DST/CD)	$10-15
Little John (DST)	$10-15
Louie (DST)	$35-50
Red shirt	
Louie (WDW)	$35-50
Red shirt, plush fabric	
Louie (DST)	$10-15
Green shirt	
Louie (WDW)	$15-20
Green shirt, plush fabric	
Lucky (DST) No Y Face	$10-15
Lucky (DST)	$25-35
Y face	
Lucky (ED)	$25-50
Red collar	
Mad Hatter (DST)	$15-25
Maid Marion (DST)	$10-15
Marie 7" (DST)	$20-35
CDN $10	
Marie 8" (DST)	$15-20
Marie 7" (DST)	$10-15
CDN $9	
Merlin (CDN)	$25-45
Merlin signed	
Merlin - (CD)	$150-250
Stamped-LE 5,000	
CD/LE tag	
Mickey 9" (DST)	$100-150
TEST version	
NO black around eyes	
Retired June '98	
Mickey (DST)	$20-35
NO inch mark (approx. 8")	
Black around eyes	
Retired June '98	
Mickey 7" (DST)	$35-65
Black around the eyes	
Retired June '98	
Mickey (MKT)	$25-30
Plush fabric, plastic eyes	
Mickey - Grad Night (MKT)	$45-75
Red shorts, seasonal product '98	
Mickey - Grad Night (WDW)	$65-95
Tropical shorts, seasonal product '98	
Mickey - Pilot (DST)	$15-25
Mickey - 1930s (JAP)	$50-75
Mickey - Valentine (DST)	$35-45
Retired Feb. '98	
Mickey - Chinese New Year (JAP)	$400-500
Seasonal '98	
Mickey - Cast Member	$400-500
NO tag, given to cast members in 1998	
Mickey - Santa (DST)	$20-35
Retired Dec. '97	
Mickey - Santa 7" (DST)	$20-35
Retired Dec. '97	
Mickey - Soccer (INT)	$100-150
Europe Exclusive HTF	
Mickey Sorcerer (DST)	$20-35
Spirit of Mickey (DST)	$25-35
Given away with pre-order	
of Spirit of Mickey movie 1998	
Mickey Space Suit (MKT)	$20-35
Tomorrowland	
Mickey - Toga (DST)	$15-25
Mickey - Tourist (DST)	$15-25
Minnie 9" (DST)	$100-150
TEST version	
NO black around the eyes	
Retired June '98	
Minnie (DST)	$20-35
NO inch mark (approx. 8")	
Black around the eyes	
Retired June '98	
Minnie (DST)	$35-65
7" Black around the eyes	
Retired June '98	
Minnie (MKT)	$15-25
Plush fabric, plastic eyes	
Minnie - Chinese New Year (JAP)	$400-500
Seasonal '98	
Minnie - Hula (DST)	$15-25
Minnie - Liberty (DST)	$15-25
Minnie - 1930s (JAP)	$50-75
Minnie - Santa (DST)	$25-35
Seasonal Product Dec. '97	
Minnie - Santa 7" (DST)	$25-35
Seasonal Product Dec. '97	
Minnie - Valentine (DST)	$35-45
Retired '98	
Spirit of Minnie (DST)	$25-35
Given away with pre-order of	
Spirit of Mickey movie 1998	
Minnie Space Suit (MKT)	$20-35
Tomorrowland	
Mr. Smee (DST/CD)	$10-15
Mushu (WDW)	$20-25
NON-talking	
Mushu (DST/CD)	$25-50
Talking	
Nala (DST)	$10-15
Nala (WDW)	$15-20
Short plush fabric, slightly different color than DST version	
Nana (DST)	$10-15
101 Dalmatian (DST)	$65-85
TEST CDN	$10
Footpads, NO spots on belly, Y on face	
101 Dalmatian 2nd (DST)	
NO Y on face, NO footpads	
101 Dalmatian 3rd (DST)	$25-35
Y face, NO footpads	
Owl (DST)	$10-15
Owl (WDW)	$15-25
Fur on chest	
Panic (DST)	$20-30
Pain (DST)	$20-30
Pain and Panic	$50-85
NO tag, bagged given away with pre-order of Hercules movie	
Patch (ED)	$25-50
Green collar, smaller than DST version	

Flubber

Tigger

DISNEY continued

Penny (ED) $25-50
Pink collar, smaller than DST version
Peter Pan (DST) $10-15
Piglet (DST) $55-75
TEST CDN $10
footpads
Piglet (DST) $10-15
Piglet (INT) $45-65
Pinocchio (DST) $10-15
Pegasus (DST) $55-85
Mane tapers down the neck
Retired Dec. '97
Pegasus (WDW/MKT) $45-75
mane is squared off at the neck
Retired Dec. '97
Penny (ED) $35-50
Pink collar, smaller than
DST Dalmatians
Pluto (DST) $45-65
TEST CDN $10
Pluto (DST) $15-25
Pluto (MKT) $15-25
Plush fabric, plastic eyes
Pluto - Reindeer (MKT) $40-50
Seasonal product '98
Pluto Space Suits (MKT) $25-35
Tomorrowland
Prince John (DST) $10-15
Pumbaa (DST) $15-25
Pumbaa (WDW) $15-25
Short plush fabric, slightly different color
than DST version
Rabbit (DST) $10-15
Yellow tail
Rabbit (WDW) $15-25
White tail

Thumper

Queen of Hearts (DST) $15-25
Red Card (DST) $15-25
Rex (DST/CD) $10-15
Robin Hood (DST) $10-15
Sebastian (DST/MKT/INT) $35-50
TEST version CDN $10
Seam down the middle of shell
Retired Dec. '97
Sebastian (DST) $20-35
NO seam down shell
Retired Dec. '97
Simba (DST) $15-25
Simba (INT) $45-65
Same as DST version
Simba (WDW) $15-25
Short plush fabric, slightly different
color
than DST version
Sleepy (DST/CD) $20-35
Retired June '98
Sneezy (DST/CD) $20-35
Retired June '98
Suzy (DST) $10-15
Thumper (DST) $20-35
Retired June '98
Thumper (INT) $50-75
Retired June '98
Thumper (WDW) $35-60
Short fur on chest
Retired June '98
Tigger (DST) $75-95
TEST CDN $10
Straight tail, air-brushed stripes,
footpads
Tigger (DST) $55-85
Corkscrew tail, air-brushed stripes
Tigger (DST/WDW) $10-15
Pre-printed fabric, cork screw tail, NO
footpads
Tigger (INT) $45-65
Tigger (WDW) $30-50
Pre-printed fabric, straight tail, footpads
Tigger (DST) $20-30
Pre-printed fabric, corkscrew tail,
footpads
Tigger - Santa (MKT) $40-60
green scarf, seasonal product '97
Timon (DST) $10-15
Timon (WDW) $15-20
Short plush fabric, slightly
different color than DST version
Timothy (QDST) $15-25
Standing
Timothy Q (MKT) $35-50
Sitting
Tramp (DST) $25-35
Brown collar, measures
approx. 8" (tags says 6.5")
Tramp (DST) $15-25
Brown collar, measures
approx. 7" (tag says 6.5")
Tramp (DST) $10-15
Rust collar, measures
approx. 7" (tag says 6.5")
Tramp (INT) $40-50
T-Rex (MKT/WDW) $35-55
Animal Kingdom Exclusive
Triceratops (MKT/WDW) $35-55
Animal Kingdom Exclusive
Trusty (DST) $10-15
Tweedle Dee (DST) $15-25
Tweedle Dum (DST) $15-25
Vulture (WDW) $15-25
White Rabbit (DST) $15-25
Winnie The Pooh (DST) $55-75
TEST CDN $10
Footpads
Winnie The Pooh (DST) $35-45
NO footpads, stitched nose
Winnie The Pooh (DST) $10-15
NO footpads, hard button nose
Winnie The Pooh (DST) $25-45
Mega-Pooh,
large body and head
NO neck
Winnie The Pooh (INT/JAP) $45-65
Winnie the Pooh - Pilot (DST) $25-35
Winnie The Pooh Bumble Bee (DST) $20-35
Winnie The Pooh - Grad Night (MKT) $45-75
Red T-shirt, seasonal product '98
Winnie The Pooh - Grad Night (WDW) $65-95
Red shorts, seasonal product '98
Winnie The Pooh Valentine (DST) $125-175
Retired Feb. '98
Winnie The Pooh Easter(DST/JAP) $125-175
Purple bunny suit, seasonal
product April '98
Winnie The Pooh Easter (MKT) $75-95
Red T-shirt, bunny ears, seasonal
product April '98
Winnie The Pooh - Santa (DST) $65-85
Hard nose
Retired Dec. '97
Winnie The Pooh - Santa (DST) $55-75
Stitched nose
Retired Dec. '97
Winnie The Pooh - Santa (MKT) $35-55
Green scarf
Retired Dec. '97
Woody (DST/WDW) $20-35
Buttons on shirt, back of vest NOT
attached, cuffs
Woody (DST) $10-15
NO buttons, vest attached in back,
NO cuffs
Woody (DST) $10-15
2 tush tags, larger squares on shirt
Woody (DST) $10-15
2 tush tags, small squares on shirt

GRATEFUL DEAD

The Grateful Dead Bears by Liquid Blue have generated a lot of excitement in the collectibles community. This list – which includes the 10 new releases – is alphabetized by character name. For each character there is a description where needed, limited edition quantity (where applicable), and median market price.

Althea fuschia $25
Retired 6-98 LE 49,920
Bertha $15
Cassidy $15
Cosmic Charlie $25

Crazy Fingers	$10
Dark Star purple with Stars	$10
Daydream	$10
Dupree	$10
Delilah leopard LE 45,000 Black front paws Retired June '98	$35
Delilah leopard LE 11,000 NO black front paws Retired June '98	$50
Franklin	$10
Irie	$10
Jack Straw yellow-gold LE 49,920 Retired June '98	$35
Jerry	$15
Peggy-O	$10
Ripple	$10
Samson	$15
Stagger Lee	$15
St. Stephen	$15
Sugaree Tie-Dye LE 57,600 Retired June '98	$50
Sunshine	$10
Tennessee Jed blue LE 56,256 Retired June '98	$35

GUND

Gund's bean bag toys are listed alphabetically by product line, from Babar to String Beans. Each section includes a character name and median market price.

ALVIN AND THE CHIPMUNKS

Alvin	$8
Simon	$8
Theodore	$8

BABAR

Babar	$12
Celeste	$10

BABE

Babe Pig	$8
Fly	$8
Ferdinand	$8
Maa/Sheep	$8

BARNEY

Barney	$8
Baby Bop	$8

CLASSIC POOH

Eeyore	$12
Kanga	$12
Owl	$12
Piglet	$12
Pooh	$12
Rabbit	$12
Tigger	$12

CURIOUS GEORGE

Curious George	$12

DILBERT

Alice	$10
Boss	$10
Catbert	$10
Dilbert	$10
Dogbert	$10
Ratbert	$10

HOTSHOTS

Light Pink	$8
Dark Pink	$8
Bright Pink	$8
Dark Purple	$8
Violet	$8
Orange	$8
Apricot	$8
Red	$8
Lime Green	$8
Blue	$8
Red with green scarf	$10
Yellow with red scarf	$10
Green with yellow scarf	$10

MICKEY & COMPANY BABY MICKEY

Mickey	$10
Minnie	$10

MISS SPIDER

Miss Spider	$12

POOH

Baby Roo	$10
Eeyore	$10
Piglet	$10
Pooh	$10
Rabbit	$10
Tigger	$10

MISCELLANEOUS

Dahling	$6.50
Flash	$9.50
Quack-A-Moley 5"	$5
Quack-A -Moley 8"	$10
Rainbow Racer	$6.50
Tinkle Crinkle	$6.50

RICHARD SCARRY

Hilda Hippo	$10
Huckle Cat	$10
Lowly and Apple	$10

STRING BEANS

Berry Punch	$5
Bleu cheese	$5
Black Beans	$5
Bubble Gum	$5
Candy Apple	$5
Caramel	$5
Cherry pop	$5
Chicken Fingers	$5
Chili	$5
Corn chips	$5
Cotton Candy	$5
Drumstick	$5
Goat Cheese Pizza	$5
Grape Jam	$5
Honeycomb	$5
Juicy Grape	$5
Key Lime Pie	$5
Lemon Squash	$5
Peanut Brittle	$5
Pickles	$5
Sweet Tarts	$5

OTHER STRING CHARACTERS

Jingles	$6
Mickey Mouse	$6
Mickey Mouse String legs	$6
Minnie Mouse String legs	$6
Minnie Mouse	$6
Christmas Mickey	$6
Christmas Minnie	$6
Snowcone	$6
Santa	$6

WINTER BEAN BAG

Jingles	$10
Snowshoes	$10

Penguily	$10
Kringle	$10

HARLEY-DAVIDSON

Like the Coca-Cola products, Harley-Davidson toys are produced by Cavanagh Group International. The list of products includes Series I, Series II and Exclusives. Names and median prices are provided for each available character. Retired products are in red type.

SERIES I INTRODUCED 1997 AND RETIRED JUNE 1998

Big Twin	$25
Motorhead	$15
Roamer	$15
Punky	$15
Rachet	$15
Racer	$15

SERIES II INTRODUCED JULY 1998

Clutch Carbo	$8
Evo	$8
Fat Bob	$8
Kickstart	$8
Manifold max	$8
Spike	$8

EXCLUSIVES

Kissing Pair	$15
White's Guide LE 15.000	
Chopper	$35
GCC Exclusive LE 5,000	

MEANIES

These off-the-wall bean bag toys from The Idea Factory are very popular. This list includes the original Series I Meanies as well as the newly released Series II. Toys are alphabetized by character name and include an estimated secondary market prices for each. Retired products are in red type.

INFAMOUS MEANIES

Bull Clinton	$8
Mike Bison	$8
Donkeying	$8
Buddy the Dog	$8

SERIES 1

Armydillo Dan	$20
Bart the Elephant	$20
Boris the Mucousaurus	$8
Fangaroo	$25
LE - Mystery Meanie	
Fi & Do the Dalmutation	$8
Hurly the Pukin' Toucan	$8
Matt the Fat Bat	$18
Navy Seal	$8
Otis the Octo-punk silver earring LE 10,512	$20
Otis the Octo-punk gold earring	$8
Peter Gotta Peegull	$8
Sledge the Hammerhead Shark 6 red gills LE 10, 512	$20
Sledge the Hammerhead Shark 5 red gills	$20
Snake Eyes Jake	$20
Splat the Road Kill Kat	$15

SERIES 2

Bare Bear	$8
Bessie Got Milked	$8
Burny the Bear	$8
Chicken Pox	$8

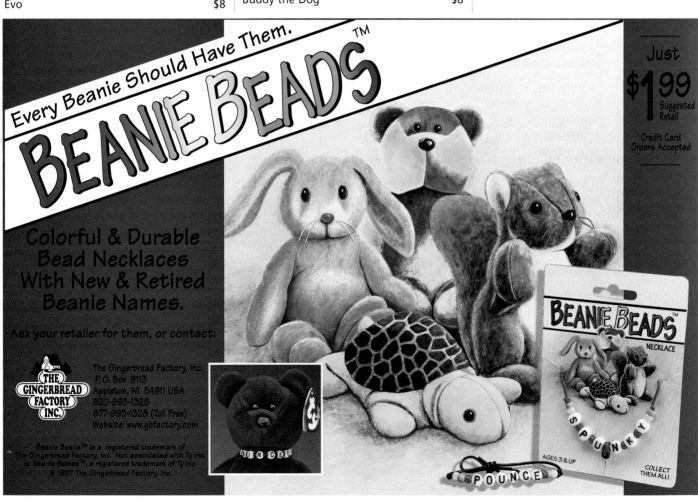

Digger the Snottish Terrier	$8
Donnie Didn't Duck	$8
Floaty the fish	$8
Lucky the Rabbit	$25
Lucky the Rabbit 1 1/2 series swing tag LE 45,000	$20
Peeping Tom Cat	$8
Phlemingo	$8
Sunny the Preemie Chickie	$8
Velocicrapper - dinosaur	$8

EXCLUSIVES

Codfather White's Guide LE 10,000	$10

BEANIE RACERS
Jones Group, Inc.

The NASCAR Beanie Racers by Jones Group, Inc., started arriving in retail stores in June 1998. The complete list of toys includes NASCAR driver name and car number, corporate sponsor, and a median market price for each.

SERIES 1

Bobby Hamilton #4 Kodak	$10
Mark Martin #6 Valvoline	$10
Hut Stricklin #8 Circuit City	$20
Ricky Rudd #10 Tide	$10
Bill Elliott #94 McDonald's	$10
David Green #96 Caterpillar	$20

SERIES 2

Dale Earnhardt #3 Goodwrench Plus	$10
Jerry Nadeau #13 First Plus Financial	$10
Ted Musgrave #16 Primestar	$10
Bobby Labonte #18 Interstate Batteries	$10
Derrike Cope #30 Gumout	$10
Jeff Burton #99 Exide Batteries	$10

PUFFKINS

The Puffkins characters by Swibco are listed alphabetically by name along with the type of animal it is and the product's estimated secondary market price. Descriptions are provided as needed for distinction. Retired products are in red type.

Albert - Alligator	$6
Amber - Brown Monkey	$6
Armour - Armadillo	$30
Aussie - Koala	$6
Bandit - Raccoon	$6
Benny - Black Bear	$6
Biff - Buffalo	$6
Bosley - Bulldog	$6
Bruno - Bull	$10
Chomper - Beaver	$6
Cinder - Dalmatian	$6
Cinnamon - Tan Cat	$6
Crystal - White Bear	$6
Ding - Bat LE Oct. 1998	$10

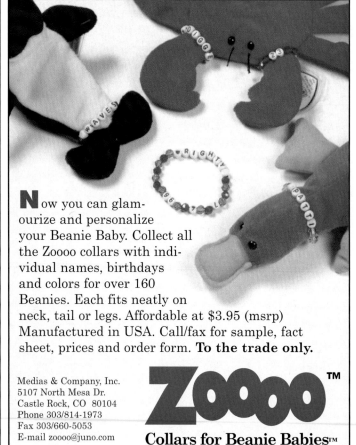

Dinky - Dinosaur yellow $22
Retired 1998
Dottie - Ladybug $6
Drake - Dinosaur red $22
Retired 1998
Elly - Elephant $6
Fetch - Dog $6
Flo - Flamingo $6
Flurry Snowman $6
LE Dec 1998
Franklin - Red Fox $6
Ginger - Giraffe $6
Gourdy - Pumpkin $10
LE Oct. 1998
Grizwald - Brown Bear $6
Gus - Moose $6
Hazel - Witch $10
LE Oct. 1998
Henrietta - Hippo $6
Honey - Tan Bear $6
Ho-ho Santa $6
LE Dec 1998
Jingles Green $6
LE Edition Dec 1998
Lancaster - Lion $10
Lily - Frog leap year $60
Lily - Frog bright green feet $40

Lizzy - Lamb $6
Lucky - Rabbit $6
Magic - Unicorn $6
Meadow - Cow $6
Milo - Black Monkey $6
Murphy - Gorilla $6
Nutty - Squirrel $6
Odie - Skunk $6
Olley - Owl $6
Omar - Orangutan $5
Paws - Cat $6
Peeps - Chick $6
Percy - Pig $6
Peter - Panda $6
Pickles - Dinosaur green $22
Retired 1998
Quakster - Duck $6
Red - Devil $10
LE Oct. 1998
Shadow - Black Cat $6
Shelly - Turtle $6
Shelly - Turtle bright green feet $40
Slick - Seal $6
Snowball - White Tiger black nose $80
Snowball - White Tiger lavender nose $45
6615 Retired
Snowball - White Tiger pink nose $50

Spike - Porcupine $6
Strut - Turkey $5
Swoop - Falcon $6
Tasha - White Tiger $6
Tibbs - Brown Rabbit $6
Tipper - Tiger $6
Toby - Whale $15
Trixy - White Monkey $6
Tux - Penquin $6
Whiskers - Walrus $5
Zack - Zebra $6

SAVE THE CHILDREN

There are only six of these special toys — the first-ever bean bag plush "people" — produced by Cavanagh Group International. This list includes each character's name and median price.

INTRODUCED JULY 1998

Haruko $8
Juji $8
Mackenzie $8

Patrick $8
Paz $8
Sila $8

Haruko

SILLY SLAMMERS

Introduced in 1997 by Cincinnati-based Gibson Greetings, Silly Slammers have charmed toy collectors with their wacky phrases.

B. Earp	$5
Botch	$5
Chaz the Spaz	$5
Cool Clyde	$5
Crash	$5
Fitz Gerald	$5
Ima Whiner	$5
Jammer	$5
Julius Seizure	$5
Lloyd	$5
Ms. Administrative Assistant	$5

Pinky	$5
Polly	$5
Striker	$5
The Boss	$5
Tiffany	$5
Yada	$5

STAR SACKS

These new bean bag collectibles based on sports figures are certain to be hot items. This list includes the name of the athlete, edition (1E means First Edition), quantity produced, and median secondary market price.

Al Capone	$20
Babe Ruth	$20
Buffalo Bill	$20
General Custard	$20
General Lee	$20
James Dean	$20
Kordell Stewart	$20
Chipper Jones 1E Baseball LE 6,000	$20
Dennis Rodman 1E Basketball LE 8,500 - red, blue or blonde	$25
Reggie White 1E Football LE 6,000	
Warrick Dunn	$20

Reggie White

WARNER BROS.

The Warner Brothers bean bag line has many interesting characters that people of all ages will recognize, from Daffy Duck to Scooby Doo. This list is alphabetized by character name and includes descriptions as needed and secondary market prices for each. Retired products are in red type.

Astro	$10
Bugs	$10
Bugs Easter Retired April 1998	$40
Bugs Talking	$15
Brain	$10
Daffy	$10
Devon and Cornwall	$35
Dino	$10
Dorothy	$8
Dot	$10
Droopy	$10
Flying Monkey	$8

Glinda	$8
Gossamer	$10
Jerry	$10
K9	$10
Lion	$8
Lollipop Boy	$8
Lollipop Boy	$8
Marvin	$15
Marvin Talking	$15
Michigan J. Frog	$10
Muttley	$10
NY Tweety LE NY Stores	$50
Penelope	$10
Pepe	$10
Pinky	$10
Road Runner	$10
Scarecrow	$8
Scooby "S" on Collar HTF	$45
Scooby "SD" on Collar	$10
Scooby Baseball	$40
Scooby Easter Retired April 1998	$40
Scooby I Love NY LE NYC	$50
Scooby Reindeer Retired Dec. 1997	$65
Scooby Talking Talks	$15
Scooby Vampire Oct. 1998	$15
Speedy	$10
Sweet Tweety Seasonal May 1998	$40
Taz	$15
Taz Birthday	$45
Taz Devil	$15
Taz dressed as devil Seasonal Oct 1998	$15
Taz Talking	$15
Tin Man	$8
Tom	$10
Toto	$10
Tweety	$10
Tweety Birthday	$45
Tweety NY LE NYC	$50
Tweety Pumpkin Seasonal May 1998	$15
Tweety - Talking	$12
Wakko	$10
Yakko	$10
Wizard	$8
Wicked Witch	$8

Tweety

MISC.

Paddington Bear	$16
Smokey the Bear	$10

BEAN BAG COLLECTORS!

Janet Leopold covers news in the world of non-Ty bean bags for "Mary Beth's Beanie World Monthly." If there is a product you would like to see featured in this Buyer's Guide, contact Janet via e-mail at janet@janetlynn.com.

This product is not sponsored or endorsed by Ty Inc. Beanie Babies™ is a registered trademark of Ty Inc.

A PORTION OF PRINCESS SALES WILL BENEFIT

FRONT PANEL	BACK PANEL		FRONT PANEL	BACK PANEL

(I)

LOVLIN FARM
ARTIST: DONNA BUSCHER

This collectible series of totes for kids and adults is created by Linda Addi to protect and show off your favorite BEANIES in their own environment!

(M)

ARCTIC FRIENDS
ARTIST: ZOLTAN

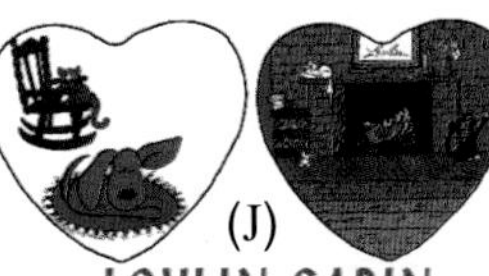

(J)

LOVLIN CABIN
ARTIST: DONNA BUSCHER

Signature Series #1 still limited call for availability.

(N)

UNDER THE SEA
ARTIST: ZOLTAN

(K)

LOVLIN POND
ARTIST: DONNA BUSCHER

Totes are made of durable PVC vinyl and include one keychain

(O)

PEACEFUL RAINFOREST
ARTIST: ZOLTAN

ORDER DESK
1 (888)
6-LOVLIN

TO FAX ORDERS
(702) 323-5111

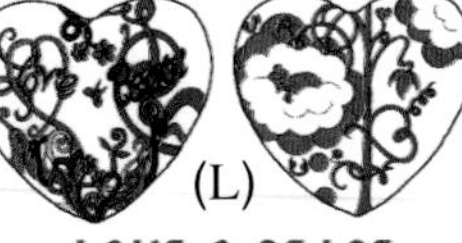

(L)

LOVE & PEACE
ARTIST: LINDA NOVEROSKE

(P)

HOO'S IN THE WOODS
ARTIST: ZOLOTAN

LOVLIN INC. • BOX 11006 • RENO, NV • 89510 • www.lovlin.com Patent and Design Registration Pending. All Rights Reserved.

A Princess' Crown

"A crown of jewels is worn
When one is Royalty
So Princess we place this on your head
Out of love and memory."

- Poem on the card included with every Princess Crown

This miniature tiara is a truly exquisite piece that would complement any collection. The Princess Crown contains 38 Austrian Swarovski crystals: 33 crystals are 4 mm in size and five crystals are 6 mm in size. The crystals are set in a metal base of pewter with a silver tone, and there is a dated and signed engraving on the inside of the base (Princess '97 USA). The Princess Crown comes complete with a poem within a velvet jewelers bag and jewelers box. Add this lovely crown to your collection to give it that royal touch.

A 6 mm crystal charm necklace and 4 mm pair of clip-on earrings also made with Austrian Swarovski crystals, are offered as a set for $13.99. A beautiful gold mounted set of Pearl clip-on Earrings & Necklace, modeled by Erin, $13.99.

Princess Crown
$24.99

"Princess '97 USA"
is engraved inside the crown.

These original designs are truly brilliant pieces of jewelry.

Swarovski Crystal
Earrings & Necklace Set $13.99

Pearl Earrings &
Necklace Set
$13.99

The jewelry is modeled by Ty's Princess ™ & Erin ™ Beanie Babies

Crown, Earrings, & Necklace $38.98

Barbi's Collectibles Inc.

P.O. Box 29097, Columbus, OH 43229

Phone (614) 901-9304

Fax (614) 895-0471 • E-mail: indenv@aol.com

Web site: http://members.aol.com/indenv/index.html

Dealer quantity discounts are available

Shipping and handling is $4.00 per order extra Please allow 2 weeks for delivery
We accept Mastercard, Visa, Discover, Checks and Money Orders.
Ohio residents add 5.75% sales tax.

Designed by Gold Plus Inc. and Barbi's Collectibles Inc.

The Web Watcher

A systematic look at Beanie-related sites on the Internet

BY JACKIE LA BERG

"Mary Beth's Beanie World Monthly" is proud to offer monthly coverage of Beanie/Plush sites on the World Wide Web. In this month's section, in honor of the first anniversary of "Beanie World," we are providing closer looks at two main sites: The "Beanie World" site and the Ty Inc. site. Of course, we also have "The Web List" and a comprehensive list of URL for sites run by our advertisers.

For a closer look at Web sites operated by young Webmasters, check out the "Web Watcher Jr." page in every issue in the "Mary Beth's Beanie World For Kids" section!

The Official "Mary Beth's Beanie World Monthly" Web Site

You can find official Web site for this magazine at http://www.beanieworld.net. There you will find all the hottest, up-to-date Beanie information covered in many popular pages. Under "Beanie Happenings" you'll find quick news, from new product announcements and retirements to updates on Beanie shows and other events. Under "Beanie News Service" you'll find Beanie-related clips

from newspapers and wire services around the world. Instead of surfing the Internet to find a variety of articles, you can now turn to one location to get all the news.

Of course, you can also get information on the site about how to advertise, how to subscribe and how to carry "Beanie World" in your store. The site also offers you the opportunity to correspond with us via direct e-mail link. The e-mail address for all correspondence is beaniew@interaccess.com.

Finally, you won't want to miss out on the "Beanie World" $100,000 giveaway, which is available only through the Web site. You can enter as often as once a week for your chance to win a COMPLETE set of Ty Beanie Babies.

The Official Ty Inc. Web Site

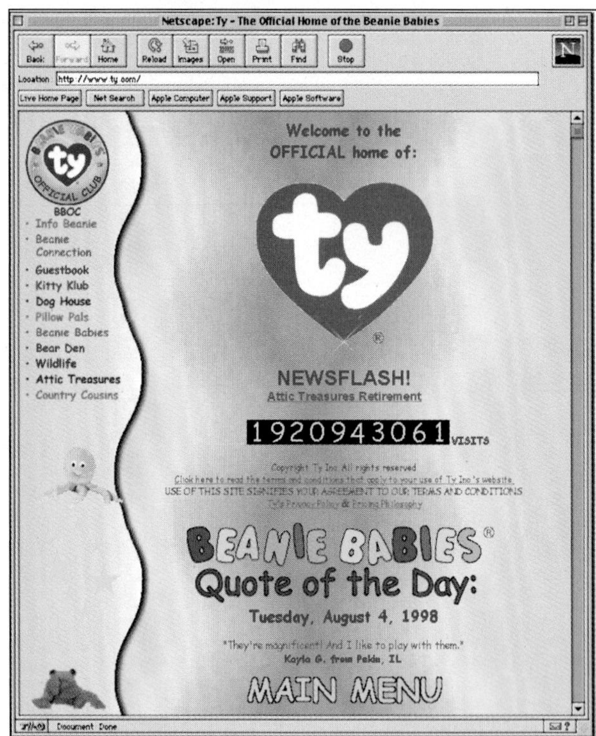

You can find the official "home" of Ty Inc. at http://www.ty.com. Since its inception in July of 1996, this popular Web site has entertained millions of users. In fact, at press time, the number of "hits" at the site was nearly 2 BILLION!

Visit Ty's Web site to catch surprise announcements under NEWSFLASH, plus "read all about it" with the Info Beanie of the month, and register to join the Beanie Connection, Ty's official communication forum for collectors of all ages! Other "mirror" Web sites for Ty Inc. are http://bow.ty.com, http://neck.ty.com, http://www.beaniebabies.com and http://cable.ty.com.

The Web Watcher continues on page 180

WIN a complete set of Beanie Babies™!!

go on-line today!

$100,000 GIVEAWAY!

(Complete set of Beanie Babies valued at $100,000)
Contest available only on our Web site.
Keep coming back to beanieworld.net for more details.

See Web Site for Contest Rules

Valued at $100,000!
You can ONLY enter on the web
See our address below...

- Current Issue On Newsstands
- Late Breaking News
- Interact with Us
- Beanie Show Updates
- What's Coming Soon
- Frequently Asked Questions
- Chicago Sun-Times Weekly Columns by Mary Beth

The Web Watcher

"MARY BETH'S BEANIE WORLD MONTHLY" WOULD LIKE TO FEATURE THE FANTASTIC WEB SITES SET UP BY OUR DEVOTED ADVERTISERS. VISIT THEM OFTEN TO FIND DETAILS ABOUT THEIR BEANIE-RELATED PRODUCTS!

ADVERTISER	Web address (add http:// to the beginning of each)
American Beanie Farm	www.beaniefarm.com
Auction Universe	www.auctionuniverse.com
Barbi's Collectibles	members.aol.com/indenv/ index.html
BB Collectibles	www.bean-stalk.com
Beanie Arc Co, The	www.beanieark.com
Beanie Central	www.beaniecentral.com
Beanie Connection, The	www.beanieconnection.com
Beanie Dad USA	members.aol.com/ashsta1/
Beanie Do-Dads	www.beaniedodads.com
Beanie Jeanie	www.beaniejeanie.com/ resellers.htm
Beanie Nation	www.beanienation.com
Becketts	www.beckettsassociates.com
Brian Wallos and Co.	www.wallos.com
Buckaroo Books	www.encyclobeaniea.com
Buckman Holding, Inc./Trends	www.polygon.net/~2853
Cat and the Fiddle, The	www.catandthefiddle.com
Collection Connection, The	www.d56cyber.com
Country Cottage	www.countrycottage.org
Creation Entertainment	www.creationent.com
DHD Designs	www.gojoplin.com/cherish
Diana Petersen's Collectibles	www.wefindit4u.com
E-Bay	www.ebay.com
Evies Beanie Raffle.Com	www.eviesbeanieraffle.com
FarleysArt	www.swiftsite.com/ heartsview
Fuzzies	www.beanieduds.com
Giddy-Up!, Inc.	www.tagbags.com
Gingerbread Factory, The	www.gbfactory.com
Hobby Heroes	www.hobbyheroes.com
Iguana's	www.iguanas-cbc.com
Imagination Unlimited	www.beaniehouse.com
Innovative Thinking	www.beaniebios.com
Knoch Designs	www.knochdesign.com
Limited Connection, The	www.thelimitedconnection.com
Limited Treasures	www.limitedtreasures.com
Lin Terry	www.linterry.com
Marcia's Originals	www.babyhotel.com
Med Files Publishing	www.planetbeanie.com
Mitchell Enterprises	www.btp-tags.com
My Collectibles	www.lovemycollectibles. com/~myc/
National Collector, The	www.tncbeanie.com
No Swetts	www.bananajunction.com
Paul and Judy's	www.pjcc.com
PCI	www.heart-tite.com
PurrFection by MJC	www.cushycritter.com
Qcom, Inc.	www.justbeanies.com
Rainbow Tags	www.heartkeeper.com or www.rainbowtag.com
Rayn or Shyne	www.raynorshyn.com/kids/ index/html
RCS Enterprises	www.jacamac.com
Sav-A-Tag	www.savatag.com
SMD	www.beanieaccessories.com
Sportscards, Supplies, Dolls	www.ssnd.com
Star Marketing	www.bug-me.com
Storage Solutions	www.beaniemotel.com
Swibco	www.swibco.com
Tag Preservers	www.tagpreservers.com
Tailor-Made	www.expage.com/page/ tailormade
Toys for Toddlers	www.toysfortoddlers.com
UCC Distributors	www.uccdist.com
Varcon Systems	www.varcon.com
Wenc Industries	www.beaniebabybeanpole.com
West Coast Cards	www.wccg.com
World's Lil' Treasures	www.worldsliltrs.com
Zinc	www.cosmocritters.com

THE WEB LIST

With the growth of the Internet, a wealth of Beanie/Plush information is at your fingertips. Access these popular Beanie/Plush Web sites to view informative articles by collectors around the world, auction or buy/sell/trade your collector pieces with fellow on-liners, find merchants who stock Beanies/Plush, or send a collector friend an on-line virtual Beanie card. Don't forget to stop by the official "Mary Beth's Beanie World Monthly" site, where you find a lot of exclusive new AND access links to many other Beanie/Plush sites!

The official "Mary Beth's Beanie World Monthly" Web site
(Remember that the URL ends with ".net" not ".com.")
http://www.beanieworld.net

The Ty Inc. Web site
http://www.ty.com

The popular "Beanie Mom"
http://www.beaniemom.com

Peggy Gallagher and Paula Abrinko's Beanie Phenomenon
http://www.beaniephenomenon.com

Lemon Lainey Design (England)
No. 1 Beanie Baby site in the United Kingdom
http://www.lemonlaineydesign.com

THE WEB LIST continued...

CToys News
(Formerly titled Meghan's Beanie Baby site)
http://www.ctoys.com

Beanie Bits and Pieces
http://www.beaniebits.com

Marcia's Beanies 101
http://www.beanies101.com

The Beanie Philes
http://www.beaniephiles.com

RJW's Beanie Mania Canadian Web site
http://www.beaniemania.com

Beanie Baby Universe
http://www.geocities.com/~beanieuniverse

BeanieShop.com's Virtual Beanie Card Shop
http://www.beanieshop.com

Electronic Worldwide Beanie Baby Exchange
(Modeled after various stock exchanges)
http://www.ewbe.com

WALT DISNEY WEB SITES

Disney Mini Bean Bag Plush Page
http://www.shop.disney.com

Janet Lynn's Collectibles
http://www.janetlynn.com

The Disney Beanie Report
http://www.dizBeanies.com/

AUCTION WEB SITES

Just Beanies Safe and Secure On-line Auctions
http://www.justbeanies.com

Beanie Nation Auctions
http://www.BeanieNation.com

E-Bay Auctions
http://www.ebay.com/aw/index.html

Auction Universe
http://www.auctionuniverse.com

One Web Place Auctions
http://www.onewebplace.com/home.asp

Up4Sale Auctions
http://www.up4sale.com/beaniebabies.htm

Check out **America Online**'s terrific newsgroup dedicated to Beanies. (Keyword: Collecting OR Collectibles, then click Beanbag Collectibles)

NOTE: As always, please sit with your children if they are using the Internet.

PLACE YOUR MAGAZINE ORDERS NOW!

"Mary Beth's Beanie World Monthly" is available for sale to gift and specialty market stores.

METRO MARKETING - U.S.A.
Suggested Retail Price
$5.99 (U.S. funds)

HONEY 'N LEMON MARKETING - U.K.
Suggested Retail Price
£3.50 (U.K. funds)

ZIBBERS INC. - CANADA
Suggested Retail Price
$8.99 (Canadian funds)

ORDER DEADLINE:	PRINT DATE:	ARRIVAL IN STORE:
Nov. Issue (9811) - Sept. 1, 1998	**Nov. Issue** (9811) - Sept. 22, 1998	**Nov. Issue** (9811) - Oct. 20, 1998
Dec. Issue (9812) - Sept. 29, 1998	**Dec. Issue** (9812) - Oct. 20, 1998	**Dec. Issue** (9812) - Nov. 17, 1998
Jan. Issue (9901) - Oct. 27, 1998	**Jan. Issue** (9901) - Nov. 17, 1998	**Jan. Issue** (9901) - Dec. 15, 1998
Feb. Issue (9902) - Nov 29, 1998	**Feb. Issue** (9902) - Dec. 15, 1998	**Feb. Issue** (9902) - Jan. 12, 1998

Wholesale Orders ONLY Contact:

METRO MARKETING
Info: (502) 360-1040
Fax: (502) 360-0052
Orders: (800) 995-7197
E-mail: metromkt@ne.infi.net

HONEY 'N LEMON MARKETING
16 High Street • Lyndhurst
Hampshire • SO43 7BD
Phone: ++44 1703 283666
Fax: ++44 7070 711746
Freefone: ++44 0800 146345

ZIBBERS INC.
20 Eglinton Avenue West
Suite 1600
Toronto, Ontario M4R 2H1
Phone: (416) 787-8516
Fax: (416) 932-1601

ODDS 'N ENDS

BY JACKIE LA BERG

OOPS! HOW DID THAT HAPPEN?

Companies that manufacture popular "Beanie/Plush" toys (such as Ty, Disney, etc.) are known for their commitment to high quality production. Due to thousands of styles being generated, however, some errors can be expected. The ODDS 'N ENDS (manufacturing mistakes) that are surfacing can be comical, interesting and collectible.

What is the value of a particular Beanie error? Some ODDS 'N ENDS prices are highlighted for your convenience within our Buyer's Guide. While we are unable to stipulate prices for virtually all error Beanies, the best rule of thumb is: Your ODDS 'N ENDS is worth what a collector is willing to pay for it. There is no guarantee that a higher value will be placed on an error Beanie. In fact, cases exist where the mistake actually depreciates the worth. Some specific examples would be Snowball, a pink Inky without a sewn-on mouth (it could easily be removed) or a Beanie missing its tush tag.

NOTE: The reversed mistags on Rainbow/Iggy are a common error and is not considered an ODDS 'N ENDS. At the present time, their value remains unchanged.

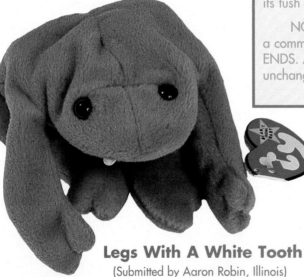

Spike Without Eyes
(Submitted by Mary Halls Connecticut)

Legs With A White Tooth
(Submitted by Aaron Robin, Illinois)

Nip Without A Tail
(Submitted by Jeralyn Flores, California)

ABOVE: **Blizzard Without A Tail** (Submitted by Joyce Lindemann, Michigan) LEFT: **Peace With A Solid Brown Upper Arm** (Submitted by Stephanie Valdes, Illinois)

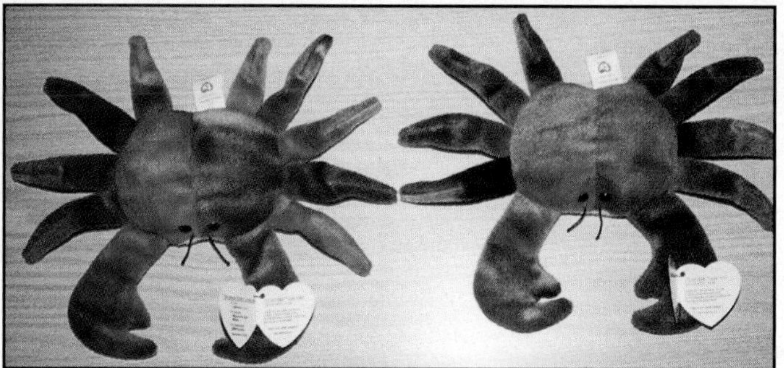

LEFT: **Claude With Nine Legs (on left)** (submitted by Daniel Skoff, Illinois)
RIGHT: **Snowball Without A Mouth** (Submitted by Barbara Cooley, Oklahoma)

Glory Without A Flag Patch On Its Chest
(Submitted by Tim LaPresto, Missouri)

Rainbow With Untrimmed Felt Around The Mouth (on right) (Submitted by Barbara Burkemper, Missouri)

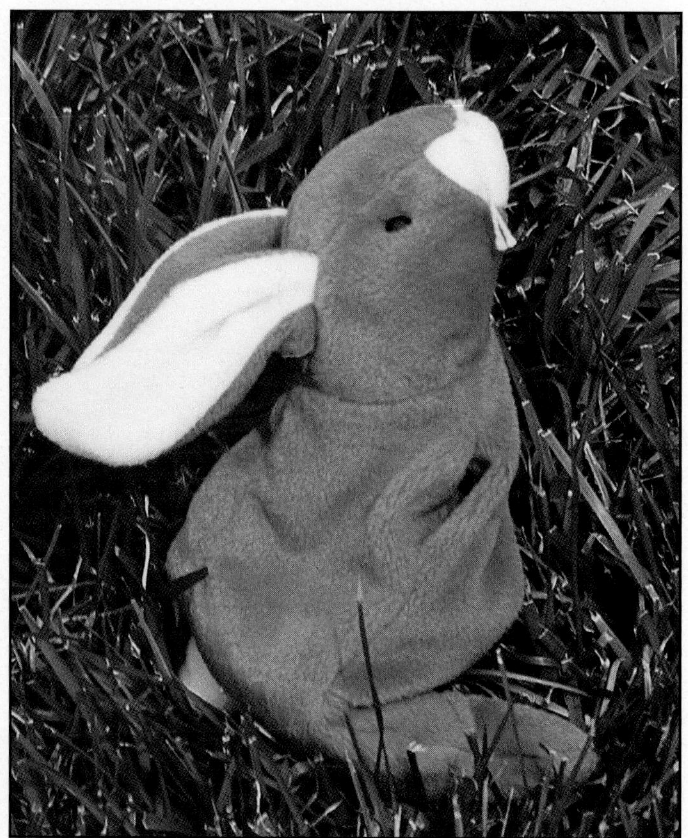

Ears With Strangely Sewn Legs
(Submitted by Barbara Cooley, Oklahoma)

If you own a Beanie/Plush ODDS 'N ENDS, "Mary Beth's Beanie World Monthly" would like to consider a photo of it for publication. Please follow these guidelines for submission: Write a brief description and send it along with a VERY CLEAR photo (instant/Polaroid photos cannot be used) to: ODDS 'N ENDS, c/o "Mary Beth's Beanie World Monthly," P.O. Box 68729, Schaumburg, IL 60168-0729. Be sure to include your caption/credit information – including your full name, postal address and daytime phone number – with your submission. Address and phone numbers are for office use only and will not be published. We regret that photos cannot be returned.

IMPORTANT NOTE: Please try to avoid duplication. It is unlikely we will repeat a Beanie error featured in a current or previous "Beanie World" issue. A mistagged Beanie – such as one bearing an incorrect swing tag (which can easily be switched) or misprinted tush tag – is NOT considered a candidate for ODDS 'N ENDS. It needs to be an apparent mistake on the Beanie itself. Additionally, the Beanie product cannot show signs of having been altered. For example, if a Glory bear is missing a chest flag patch, the material needs to be perfectly smooth throughout that area, without stitch holes showing.

We regret that we are unable to answer questions regarding the value of your ODDS 'N ENDS. This section is offered for your general interest. "Mary Beth's Beanie World Monthly" is not responsible if a printed photo results in a discrepancy.

NEW RELEASES!

- Limited production – Only 36,000 of each bear!
- Each hangtag sequentially numbered!
- Each hangtag has a hologram to ensure authenticity to deter counterfeiting!

INTRODUCING

Sam!

Elvis!

Gordon!

The Mystery Bear!

Visit our Web site to find out who the Mystery Bear is.

Extremely limited production – Only 36,000 of each bear produced!

OscoDrug
Sav-on drugs.

TOTALPHOTO

ONE HOUR PHOTO SERVICE AVAILABLE IN MANY OSCO/SAV-ON STORES. CALL 1-800-443-5701 FOR THE OSCO/SAV-ON LOCATION NEAREST YOU.

Kodak Moments Make Great Memories!

Using Kodak paper the Osco/Sav-on Photo Shop provides state-of- the-art photo processing for all your memories!

$6.99 24 exp. Jumbo Prints

One-Hour*
Color Print Processing

#002

Order 2 Sets, 2nd Set ONLY! 8¢ per print
ANY EXP. ROLL!

1-Hour Jumbo Size Color Print Processing

35mm only

OscoDrug
Sav-on drugs.

One Hour Service Only!
Good thru Sat., October 17, 1998.
Coupon must accompany order.

*Limited to Machine Capacity. 35 mm only.

High quality Kodak Royal Gold Paper helps keep images sharp and colors true. It's the only paper we use at Osco One Hour Photo Express.

PHOTO EXPRESS™

Next Day Color Print Processing
7 Days a Week or They're FREE!*

Regular Size
Color Print Processing

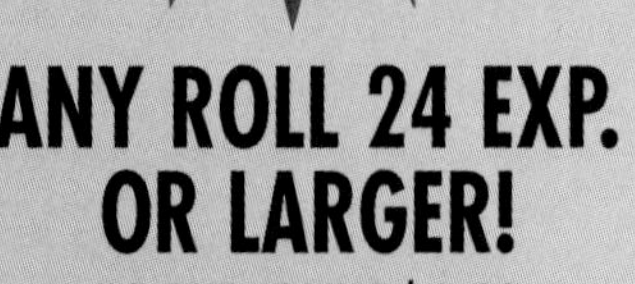

Hot Price
$2.99
Offer Good With Coupon #164

ANY ROLL 24 EXP. OR LARGER!
12 EXP. ONLY $1.99

*Some restrictions may apply.
Details in Store.

PHOTO EXPRESS™

#164
Good thru Sat., October 17, 1998
Coupon must accompany order

$2.99 Any Roll 24 exp. & Larger

2nd Set 8¢ per print
• 12 Exp. $1.99

RegularSize
ColorPrintProcessing
35mm and 110 only

OscoDrug Sav-on drugs.

A closer look at bean bag toys made by companies worldwide

CONTENTS

WARNER BROTHERS

Follow the yellow brick over to your Warner Brothers store to find the latest Wizard of Oz bean bags! These bean bags are based on the Oz children's books, first published in the United

Dorothy

States in 1900. When L. Frank Baum's first book, "The Wonderful Wizard of Oz," was published, it became one of the best-selling American children's books of all time. Baum wrote 13 more books and a few short stories about the Land of Oz, and there are about 40 books considered part of the Oz series, as many writers continued to write Oz books after Baum's death.

Scheduled for release in October 1998, these Wizard of Oz bean bags are sure to be hot sellers among bean bag collectors and "Wizard of Oz" memorabilia collectors alike. The bean bag line will include Wizard, Glinda, Wicked Witch, Flying Monkey, Scarecrow, Tin Man, Cowardly Lion, Dorothy, Toto, Lollipop Girl and Lollipop Boy.

This set will join the more than 45 Warner Brothers bean bags currently in stores, but do not delay your purchase because Warner Brothers retires characters regularly.

Glinda

Wicked Witch

Toto

Cowardly Lion

Tin Man

Scarecrow

APPLAUSE

With its large number of licensees – including such big names as Walt Disney, Looney Tunes, Sesame Street, Raggedy Ann & Andy and Peanuts – Applause has become a major player in the bean bag toy business. The variety of affordable, recognizable products makes the Applause line very appealing to collectors of all ages.

Among the biggest of the news flashes from Applause is the announcement of a September 1998 launch date for five new Disney bean bag toys: Mickey, Minnie, Donald Duck, Goofy and Pluto (see photo, left). Each new mini plush has a laminated hang tag with the character's signature on the inside left and some short statements about the character on the inside right. Mickey's tag reads, "Mickey Mouse is proof that good guys finish first. An optimistic outlook on life, an enthusiastic nature – these are the traits that make Mickey a real winner."

New Disney toys from Applause

Another Disney favorite – with a September 1996 launch date – was the popular 101 Dalmatians bean bag plush (see photo, right). With only 305,000 made, production of these adorable pups came to an abrupt halt in July 1997, when Applause discontinued them. There were six in the set of 7-inch playful pups – named Dipstick, Two-Tone, Jewel, Wizzer, Fidget and Lucky. The suggested retail price for each was $5, but each now is worth $8-$10 on the secondary market.

101 Dalmatians set

With the introduction of the animated movie "Hercules," Disney approved a license for Applause to produce Pegasus, a small white horse with bright, sea-blue wings and mane. Pegasus, launched in May 1997, was in production for only that month and had only 343,000 pieces produced. Pegasus' secondary market value is $8-$10.

The Little Mermaid set, launched in September 1997, featured four characters from the popular Disney film. They were Ariel the mermaid (10 3/4 inches long; 438,000 produced), Flounder the fish (7 1/2 inches long; 374,000 produced), Scuttle the bird (7 1/2 inches long; 267,000 produced), and Sebastian the crab (5 inches long and 6 inches wide; 362,800 produced). The entire set ceased production in December 1997. The suggested retail price for each toy in the set was $5, but each now can is worth $8-$10 on the secondary market.

Kiara and Kovu

The sequel to Disney's "The Lion King," called "Simba's Pride," features two darling characters who have been made into mini plush bean bags. Introduced in June 1998, Kiara and Kovu (see photo, left) are still in production and have a suggested retail price of $5 each.

Among the hardest-to-find Applause bean bags are the characters from Disney's "Beauty and the Beast." Released in October 1997, only 9,864 Belles and 7,920 Beasts were produced. The secondary market value for each toy is $10-$12.

Applause also has introduced several Looney Tunes characters in the bean bag market. Bugs Bunny, Sylvester, Tweety Bird, Tazmanian Devil and Michigan J. Frog were introduced to the retail market in January 1998.

The gang from Charlie Brown's neighborhood also occupies a big spot in Applause's lineup. Charlie, Woodstock and Snoopy were launched in June 1998 and remain in production. Each toy has a suggested retail price of $5.

In the August 1998 issue of "Mary Beth's Beanie World Monthly" we introduced you to the Nickelodeon Rugrats bean bags (see photo, right). With a launch date of September 1997, they remain in production. Angelica seems to be the favorite among collectors and thus is very hard to find. The secondary market value for Angelica is up to $15 even though the toy technically is still in production. Tommy, Spike, Chuckie and Reptar are not quite as hard to find and have a retail value of $5 each.

The Rugrats gang

Applause also manufactured a limited quantity of Raggedy Ann & Andy bean bags, with only 12,000 sets distributed in the six months they were in production. Launched in June 1997 and and discontinued in January 1998, Raggedy Ann & Andy are a tough couple to find. The couple's market value is $15-25.

Sad Sam and Honey are a pair of pups you would definitely want to take home. With big, droopy eyes and adorable faces, these 7-inch pups were released in June 1997 and remain in production. Each toy has a suggested retail price of $5.

Applause introduced the Hush Puppies mini bean bag plush in November 1997 as a marketing tool. The line, retired in May 1998, included six small Basset Hounds in the colors that Hush Puppies shoes are available in. They were each 4 1/2 inches tall and 6 inches long and came in the colors Miami Coral, Royal Purple, Salad Green, Beet, Blue Bayou and the Logo Basset. This original series was considered "hard to find" since its introduction, and on the secondary market each commands a price of $12-$20 each.

The Logo Basset

Applause introduced a new Hush Puppies series in July 1998

New Hush Puppies, clockwise from upper left: Berry Frappe, Bunting Blue, Chantilly and Jet Black.

with four new colors and the Logo Basset. The new lineup colors are Berry Frappe, Bunting Blue, Chantilly and Jet Black. These new toys sell for $5 each wherever Hush Puppies shoes are sold.

Finally, Applause put the Sesame Street gang into production in 1997. The word is, however, that Big Bird, Elmo, Cookie Monster and the rest are poised to retire by the end of 1998, so if you see any Sesame Street bean bags on store shelves, purchase them before it's too late!

DISNEY

"THE LADY AND THE TRAMP"

Disney introduced "The Lady and the Tramp" bean bags in December 1997. Since then, Tramp has undergone several design changes.

Although the Tramp swing tag says 6.5", it appears that Tramp continues to shrink. It seemed strange that Disney would list such an odd size on Tramp's swing tag because most Disney Mini Bean Bag Plush have a size of 7" or 8". The original Tramp measured approximately 8" and wore a brown collar, yet his tag said 6.5". This Tramp is very hard to find and even harder to identify. He is very tall and full. You can measure your Tramp from the tip of his head to the front paw to determine his size.

The Tramp variations

The second Tramp was produced slightly smaller than the first and measures 7". His swing tag, however, still says 6.5". His collar is brown.

Finally, Disney changed the color of Tramp's collar to a rust color. He measures approximately 7".

Released in Europe in July 1998 is a much smaller Tramp that wears a brown collar. His tag says 8".

Lady has remained the same during all of Tramp's changes.

"Lady and the Tramp" characters

In July 1998, Disney added two more characters from the movie "The Lady and the Tramp." Trusty is a light brown dog in a sitting position. His collar is black and features the name Trusty. Jock is a wonderful, dark brown dog with a furry mustache and eyebrows. He wears a rust-colored collar.

"TOY STORY"

The "Toy Story" characters – Woody, Buzz Lightyear and Alien – were introduced at Disney Stores in December 1997.

("TOY STORY" continued on page 196)

Woody: With and without buttons

This threesome was very hard to find when first released.

Woody originally had buttons on his shirt, cuffs on his shirt and one tush tag. When he finally began to ship again after a long absence, Woody had lost his buttons and cuffs. But before collectors could scramble to find the second variation of Woody, Disney released the third Woody with buttons, cuffs and TWO tush tags. The third version also has larger squares on Woody's shirt, though you can still find the third version in some locations with the original, smaller squares.

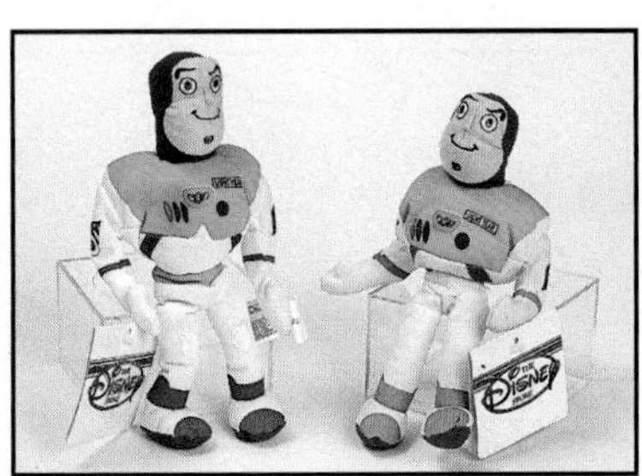

Buzz Lightyear: "V" and "No V"

Meanwhile, buddy Buzz Lightyear was also going through some changes. The original Buzz has kneepads and an upward "V" on the green part of his shirt. The second version of Buzz has NO upward "V" and NO kneepads. Three variations have been found in the color of Buzz's shoes: light green, dark green and lime green.

Alien: With sticker eyes (Japan) or with stitched eyes (U.S.)

There has only been one version of Alien in the United States. The Japanese version of Alien has sticker eyes instead of the stitched eyes found in the United States.

Buzz, Rex, Hamm and Woody from "Toy Story"

Available for many months only at Disney Stores in Japan is Hamm from "Toy Story." The Japanese version of Hamm is larger than the version released to U.S. Disney Stores, theme parks and Club Disney in July 1998. Many collectors want all variations of the "Toy Story" characters.

Also released in July 1998 is Rex from "Toy Story." This green dinosaur has disappeared quickly from store shelves.

To learn more about the Disney Mini Bean Bag Plush variations, jump on the Web and visit http://www.janetlynn.com.

DISNEY NEW RELEASES

Walt Disney continues to fulfill collectors' wishes to see all Disney characters as bean bag toys. Some of the latest releases are shown here.

Hen Wen, Gurgi and Fairfolk from the movie "Black Cauldron"

Robin Hood, Lady Kluck, Little John and Maid Marion (also available but not pictured: Prince John)

Pilot Mickey Mouse and Pilot Winnie the Pooh ... Pilot Pooh continues in the path of all Pooh bean bags. He is very sought after and demands a high price on the secondary market.

Tourist Mickey Mouse

Toga Mickey Mouse

Liberty Minnie Mouse

Hula Minnie Mouse

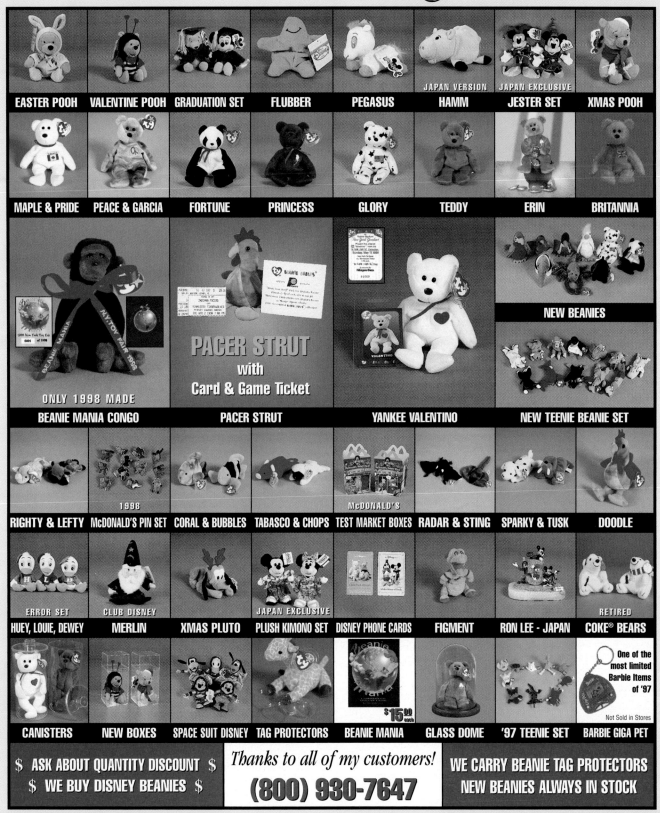

SPECIAL REPORT: Merlin signing at Club Disney

The first Club Disney event to focus on Disney's Mini Bean Bag Plush was a huge success!

From 8 a.m. to 11 a.m. on July 25 and August 1 at both Club Disney locations in California – West Covina and Thousand Oaks – collectors had the opportunity to purchase one Merlin bean bag with a special swing tag for only $6. The front of the gray tag says, "This Merlin Bean Bag was stamped at Club Disney and is authenticated with Merlin's signet. Do not duplicate. © Disney 1998." It has the Club Disney logo on the front and Merlin's stamp on the back. The second swing tag is the traditional Club Disney price tag.

The front of special Merlin tag

The back of special Merlin tag

Collectors lined up outside Club Disney in Thousand Oaks, CA, the night before the Merlin event.

The front of Club Disney

At one location, a line of about 300 Disney bean bag collectors had formed overnight. Everyone was in great spirits, and no one seemed to mind the wait for a limited edition Merlin. The entire cast from Club Disney was well prepared for the event, offering collectors tattoos of their favorite Disney characters and selling fresh donuts, coffee and juice to everyone in line. Once the event began, cast members escorted collectors to Merlin, who personally stamped his signet on each Mini Bean Bag Merlin purchased.

Merlin stamps one of the limited edition Merlin bean bags.

This stamped, limited edition Merlin is special for several reasons.

1. Currently, Merlin is sold at only two Club Disney stores in California.

2. The stamped, limited edition Merlin was available only to collectors that attended the events on July 25 or August 1 between 8 a.m. and 11 a.m.

3. Only 5,000 stamped Merlins were made available, meaning this toy may become one of the most sought after of all Disney Mini Bean Bag Plush characters.

The Merlin bean bag

After talking to collectors at the Club Disney event, it's clear that Disney bean bag collecting has become a hot hobby. Douglas Gee said he arrived at Club Disney around 6:30 p.m. the evening before the signing to await his opportunity to purchase the limited edition Merlin. Cheryl Schulman brought her entire family to the event, arriving at 11:00 p.m. for the night-long campout. Another collector brought her two sisters that were visiting from Hong Kong to the event. She said she wanted to show her sisters "just how crazy Americans are about their Disney Mini Bean Bag Plush!"

That line really says it all!

CAVANAGH GROUP INTERNATIONAL COCA-COLA

August 1998 marked the retirement of the first six bean bags in the Retail Gift Collection by Coca-Cola. These first edition 1998 Coca Cola Bean Bag plush characters were the first releases of Coke's plush line from Cavanagh Group International. They are:

- Coca-Cola Seal in Ski Cap, style CS0114
- Coca-Cola Polar Bear in Sweater, style CS0116
- Walrus with Coca-Cola Bottle and Logo Shirt, style CS0124
- Coca-Cola can in Shades, style CS0132
- Reindeer in Coca-Cola T-shirt, style CS0133
- Coca-Cola Polar Bear in Driver's Cap and Bow Tie, style CS0140

This set joins the already-retired sets from May 1997, September 1997, November 1997 Blockbuster Exclusives and the 1st edition of the White's Guide Kissing Bears. For more information on the secondary prices of these retired characters, see the bean bag toy buyer's guide in the center of this and every issue of "Mary Beth's Beanie World Monthly."

Enjoy 360 Degrees of Beanie viewing while protecting them from the elements with Crystal Display Tumblers and Crystal Display Boxes from Transparent Container Company. Need tag protectors? Just ask! Mini Beanie Baby products are also available. Minimum order for containers is one case. Join the serious collectors who buy factory direct from Transparent Container Company.

Protect the Ones
You Love Most.

Price Chart	0-250 pieces	250-500 pieces	500-1,000 pieces	1,000-2,500 pieces
400 x 608 MPP	$2.10	$1.85	$1.60	$1.45
300 x 500 MPP	$1.80	$1.55	$1.40	$1.25
608 x 408 x 400	$1.35	$1.15	$1.05	.90
514 x 302 x 200	$1.10	.90	.80	.65
SFC-BB	$1.95	$1.70	$1.55	$1.40
SFC-MBB	$1.75	$1.50	$1.35	$1.20

For orders over 2500 pieces, call for special pricing. Prices do not include shipping. Only full cases can be sold.

Buy Factory Direct and Save!

Crystal Display Tumblers
w/metal bottom
400 x 608 MPP
4" dia x 6 1/2" H
36 pieces/carton

Crystal Display Tumblers
w/metal bottom
300 x 500 MPP
3"dia x 5" H
32 pieces/carton

Crystal Display Boxes
608 x 408 x 400
6 1/2"L x 4 1/2"W x 4"H
36 pieces/carton

Crystal Display Boxes
514 x 302 x 200
5 7/8"L x 3 1/8"W x 2"H
40 pieces/carton

Crystal Display Cartons
SFC - BB
5"L x 4"W x 6 1/2"H
36 pieces/carton

Crystal Display Cartons
SFC - MBB
3 1/8"L x 2"W x 5 7/8"H
72 pieces/carton

Tag protectors available on request!

We accept  
MasterCard
VISA

Call toll free:
1-888-393-4413

Illinois residents call:
312-666-4413

Transparent Container Company

Transparent Container Company

345 North Western • Chicago, Illinois • www.transparentcontainer.com

CAVANAGH GROUP INTERNATIONAL HUMBUGS

Humbugs creator Tobin Fraley

In December 1995, Tobin Fraley turned to his wife, Rachel Perkal, and said, "You know what would make a great Christmas ornament? A Humbug!"

Not sure what he was talking about, Rachel asked him to elaborate.

Meet the Humbugs

"Well," he said, "A Humbug is a little character that runs around at Christmas time causing all kinds of mischief."

And that is where it all began.

Tobin Fraley began sketching, trying to determine exactly what a Humbug would look like. After several attempts, however, Fraley still did not feel he had captured the true Humbug. So, he decided to sit down and write a book about Humbugs and through the story somehow bring out what a true Humbug should look like.

As the book developed, Fraley met Betty Reichmeier, an artist from Kansas City, MO. Within weeks, Reichmeier had captured the look of the Humbug. Fraley described the look as "a cute, adorable little bug with a twinkle in his eye and mischievous sly smile."

This Humbug ornament is a holiday season offering.

Collectors will properly agree that Fraley has captured the essence of a Humbug in his new book, "A Humbug Christmas," and that the new Humbugs bean bags distributed through Cavanagh Group International are sure to be a big hit.

The Humbugs bean bags were to be introduced at collectibles shops in September 1998 with a suggested retail price of $8 each.

The line consists of four bean bags:

- Humbug, style AS9202
- Santa, style AS9201
- Scroogy, style AS9204
- Sleepy, style AS9203

Each bean bag is produced with the same attention to detail and quality that collectors have grown accustomed to in all Cavanagh products, such as Coca-Cola, Harley-Davidson and Save the Children bean bags.

The original four Humbug bean bags are current releases, but there are plans to retire bean bags and add new Humbugs to the line.

Fraley, of course, is best known for his American Carousel Collection. And yes, for all of you who are followers of Fraley's work, there will be a Humbug Ornament, Ride 'em Cowboy, featuring the mischievous little Humbug on a carousel. Other Humbugs products to be available for the 1998 holiday season include figurines, snow globes, cookie jars, ornaments and plush characters.

BEANY BEETLES

The Beany Beetles

Collectors have long loved their bears, dogs, cats and other animals in various bean bag toy lines. But now there is something a little different – the new "Bug-me" Beany Beetle. These highly detailed cars are introducing a whole new group of collectors to bean bags.

This line was designed and created by the owner of Starr Marketing, Peter Golesteanu, who first thought of the Beany Beetle when he learned about the new "Beetles" being introduced by Volkswagen. In January 1998 in Chicago, Starr Marketing unveiled a drawing of the "Beany Beetle," and the response was phenomenal.

Each Beany Beetle comes with a numbered tag and brief description. The original Beany Beetles are Junior (yellow and black), Bear (blue and white), Ken (green and white), Ray (red, blue and white), Dream (black and gray) and Larry (green and blue). The first Beany Beetles were to begin shipping in August 1998, and you can buy them at collectibles shops for a suggested retail price of $8.95 to $10.95.

Beany Beetles will be retired on a regular basis as each style sells out, and only about 50,000 beetles of each style will be produced. In addition, a limited edition, black-and-gray (Route 66) Beany was to be made available in September through "White's Guide to Collecting Figures." This piece will be limited to 15,000.

There are several deals in the works for other limited edition beetles to be offered through sports teams and various events in 1999. Collectors will also have several Beany Beetles to look for during the 1998 holiday season, including the Greatfull Vans, Single Cab, Pick-ups and Rollsbug.

To learn more about the Beany Beetles, visit the Web site at http://www.bug-me.com.

SILLY SLAMMERS

Drop them, throw them, whatever! Silly Slammers are bean bags with an attitude, and they are quickly taking over homes and offices around the United States. These round little balls are filled with attitude, and they don,t mind telling you. Some are round (about the size of an orange), while others are human-shaped with arms and legs.

Introduced in 1997 by Cincinnati-based Gibson Greetings, Silly Slammers have charmed toy collectors with their wacky phrases. Pinky, with its pink round face with bright red lips, tells you, "No way!" or "As if!" Ima Whiner, a purple fur ball with arms and legs, shouts "No fair." There appears to be a comment for everyone in the Silly slammers line. Each bean bag comes with its own swing tag featuring the Silly Slammer's name and some descriptive notes.

Some of the Silly Slammers currently available are:

- POLLY – Pucker up? You betcha! Her smacker's gonna getcha!
- BOTCH – He sounds apologetic, but he's really just pathetic!
- LLOYD – This yellow fellow says, "Hello?" and "You're bothering me!" because he's always a bit annoyed!
- STRIKER – Behind his soccer player's screams are World Cup dreams!
- JULIUS SEIZURE – If he doesn't get his way, you can bet someone will pay!
- COMPUTER – This one says, "Crash!" and "Goodbye, files!"

These and the rest of the soft, wide-eyed characters have made appearances on "The Rosie O'Donnell Show," "Live With Regis and Kathie Lee" and "Talk Soup" on E! Available through retailers such as Kmart, Wal-Mart and Toys 'R Us for a suggested retail price of $4.99 each, Silly Slammers are ready to talk back to you!

WISHBONE (Denny's)

Available exclusively from Denny's restaurants are two Wishbone bean bags. The first Wishbone is sitting down, and the second is in a prone position. Both bean bags have a leather-like collar with the name Wishbone on it. The dog is white with one black spot on his back. He has one brown ear, and the other ear has a brown paw print. The Wishbone bean bag has a swing tag that reads,

The two versions of Wishbone

My name is:
WISHBONE™
My TV show debuted
October 9, 1995
My buddy's name is:
(Here is a space to write your name)

The Wishbone bean bags are available for a limited time at participating Denny's restaurants for $2.99 each.

PUFFKINS

Swibco, the maker of Puffkins, announced in late July that Toby the whale would be joining Armour, Dinky, Drake, Pickles and Snowball in a life of retirement. Toby was born on October 11, 1997, and his poem reads:

Toby likes to splash and play,
He roams the seven seas all day.
With water blowing out of his spout,
He makes you want to jump and shout.

Toby the whale is the latest Puffkin to be retired.

The four new Puffkins from Swibco are, from left, Strut the turkey, Swoop the falcon, Omar the orangutan and Whiskers the walrus.

In addition to the retirement, Swibco also announced the release of four new Puffkins. They are Omar the orangutan, Strut the turkey, Swoop the falcon and Whiskers the walrus. This comes right on the heels of another new release announcement in late spring. Those five new toys were Bruno the bull, Bosley the bulldog, Crystal the white bear, Flo the flamingo and Grizwald the brown bear.

(PUFFKINS continued on page 202)

Bean Bag Bonanza

Amid all the new releases and the retirement announcement for Toby, don't forget the four limited edition Halloween Puffkins, which were to be shipped to collectibles and card shops in September. The limited edition toys are Ding the bat, Gourdy the pumpkin, Hazel the witch and Red the devil.

For Puffkins information, visit the official Web site at http://www.swibco.com.

SALVINO'S BAMM BEANO'S

Salvino's has hit a home run with the 3 Bs: BEARS, BEAN BAGS AND BASEBALL! What could spell success better than making a top-notch product that appeals to collectors of all three.

Each colorful bear comes with its own swing tag with a brief biography of the baseball player it represents and a Web site that can be accessed to get more information about that player. The bears are about 8 inches high and have the player's name and uniform number embroidered on the back. The player's number and "Denver Colorado, July 7th" are embroidered on the front chest. All embroidering is done in gold stitching.

Mark McGwire – St. Louis Cardinals – Red Bear
Don't miss the pullout of this bear in this issue!

The first series of Bamm Beano's were officially "sold out" before even one bear was shipped to stores! The first 12 bears were retired at the All-Star Fanfest in Denver on July 7, 1998. Salvino's took no orders after that date, and the production run was limited to the number of bears ordered in a three-week period. The bears were to begin shipping to retailers in mid-September. The first 12 bears are:

Dante Bichette – Colorado Rockies – Purple Bear
Juan Gonzalez – Texas Rangers – Red Bear
Ken Griffey Jr. – Seattle Mariners – Green Bear
Tony Gwynn – San Diego Padres – Tan Bear
Derek Jeter – New York Yankees – White Bear
Greg Maddux – Atlanta Braves – Tan Bear
Mark McGwire – St. Louis Cardinals – Red Bear
Mike Piazza – New York Mets – White Bear
Cal Ripken Jr. – Baltimore Orioles – Orange Bear
Gary Sheffield – Los Angeles Dodgers – Blue Bear
Frank Thomas – Chicago White Sox – White Bear
Kerry Wood – Chicago Cubs – Blue Bear

The Bamm Beano's

A second set of three Bamm Beano's – all representing members of the Colorado Rockies – were designed for fans attending the 1998 All- Star Game in Denver. This set consists of Dante Bichette, Vinny Castilla and Larry Walker. Each of these three bears is gray with purple stitching, which corresponds with the Rockies' team colors.

The next series of Bamm Beano's to be released for public sale will consist of:

Barry Bonds – San Francisco Giants
Roger Clemens – Toronto Blue Jays
Jim Edmonds – Anaheim Angels
Ken Griffey Jr. – Seattle Mariners
Chipper Jones – Atlanta Braves
David Justice – Cleveland Indians
Tino Martinez – New York Yankees
Mark McGwire – St. Louis Cardinals
Cal Ripken Jr. – Baltimore Orioles
Alex Rodriguez – Seattle Mariners
Ivan Rodriguez – Texas Rangers
Sammy Sosa – Chicago Cubs

With the very limited number of bears produced in the first set, watch for the prices of these bears to increase quickly and significantly in the secondary market. **To order Bamm Beano's, call toll free at (877) 725-8466.**

EDEN TOYS - BLUE'S CLUES

Since its premiere in September 1996, the television show "Blue's Clues" continues to grow in popularity. In fact, the Nickelodeon program attracts more than 12 million viewers per week. Episodes of the program, designed for preschoolers, air every day for a week to help youngsters learn through repetition.

A variety of Blue's Clues products

The show's star is Blue, a blue puppy who places clues around the world for viewers to find and figure out "what Blue wants to do." Another character, Steve, runs around looking for clues. Among the other characters are Mr. Salt and Mrs. Pepper (who stir up fun for Steve and Blue), a clock named Tickety Tock (clock), Shovel and Pail (who live in the garden), and Snail, who appears three times in every episode but is difficult to find..

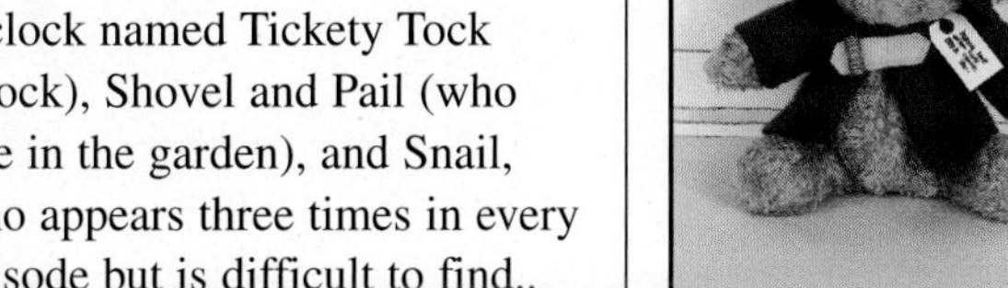

Blue's Big Birthday Book

Eden Toys has introduced a great line of "Blue's Clues" products, including Blue's Big Birthday Book, Clue Cards, Blue's Clues Utensils, Place Setting and Mat, Blue's Clues TV Play-Along Kit, 7-inch Velour Little Blue, and 10-inch Velour Big Blue with embroidered face and appliqued signature paw print.

TV Play-Along Kit

For a limited time, Subway sandwich shops offered four Blue's Clues toys in their kid's meals. The set of four included Mailbox, Blue, Tickety Tock and Handy Dandy. In addition, Blockbuster Video stores are selling a stuffed Blue that is about 10 inches tall and has Handy Dandy notebook tied around its neck.

To learn more about "Blue's Clues," visit Nickelodeon's Web site at http://www.nickjr.com.

EDEN TOYS - PADDINGTON BEAR

Paddington books by Michael Bond

Based on the classic book series written by author Michael Bond, Paddington Bear is celebrating his 40th anniversary this year. In 1958, Bond introduced this bear to the world in his first book, "A Bear Called Paddington," and since then more than 70 Paddington books have been published in 18 languages.

Paddington 40th Anniversary Bear

In conjunction with the anniversary, Eden Toys has released a 13-inch plush Paddington Bear that has the words "40th Anniversary Edition" embroidered on his coat.

Paddington Bean Bag

Of course, Paddington could not celebrate his anniversary without a Paddington Bean Bag. Also by Eden Toys, this bean bag is 9 inches high and produced from a tumbled plush. Paddington wears his classic blue coat and red bush hat and, yes, he has his trademark tag that reads, "Please watch after this Bear. Thank You."

This classic bear can be found for a suggested retail price of $16 wherever Eden products are sold.

EDEN TOYS - TELETUBBIES

First introduced in the United Kingdom in March 1997, the Teletubbies have become an incredible phenomenon, and their TV program first started airing on PBS affiliates in the United States in April 1998. The show, billed as the first to be aimed at children as young as a year old, focuses on the antics of four characters – Tinky Winky, Dipsy, Laa-Laa and Po – who live in cheerful Teletubbyland.

The small bean bag Teletubbies

Eden Toys was preparing to introduce the four Teletubbies Bean Bags in late August 1998. The small bean bag Teletubbies will measure about 9 inches high and will have beans inside. The suggested retail price for these bean bags is $8 each. The larger toys that Eden is producing are 16-inch plush Teletubbies made out of a soft velour fabric. The larger Eden Teletubbies, which will have unique textured faces and hologram TV screens in their bellies, have a suggested retail price of $20 each.

The plush Teletubbies

After Eden's initial shipment of Teletubbies, the next shipment will not be until late October, officials say, so if you want to purchase these toys, act quickly. Last year in England, the demand for the Teletubbies was so great that stores could not keep up with the demand. These highly-sought-after bean bags should be available in most collectibles shops.

SMOKEY BEAR

Smokey Bear has been part of American history for years. What child cannot answer the question, "Which bear helps prevent forest fires?" Smokey, of course!

Now you can have your own Smokey Bear bean bag. First introduced in June 1998 by Colorado's Bright Ideas, Inc.,

Smokey Bear products include, from left, the 15 1/2-inch 'Talking Smokey, the Smokey with Key Chain and the Smokey bear Bean Bag.

Smokey has a suggested retail price of $9.00. The tag on the toy says a portion of the proceeds from the sale of Smokey bean bags will be donated to the U.S. Forestry Service to help the agency promote fire prevention and forest preservation efforts.

You can find Smokey Bear bean bags at specialty stores and in many mail-order catalogs. You may also want to look for Bright Ideas' other Smokey-related products, including a Smokey with Key Chain and a 15 1/2-inch Talking Smokey.

GIRL SCOUT BEAN BAGS

Available exclusively through the Girl Scouts Catalog and local Girl Scouts stores are four cuddly Belly Beans. Produced by Mary Meyer Corporation in Townsend, VT, these Belly Beans are not just for Girl Scouts. The set of four was introduced in March 1998 and has been a top seller at stores nationwide. The set of lovable characters includes:

- DAISY GIRL SCOUT COW – a blue-and-white cow with tan horns and nose
- BROWNIE GIRL SCOUT BEAR – a brown bear with blue inside his ears and blue footpads
- GIRL SCOUT DOG – a green dog with blue ears, nose and footpads
- CADETTE GIRL SCOUT – a light blue cat with white inside his ears and on his footpads and nose

Each Belly Beans toy is embroidered with I ❤, followed by Daisy, Brownie, Junior or Cadette/Senior Girl Scouts.

There are no immediate plans to introduce new Belly Beans or change the first released beans. You can order your Belly Beans by calling toll free 1-800-221-6707 or by visiting your local Girl Scouts store.

Daisy Nicolette Solano, Brownie Amanda Ledvora, Junior Connie Ledvora and Cadette Kim Accurso pose with their Girl Scouts Belly Beans.

The Girl Scouts Belly Beans

Janet Leopold covers news in the world of non-Ty bean bags for "Mary Beth's Beanie World Monthly." She specializes in a wide variety of retired and limited edition collectibles. Her Web page can be found at http://www.janetlynn.com.

Introducing

THE ONLY CUSTOM BEANIE PROTECTION

CRYSTAL CLEAR
20 ML PVC
DESIGNED SPECIFICALLY
TO CUSTOM FIT
TY BEANIE BABIES ™

PROTECT
YOUR
TOTAL
BEANIE BABIES ™
INVESTMENT

ONLY
$ 1.29
ea.

- *SPACE SAVER*
- *FOR* ⟨ *STORAGE / DISPLAY / TRANSPORT*
- *PROTECTS BEANIE AND TAG*

SHELL 5

SHELL 4

SHELL 3

SHELL 2

SHELL 1

BEANIE SHELL™ MATCH LIST

Shell 1
st Dogs
Shell #5)
ll Cats
lackie
lizzard
ucky
Chilly
ocolate
runch
ubbie
Daisy
erby
Ears
Flash
leece
reckles
Grunt
appy
mphrey
Iggy
Inch
Lefty
Legs
anny
Mel
ystic
eking
ainbow
ingo
oary
eamore
Sly
noochy
Snort
plash
uealer
tinky
tripes
abasco
Tusk
elvet
Ziggy

Shell 2
Bessie
Bongo
Britannia
Curly
Erin
Floppity
Fortune
Garcia
Glory
Hippity
Hoppity
Libearty
Maple
Peace
Princess
Teddy (All)
Valentino

Shell 4
Bubbles
Bumble
Claude
Coral
Digger
Flutter
Goldie
Lucky
Speedy
Spinner
Sting
Web

Shell 5
Ants
Gigi
Rover
Scottie
Spike
Steg
Tank
Tuffy
Tracker
Trap
Weenie

Shell 3
Baldy
Batty
Bronty
Caw
Congo
Doodle
Early
Echo
Gobbles
Gracie
Hissy
Hoot
Inky
Jabber
Jake
Jolly
Kiwi
Kuku
Nuts
Peanut
Pinky
Pouch
Puffer
Quackers
Radar
Rex
Righty
Rocket
Seaweed
Slither
Snowball
Strut
Twigs
Waddle
Waves
Whisper
Wise

THE BEANIE SHELL™

NAME- ______________________
ADDRESS- ______________________
CITY ____________ STATE ___ ZIP ______
PHONE _____ - ______________________
FAX TO • (619) 265-7566 (24 HOURS)
TOLL-FREE PHONE ORDERS 1-800-552-3322
9-5 Pacific Standard Time (M-F)

MAIL TO -CREATIVE PROTECTION
5173 WARING RD. BLDG 28, SAN DIEGO, CA 92120

CREDIT CARD # ______________________
MC ______ VISA _____ DISCOVER _____
EXP. DATE ____________
SIGNATURE ______________________

WE ALSO ACCEPT MONEY ORDERS, CASHIER'S CHECKS
25 PIECE MINIMUM

Shell 1	
Shell 2	
Shell 3	
Shell 4	
Shell 5	
TOTAL # OF BEANIE SHELLS	
@ $ 1.29	
SHP./HAND.$ 25-100 pcs ($6.00) 101-200 pcs ($9.00)	
CA.RES ADD SALES TAX 7.75%	
TOTAL $	

Paul & Judy's

PJCC World Wide
"The Collector's Superstore"

Coins & Cards, Inc.

Phone (217) 543-3366

Can you spot the fake Flutter™?

Paul & Judy's did.

Paul & Judy's has been in the collectibles business for over 16 years and has a wealth of experience in evaluating everything from coins to Beanie Babies.™

Spotting counterfeits is part of our everyday work, and we use every technique available to us to provide our customers with the assurance that a product from PJCC is a product in which the buyer can have complete confidence.

As the first step toward instilling that confidence in our product, every Beanie Baby™ valued at $100.00 or more will include this tag.

The tag is your guarantee that you have a Beanie Baby™ from Paul & Judy's that has been carefully inspected to assure both its quality and its authenticity.

Every Beanie Baby,™ regardless of its cost, still has Paul & Judy's guarantee that it is an authentic Beanie Baby.

If you are not satisfied with your Beanie Baby™ for any reason, contact Paul & Judy's within seven (7) days of receiving your order and we will replace it or refund your money.

Get the PJCC guarantee.

Protect yourself.

Protect your investment.

This tag is your best defense against counterfeits.

BEANIES DRESS UP COUPLES' WEDDING DAYS

Ty-ing the Knot

Set the wedding date. Plan the ceremony. Hire the music. Reserve the reception hall. Order flowers. Shop for gowns and tuxedos. Hire the photographer. Mail the invitations. Buy the Beanie Babies.

BY JACKIE LA BERG

Buy the Beanie Babies?

That's right! Beanie Babies are a hit at birthday celebrations, within school classrooms, and now those adorable toys are standing witness as couples state, "I do." Step aside almonds, bells and netting, Beanie Babies are now capturing hearts at weddings.

Before tying the knot, engaged couples have many details to organize, and many are integrating fun into their festivities by using Beanie Babies as part of their matrimonial theme. Beanie bridal attendant gifts, centerpieces, balloon holders, and cake toppers are just the way to bring harmony to their special day.

Bridesmaid Veronica Cullen and other party guests are thrilled with George's roaring gift!

Sly and Roary: The Perfect Gifts!

In the fall of 1997, Cyndi McPike and George King were introduced on the world-famous Internet site www.match.com. Each was the first and only person the other met through the site – you could say it was "love in cyberspace." They got engaged soon after, and chose June 20, 1998, for their wedding date in California. During that same time frame, Cyndi found yet another love, Beanie Babies! Three weeks later, George couldn't resist and began collecting them along with his fiancée.

Roary and Sly show off their fancy ribbons for Cyndi & George's wedding.

The topic of wedding favors came up during arrangements for the Kings' upcoming marriage. Cyndi said, "We didn't wish to do the typical thing. ... We wanted to give a wedding memento that our guests would remember, something '90s." While on a Beanie Baby hunt, the future bride realized the answer to their dilemma – BEANIES! George liked the idea, and together, the couple decided that Cyndi would give Sly the fox to the male guests at the wedding (because her e-mail address is CyberFox), and George would present the ladies with Roary the lion (his handle being Bigcat).

Cyndi also decided that her Maid of Honor, Mayra Bernebe, and Bridesmaid Veronica Cullen would receive a Princess Bear as their attendants' gift – a perfect match with their purple gowns. In addition, Tawny Mears would receive a Valentino for her assistance with the guest book.

The next project on the agenda was to find 30 Slys and 30 Roarys. It took three weeks of Beanie runs to Casey's Ice Cream & Candy Shop, Beanie shows, and local stores to get the quantities needed. The couple ordered white and gold ribbons that would be

“WE DIDN’T WISH TO DO THE TYPICAL THING ...WE WANTED TO GIVE A WEDDING MEMENTO THAT OUR GUESTS WOULD REMEMBER, SOMETHING ’90s.”

(Left to Right) Veronica Cullen, Cyndi McPike (now Mrs. King), Barbara Bowman (the bride's mother), and Karen Butler pose with the tower of Beanie wedding favors they created.

“ty’d” around each Beanie’s neck. The ribbons read “Cyndi & George – June 20, 1998” in plum-colored writing. Cyndi hosted a pizza/Beanie favor making party, and photographer Jim Penrod was there to capture this enthusiastic event.

Mr. and Mrs. George King are ready to present their Beanie keepsakes.

Cyndi and George’s wedding went off without a hitch. Following the cake cutting, the bride and groom carried their baskets of Beanies throughout the reception. The reaction from the guests was pure delight!

“When we handed them a Beanie keepsake, the expression on their faces were priceless!” Cyndi said. Beanies were seen peeking out of pockets, displayed over people’s shoulders, and many even joined guests on the dance floor.

How did Mr. and Mrs. King spend their monetary wedding gifts? A portion went to (what else?) Beanies! The newlyweds added the “Mary Beth’s Beanie World Monthly” Pasadena Beanie Show to their honeymoon itinerary. There they purchased Tank and Goldie for Cyndi and Inky, Hippity, Floppity and friends for George.

Make That Happy Meal To Go!

May 22, 1998. Does this date ring a bell? It does for Erin Muench. Not only did her last name change to Silva on May 22, it was also the debut day for the second Teenie Beanie Babies promotion by McDonald’s. The game plan was for the limousine to pick Erin and her parents up at 3:30 p.m., pull into the McDonald’s

RSARY OF "MARY BETH'S BEANIE
:D EDITION HARDCOVER BOOK!

Only 25,000 copies of the October 1998 issue were printed in hardcover.

Available at select gift and specialty stores, at Beanie shows where "Beanie World" is in attendance, and on the Web ...
NOT available by mail or phone order!

Cover price: $19.95
(plus shipping and handling on Web orders only)

Don't miss out on this hot collectible edition!

To order this book on the Web, visit our site at http://www.beanieworld.net

CELEBRATE THE FIRST ANNIVE
WORLD" WITH THIS LIMITE

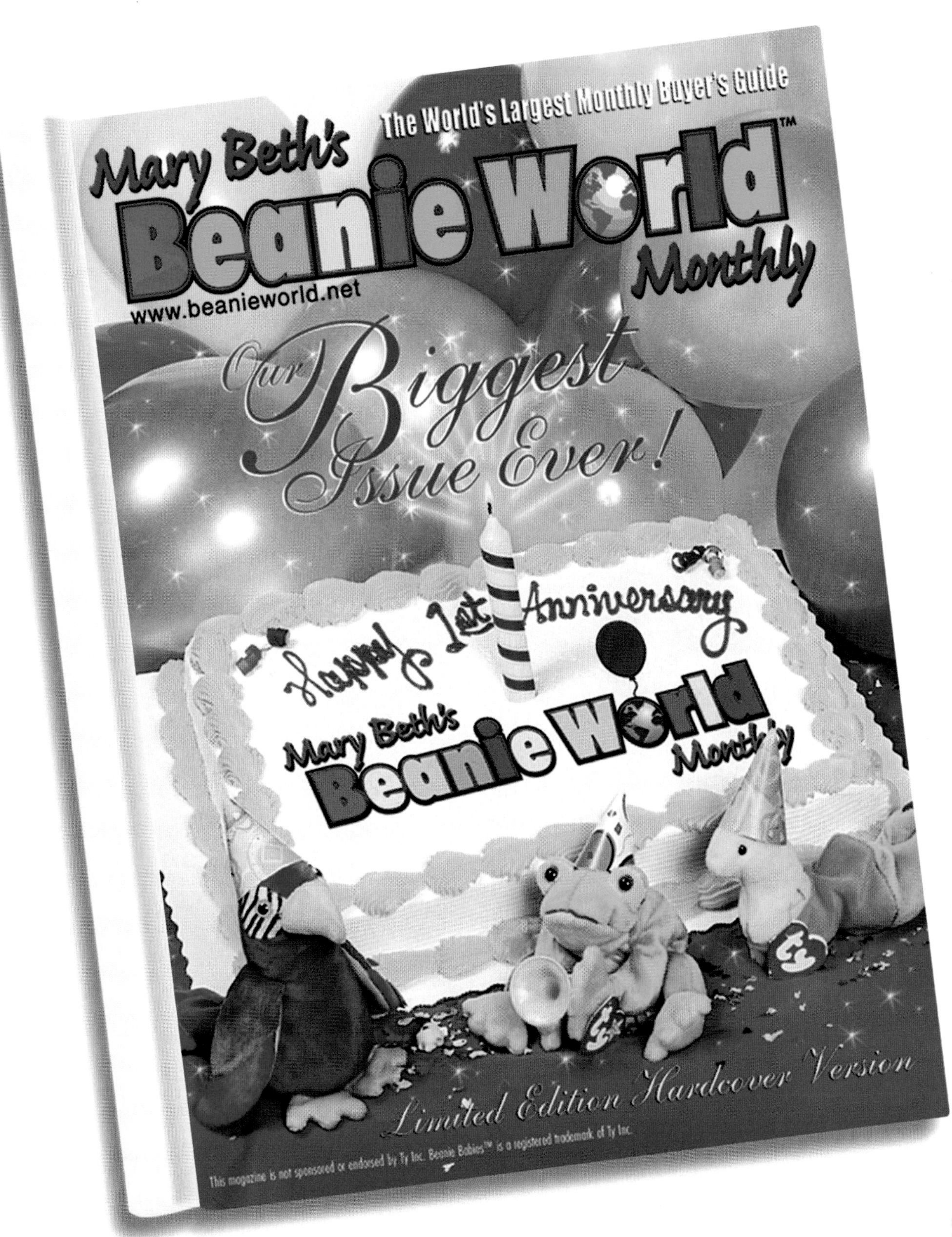

drive-thru to obtain Teenies, then proceed to Erin's wedding ceremony.

That arrangement soon changed as Erin and her mother, Eileen, drove home from their morning beauty shop appointment and saw the long line at one Chicago area restaurant. If they waited until later, chances were they would get stuck in line and be late arriving at the church. Mom immediately pulled into McDonald's parking lot and left Erin, who was wearing her bridal veil, in the car. Mom bought Happy Meals along with Teenie Beanies Bongo and Twigs. They missed out on Doby, the first Teenie.

An important phone call was made. The prior arrangement was for family friend Maureen Fiore to meet the bride and her parents at the McDonald's soon after 3:30 p.m. Maureen would snap an entertaining photo of the bridal bunch purchasing Teenies while riding in the limo.

Unfortunately, Maureen never stopped at home to retrieve the Muenches' answering machine message, and she waited at the McDonald's drive-thru for more than an hour. As a result, Maureen missed the entire church ceremony.

Now, let's rewind the story a bit. Upon Eileen and Erin's arrival home following the Teenie Beanie run, the father of the bride announced there was an important phone call from a local Beanie retailer. Eileen's order for an Erin and Princess bear had finally been filled. Glancing at the clock, Eileen realized she had only one hour until the florist and photographer were to arrive, and she still needed to get ready! She looked at Erin and said, "Honey, I'll be back in 10 minutes."

Well, Erin Silva (of Irish decent) was given her "namesake" Erin bear by Mom on her wedding day. In addition, Eileen's niece, Cathleen Anderson, presented them with Teenie Beanie Doby at the wedding reception. This bride's family never missed a beat on Teenie Beanie day!

From wedding arrangements to the ceremony and reception, Beanie Babies can offer joy and harmony to a couple's special day. I wonder how the newlyweds will celebrate their 1st Anniversary! ❤

Eileen Muench and daughter Erin (now Mrs. Silva) pose for fun with their Teenie Beanies, purchased on the way home from the beauty salon on Erin's wedding day.

Check out the romantic Valentino bear cake created for Shirley and Brian Gwynn's 5th Wedding Anniversary. (Photo compliments of Roger Pierce of Florida.)

Jackie LaBerg is a staff writer for "Mary Beth's Beanie World Monthly." She specializes in human-interest stories and is an expert on Beanie-related Web sites.

Wear the HOTTEST Tee's Around!

Here's Our Tush Tag!

SPECIALLY PRICED
Anniversary Sale!!!
Hanes Heavyweight 50/50.

Youth S,M,L. . . . . $10.99 + S&H
Adult S,M,L,XL. . $14.99 + S&H
Adult Tie-Dye . . . $19.99 + S&H
2X & 3X available for an extra $2

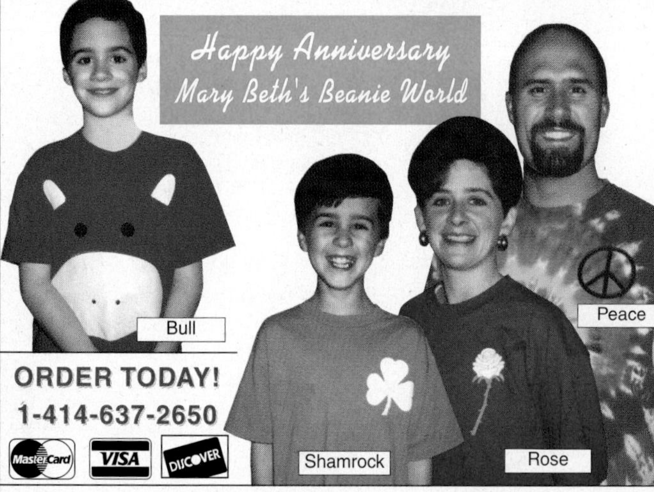

ORDER TODAY!
1-414-637-2650

Visit us at www.knochdesign.com
All designs © Copyright 1998, Knoch Design Corp.

S&H $3.00 per shirt in the U.S.
Call for outside U.S. shipping.
2-4 weeks delivery.

Rounding Third

4688 SE Harrison St. Milwaukie, OR 97222
(503) 794-6839 E-mail: rndg3rd@aol.com
Web site: Http://members.aol.com/~Rndg3rd
Visa/MC/Discover cards accepted

BEANIE ACCESSORIES

B & Z Heart Safe Tag Protectors
This is not a MISPRINT!!!
100 ct $12.00
1000 ct $80.00

Shipping charges: Up to 300 - $3.00
400 - 1000 - $5.00
CALL FOR QUANTITY DEALER PRICING!
Call us about our new Disney Tags!!!

Acrylic Storage Boxes
4"x4" x 7 1/4"

1-10 Boxes $2.35 ea.
11-20 Boxes $2.20 ea.
21-49 Boxes $2.10 ea.
50 or more Boxes $2.00 ea.
Shipping charges $3.00 for first 3. Each additional box, add .50 cents each.

Posters
$6.00 each
Shipping $3.00 for up to 5 posters

Coloring Books
Set of 4/$8.00
Shipping $3.00/set

Tags	Qty____	Total____
Boxes	Qty____	Total____
Posters	Qty____	Total____
Color Bks	Qty____	Total____
	Shipping	Total____
	Grand	Total____

Ship to:______________________
Address______________________
City______________ST__________
Zip__________Phone (   )__________
Credit card#______________________
Exp.Date________Signature__________

Make checks payable to: Rounding Third
4688 SE Harrison St. Milwaukie, OR 97222

The **BEANIE BABIES®** *Specialists*

Thousands Of Beanie Babies® In Stock, Including:
New Releases, Currents, Retireds,Teenie Beanies,
Meanies, Disney, and Grateful Dead Bears!!

http://www.toysfortoddlers.com

Protective Cases and Tag Protectors Available in Small or Large Quantities

"ALWAYS BUYING"

Phone: (813) 538-0015 or Fax: (813) 546-2006
7500 Ulmerton Road Suite 26
Largo, FL 33771
If we can't find it,
they don't make it!

Lending A Helping Hand

'SUMMER BEANIE BASH' IS A SMASH

A Beanie party takes the cake at Cedars-Sinai Medical Center in California

By Rena Wish Cohen
Photos By Mitch Cerrone

The limousine pulled up to the Cedars-Sinai Medical Center in Los Angeles, and for all the excitement inside the car, you would have thought it was Oscar night. After a 90-minute ride, pediatric oncologist Dr. Alba Sanmarco stepped out with four of her young patients and their mothers. Their Destination was the "Summer Beanie Bash," a Beanie Baby party designed to light up the lives of children who have had more than their fair share of darkness.

Sponsored by "Mary Beth's Beanie World Monthly" and magazine publisher H&S Media, Inc., the June 27 party gave inpatients and outpatients alike the opportunity to forget their troubles for a few hours and engage in a little hard-won revelry. From arts and crafts activities to visits with the Los Angeles Dodgers mascot and entertainment by an unusual magic act called Big Jerry and Little Jerry, the watchword was "fun."

In keeping with the Beanie theme, there were Beanies or Beanie-inspired trimmings everywhere: in the Beanie-filled centerpieces on the tables, in the animal-shaped balloons that adorned the room, in the Beanie-lookalike cookies, and – best of all – in the goodie bags the children took with them after the party had ended. Each child received a new Ty Beanie Baby and a copy of "Mary Beth's Beanie World Monthly" as a mementos.

"For families with children in the hospital, it can be such a stressful time. Days often seem to run together, and the only reprieve from a child's hospital room is usually the playroom," said Vicki Brunn, childlife specialist at Cedars-Sinai. "But when it was time for the Beanie Bash, the kids got dressed and went with their families to a completely different area of the hospital that they didn't even know existed. It was like going to a party at home, and it was an unexpected opportunity for an outing. Something like that can change a child's whole outlook on being in the hospital."

It was like going to a party at home, and it was an unexpected opportunity for an outing.

The fun began as soon as the children entered the party room at the hospital's Educational Conference Center, in a separate wing from where patients are housed. Girls were immediately outfitted with magic wands and glittery, ribbon-bedecked halos designed to make them feel like princesses. Boys received red baseball caps that in some cases covered heads made bald through chemotherapy.

Then Heart Throb the Clown (aka Linda Berman), made her Benjy the Dog puppet "talk" to the children and transformed their faces into butterflies and other creatures with special washable paint. 643DP, the Dodgers' talking-robot mascot, distributed action figures of Dodgers baseball players and radio headphones that one child clamped on the mascot's head under the misguided notion that the robot would be able to hear. Big Jerry (Robert Hartley) and Little Jerry (Robert Jackson), a 12-year-old boy with Down's syndrome (continued on page 214)

Lending A Helping Hand

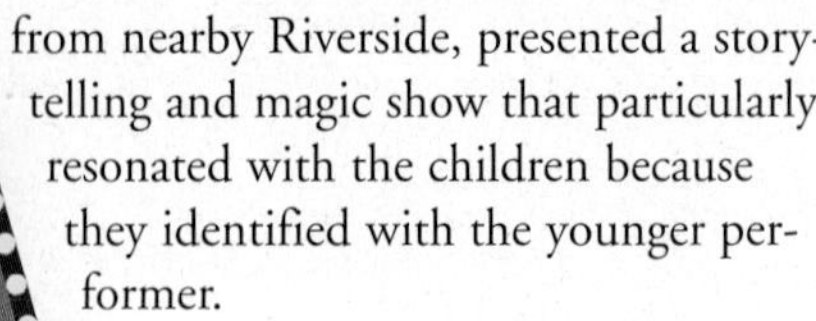

from nearby Riverside, presented a story-telling and magic show that particularly resonated with the children because they identified with the younger performer.

During breaks in the entertainment, the children busied themselves with making ladybug and bumblebee hand puppets, a "bubbly bug" noteholder that resembled the Inchworm Beanie Baby and picture frames decorated with rhinestones, animal buttons, stickers and pompons. The completed frames then were filled with Polaroids of the party guests snapped by volunteers from the nursing staff. The pictures were such a popular attraction that some children made two or three picture frames, and even some of the dignitaries attending the party got into the act.

The party was unusually rewarding for everyone involved.

The party also was a coming-out of sorts for A Special Wish Foundation, the third-largest wish-granting organization in the United States and the only one granting wishes to children from birth through age 20. Founded in 1982 in Ohio by Ramona Fickle, a hospice volunteer who recognized there was a special need to help children with life-threatening disorders, A Special Wish is just setting up its first chapter in California, and it assisted in preparations for the Cedars-Sinai Beanie Bash as a means of spreading the word of its new local presence.

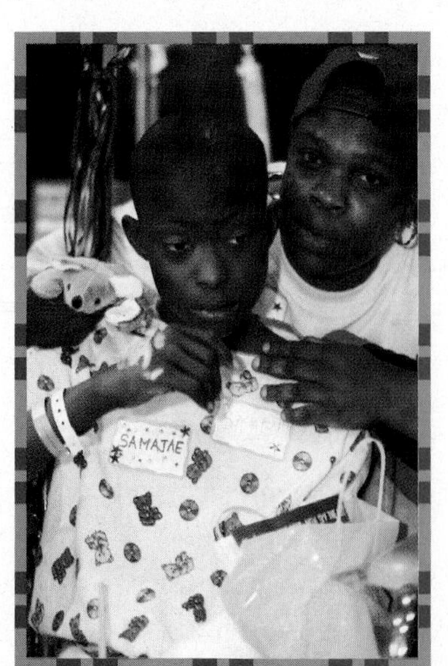

"There was never a dull moment at the party, and even some of the moms didn't want to leave," said Ginger M. Hall, representative of the foundation's new Inland Empire Chapter in San Bernardino and Riverside counties. "It was wonderful to see the children's eyes light up and to know they were having such a good time that even the most seriously ill could transcend their troubles for a while."

In addition to Hall and Dr. Sanmarco, a national executive board member of A Special Wish and a member of the oncology/hematology department at Kaiser Permanente in Fontana, the foundation was represented by Leonard Rodriguez, the organization's national director of program and chapter services, and Lisa Hardin, the national wish coordinator. Also in attendance were Dr. Joel Geiderman, medical director of the emergency department at Cedars-Sinai; Harvey Wasserman, president of H&S Media; Paula Eisen, president of Chicago-based DreamMakers and event coordinator for "Mary Beth's Beanie World;" and various childlife and pediatric nursing staff from Cedars-Sinai.

CEDARS-SINAI MEDICAL CENTER

July 1, 1998

Harvey Wasserman
H&S Media
3400 Dundee Road, Ste. 245
Northbrook, IL 60062

Dear Mr. Wasserman:

On behalf of the pediatric patients and their families of Cedars-Sinai Medical Center, I would like to thank you for hosting the Summer Beanie Bash. As you can imagine, spending time in the hospital can be a difficult experience for a child. Having normal and special activities during this time can be of great benefit to the children.

The party was a wonderful treat for the kids and their families. The arts and crafts were wonderful, as was the entertainment. I appreciate all the work and energy that Paula put into making this event a success. Thank you for ...onsorship and sharing the fun of beanie babies with our children.

... children, and Cedars-Sinai ... is greatly appreciated.

The party was unusually rewarding for everyone involved.

"There was one young man in a wheelchair with lots of tubes in him, and it was hard for him to sit up, so I just painted his hand," said Berman, the woman underneath all the greasepaint that turns her into Heart Throb the Clown. "It made me feel good just to be a little bit of sunshine in his day, and that's how I felt about all the children. It was really a special experience." ❤

For more information on A Special Wish Foundation, call (800) 486-WISH.

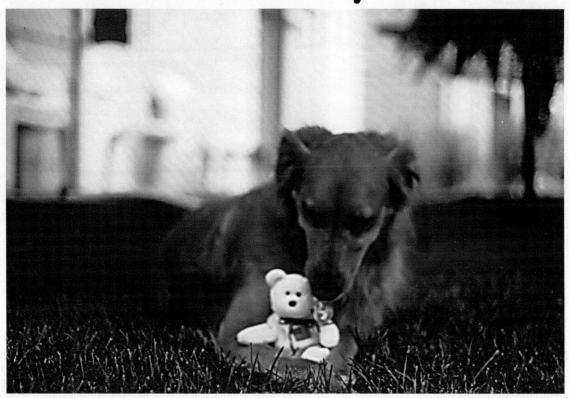

Lending A Helping Hand

Ballpark Beanies Thrill Kids

"Beanie World" and A Special Wish Foundation team up for special game

By Sarah Juon
Photos By Mitch Cerrone

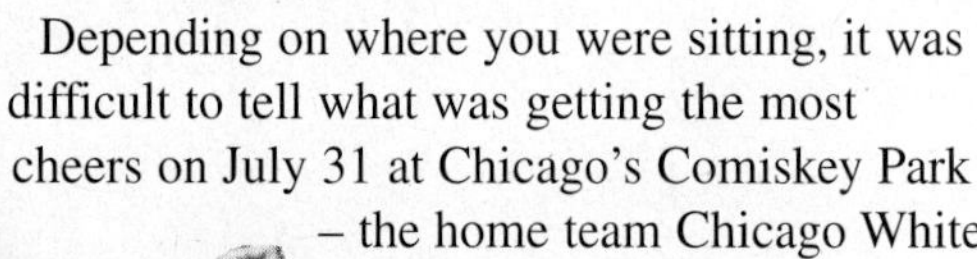

Depending on where you were sitting, it was difficult to tell what was getting the most cheers on July 31 at Chicago's Comiskey Park – the home team Chicago White Sox or Blizzard the tiger.

Twenty-five Beanie Baby collectors arrived early at the stadium on that hot, sunny day to be among the first 10,000 children ages 14 and under to receive Blizzard the tiger as part of a Chicago White Sox promotion. They all got Blizzard, and because they also were the special guests of "Mary Beth's Beanie World Monthly," they received a second Beanie Baby before the day was over.

The 25 children, ranging in ages from five to 13, were also the guests of the Chicago chapter of A Special Wish Foundation, a national not-for-profit organization dedicated to granting wishes for children who have a life-threatening or terminal disorder that is life-altering. Founded in 1982 and based in Ohio, the foundation is the third-largest wish-granting organization in the United States, serving children from birth to age 20.

Even though taking the children to the White Sox baseball game was not part of the official "wish granting" program (it fell into the "extra event" category), the outing that day did fulfill several wishes, foundation volunteer Kathy Taylor said.

"I've never seen them so happy," Taylor said. "I don' t think they sat down once. They cheered wildly for every home run and were dazzled by the fireworks displays. And since every single one of them is a Beanie Baby collector, they were unbelievably thrilled to receive those Beanies."

Taylor reported that most of the children had never attended a baseball game before.

It was a special treat for them to just be with their friends, or their brother or sister, acting like any excited kid for the day."

Taylor said one of the biggest highlights of the day was meeting "Beanie World" Editor-In-Chief Mary Beth Sobolewski, who visited a private skybox to talk with the children.

Paula Eisen of DreamMakers played hostess, making sure the children got all of the hot dogs, sodas and treats they wanted, in addition to their gift bag from "Mary Beth's Beanie World Monthly."

"Because they all loved Beanies so much, this was particularly fun for me," Eisen said. "Two of the children, Colleen and Daniel, are big-time Beanie Baby collectors. Colleen and Patrick were excited about recently receiving the Princess Diana Beanie."

The littlest children – Christopher and Kevin – were "blown away" by the whole experience of the game and receiving the two Beanie Babies, Eisen said, adding, "This is why I love my job." Helping Eisen that day were two other Special Wish volunteers, Lindsey Kleiman and Craig James.

The Chicago chapter of the foundation is unique because it is run solely by volunteers. Rory Dunne, a lawyer, serves as the chapter's president.

"I got involved because, when I was a child, I was given a wish by family friends at a time before all the wish organizations existed," Dunne said. "So I appreciate the values these wishes have for seriously ill children and their families."

(continued on page 217)

The most commonly granted wish, he said, is a family trip to Walt Disney World. The foundation arranges for the families to stay at the Give-Kids-the-World Village, an independent organization located about 20 minutes from Disney World that lodges, feeds and provides transportation for up to 30 families at a time.

The next most popular wish granted is for computers, Dunne said, adding that, "We are always looking for individuals and vendors to help us with granting this wish."

Foundation volunteer Taylor, who served for many years as the coordinator of wish granting for the organization, said that one of her favorite wishes was a 12-year-old's request for a shopping spree.

"We had a limousine pick her up, and she shopped to her heart's content in Woodfield (a shopping mall) for a TV, a bike, clothes, you name it." Another wish Taylor said she enjoyed was a bedroom makeover – new wallpaper, bedspread and decorations – for an 8-year-old.

The Chicago White Sox game, too, will be one of her happy Special Wish memories, she noted.

"You should have seen those kids dancing to the 'YMCA' song and how they screamed with delight when the TV camera zoomed in on them and they saw themselves up on the big screen. The whole time they were hugging those Beanie Babies for dear life." ❤

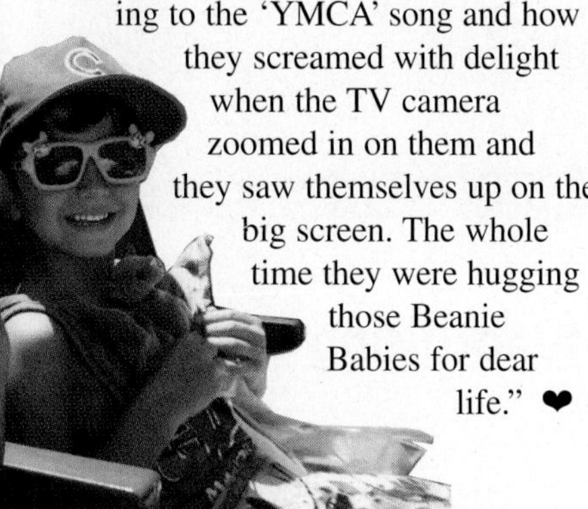

For more information about A Special Wish Foundation, call (800) 486-WISH. The Chicago chapter of the foundation can be reached at (312) 946-4328.

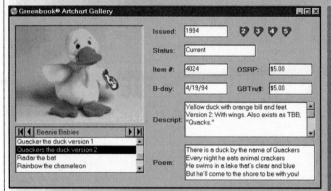

Lending A Helping Hand

Making A Difference

Youngster's limited-edition Mel raises $10,000 for Cystic Fibrosis Foundation

By Lauren Springer

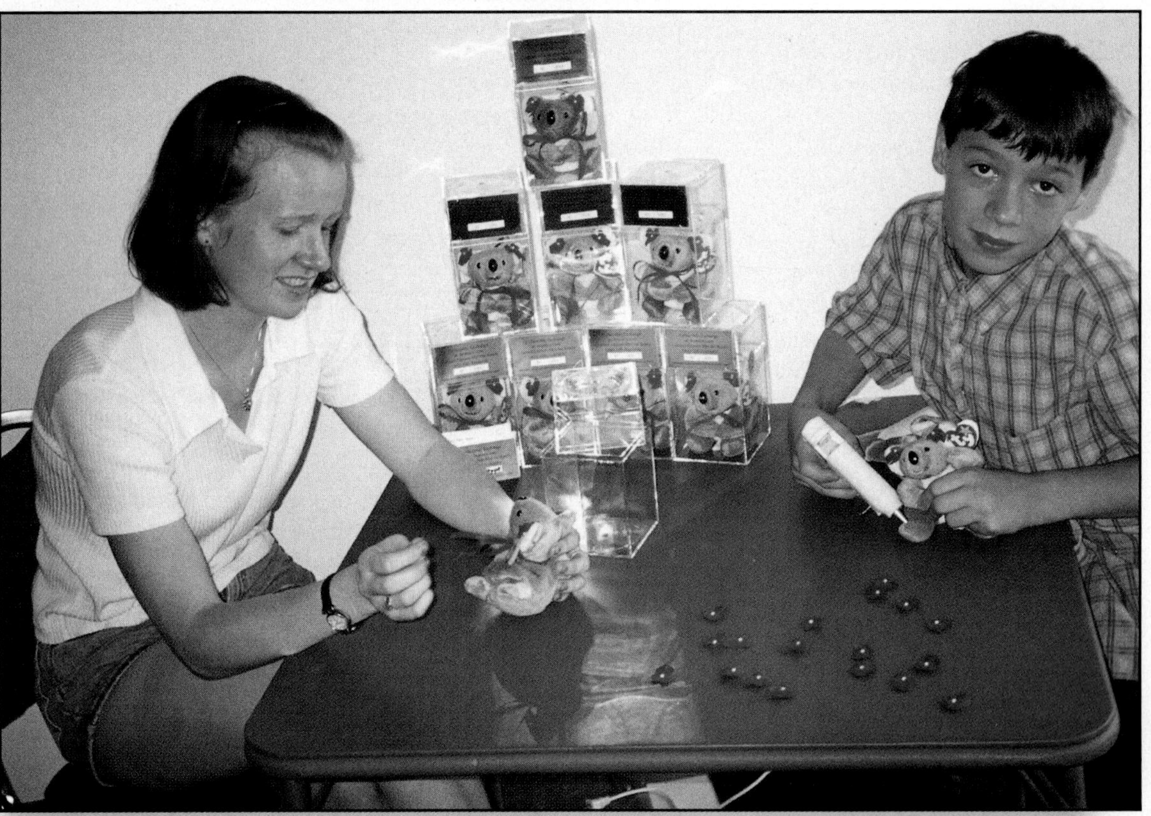

Heather and Michael Podraza with the fundraising Beanies

Imagine a child only 11 years old raising $10,000 and touching more than 30,000 lives. Well, that is exactly what Beanie collector Michael Podraza of Schaumburg, IL, did!

When Cystic Fibrosis, one of the world's most deadly genetic diseases, took the lives of two family members and afflicted a friend, Michael decided he wanted to do something about it. Michael, who is also the creator of the Collectible Exchange (a Beanie buy, sell and trade Web site that gets more than 50,000 hits a day), worked diligently to come up with a unique Beanie fundraising idea. He picked the Ty Beanie Baby Mel, his favorite Beanie, to offer with special limited edition cards. Proceeds from the sale of these Mels were to be donated to the Cystic Fibrosis Foundation.

The Mels, 100 in all, were packaged in acrylic cases with numbered Collectible Exchange Certificates of Authenticity. These acrylic boxes were designed with a special mount to display the certificate and sealed on each side with two limited edition Mel official stickers.

When asked why the certificate did not actually mention the Cystic Fibrosis Foundation, Michael's father, Dan, laughed. The senior Podraza replied that you just had to understand Michael. Apparently, when Michael gets an idea, he goes with it. Before Dan got a chance to confirm the details (continued on page 220)

Lending A Helping Hand

Michael Podraza's limited edition Mel

with the Cystic Fibrosis Foundation, gung-ho Michael was already in the process of getting the certificates printed.

A black-tie affair was scheduled at the Fairmont Hotel in Chicago on September 19, 1998, where Michael intends to present his big check to the Cystic Fibrosis Foundation.

Not content to sit back and merely reflect on his accomplishments, Michael is already busy planning his next fundraiser, which involves famous bear designer Sally Wincy. Michael is commissioning Sally to make 10 limited edition sets of bears called "Beanie John and Beanie Jean." The 8-inch stressed mohair bears are being named after Michael's grandparents and are said to be "Beanie experts." ❤

Information about Michael's fundraisers can be found at the Collectible Exchange Web site, http://www.beaniex.com.

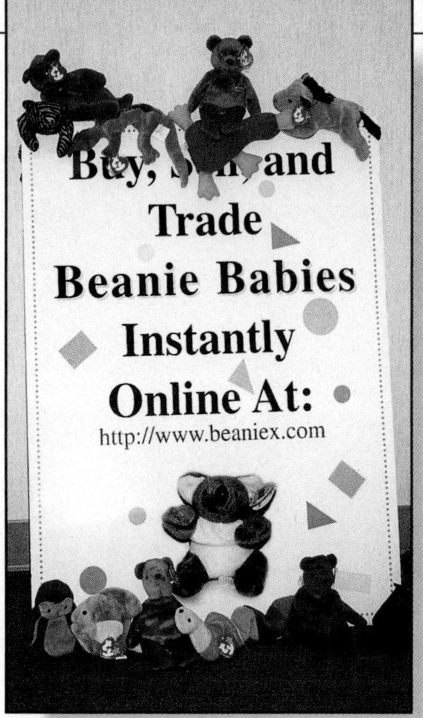

Lauren Stringer of Memphis, TN, and has been collecting Beanie Babies since spring of 1996. She is now the proud owner of a complete collection. She is an especially avid collector of the special edition Beanies and the sports promotion commemorative cards. She can be reached via e-mail at Snoop4BB@aol.com.

Mary Beth's BEANIE WORLD For Kids

HEY KIDS! Watch for our new spinoff magazine on newsstands in late October 1998!

CONTENTS

Mary Beth's BEANIE WORLD For Kids

MAIL FROM THE KIDS

DEAR BEANIE WORLD,

I'm 11 years old and another Beanie-holic! I have one suggestion about your price guide. I think you should put the Canadian market prices alongside the UK market prices. I would really appreciate it and think it would be very helpful to Canadian collectors. Thanks and keep up the good work!

Nadia Pawlosky
Winnipeg, Manitoba

Editor's note: Thank you so much for the great suggestion! You will notice that we now have Canadian values listed for the median values in our Buyer's Guide.

DEAR BEANIE WORLD,

We were excited to find your Teenie Beanie World Special Edition magazine during the McDonald's Teenie craze! It is a very informative and interesting magazine. It was the first place we have seen anything in print about the 1997 McDonald's 77 Beanie Baby display case. At 6 a.m. the first day the Teenies were available in 1997, my 5-year-old son and I saw the local store manager set this display up in front of this restaurant. My son was so excited to find out that he could win it and filled out an entry card right away. Two weeks later, the store manager called and told him we had won! We know there aren't many of these around and we feel fortunate to have one.

Ben Beach is the lucky owner of this valuable McDonald's display!

Lori and Benjamin Beach
Plymouth, MN

DEAR BEANIE WORLD,

I wanted to tell you about what happened to my friend. We were having a carnival at school and there was a place for people to bring in their old toys and sell them for cheap. My friend saw a kind of dirty Beanie Baby without an ear tag and bought it for 75 cents.

About five months later, his Dad called a Beanie store and asked how much it was worth. It ended up my friend had bought the Spot with no spot and sold it for $550 because it had no tag and was dirty. But remember, he only paid 75 cents for it!

Jarrett E. Fisher-Forester
Via E-mail

DEAR BEANIE WORLD,

I have been collecting Beanie Babies since 1995. I'd like to congratulate you on your magazine, which is Da Bomb! My life revolves around everything having to do with Beanie Babies. I have 30 Beanies and all 12 Teenie Beanies, along with your special edition, "Teenie Beanie World." Guess what? I have eaten McDonald's every night for the past three weeks. See, my life really DOES revolve around Ty Beanies!

Christine Calace, 11
Sound Beach, NY

DEAR BEANIE WORLD,

These energetic second- and third-graders of Hawaii Baptist Academy packed their Beanie Babies and went back to school for a writing workshop during their vacation. They thank "Mary Beth's Beanie World Monthly" for inspiring them to read, draw and write about the adorable animals.

These youngsters in Hawaii are proud to be learning with Beanies!

Dale G.
Honolulu, HI

DEAR BEANIE WORLD,

We wanted to do an interesting project for our Social Studies Fair. We decided to share Beanie Baby information with our fellow students. The judges seem to share our interest.

We named our project Beanie Baby Phenomenon and entered it into the Sociology division for group projects. We won second place in our division and third overall! We qualified for regionals and won second in our division, which qualified us for state competition. Although our project is now over, we will continue to collect Beanie Babies.

Abby and Ashley were big winners with their Beanie Baby project!

Abby Allums and Ashley Jayroe
Benton, LA

DEAR BEANIE WORLD,

I absolutely adore your magazine! I love that you have some places where your readers can have an opportunity to send in things for other people to see.

Kaitlyn McConnell, 10
Niangua, MO

DEAR BEANIE WORLD,

I am not a "serious" collector. I like to play with Beanies, so I won't buy them for an outrageous price. The one Beanie I really want badly is Erin. I think she's cute. I love your magazine because it keeps me updated on Beanie Babies and other bean bag toys, while at the same time makes reading the magazine fun and interesting! Thanks for creating a wonderful magazine.

Halle Bauer
Shaker Heights, OH

WRITE TO US

Hey kids! We welcome your mail. Please send your correspondence to: "Kids Mail," c/o "Mary Beth's Beanie World Monthly," P.O. Box 551, Mt. Prospect, IL 60056-0551. Make sure to include your full name, age, postal address, e-mail address (if any) and daytime phone number with your correspondence. Address and phone information are for office use only and will not be published. We regret that letters cannot be answered personally.

Have You been to ?

(the amazing new place to buy, sell, and collect)

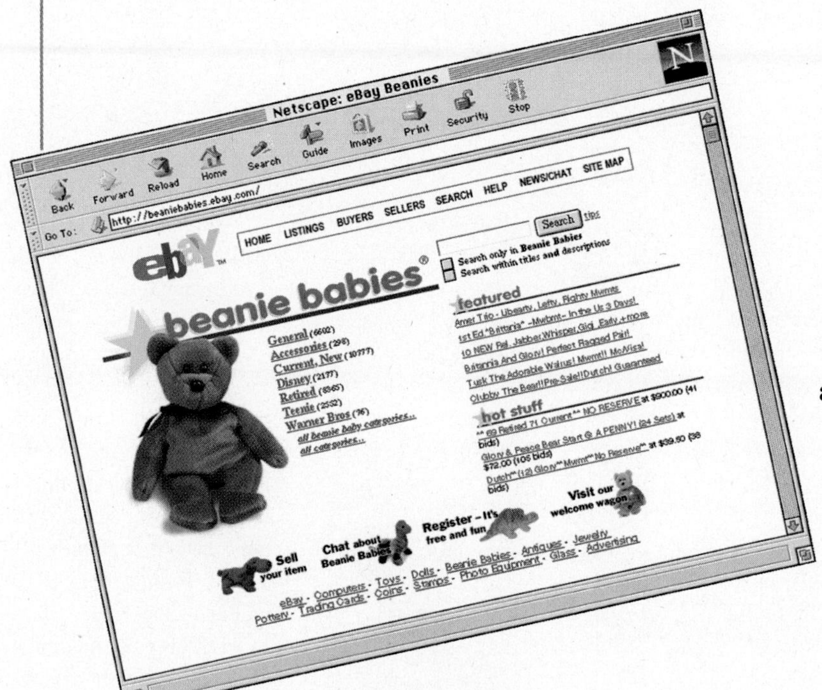

Welcome to the place where millions of people have already found success. The place where you can hunt through about 25,000 Beanies,

(thAt's a lOt of Stuff!)

where it's always the fun of the auction,

(YOU set tHe pRice!)

and where you're dealing with someone who loves the same stuff you do.

(who knows? You might make a frieNd!)

Welcome to eBay.

The online auction with 80,000 new things to see every day.

(you wouldN't want to miss a day!)

This is the one you've been hearing about – where millions of registered buyers and sellers get together to do business.

(whAt are you waitiNg for?)

So try it out – because even if you could find it somewhere else... what fun would that be?

here's how You Get there

www.ebay.com

and click on Beanie Babies

yoUr perSONaL tradiNg CoMmunitY™

Mary Beth's BEANIE WORLD For Kids

KIDS ASK THE EDITOR

Dear Mary Beth,

Are Disney Beanies worth the same amount if they do not have the swing tags attached?

Deanna Sommella, 11
Lehigh Acres, FL

Dear Deanna,

A Disney bean bag missing its tag is worth about half the normal price on the secondary market unless it is a character that was sold only without tags. Examples of these are Pain and Panic in their original bags and Duchess with a hard nose and whiskers sold only through the Disney Catalog.

Dear Mary Beth,

Is is possible to purchase only the tags for Ty Beanie Babies? I have a Nana and a Blizzard without any tags.

Nina Pomeroy
Alamogordo, NM

Dear Nina,

Swing tags for Beanie Babies are not available for individual sale through official Ty Beanie Babies retailer outlets. They are all attached to the Beanies in the factories in China, Korea and Indonesia. No Beanie tags are shipped to the United States without the Beanies.

Dear Mary Beth,

I was looking at a friend's Libearty and I noticed the tush tag had "Beanie" spelled "Beanine." Is this legitimate? If so, is it worth more?

Erin Crouse, 13
Asheville, NC

Dear Erin,

When released in the summer of 1996, the first shipments of Libearty had the word "Beanie" misspelled on the tush tag as "Beanine." Quite popular among collectors of Beanie errors and oddities, the misspelling does NOT appear to have significant effect on the secondary market value of retired Libearty bears. Oddly enough, the misspelling is more common than the corrected version!

Dear Mary Beth,

The other day I was at a flea market and picked up a Ty jointed bear named Scruffy. He has a second generation swing tag and the color is off-white. I only paid $1 and was wondering how much (if any more) he is worth. Thank you for your help!

Letitia Phillips
Sault St. Marie, MI

Dear Letitia,

Congratulations on a wonderful flea market bargain! This beautiful Ty Plush bear (Style 5013) was only available in this particular color for retailers to order in 1992. All subsequent years, the Scruffy was manufactured in light gold (Style 5013) or dark gold (Style 5012).Currently, if in mint condition, cream Scruffy is valued at $225. Great find, Letitia!

Dear Mary Beth,

Since Britannia is a European bear, she is very expensive in the United States. What is her price in Europe? Is she expensive or regular price? I have the same question for Maple. Is he cheaper in his home country?

Kristin Groggel
Oxford, OH

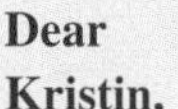

Dear Kristin,

Britannia's suggested retail price is between £3.99 and £5.99 UK pounds sterling, which is equivalent to $6.50 to $10 in the United States. Many UK retailers, however, have realized that there is an insatiable demand for these Britannias and are charging the equivalent of $200 to $500 in U.S. funds. Maple's suggested retail price is $8.99 to $9.99 in Canadian dollars (or $6.00 to $6.40 in U.S. dollars).

Dear Mary Beth,

I was looking through the August 1998 issue of Beanie World and I don't understand why it doesn't show in the Buyer's Guide about the Beanies that retired in May. Why wasn't the guide up to date?

Jodi B.
Via E-mail

Dear Jodi,

You've asked the most popular question this month! There's no getting around it, we inadvertently neglected to place the "Retired" banners on most of the May 1, 1998, Beanie Babies retirees in our Buyer's Guide. Nevertheless, the projected prices in that issue for those Beanies DO reflect that they are retired, even though they don't have the "retired" banner shown with their photos.

In addition, you may notice that some retirement or new product announcements may not appear in the issue that goes on sale soon after the announcement. For instance, the July 31 announcement of Attic Treasures retirees is not noted in our September issue. That's because our issues print about six weeks before the month shown on the cover. So, we've included that July 31 announcement in this issue (October). ❤

We welcome youngsters' questions about Beanie Babies and related toys. Please send your correspondence to: "Kids Ask The Editor," c/o "Mary Beth's Beanie World Monthly," P.O. Box 551, Mt. Prospect, IL 60056-0551. Make sure to include your full name, age, postal address, e-mail address (if any) and daytime phone number with your correspondence. Address and phone information are for office use only and will not be published. We regret that letters cannot be answered personally.

WHOLESALE

1430 E. SPRINGHILL DR.
TERRE HAUTE, IN 47802

800-334-1780
812-299-2181 • FAX 812-299-1435
www.springhillwhsle.com/beanie

Your complete Beanie Baby storage and display supplier!

All of our storage cases feature:

- Crystal clear for easy viewing
- Hard, durable acrylic
- Snug fitting snap-on lids

#48-C 4x4x8
Square Upright Boxes w/beveled edges

Packed 24 boxes per case
24 - 120 - $1.75 each
144 - 552 - $1.60 each
576 - 2376 - $1.35 each
2400 & up - $1.25 each

#570-X 4x4x8
Square Upright Boxes w/o beveled edges

Packed 25 boxes per case
25 - 125 - $1.75 each
150 - 575 - $1.60 each
600 - 1225 - $1.35 each
1250 & up - $1.25 each

Beanie Babies can represent a large investment. Whether you're a dealer or a collector, that investment needs to be protected. Springhill has a complete line of storage and display solutions!

#84-C 4x4x8
Full View Stackable
Available 9/98

Packed 24 boxes per case
24 - 120 - $2.00 each
144 - 552 - $1.75 each
576 - 2376 - $1.50 each
2400 & up - $1.35 each

#567-X 4x4x7 1/4
Square Upright Boxes

Packed 25 boxes per case
25 - 125 - $1.50 each
150 - 575 - $1.30 each
600 - 1225 - $1.20 each
1250 & up - $1.00 each

#279-C 4x8
Round Upright Boxes

Packed 24 boxes per case
24 - 120 - $1.75 each
144 - 552 - $1.60 each
576 - 2376 - $1.35 each
2400 & up - $1.25 each

HeartGuards Tag Protectors

A 1-piece locket that fits perfectly over the heart tag without crimping the red wire. With easy-open tabs.

100 pcs - 20¢ ea
500 pcs - 15¢ ea
1000 pcs - 13¢ ea
10,000 pcs - 11¢ ea

"Beanie Babies", "Ty" and the Ty Heart are trademarks of Ty, Inc. Our products are not sponsored or endorsed by Ty, Inc.

Tag Guards

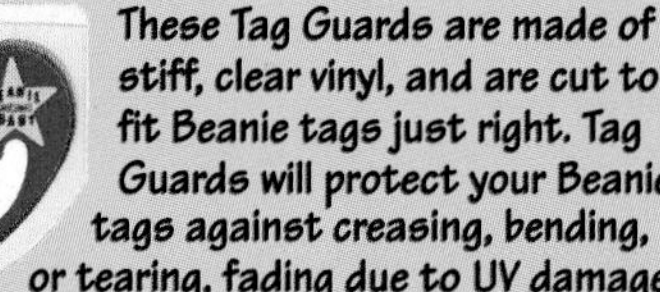

These Tag Guards are made of stiff, clear vinyl, and are cut to fit Beanie tags just right. Tag Guards will protect your Beanie tags against creasing, bending, or tearing, fading due to UV damage, or yellowing with age. 20 tag guards per pack.

12 packs: $ 18.00 (1.50 per pack of 20)
25 packs: $ 31.25 (1.25 per pack of 20)
50 packs: $ 55.00 (1.10 per pack of 20)
100 packs: $ 100.00 (1.00 per pack of 20)
200 packs: $ 190.00 (.95 per pack of 20)
600 packs: $ 540.00 (.90 per pack of 20)

Get a free display case with every 100 packs purchased!

Hard Acrylic tag protectors

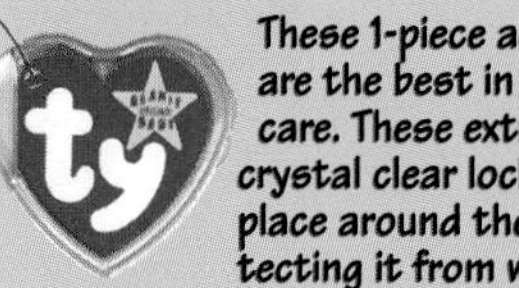

These 1-piece acrylic lockets are the best in Beanie tag care. These extra-hard, crystal clear lockets snap in place around the tag, protecting it from wear and damage. Each tag is poly-bagged for easy individual sale.

100 pcs - 30¢ each
500 pcs - 25¢ each
1000 pcs - 20¢ each
5000 pcs - 15¢ each

Mary Beth's BEANIE WORLD For Kids

YOUNG REMBRANDTS

"Mary Beth's Beanie World Monthly" is proud to showcase

"Slither the Snake" by Brad Carrabine, 10, of Wooster, OH

"Chip in a frog suit" by Jennifer Tazi, of Falls Church, VA

"Bones" by Alex Villasenor, 7, of Okinawa, Japan

"Ziggy" by Tori Carroll, 12 of Fayetteville, NC

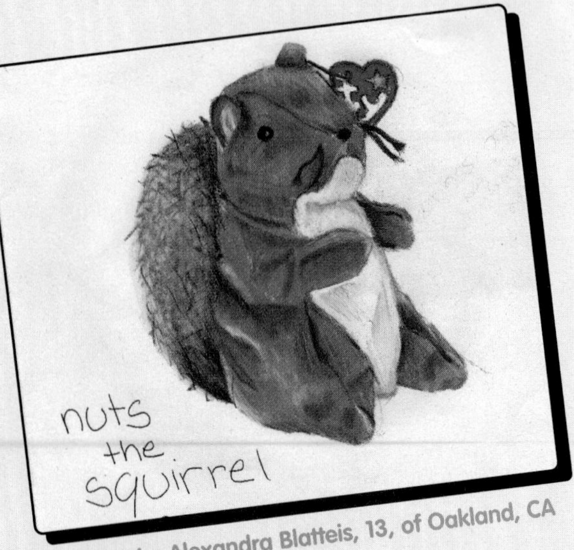

"Nuts" by Alexandra Blatteis, 13, of Oakland, CA

original Beanie artwork by youngsters from around the world!

"Seaweed" by Wendy Farrell, 13, of Fremont, OH

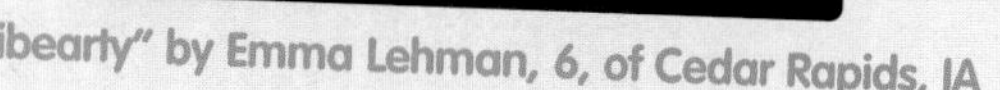

"Libearty" by Emma Lehman, 6, of Cedar Rapids, IA

"Glory" by Markie McManus, 6, of Morongo Valley, CA

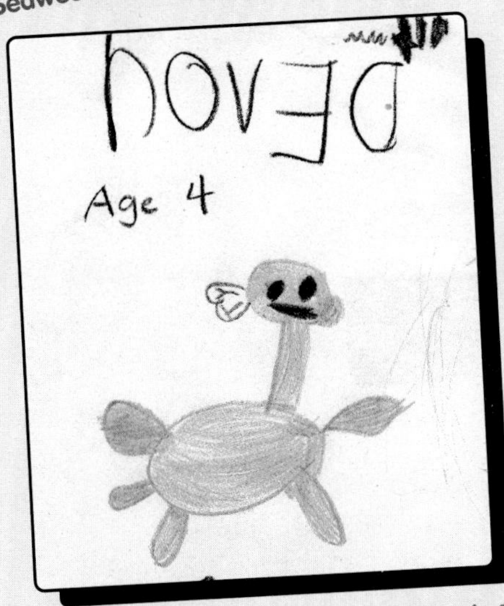

"Bronty" by Devon, 4, of Coconut Creek, FL

"Kittens in a box" by Miranda Pittman, 10, of Morristown, MN

"Jabber" by Joshua Lofgren of Amarillo, TX

"Humphrey" by Jodi Fettig, 10, of Petoskey, MI

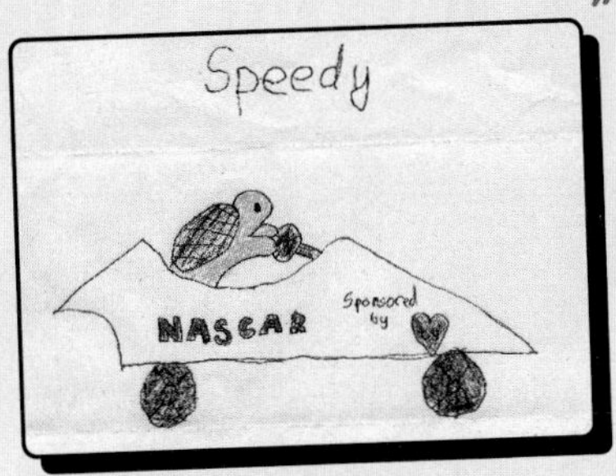

"Speedy the Racer" by Jaheed Ahmed Malik of Cheverly, MD

We welcome your original Beanie drawings. Artwork previously submitted to another publication will not be considered. Please send your drawings to:

"Young Rembrandts"
c/o "Mary Beth's Beanie World Monthly"
P.O. Box 551
Mt. Prospect, IL 60056-0551.

Make sure to include your full name, age, postal address, e-mail address (if any) and daytime phone number with all drawings. Address and phone information are for office use only and will not be published. We regret that the original artwork cannot be returned.

Mary Beth's

BEANIE WORLD For Kids

KID SPOTLIGHT

By Jackie La Berg

Oh Say Can She Sing ... for Beanie Babies!

Jamie Lynn Bence is well-known. She's so popular that on November 5, 1997, the TV game show "Jeopardy" had a question about her. Answer:"Sang the National Anthem at 18 Major League Ballparks last summer." Question: **"Who is Jamie Lynn Bence?"**

That was only the beginning. This adorable, sandy-haired girl from Hartland, WI, recently completed her ambitious "USA Tour." At age 10, Jamie Lynn is the youngest performer ever to sing at every Major League Baseball Stadium across the country. In just two short seasons, she hit all 30 ballparks in the United States and Canada, singing the National Anthem a capella.

Her reward for these performances? Beanie Babies.

At age 4, Jamie Lynn expressed a desire to sing and dance. She has taken voice lessons since age 5, and practices singing up to two hours per day. Inspired by Celine Dion, Jamie Lynn said, "I really just love to sing," and added that she hopes to have a career in singing.

Besides Jamie Lynn's performances at sporting and charity events, theater productions and festivals, this high spirited fifth-grader hit the big leagues on television. Her dedication, hard work and talent led her to numerous opportunities, including more than 215 radio and television interviews. Among them, she appeared as a guest on "Good Morning America," CNN, "The Vicki Lawrence Show," "CBS Up to the Minute." She also has starred in TV commercials.

Proving she had a song to sing, Jamie Lynn performed at a Chicago

UPPER RIGHT: Hugs and smiles are scored with Montreal Expos mascot Youppi. ABOVE: Jamie Lynn Bence hit the big leagues singing the "National Anthem." LOWER RIGHT: Jamie Lynn hugs her "Beanie" prize, Waves the whale.

White Sox game in April 1997. Her tour had begun. Jamie Lynn continued her journey singing "The Star-Spangled Banner" at ballparks across the United States. "O Canada" (sung in French) was added to her repertoire when she visited the Montreal Expos and Toronto Blue Jays, or if either of those teams was the visitor at a game in the United States. When asked how it felt singing before tens of thousands of fans, Jamie Lynn said, "It feels like you can stop the stadium."

And that she did. First the crowds drew silent, then unstoppable cheering and applause were heard, often followed by standing ovations. Jamie Lynn said she never got the jitters because "it's too much fun to get nervous."

After her performances, she always received a treasure she'll own forever: a Ty Beanie Baby from her parents.

Vicki Lawrence welcomes Jamie Lynn to her TV show in August 1997.

The Beanie prize was always a surprise. Her parents, Dr. Rich and Dawn Bence, ordinarily choose a style symbolic of the team where she performs. When she sang for the Detroit Tigers, Stripes was given; for the Florida Marlins, she received Pinky; and in Montreal, Echo and Waves were her reward (2 anthems = 2 Beanie Babies).

Jamie Lynn also received a couple of bonuses. Beanie Baby sports promotions were offered by Ty Inc. during two of her performances. She received Lucky and a commemorative card at the July 31, 1998, game in Minnesota, and Rover and a commemorative card at the Cincinnati Reds game on August 16, 1998.

Jamie Lynn now owns more than 120 Beanie Babies, and her collection keeps growing. Topping as favorites are Wrinkles and Tuffy. She finds Beanie collecting fun and challenging and hopes to soon be the proud owner of Glory, who bears the U.S. flag. Jamie Lynn also enjoys sailing, downhill skiing and of course, performing.

Rich and Dawn offer their daughter 100 percent support and are never far from her side. They tend to performance details with the help of Jamie Lynn's personal manager, Rod Beaudoin of Gerard Entertainment. There has been a lot to oversee, such as the stadium's sound system "delay," introduction copy and microphone height. All travel arrangements were planned by Dawn, and the Bences always included sightseeing excursions at each city they visited.

So what's next on the agenda for this inspiring young performer? Jamie Lynn has already cut one record, "A Kid's Christmas," in 1997. With the assistance of song writer Greg Gerard, she has original material and lyrics ready for her debut pop album. Waiting for a record label to sign, Jamie Lynn is currently busy at recording sessions. It makes you wonder how many Beanie Babies she'll earn for this performance!

You can visit the Star-Spangled girl on the Internet at http://www.JamieLynnBence.com. ❤

Mary Beth's

BEANIE WORLD For Kids

IF I WERE TY

By Jackie La Berg

Calling All Inventors

"Ty" on your thinking cap! It's time to create a new Beanie Baby – it's a snap!

KIDS, imagine yourself in H. Ty Warner's shoes. What style Beanie Baby would you invent? What name and birthdate would it have? What would the poem say? Well, here's your chance to give it a whirl. Sketch plans for your "original" Beanie drawing, using BRIGHT markers, colored pencils, or crayons on plain white paper. On a separate sheet of paper, neatly print the Beanie's name, birthdate (month, day, year), and poem. Then send us your Beanie creation! See the box at the bottom of this page for information on sending your work.

Firework the Fourth of July Bear, created by Brittany Shupe of Wyoming, MI

Wendy the Wedding Bear, submitted by 17-year-old Maron Harris of Grand Rapids, MI

Kelly the Jellyfish, submitted by Anna Woerpel of Burlington, WI

Earthia the Earth Day Bear, drawn by 10-year-old Vivie Nguyen of Diamond Bar, CA

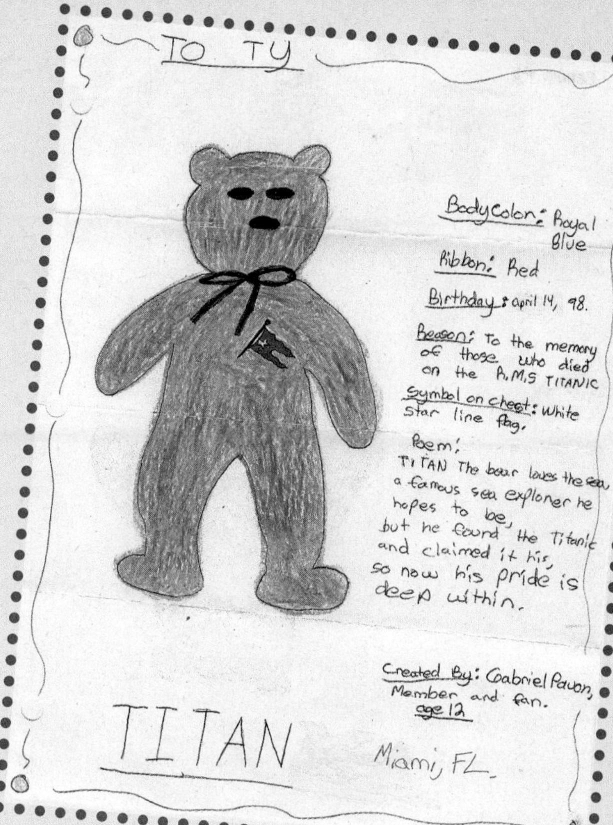

Titan the Titanic Bear, created by 12-year-old Gabriel Pavon of Miami, FL

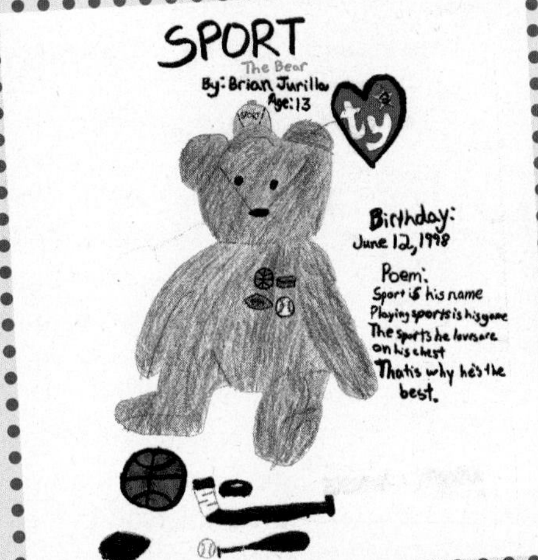

Sport the Athletic Bear, created by 13-year old Brian Jurilla of Moreno Valley, CA

Birthday: May 3, 1998

Poem:
On a tightrope, Whip will run.
She is a cat who always has fun.
As the crowd thinks she's funny,
She and her master keep all the money!

Designed by Jenna Stewart, age 9

Whip the Circus Cat, submitted by 9-year-old Jenna Stewart of San Jose, CA

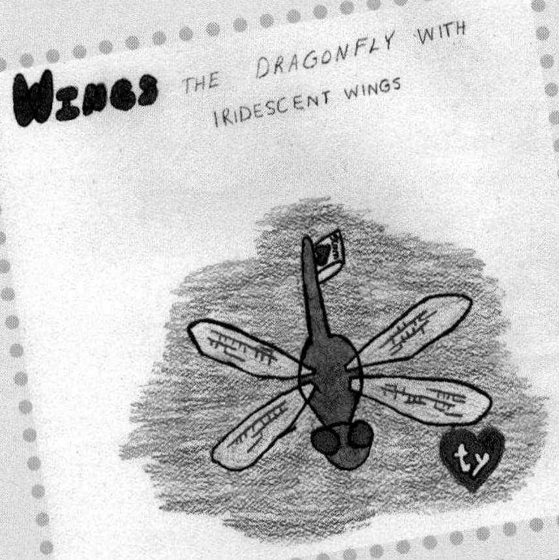

Wings the Dragonfly, drawn by 11-year-old Eric Scheller of Parma Hts., OH

WE WELCOME YOUR BEANIE INVENTIONS

Conceal your secret plans in an envelope and send to: "If I Were Ty," c/o "Mary Beth's Beanie World Monthly," P.O. Box 68729, Schaumburg, IL 60168-0729. Please be sure to include on a separate sheet of paper your name, age, postal address and daytime phone number. Address and phone number are for office use only and will not be published. We regret that your submitted idea cannot be returned. Have fun!

Mary Beth's BEANIE WORLD For Kids

LEARN ABOUT THE ANIMALS

Tracker the Basset Hound

By Lindsay Gomes, 12 years old

I love and collect all Beanies. Tracker is definitely my favorite. Normally, I'm a cat person, but I love Tracker's big eyes, droopy ears and short legs. Actually, Tracker looks a lot like a real basset hound.

A basset hound's coat is short, smooth and glossy. It is usually black, tan and brown (although Tracker is only brown and tan). The ears are very long and low set on its head. Basset hounds have large watery eyes that make them look sad. Their tails are long, thin and usually have a slight kink near the end.

The first basset hounds were bred by monks in the Middle Ages who used them to hunt small animals such as rabbits and deer. But how could such a small dog run after a fast animal like a rabbit? Their long ears and big eyes allow them to hear and see very well. Those help when they are hunting, but those aren't all that a hound relies on. A basset hound's nose can pick up almost any scent, so even if it loses sight of its target the hound can track it.

Some interesting facts about basset hounds:

- George Washington owned many basset hounds presented to him by Lafayette after the American Revolution.
- The syndicated comic strip Fred Basset features a bassethound who seems more human than many of the humans in the cartoon!
- The basset hound is used as an advertising logo for Hush Puppies shoes and accessories.

You can learn many other interesting things about basset hounds on the Internet. Visit these sites for to learn more!

- *http://www.kuai.se/~lhuntus/bh_faq.html*
- *http://www.lib.ox.ac.uk/internet/news/faq/archive/dogs-faq.breeds.bassets.html*
- *http://www.vethospital.com/fbbasset.htm*

Maybe with Tracker being released, basset hounds will become more popular and more will have homes. And all of this is why I love basset hounds! Especially Tracker!

Fortune the Panda

By Nick Mulka, 9 years old

My newest Beanie Baby is Fortune. I picked Fortune because pandas are endangered. That means there are very few left on earth.

Fortune is modeled after the Giant Panda, which lives in China in the cool, damp, bamboo forests. The bamboo forests are more than a mile up in the mountains. Bamboo is what pandas eat.

Humans are moving into the places where pandas used to live. The Chinese government made 12 reserves to protect the pandas from humans. A scientist is trying to clone pandas to keep them from being extinct. ❤

Are you a kid who has learned about an animal through Beanies and wants to share what you know with other Beanie kids around the world? We'd love to hear from you! Be sure to get permission first, then send your letter to: "Mary Beth's Beanie World Monthly - Kid Clips," P.O. Box 551, Mt. Prospect, IL 60056-0551. Please include your name, age, postal address, e-mail address (if any) and phone number. Address and phone information are for office use only in case we need to reach you and will not be published.

Mary Beth's BEANIE WORLD For Kids

WEB WATCHER JR.

Compiled by Jackie La Berg

Welcome to Web Watcher Jr., featuring kids' Web sites from across the globe. This section highlights Beanie-related sites created by Web masters ages 8 to 16. A new, rotating list of kids' Beanie sites will appear each month. Be sure to visit their fun, fantastic pages, and give them a round of applause for their dedication and hard work. Bravo JUNIORS!

PLEASE NOTE: When you retrieve a Tripod site, you may need to click the "X" in the upper right browser window box to view the specific page listed. It is recommended that children be supervised while using the internet.

Kids: just a friendly reminder that articles and text within "Mary Beth's Beanie World Monthly" – including Buyer's Guide prices and other information – cannot be reprinted at your Web sites with the written permission of the publisher. Thank you.

The Beanie News
http://www.angelfire.com/hi/BeanieNews5
Bonkers for Beanies
http://www.gurlpages.com/me/puppiedog/index.html
Beanie Barn
http://www.geocities.com/RainForest/Vines/1424
Beanie News Galore Online!
http://www.geocities.com/EnchantedForest/Tower/2808/index.html
The Beanie Universe
http://www.beanieuniverse.com
Beaniemasters Homepage
http://members.delphi.com/beaniemaster/index.html
Banks' Beanies
http://members.tripod.com/~Fleece2
Beanie Bananas
http://www.expage.com/page/BeanieBananas
Beanie World
http://www.geocities.com/EnchantedForest/Glade/6476
Beanieville
http://www.geocities.com/~beanievilleusa/

PUZZLES AND GAMES

IT'S TIME FOR RHYME...

WHAT WOULD YOU CALL...

By Dorothy Lamb

Each of the answers below includes the name of a Beanie Baby and a word that rhymes with the name. There is one line for each letter of the answer.. Can you figure out each answer from the clues provided? The first one is done for you. For the answers, see page 236. Good luck!

1. a bull who isn't very tall? SHORT SNORT
2. a flamingo who really needs a bath? _ _ _ _ _ _   _ _ _ _ _
3. a bashful fox? _ _ _   _ _ _
4. a spider who lost weight? _ _ _ _ _ _ _   _ _ _ _ _ _ _
5. a skunk who opens and closes his eyes? _ _ _ _ _ _   _ _ _ _ _ _
6. a terrier who has just been brushed? _ _ _ _ _ _   _ _ _ _ _
7. a beaver who just won the lottery? _ _ _ _ _   _ _ _ _ _
8. a unicorn who paints great pictures? _ _ _ _ _ _ _ _   _ _ _ _ _ _
9. a cow who likes to lay around and do nothing? _ _ _ _   _ _ _ _ _
10. a parrot who tells things he shouldn't? _ _ _ _ _ _ _   _ _ _ _ _ _
11. a brown bear who arrives ahead of time? _ _ _ _ _   _ _ _ _ _
12. a bat who talks a lot? _ _ _ _ _ _   _ _ _ _ _
13. a counterfeit mallard duck? _ _ _ _   _ _ _ _
14. a St. Bernard who practices law? _ _ _ _ _ _ _ _   _ _ _ _ _ _
15. a black bear who acts crazy? _ _ _ _ _   _ _ _ _ _ _ _
16. a polar bear who looks ridiculous? _ _ _ _ _   _ _ _ _ _ _
17. an iguana with bad table manners? _ _ _ _ _   _ _ _ _
18. a brown bear who just got all dirty? _ _ _ _ _ _   _ _ _ _ _ _
19. a red crab who just grew? _ _ _ _ _ _   _ _ _ _ _ _
20. a lizard who spins around too long? _ _ _ _ _   _ _ _ _ _
21. a manatee who has a grandchild? _ _ _ _ _ _   _ _ _ _ _
22. a powerful elephant? _ _ _ _ _ _   _ _ _ _ _ _
23. a turtle who eats all of the food? _ _ _ _ _ _   _ _ _ _ _ _
24. a dog who has been in the sun too long? _ _ _   _ _ _ _
25. a puffin who gets stronger? _ _ _ _ _ _ _   _ _ _ _ _ _

WHAT WOULD YOU DO IF...

26. a cockatoo gets dirty? _ _ _ _ _ _ _   _ _ _ _
27. a crab puts on a great performance? _ _ _ _ _ _ _   _ _ _ _ _ _
28. you want to keep a blue jay with you? _ _ _ _ _ _   _ _ _ _ _ _
29. you want to send a Siamese cat to a friend? _ _ _ _   _ _ _ _
30. you see a tie-dyed bear tied up? _ _ _ _ _ _ _   _ _ _ _ _
31. you want everyone to know that the brown cat has arrived? _ _ _ _ _ _ _ _   _ _ _ _ _ _
32. a sea otter gets hungry? _ _ _ _   _ _ _ _ _ _ _
33. you want to please an owl? _ _ _ _   _ _ _ _
34. you want to take a stingray with you? _ _ _ _ _   _ _ _ _ _
35. you want to give Trap for a present? _ _ _ _   _ _ _ _
36. you prefer a rhinoceros for a friend? _ _ _ _   _ _ _ _ _

Mary Beth's

BEANIE WORLD For Kids

PUZZLES AND GAMES

IT'S TIME FOR RHYME...ANSWERS

1. SHORT SNORT
2. STINKY PINKY
3. SHY SLY
4. THINNER SPINNER
5. BLINKY STINKY
6. FLUFFY TUFFY
7. LUCKY BUCKY
8. ARTISTIC MYSTIC
9. LAZY DAISY
10. BLABBER JABBER
11. EARLY CURLY
12. CHATTY BATTY
13. FAKE JAKE
14. ATTORNEY BERNIE
15. WACKY BLACKIE
16. SILLY CHILLY
17. PIGGY IGGY
18. GRUBBY CUBBIE
19. BIGGER DIGGER
20. DIZZY LIZZY
21. GRANNY MANNY
22. MIGHTY RIGHTY
23. GREEDY SPEEDY
24. HOT SPOT
25. TOUGHER PUFFER
26. SHAMPOO KUKU
27. APPLAUD CLAUDE
28. POCKET ROCKET
29. SHIP SNIP
30. RELEASE PEACE
31. ANNOUNCE POUNCE
32. FEED SEAWEED
33. SUIT HOOT
34. BRING STING
35. WRAP TRAP
36. LIKE SPIKE

LIBEARTY REPORTING

Mary Beth's BEANIE WORLD For Kids

This is Libearty reporting from the Hungarian Embassy ... I am here for a special reception for the Christian Embassy. As I stated in my last report, my plan was to tell you about this lovely place and its Ambassador, but some breaking news has pre-empted that report — I'll give you it later.

One of the couples I met during this reception was Ambassador Bogan from Papua New Guinea and his lovely wife, Lady Nora Bogan. You may have read in the newspaper that a huge disaster struck their island nation on July 19. In the town of Aitape, in the West Sepik province and on the northern side, a tsunami (sue-nah-mee) came ashore. A tsunami is a wall of water — this one was 23-feet tall — sometimes called a Tidal Wave. Caused by an underwater earthquake or volcano, a tsunami is capable of moving hundreds of miles per hour. When it crashes on to the land it will literally level everything in its path and drown hundreds, if not thousands, of people. The death toll in Papua New Guinea is over 2,000, with another 5 to 6,000 missing. The majority of people missing are children.

Papua New Guinea is one of the largest islands in the world, second only to Greenland. It is located in the southwest Pacific Ocean, just below the Equator; as part of the eastern Malay archipelago, or East Indies, it sits 93 miles north of Australia. The island covers 310,000 square miles; it's 1,500 miles long and 400 miles wide. More than 70 percent of the country is covered with a dense tropical rain forest housing many endangered species. Port Moresby is the capital and largest city. One of its most famous cities, Lae, is known as Amelia Earhart's last departure point before her disappearance in June of 1937. Today Lae is home to one of the two universities on Papua New Guinea.

The island is known for its diversity and variety, with over 700 languages spoken by the more than four million residents. Although English is the "official" language, Melanesian Pidgin and Motu are used by half of the island. Their government is led by the prime minister, who heads the majority party in the single chamber National Parliament. (Remember last month when I reported from the Capitol in Washington D.C. and I told you our government had two chambers ... the House of Representatives and the Senate?) This nation has sent the Honorable Bogan to Washington D.C. to be their representative, a kind of ambassador. It is especially important for him to be present in times of national disaster such as the one created by this horrific tsunami. The islands of the southwest Pacific are usually self-sufficient, harvesting crops like sweet potatoes, taro and coconuts — but in times of disaster we all need help. Ambassador Bogan is actively coordinating the relief effort here in the states for his nation. They are accepting cash donations, clothing, blankets and household items.

You can imagine the devastation of losing everything in such a disaster. One man was quoted as saying that they plan to rebuild on higher ground but can't because they don't have the tools to build. If you would like to help, you can send a check payable to the Aitape Disaster Relief Fund, c/o Papua New Guinea Embassy, 165 New Hampshire N.W., Suite 300, Washington D.C. 20009 or call the Embassy at (202) 745-3680 to arrange to send goods. As you can imagine, all help will be gladly accepted. ❤

Mary Beth's

BEANIE WORLD For Kids

KID CLIPS

Gracie's Day

by Amanda Weigler, Age 6 of Pennsville, NJ

Once upon a time there was a swan. Her name was Gracie. She was all alone. Then she heard some bubbles. It came up to her and it was a fish. Bubbles asked, "What are you doing and why are you standing here doing nothing?"

Gracie responded,"Oh, nothing. Just sitting here."

Bubbles the fish went away. Soon, Gracie heard some other bubbles in the water around her. It was Ally the alligator.

Ally said, "Why are you just sitting here? You should be catching fish or swimming around or doing something."

"Well Ally, I don't want to be splashing around, swimming or doing anything," replied Gracie. And then Ally said, "OK, bye ... see ya," and swam off.

Suddenly, Gracie felt splashed – it was Legs the frog! She saw some other bubbles and then up came the frog.

Gracie asked, "Why did you splash me?"

"Because frogs are SUPPOSED to splash!" said Legs.

Gracie said, "Then why don't you splash somewhere else because I don't want to get splashed or have fun right now." So, Legs swam off.

Then Gracie saw some movements from the in the water. Along came a nice, yellow duck. He said, "Hi, my name is Quackers." And he was eating Cracker Jacks and crackers. "Why are you eating Cracker Jacks and crackers?" Gracie asked.

"Can't you guess?" Quackers explained, "it's because I LIKE them! Why don't you swim around the pond instead of having all these noises everywhere?"

"Good idea! Hey, Quackers ... why don't you come with me?" said Gracie. "OK, let's go!" said Quackers. And so they swam off – together! ❤

BEANIE PROJECTS

Bumble Bee Hand Puppet

This hand puppet based on the Ty Beanie named Bumble is an easy-to-create craft that will delight young and old alike.

MATERIALS YOU'LL NEED THE FOLLOWING MATERIALS TO CREATE THE BUMBLE BEE HAND PUPPET:

* 2 - 6″x10″ Colored Felt Rectangles (used to make thehand mitt)
* 2 - 6″ x10″ Black Felt Rectangles (used to make the bug body)
* 1 - 6″x10″ Gray Felt (used to make the bee wings)
* 2 - 15 mm Wiggly Eyes
* 1 - 4 oz. Tube of Tacky Glue
* White (Material) Paint Marker (used to draw the smile on the ladybug)

1 - Pair of Scissors

Instructions To create the Bumble Bee Hand Puppet, follow these steps:

1. Cut out the hand mitt shapes using the 2 - 6″x10″ Colored Felt Rectangles
2. Glue together the two halves of the felt hand shapes to complete the mitt. This mitt will be used as the hand-puppet base to be decorated.
3. Cut bee wings out of gray felt. Place wings at the center of the neck of your hand mitt. Glue down the wings to the mitt.
4. Cut out the bug body using one of the 6″x10″ black felt rectangles. Glue the bumble bee body to the hand mitt.
5. Cut out 4 strips of yellow felt. Place the strips across the bee's body forming stripes. Glue stripes down.
6. Cut out two antennas using the scraps of black felt. Glue the antennas to top of the bumble bee head.
7. Glue the wiggly eyes to face.
8. Draw a smile on the bumble bee's face with a paint marker.

Fancy Frames

Fancy frames are a colorful way to display treasured photos of you and your favorite Beanie Baby. Everyone will have fun decorating these frames.

MATERIALS YOU'LL NEED THE FOLLOWING MATERIALS TO CREATE YOUR FANCY FRAME:

* 1 - 6″x6″ Plywood or cardboard frame for a Polaroid picture (with an easel back)
* Acrylic rhinestones of assorted color shape and sizes
* Buttons of assorted color shape and sizes
* Colorful plastic animal shaped buttons
* 1 - 4 oz. tube of Tacky Glue
* A wonderful assortment of stickers
* 1/4″ pom-poms in a variety of colors

Instructions To create the Fancy Frames, follow these steps:

1. Take a Polaroid picture of yourself with your favorite Beanie Baby(ies).
2. Glue various buttons, pom-poms, stickers all around the frame. Let dry for 5 minutes.

Fancy Frames are also a great gift idea!

✳ PROJECTS BY PAULA EISEN

Mary Beth's BEANIE WORLD For Kids

MARY BETH'S CLUBHOUSE

An Anniversary Celebration

On a cool autumn afternoon, Hoot, the wise old owl, is sitting in his favorite tree in front of Mary Beth's Clubhouse. He is enjoying the solitude now that the Beanies are all back in school. They are learning the ABCs, 123s and geography. Beanie World is a great place to live, especially because all of the Beanies are learning how to work and play with each other.

As he's sitting and daydreaming, a chorus of voices comes his way. "Now this is a diverse group if ever there was one," he mumbles under his breath as the big group approaches.

"Well ladies and gents, what brings you to my favorite tree?" Hoot asks curiously.

"Hoot, you know how much we love and respect you," Smoochy the frog schmoozes.

"Yes, Hoot, you are our role model," Bernie the St. Bernard adds.

"Enough," Hoot hoots. "What in heaven's name do you want?"

"Want!? Just because we come to pay respects to our revered leader," Dotty the Dalmatian says solemnly.

"Hoot rules! Hoot rules!" Jabber the parrot hollers.

"Flattery will get you nowhere boys and girls," Hoot states matter of factly. "What are you up to?"

"Well, Hoot, you know we all have something in common," Tuffy the terrier says, tripping over his own tongue as he tries to get the words out, but Spinner the spider beats him to the punch. "We all have October birthdays."

"So you do," Hoot says quietly.

Batty the bat spills the beans, "Could we have a sleepover birthday party at the clubhouse?"

"Mary Beth is celebrating the one-year anniversary of her magazine, 'Mary Beth's Beanie World Monthly,' " Spooky the ghost says.

Story by Mary Catherine Cosme
Illustrated by Elizabeth Slomka
Designs created and distributed by: SMD PROMOTIONS, INC.

"You know, Hoot, the magazine is about us, so we have to show our appreciation," Dotty says, always concerned about etiquette.

"Oh, all right," Hoot gives in, "A party it will be, but we have to pick a date and send out invitations from Kidd Packk to all our Beanie friends.

"Tomorrow we'll go to SMD Promotions and pick out costumes. You can't have a party in October without costumes," Hoot exclaims.

The next day, after school, they all head for the new store in town, SMD Promotions, to look at costumes and proper attire for a slumber party.

"I am so happy that SMD is located in Beanie World," Snip says with a meow.

As they open the door, they are greeted by the sight of ballerinas twirling and pirouetting. Erin the emerald green bear is doing an arabesque, while Princess the bear does a grand jetty. "I didnít know that Happy the hippo could kick that high," Spinner says, staring in amazement.

"Imagine," Smoochy says. "Inky the octopus in a tutu."

"No, not a tutu," Doby corrects him. "In a beautiful ballerina outfit."

As the group plies and leaps in the air, the Birthday

Beanies stare in respectful silence. They look at the colorful iridescent outfits with matching headbands.

"How lovely," Smoochy observes. "The colors are so intense; silver and blue, gold and black, red and silver, and look, Erin the Irish bear is wearing green, of course."

The ballerinas continue to circle the Birthday Beanies, spinning as they move to the music from "Swan Lake."

The Birthday Beanies cannot believe that so much talent exists in Beanie World. Princess is the epitome of grace and splendor as she glides by on her toes.

"You need special shoes to dance on your toes," Hoot comments.

▼ ▼ ▼ ▼ ▼ ▼ ▼ ▼ ▼ ▼ ▼ ▼ ▼

"Ooh! That must hurt," Snip observes as his sister, Flip, flips on by with her head down, counting the beats of the music.

Dotty shakes her head up and down counting along with Flip and commenting on how she has improved since the last dance recital. Yes, ballet class has given both boy and girl Beanies a sense of form and balance.

"Look," Hoot observes. "Even Pinky the flamingo, who is usually all legs, isn't tripping over her own feet."

They all nod in agreement. Ballet is the best thing to happen to Beanie World since Mary Beth's Clubhouse arrived. The Birthday Beanies think that ballerina costumes are a great idea.

"Oh my," Hoot observes in awe. "Happy the hippo is doing the splits." They all turn their heads simultaneously and applaud her efforts.

"Hip, hip, hooray for Happy!" they cheer in unison. Pretty soon the whole place is cheering her on.

"Well, if anyone else is interested in ballerina costumes, they're in aisle 2," Hoot mentions, as a group of Beanies nearly mows him down to get there first.

▼ ▼ ▼ ▼ ▼ ▼ ▼ ▼ ▼ ▼ ▼ ▼ ▼

On their way back to the Mary Beth's Clubhouse, they see more Beanies in cowboy outfits race on by. They're pretending to ride horses and lasso objects with their leashes. Hoot asks them where they found their smashing costumes.

"Why, at SMD Promotions, of course," they all respond.

"These cowboy outfits are so authentic," Hoot says as one after another gallops by.

"I love the tan naugahyde vests, and those cowboy hats are too much," Spinner spouts.

When they reach the clubhouse, the cowboys are having a rodeo in the front yard. One after another is trying to calf-rope poor Freckles, who just stands there in a daze.

"Oops, down he goes," says Dotty as Snip the cat tries to untie him. Before she knows it, Snip is on his back with feet in the air, hog tied.

"Let me go," Snip sniffles. "You can hurt a kitty cat when you play that rough."

The cowboys apologize but continue to ride roughshod. Congo the ape is trying to coax Derby the horse into joining the circle of cowboys, but Derby has other plans.

"I'm in training to be a racing horse," he insists. "I can't afford to get hurt doing something silly." They all look at him in disbelief – Derby, a racehorse!?!?

▼ ▼ ▼ ▼ ▼ ▼ ▼ ▼ ▼ ▼ ▼ ▼ ▼

Congo and Bongo take offense at this remark, as they trot by on the backs of Garcia and Curly, the bear pair. Hoot is astonished at the agility they demonstrate. The monkeys keep their balance as they do somersaults and leaps on the bears' backs. While all these shenanigans are going on, Spooky the ghost jumps out from behind the clubhouse porch, shouting "B-O-O-O" at the cowboys. The cowboys give Spooky a look of disdain. These hard-working cowpokes never show fear because it's not the manly thing to do.

Then, Hoot goes back to the party plans.

"Well, the Kidd Packk invitations are in the mail. They are the perfect touch for our party planning. Remember, the only place that they can be obtained is from SMD Promotions."

All of the Beanies are eagerly awaiting the party. Birthdays are such fun, but the big draw at this party is the celebration of Mary Beth's anniversary. Imagine that – "Mary Beth's Beanie World" is one year old. It's hard to believe!

▼ ▼ ▼ ▼ ▼ ▼ ▼ ▼ ▼ ▼ ▼ ▼ ▼

The night of the party finally arrives. All of the Beanies are arriving with their pajamas, robes and slippers. During the past week, there was a run on sleeping bags, too. SMD has everything a Beanie could want for a slumber party!

The Beanies are so excited. Some have never slept away from home. What an adventure!

Four bears are arriving with their mascot, Chip ne cat. Valentino the white bear is busy introduc- ng his cousin, Mel the koala bear, who is visiting rom Australia. Teddy the bear is introducing his ousin, Fortune the panda, who is visiting from China. Hoot is all excited about having visitors rom foreign countries at Mary Beth's Clubhouse.

The next group to arrive is the bunnies, with their friend Kiwi the tou- can. They are all wearing brand new robes made of terry cloth, and they ome with little terry loth slippers. SMD is mazing; they even ave a special acrylic ox to house individ- al Beanies, and there s a pillow to put inside for a Beanie's comfort.

▼ ▼ ▼ ▼ ▼ ▼ ▼ ▼ ▼ ▼ ▼ ▼ ▼ ▼

Hippity, Hoppity and Floppity all chose different color obes so they wouldn't get them mixed up. Ears doesn't care ne way or another what color he's wearing. He's not into natching; sometimes his colors clash, but that's OK, too. A eanie is entitled to his individuality.

There are hot dogs, chips and juice for everyone, but the est part is the cake and ice cream. After dinner, the eanies play games and win prizes courtesy of the planning ommittee. Their job is to ensure that all the Beanies have a ood time. The committee is especially concerned that Mary eth enjoys herself at the celebration. The committee is busy naking up a special bed for Mary Beth to sleep on. The heets are color coordinated, and the comforter is very soft. hey even chose a particularly soft pillow for her to lay her ead. The Beanies love her very much! They treat her like a rincess when she comes to visit.

Before bed, the Birthday Beanies march in wearing spe- ial birthday outfits. The ponchos and hats are white with ifferent colored polka dots. They are trimmed in iridescent ace, and right in the center of the poncho it says, "'HAPPY IRTHDAY BEANIE BABY from SMD."

▼ ▼ ▼ ▼ ▼ ▼ ▼ ▼ ▼ ▼ ▼ ▼ ▼ ▼

The Birthday Beanies are so happy as they march around ne room while all of the other beanies sing Happy Birthday October Beanie Babies. Smoochy the frog blows kisses to veryone as he hops on by. Bernie the St. Bernard is proud s punch in his poncho, and he looks it, too.

Rainbow the chameleon glows as she dances around the room. She has always wanted to be a ballerina. Spinner the spider spins a silky web around Batty the bat as the two of them meander through the crowd.

The Beanies are having a ball. The October Birthday Beanies are in the spotlight this month. They are all waiting to sing "Happy Anniversary" to Mary Beth for her maga- zine, "Mary Beth's Beanie World Monthly."

The excitement mounts, and as they complete the last verse of the song, Mary Beth waves and blows them all a kiss. This has been the best party, but even Beanies get sleepy. Slowly, they all head for their sleeping bags, climb- ing in, wiggling till they get comfortable and closing their eyes. Pretty soon there is a chorus of zzzzs throughout the clubhouse. A good time was had by all! ❤

Tag protectors designed specifically to fit Disney's Mini Bean Bag Collection. They are a sturdy rigid vinyl with 1/8 inch lip which allows for both a snug fit yet easy insertion of the tag into the protector. No more bent tags, lost prices, or unsightly curls.

Protectors that fit the Disney Store tags

Pricing:	S/H:
25 for $9.99	$3.25
50 for $14.99	$3.25
100 for $24.99	$3.50
200 for $49.98	$4.00
300 for $74.97	$4.50
500 for $100.00	$6.50

Made in the U.S.A.

Theme Park

tag protectors that fit mousketoy, WDW, and Club Disney

Cherish mini bean bag protectors are endorsed by Disney Beanie Report, www.dizbeanies.com, the best source on the Net for Disney Beanie Information...

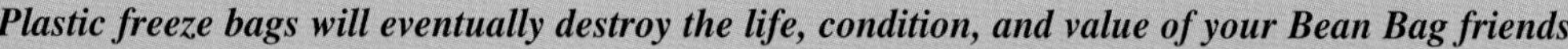

We are an authorized retailer of beanibags ™

DID YOU KNOW!!

Plastic freeze bags will eventually destroy the life, condition, and value of your Bean Bag friends.

archival
acid free
attractive
affordable
all beans fit

ITEM	Pricing:	S/H:
25 beanibags	$7.99	$3.00 priority shipping
50 beanibags	$13.99	$3.00 priority shipping
100 beanibags	$25.99	$4.00 priority shipping
200 beanibags	$48.99	$5.00 priority shipping

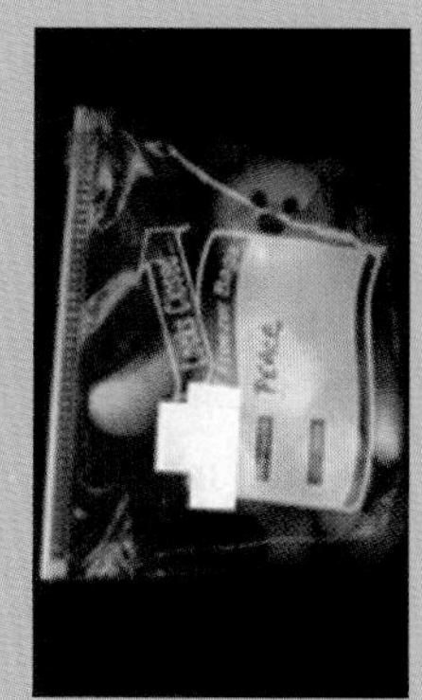

Costs up to 95% Less than Plastic Cubes.
Metallic Gold twisty closures. and an Exclusive Information Sheet.
Caring for your Beanie Bag Plush are included with your Beanibag™ order!

24 hr. ORDER LINE

1-800-807-4437 www.gojopin.com/cherish

Dealer inquiries, questions & comments 1-800-806-7602

'es! I want to protect my collection!
'lease send me...

TY ________ CHERISH MINI BEANBAG PROTECTOR™
PECIFY TYPE **(THEME PARK)** OR **(DSTORE)**

TY___________BEANIBAGS™

* IL RESIDENTS ADD 7.50% SALES TAX
* Out of country add an additional $3.00 for shipping

ease CHARGE __________ to my:
VISA DISCOVER AMEX MASTERCARD

__________ +S/H __________
TOTAL

__________ +S/H __________
TOTAL

__________ +S/H __________
TOTAL

Card number Exp. date Signature

Please ship my order to:

NAME: ____________

ADDRESS: ____________

CITY: ____________

STATE: ______ ZIP: ____________

PHONE: ____________

Send this order form with payment or credit information to:
DHD Designs
P.O. Box 1268
Granite City, IL 62040-1268

Cherish and DHD DESIGNS are by no means associated or endorsed by the Walt Disney Company Disney©

Beanie Shows

ARIZONA

October 17th – Tucson. R & J Collectible Show: Beanie Babies, Hot Wheels, Dolls, Toys & More. 9 am - 3 pm. Doubletree Guest Suites (formerly the Radisson) Catalina Ballroom 6555 East Speedway Boulevard (east of Wilmot). Free Admission. Free drawings! Vendor tables are $45, and after Sept. 19th they are $50. Contact Roberta or John at (520) 292-9458 or 408-2470. E-mail: babytyler@juno.com or floresj@gci-net.com.

CALIFORNIA

September 5th & 6th – Simi Valley. "Ventura County's Largest Monthly Show" Simi Valley Mountaingate Plaza Mall Show: Located at First & Los Angeles St. inside the Mountaingate Plaza Mall. (1/2-mile South of Hwy 138, exit First St.) Show hours are Saturday 10am - 5pm, Sunday 11am - 4pm. Free admission & plenty of free parking. 50 dealer tables (8-foot tables: $45 for 1 Day, $80 for 2 Days). Special credit card system where you can use your Visa/Mastercard/Discover & American Express at all dealer tables. Also, ATM available for cash back. For more information, contact Eric Beckerman or Golden State Promotions at (310) 454-5030.

Every 1st and 3rd Sunday, Sept. 6th & 20th, Oct. 4th & 18th – Fresno. Step Above Presents Beanies. Beanies. Beanies. Ramada Inn. 41 Fwy & Shaw Ave. $1.00 Admission. Kids Free. Door Prizes Every Half Hour. Winners must be present. Dealer 8' tables: $45 includes city tax. Over 50 tables of the finest dealers across America. Please call or visit our Web site for more info at http://www.ctsite.com/beaniebabies. Or call (909) 944-7628 or (209) 322-0407.

Every 2nd & 4th Sunday, Sept. 13th & 27th, Oct. 11th (no show 25th) – Bakersfield. Doubletree Hotel, 99 Fwy & Rosedale Hwy. 9 am - 3 pm. $2.00 Admission. Kids Free. Door Prizes Every Half Hour. Winners must be present. Dealer 8' tables: $45 includes city tax. Over 50 tables of the finest dealers across America. Please call or visit our Web site for more info at http://www.ctsite.com/beaniebabies. Or call (909) 944-7628 or (209) 322-0407.

September 20th – Anaheim. Kim's Southern California Beanie Baby Trade Shows. 9 am - 3 pm. The Disneyland Pacific Hotel. 1717 S. West Street. Right behind Disneyland. Admission $3. Children 7 and under are free. For additional information, call (714) 754-0518 or 24-hour info line (714) 568-2952. Visit our award-winning Web site: kimsbeanieshows.com

September 20th – Orange County/Buena Park. Orange County's Largest Monthly Beanie Baby, Sports Card, & Collectibles Show. Every 3rd Sunday of the Month at the Buena Park Holiday Inn. Located at 7000 Beach Blvd. at Hwy 91, 1/2-mile West of the 5 Fwy. Show hours are 10 am - 4 pm. Admission $1.00 (kids 8 & under are free) Early admission: 9 am - 10 am, $3, with plenty of free parking. 75 dealer tables (8-foot tables: $45 ea.). Show sells out 1 week prior to show date. Over $500 in door prizes, plus the very popular Beanie & Pack War Tournaments. Special credit card system where you can use your Visa/Mastercard/Discover & American Express at all dealer tables. Also, ATM available for cash back. For more information, contact Eric Beckerman or Golden State Promotions at (310) 454-5030.

September 26th – Westlake Village. All Beanie Baby Fun Fest Show. 9 am - 3 pm. Hyatt Westlake Plaza Hotel. 880 S. Westlake Blvd. Admission $3.00/9-10 am Early Bird Admission $4.00, 7 & under free. Grand Prize Raffle: Britannia bear. E-mail: Imagine12@aol.com.

September 27th – West Covina. Gabe Frimmel Promotions Monthly Beanie Babies & Collectibles Show. 10 am -3 pm. Adm $5, Under 7 Free. Radisson Hotel, 14635 Baldwin Park Towne Center (10 Fwy-Puente Exit). First 100 customers will receive a free Beanie Babies Exclusive Trading Card. For additional information, call (626) 967-5744 or fax (626) 967-5745.

September 27th & October 11th & 25th – Los Angeles/Van Nuys. LA's Largest Monthly Beanie Baby, Sportscard, & Collectibles Show. Every 2nd & 4th Sunday of the month at the Van Nuys-Airtel Plaza Hotel & Conference Center. Located at 16201 Sherman Way (1/2-mile west of the 405 Fwy exit Sherman Way-West). Hours are 10 am - 4 pm, Admission $1 (kids 8 & under are free). Early Admission: 9 am - 10 am, $3. Plenty of free parking. Three Rooms and 130 dealer tables (6-foot tables: $45; 9-foot: $60; Two 6-foot tables in an L-shape: $70). Show sells out 2 weeks prior to show event. Over $750 in door prizes, plus the very popular Beanie & Pack War Tournaments. Special credit card system where you can use your Visa/Mastercard/Discover & American Express at all dealer tables. Also, ATM available for cash back. For more information, contact Eric Beckerman or Golden State Promotions at (310) 454-5030.

October 4th – Ontario. The Inland Empire Beanie Baby & Hallmark Show. 9 am - 10 am $7, 10 am - 3 pm $5, kids 12 & under $1 all day. Free parking. Doubletree Hotel, 222 N. Vineyard Ave. Off the 10 Fwy. Buy, Sell & Trade. For more information, e-mail beaniesho@aol.com or (714) 536-6437. Or see Web site at http://members.aol.com/MHOKA/wep.html.

October 11th – Fullerton. Gabe Frimmel Promotions Monthly Beanie Babies & Collectibles Show. 10 am - 3 pm. Four Points Sheraton Hotel. 1500 So. Raymond Ave. (91 Fwy-Raymond Exit). Admission $5, Under 7 Free. First 100 customers will receive a free Beanie Babies Exclusive Trading Card. For more information, call (626) 967-5744 or Fax (626) 967-5745.

October 16th, 17th & 18th – Los Angeles. Southern California's Largest Beanie Baby, Sportscard & Collectible Show Ever! Over 300 Dealer tables of the nation's best dealers at the magnificent Hollywood Park Convention Center and Casino, located at 3883 Century Blvd & Prairie. From 405 Fwy, exit Century Blvd. East. From 105 Fwy, exit Prairie Blvd North. Show hours: Friday 3 pm - 9 pm, Saturday 10 am - 7 pm, Sunday 10 am - 5 pm. Admission: $5 (Kids 12 & under free). Plenty of free parking. 300 Dealer Tables (8-foot tables $75/day or $195 for 3 days). Autograph guests to be announced. Free seminars on Beanie collecting, investing and counterfeits. Over $5000 in door prizes to be given away including a Grand Prize $1000 shopping spree, plus the very popular Beanie & Pack War Tournaments. Special credit card system where you can use your Visa/Mastercard/ Discover & American Express at all dealer tables. Also, ATM available for cash back. For more information, contact Eric Beckerman or Golden State Promotions at (310) 454-5030.

October 25th – Costa Mesa. Kim's Southern California Beanie Baby Trade Shows. 9 am - 3 pm. The Countryside Inn Hotel. 325 S. Bristol St. Admission $3. Children 7 and under are free. For additional information, call (714) 754-0518 or 24-hour info line (714) 568-2952. Visit our award-winning Web site at kimsbeanieshows.com.

DELAWARE

TBA – Beanie Fest. Dates, locations to be announced. 10 am - 4 pm. Admission $4/kids 3 to 12 years $2/family pass $8. For information, call (609) 778-3601 and ask for Dave or visit www.BeanieFest.com on the Web. Great selections of retired & new Ty Beanies, Attics, Disney and other bean bag toys, supplies and accessories. Free door prizes every half hour. Free parking, easy access, ample aisle space.

FLORIDA

September 19th – Fort Lauderdale. Beanie Spectacular IV. 9 am - 4 pm. Turnpike Holiday Inn, 5100 N. State Rd. 7 on 441 just north of Commercial Blvd. Admission $5 for adults, $2 for children, children 5 & under are free. $1 off for kids that mention "Mary Beth's Beanie World." Beanie Grab Bags for first 50 paid admissions. "Beanie Bucks" for all kids through the door. Scheduled to appear: author and writer Ms. Janie Daniels, "The Beanie Invasion," and writer Vicki Krupka, counterfeit expert and writer for Beaniemom.com. Representatives from "Mary Beth's Beanie World" are scheduled to attend. Beanie bingo, giveaway for kids every 15 minutes, Bear drawing every hour, free balloons. Raffle for "Flag Bear Set" – Maple/Glory/Britannia – $1 a chance or $5 for six chances. Contact Mike or Shelley at (954) 792-0714, or send e-mail to mnsbeanies@webtv.net. Visit the Web site at http://www.mnsbeanies.com.

September 20th – Kissimmee. Beanie Baby Collectible Expo. Show hours 10 am - 5 pm. Holiday Inn on 2009 West Vine Street. Admission $3 (Early Buyer 9 am admission: $10). Kids 6 and under free. Collectibles at the show will include Beanie Babies Retired & Current, Teenie Beanies and accessories. Grand Prize Britannia and door prizes every half hour. More than 40 8-foot tables and over 25 vendors. For more information or dealer inquiries, call Mike at (407) 592-9753 or (407) 228-6456 or send e-mail to mpries8354@aol.com.

September 27th – Fort Myers. Beanie Baby Collectible Expo. 10 am - 5 pm. Radisson Inn, 12635 S. Cleveland Ave. Admission $5 (Early Buyer 9 am admission: $10). Collectibles at the show will include Beanie Babies, Teenie Beanies and accessories, toys, Barbies, Hallmark ornaments and much more. Charity raffle to include all 14 of the new Beanie Babies, Grand Prize will be Britannia. 60 dealer tables. Come buy, sell and trade. For more information or dealer inquiries, call Mike at (407) 592-9753 or (407) 228-6456 or send e-mail to mpries8354@aol.com.

September 27th – Largo. Chris' Beanie Baby Show. 10 am - 4 pm. Honeywell Minnreg Building, 6340 - 126th Ave. North, near the intersection of 126th Ave. & US 19. Admission $2. New, current and retired Beanies for sale or trade as well as supplies, accessories and a variety of other types of collectibles. Dealer tables (65 in all) are still available. Contact D. Walent at P.O. Box 82254, Tampa, FL 33682-2254 or call (813) 932-0494 or send e-mail to Ephemera@gte.net,

October 3rd & 4th – Kissimmee. Beanie Baby Collectible Expo. Show hours 10 am - 5 pm. Holiday Inn on 2009 West Vine Street. Admission $3 (Early Buyer 9 am admission: $10). Kids 6 and under free. Collectibles at the show will include Beanie Babies Retired & Current, Teenie Beanies and accessories. Grand Prize Britannia and door prizes every half hour. More than 40 8-foot tables and over 25 vendors. For more information or dealer inquiries, call Mike at (407) 592-9753 or (407) 228-6456 or send e-mail to mpries8354@aol.com.

October 4th – Key Largo. 10 am - 4 pm) at the Key Largo Marriott, Mile Marker 103.8. Admission is $4 (kids under 7 free). Early bird admission at 9:30 am is $7 per person. All proceeds will be donated to the Friends of the Pool Committee. Hourly raffles, plus Maple the Canadian bear will be raffled. Vendors needed. Contact Tonia Sledd at (305) 852-1183 or via e-mail at tsledd@gate.net.

October 11th – Ocala. Ocala Beanie Baby and Collectibles Fall Show. 10 am - 5 pm. The National Guard Armory. 900 SW 20th Str. Admission $3 for adults, $1 for children 5-12, children under 5 admitted free. Approximately 50-75 vendors. Beanie Babies, Barbies, Hot Wheels, Starting Lineups, Sports Cards and more. Concessions available, plus door prizes. For more information, contact Jorge or Carmen at (352) 861-2595 after 6 pm or send e-mail to Kito0712@aol.com. Vendor tables $30 for an 8-foot table.

October 18th – Orlando. Beanie Baby & Hallmark Collectibles Expo. 10 am - 5 pm. Orlando Marriott Inn, 8001 International Drive, at the intersection of International Drive and State Road 482, Exit 29 off I-4. Admission $4 with this ad, kids 6 and under free. Collectibles at the show will include Beanie Babies, Teenie Beanies and accessories, toys, Hallmark ornaments, Barbies and much more. 125 tables with over 70 vendors. There will be a charity raffle and door prizes every 30 minutes. The Grand Prize will be Britannia. For more information or dealer inquiries, call Mike at (407) 592-9753 or (407) 228-6456 or send e-mail to mpries8354@aol.com.

HAWAII

October 3rd – Honolulu. West Coast Trade Show Presents "Humphrey's Hawaiian Holiday." 9 am - 4 pm. Blaisdell Convention Center, Honolulu. Admission $5, children 7 and under are free. Raffle for Humphrey the camel. All raffle proceeds donated to Hawaii Youth Services Network. Call (714) 754-0518 for information.

ILLINOIS

September 27th – Crystal Lake. Beanie Extravaganza. 10 am - 3 pm. Holiday Inn, Route 31 & Three Oaks Road, 2 miles south of Rt. 176. Admission $3; Preteens $1; Early Bird $10 (9 am -10 am). 50 Tables; table fee $40. For more information, contact First Chance Promotions, P.O. Box 56, Waucondail, IL 60084, or call (847) 361-1737.

IOWA

October 11th – Des Moines. Des Moines 1st Annual Central Iowa Beanie Baby Show. Regular hours 9:30 am - 5:30 pm. Early Bird 8:30 am - 9:30 am, $6.00; Adults $4, children $1, under 4 free. Marriott Grand Ballroom.1250 74th Street, West Des Moines, just West of I-235/I-80-35 interchange, exit 121. Coloring contest with Beanie Baby prizes for children ages 3-8. Door prizes all day long. The Marriott also features a Sunday buffet. For more information, call Marriott at (515) 267-1500 or call Donna Batterton at (515) 270-9626.

KANSAS

October 3rd – Lawrence. Beanie Baby Bonanza. 9 am - 4 pm. Douglas County Fairgrounds, 2120 Harper. Admission $3 for adults, kids under 12 free. Lots to raffle. Vendors inquire within. Contact Hafid Saba (785) 841-9844 or visit the Web site at www.sunflower.com/~hafids for more information.

KENTUCKY

October 17th – Marion. Beanie Baby Show. 10 am - 5 pm. Town and Country Riding Club and Fair Grounds. Admission $2 for adults, children 12 and under free. For more information, call (302) 667-9889 or send e-mail to ltinsley@kih.net.

MARYLAND

TBA – Beanie Fest. Dates, locations to be announced. 10 am - 4 pm. Admission $4/kids 3 to 12 years $2/family pass $8. For information, call (410) 761-3378 and ask for Dave or visit www.BeanieFest.com on the Web. Great selections of retired & new Ty Beanies, Attics, Disney and other bean bag toys, supplies and accessories. Free door prizes every half hour. Free parking, easy access, ample aisle space.

MISSOURI

September 19th – Branson. Beanie Baby Extravaganza ... Buy, Sell, Trade. 9 am -5 pm. Located at Branson High School on North Highway 65 and Bee Creek exit. One mile north of downtown Branson on busy highway. Great location! Admission $3, children under 11 free. Vendor tables $25 each. For more information, call Paula or Paul at (417) 334-0687 or fax (417) 334-2050 or send e-mail to 4aparty1@gte.net. Door prizes. Snacks available.

NEVADA

October 10th and 11th – Las Vegas. West Coast Beanie Babies, Collectibles, and Sports Cards Extravaganza! 9 am - 4 pm Saturday and Sunday. Vacation Village Hotel and Casino, 6711 Las Vegas Blvd. South, just off the 215 Las Vegas Blvd. exit. Show is located on the 2nd floor in banquet room. Admission is $1.00 off with flier, children under 10 free. Ask for Mark at (702) 837-1827 or Ivan at (702) 433-1134, or e-mail Mark at Sidout98@aol.com. Beanie Babies new, retired, current, Sports collectibles, comics and more!

NEW JERSEY

September 26th – Neptune. Beanies! Beanies! Beanies! 10 am - 3 pm. Jumping Brook Country Club. Jumping Brook Road between Route 66 and Route 33. Admission $5 for ages 13 and up, $3 for 12 and under. New, old, hard to find, current and accessories. For information, call (732) 888-4681.

October 10th – Pennsauken. Beanie Fest. South Jersey Expo Center, Routes 73 & 130. Admission $4/kids 3 to 12 years $2/family pass $8. For information, call (609) 778-3601 and ask for Dave or visit www.BeanieFest.com on the Web. Great selections of retired & new Ty Beanies, Attics, Disney and other bean bag toys, supplies and accessories. Free door prizes every half hour. Free parking, easy access, ample aisle space.

NEW YORK

TBA – Beanie Fest. Dates, locations to be announced. 10 am - 4 pm. Admission $4/kids 3 to 12 years $2/family pass $8. For information, call (609) 778-3601 and ask for Dave or visit www.BeanieFest.com on the Web. Great selections of retired & new Ty Beanies, Attics, Disney and other bean bag toys, supplies and accessories. Free door prizes every half hour. Free parking, easy access, ample aisle space.

OHIO

September 20th – Akron. Beanie Fest 5. 10 am - 3 pm. Holiday Inn Arlington Road, I-77 Exit 120. 30 Tables. Admission $2, under 12 free. For more information, call Doug Hapstak at (330) 854-5110 or send e-mail to Dugbowl@aol.com.

September 27th – Canton. Beaniepalooza. 10 am - 3 pm. Sheraton Inn Belden Village, I-77 Exit 109. Across from Kent State. 30 Tables. Admission $2, under 12 free. For more information, call Doug Hapstak at (330) 854-5110 or send e-mail to Dugbowl@aol.com.

October 17th – Kirtland. The Cleveland National Beanie Baby Show. 9 am - 3 pm. Lakeland College. (I-90 E/State Route 306) For dealer information, call (440) 256-8141. Last attendance for this show was 2,380 with 102 dealer tables.

October 18th – Akron. Beanie Fest 6. 10 am - 3 pm. Beanie Fest 5. 10 am - 3 pm. Holiday Inn Arlington Road, I-77 Exit 120. 30 Tables. Admission $2, under 12 free. For more information, call Doug Hapstak at (330) 854-5110 or send e-mail to Dugbowl@aol.com.

October 25th – Canton. Beaniepalooza. 10 am - 3 pm. Sheraton Inn Belden Village, I-77 Exit 109. Across from Kent State. 30 Tables. Admission $2, under 12 free. For more information, call Doug Hapstak at (330) 854-5110 or send e-mail to Dugbowl@aol.com.

OKLAHOMA

September 26th – Oklahoma City. 10 am - 4 pm. Craft Street Craft Mall, 7503 S. Walker. Admission $1. Fifteen vendors by invitation only. For consideration, list your last five shows to above address. Attendance: Averaged more than 1,000 at each of six previous shows. Vendors from around the region will be bringing everything from older retireds to new releases, plus accessories at low prices you won't find in stores. Call (405) 631-2115 or toll free (877) 272-3878.

PENNSYLVANIA

October 4th – Pittsburgh. Beanie Babies Show. 10 am - 4 pm. Holiday Inn South. Admission: $3 for adults, $1 for children under 12. Early Bird at 9:30 am - $8.00. For table information, call Paul at (724) 872-0512 or Marcy at (412) 835-1289.

TBA – Beanie Fest. Philadelphia, Reading, Allentown, Harrisburg. Dates, precise locations to be announced. 10 am - 4 pm. Admission $4/kids 3 to 12 years $2/family pass $8. For information, call (609) 778-3601 and ask for Dave or visit www.BeanieFest.com on the Web. Great selections of retired & new Ty Beanies, Attics, Disney and other bean bag toys, supplies and accessories. Free door prizes every half hour. Free parking, easy access, ample aisle space.

TEXAS

September 26th – Hurst (Dallas-Fort Worth metroplex area). Beanie Baby Show by Paradise Events, Etc. Best Western Inn. 183W and 820S, exit 24A. 10 am - 4 pm. Admission $2 for adults, children 12 and under free. Free kids raffles! Door prizes every 30 minutes! Bring this ad to enter special drawing! Vendor space available. If in the Fort worth area, call Ellen Tennyson (817) 220-3122. People from other areas, call toll free (888) 993-4990, PIN #3338.

October 24th – Grapevine (Dallas-Fort Worth metroplex area). Big Collectible Toy Show by Paradise Events, Etc. 10 am - 4 pm. Grapevine Convention Center. 1209 S. Main St. Featuring Beanies, Barbies, Hot Wheels, Baseball Cards, Dolls, Comic Books, Trains, Marbles, Disney, Nascar and more. Fun for the whole family! Over 100 Vendors. Vendor space available. If in the Fort worth area, call Ellen Tennyson (817) 220-3122. People from other areas, call toll free (888) 993-4990, PIN #3338.

VIRGINIA

TBA – Beanie Fest. Dates, locations to be announced. 10 am - 4 pm. Admission $4/kids 3 to 12 years $2/family pass $8. For information, call (703) 761-1124 and ask for Dave or visit www.BeanieFest.com on the Web. Great selections of retired & new Ty Beanies, Attics, Disney and other bean bag toys, supplies and accessories. Free door prizes every half hour. Free parking, easy access, ample aisle space.

WASHINGTON

September 26th – Mukilteo. Jerry's Beanie Baby Show. 10 am to 4 pm. Games Family Fun Center. 3616 South Road. Admission $1, children 10 and under free. Lots of door prizes! This will be our second show and promises to be even bigger and better than the last. For information and/or table rental, call Jerry Day at (425) 356-1099.

October 24th & 25th – Spokane. Ann & Debbie's Beanie Affair. Saturday, 10 am - 9 pm; Sunday 11 am - 6 pm. Spokane Valley Mall. Free Admission. Costume contest for the kids, raffles and much more. Vendor space available. For more information, call Debbie Motz at (208) 667-6903 or send e-mail to DM14139@aol.com, or call Ann at (208) 765-5052 or send e-mail to pszmania@aol.com. Come join the fun!

WISCONSIN

September 19th – Milwaukee. 1st Annual Beanie Baby National Convention. At Serb Hall (51st and Oklahoma). 9 am - 2 pm. The biggest door prize ever – Peanut the Royal Blue Elephant (mint) to be given away to one lucky winner. 100 tables of quality Beanies, Teenies, Disney and others. Admission $5. For dealer tables, call (414) 783-4339.

CANADIAN SHOWS - TORONTO

October 4th – Toronto. Beanie Baby Extravaganza (Canada's Largest). 10 am to 5 pm. Holiday Inn Toronto. Admission: Adults $5, kids under 12 $3. 7095 Woodbine Ave. (Hwy 404 & Steeles). "GET YOUR MAPLES HERE." For more information, call Rob at (416) 243-1500, or send e-mail to Robdan@netcom.ca.

U.K. SHOWS - SURREY

October 18th – Surrey. Beanie Collector's Show. 10 am - 4 pm. Lingfield Park Racecourse. (Signs from M25 Junction 6). Admission £2.00. For inquiries and stand details, Tel/Fax: 01342-892770

(continued on page 244)

Beanie Shows

"BEANIE WORLD" ON THE ROAD!

Representatives of "Mary Beth's Beanie World Monthly" plan to be in attendance at the following Beanie shows. Be sure to stop by the "Beanie World" booth and say hello! Check our Web site at http://www.beanieworld.net for periodic updates to this list. At most of these shows, retired and current issues of "Mary Beth's Beanie World Monthly" will be available for purchase.

September 5-7, 1998 Saturday - Monday (Labor Day weekend)
Starr Marketing presents "Bugs on Navy Pier" Beanie and Collectible Show. Staff writer Claudia Dunne will be available to sign autographs and answer your Beanie Baby questions on Sunday the 6th and Monday the 7th. Meet show representatives Laura Grimaldi and Meri Lauterbach.
WHERE: Navy Pier, downtown Chicago, IL
TIME: 10 am - 4pm each day
CONTACT: (708) 692-0691

September 6, 1998 Sunday
Carol Ann's Beanie Expo "Labor of Love." Staff writers Karen Gomes and Jackie La Berg will be in attendance signing autographs and answering your Beanie Baby questions.
WHERE: Holiday Inn, 3405 Algonquin Road, Rolling Meadows, IL
TIME: 10 am - 4 pm
COST: $5
CONTACT: Carol Ann or Don at (847) 520-1412 (after 11 am)

September 12-13, 1998 Saturday-Sunday
Kim's Southern California Beanie Baby Trade Show. Staff writers Claudia Dunne and Karen Gomes will be in attendance signing autographs and answering your Beanie Baby questions. Counterfeit authority Claudia Dunne will offer a seminar on "fake" Beanies at 1 pm on both days of the show.
WHERE: Orange County Fairgrounds, 88 Fair Drive, Building 10, Costa Mesa, CA
TIME: 10 am - 4 pm
COST: $5, Children 5 and under free, Early bird admission, 9-10 am, $7
CONTACT: Kimberly Barlow at (714) 754-0518 or Theresa Webster (714) 751-3102

September 12-13, 1998 Saturday and Sunday
Carlton Productions presents "Collectibles By The Sea." Featuring Beanie/Attics/Plush author and expert Peggy Gallagher, who will speak on "Granny's Beanie Addiction" - how the collecting craze moved from children to adults. You can also meet "Beanie World" show representative Laura Grimaldi.
WHERE: Myrtle Beach Convention Center, Myrtle Beach, SC
TIME: Saturday 9 am - 6 pm, Sunday 10 am - 4 pm
CONTACT: (888) 299-4631

September 19, 1998
Beanie Spectacular IV. "Beanie Mom" Sara Ann Nelson – the new editor in chief of "Mary Beth's Beanie World For Kids" – will attend this "spectacular" event to sign autographs and answer all of your Beanie Baby questions. Also, meet "Beanie World" show representative Laura Grimaldi.
WHERE: Turnpike Holiday Inn, 5100 N State Road, Fort Lauderdale, FL
TIME: 9 am - 4 pm
COST: Adults $5, children over 5 years old $2, children under 5 free!
CONTACT: Show hotline (954) 316-2149 or go to http://www.mnsbeanies.com

September 27, 1998 Sunday
Cosmic Endeavors "Change of Seasons" Beanie and Plush Collectibles Show. Meet staff writers Jackie La Berg, our "ODDS 'N ENDS" and Beanie Web site expert, and Karen Gomes, our Canadian market expert. They will be available to sign autographs and to answer your Beanie Baby questions.
WHERE: Marriott Hotel, 50 N. Martingale Road, Schaumburg, IL
TIME: 9 am - 3 pm
COST: $5 Adults, Kids under 12 FREE
CONTACT: Greg or Lisa Koch at (847) 590-8908 or via e-mail to tyedyeduo@aol.com

September 27, 1998 Sunday
Dallas-Fort Worth Ty Collectibles Expo. Retired Beanie Babies, Attic Treasures, Plush, Pillow Pals
Staff writer and author Peggy Gallagher will be available to sign autographs to speak on Counterfeit Beanies, Attic Treasures and Ty Plush.
WHERE: Holiday Inn Select DFW Airport North, 114 & Esters Blvd., Irving, TX
TIME: 10 am - 4 pm
Cost: Adults $6, Children 6-12 $4 ... Early bird admission 8:30 am - 10 am, Adults $12, children 6-12 $6
CONTACT: Diane Eberly (972) 867-INFO or via e-mail to deberly@flash.net

October 16-18, 1998
Golden State Promotions presents Southern California's Largest Beanie Baby & Sportscard Expo. Staff writer Claudia Dunne, counterfeit expert and co-author of "Tag Training 101" and show representative Laura Grimaldi will be available on the 17th and 18th for autographs and to answer Beanie Baby questions.
WHERE: Hollywood Park Convention Center & Casino, 3883 W. Century Blvd. & Prairie
TIME: Friday 3 pm - 9 pm, Saturday 10 am - 7 pm, Sunday 10 am - 5 pm
CONTACT: (310) 454-5030

It's showtime!

Let "Mary Beth's Beanie World Monthly" list your show. There will be a $150.00 charge for each listing. The cost includes the show listing and 25 complimentary copies of the issue your show is listed in. That alone is a retail value of $150.00! Use the issues as door prizes, giveaways, or sell them at a retail price at your show! All show listings may be submitted via fax, regular mail or e-mail. Contact name and phone number required for all submissions.

For the November issue, you may submit information for shows being held between October 20 and November 22, 1998. The due date for these submissions is September 4. For the December issue, you may submit information for shows being held between November 23 and December 27, 1998. The due date for these submissions is October 9.

Listings in the November and December issues will include shows held only during the previously stated date ranges. For credit card payment, be sure to include card number, name on card and expiration date.

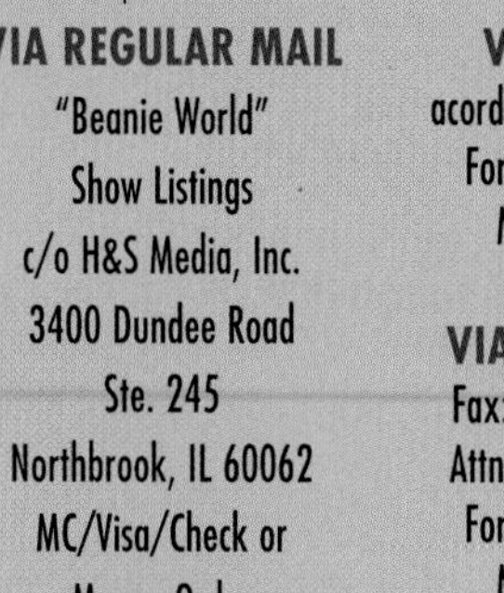

VIA REGULAR MAIL
"Beanie World"
Show Listings
c/o H&S Media, Inc.
3400 Dundee Road
Ste. 245
Northbrook, IL 60062
MC/Visa/Check or Money Order

VIA E-MAIL
acordero@adspub.com
Form of payment:
MC/Visa only

VIA FACISIMILE
Fax: 847-291-0612
Attn: Aileen Cordero
Form of payment:
MC/Visa only

Beanie Display Cases: 9"x5"x4" Made of Clear Plastic. Protects your investment. Reg. $1.29 ea. On Sale $0.89 ea. 10 cases per carton for $10.50, Inc. S&H. PFM Co., 20008 Kelly, Harper Woods, MI 48225. CK/mon. order 313-521-1002

Brand New! I Luv Beanies Slide Bracelet with accurate renditions of your favorite Beanies. Multi-color, enameled, in goldtone or silver. Fun to wear! Many styles available! For more info call: The Majic Garden. 1-800-376-0991. V/MC accepted.

At Shazam! — Specialists in Retired Beanies. Great Selection of Currents and Hard to Finds. Buy and Sell. 614-488-8712 or E-mail us at mjacks@netset.com

B&H Specialty Co.
"Your Beanie Baby Connections"
1000s in stock - BUY - SELL - TRADE
CURRENTS - RETIRED - RARE
E-mail us at Boschebuss@aol.com or call Harold at (610) 434-1248

Beanie Babies over 50 styles in stock Genuine TY products- No bears, retireds or new issues 800-243-9709 www.nostalgicks.com nostal@greene.xtn.net

BEANIES-MAPLE, ERIN, PRINCESS PLUS 96 MORE CAN BE YOURS FOR $10. SEE WWW.BEANIEADV.COMTY dealer for Beanies and plush.

CHECK THIS OUT! Ty BB's FROM GERMANY! 10%-50% less than USA price! Cur.+Ret.+Erin+Valentino+ Peace+Princess(PVC). Only one per customer. +P&H. NO DEALERS! EMail:MMarkow@t-online.de or write:Markow, Neunkircherweg45, D-64397 MODAUTAL

7 CENT OR LESS TAG PROTECTORS. Buy Direct. Our semi rigid 15 mil, heart shape protectors are the best value and quality. 100% satisfaction assured! 100 @ $8, 200 @ $15+$3 air, Buy 250 @ $22.50 get 50 free! Case 4000 @$200 Dealer Special! E-mail cweidmark@aol.com or call 613-786-1000. Buy now! Loon Lake Design.

THE BEST LOCKET STYLE TAG PROTECTOR ON THE MARKET. MADE OF 15 MIL PVC, UV COATED TO PROTECT TAGS FROM FADING, TABS ON THE SIDES FOR EASY OPENING, THE LOCKET SHUTS TIGHT AND OPENS EASY (NO MORE PRYING THE LOCKET OPEN). OUR PRICE FOR 1000 LOCKETS IS $115 WITH FREE DELIVERY! TO ORDER 1000 LOCKETS PLEASE SEND A MONEY ORDER TO: BEANIE SAFE, 1659 WEST TURKEYFOOT, BARBETON, OHIO 44203 1-800-576-9162, safe1111@aol.com

Wisconsin's 1st Annual Beanie Baby National Convention Sat. Sept. 19, 9am-2pm at Serb Hall (51st and

THIS AD CONTINUES ON PAGE 246

HOW TO SUBMIT ITEMS FOR BEANIE MARKETPLACE

Marketplace classifieds cost $15 per line (*min. 5 lines, max. 46 characters per line*)

Materials must be received by: **Sept. 4, 1998**, for the **November** issue, **Oct. 2, 1998**, for the **December** issue

Send the text for your Beanie Marketplace ad with payment. (*check, money order, or MasterCard/VISA*)

H&S Media, Inc.
Attn. Patrick Julian
Beanie Marketplace
3400 Dundee Road, Suite 245
Northbrook, IL 60062
PH: (847) 291-1135, Ext. 307
FAX: (847) 291-0612

Or submit your ad via e-mail: **pjulian@adspub.com**

Oklahoma) in Milwaukee. The Biggest Door Prize Ever: Peanut the Royal Blue Elephant (mint) to be given away to a lucky winner. 100 tables of Quality Beanies, Teenies, Disney, and others $5 admission. For dealer tables, call 414-783-4339

Beanies: Selling + Buying all older Ty Retired
Our daily inventory includes retireds, new releases and currents. Call for difficult and hard to find, 920-467-6662. Also availableolder Hummels, Cherished Teddies, Prec. Moments

---

Chicagoland Beanie Source
All Current Beanies
New And Retired, Buy-Sell-Trade!
Top $$ Paid — Cash! 847-674-6570
4753 W. Touhy, Lincolnwood, IL 60646

Beanie and Teenie Accessories Galore
Sleeping Bags, Bean Bag Chairs, Pouches, Leases, Snuggle Me Harnesses. Outfits of all kinds: Sleep Wear, Super Hero, Rain Gear, Jeans, T-shirts and much more. Also Screen Savers, Mouse Pads, Key Chains, Magnets, Buttons, Transfers. Send SASE for info or call
A La Carte Designs
P. O. Box 311
St. Michaels, MD 21663
410-745-2722

TY BEANIES: RETIRED, CURRENT, HARD TO FIND, AND NEWLY RELEASED. DISNEY, TEENIES, NASCAR, HARLEY, COCA COLA, ALSO RETIRED DREAMSICLES AND PRECIOUS MOMENT DOLLS. 414 626-2022 6PM-9:PM CST WEEKDAYS.

BRITANNIA BEAR, PRINCESS (PVC PELLETS), CURLY, PEACE, HOLIDAY, AND VALENTINO BEARS PLUS THE RECENTLY RETIRED BEANIES AND RECENTLY RETIRED

PILLOW PALS FOR SALE — BEST OFFERS TO FAX (ENGLAND) 011-44-1543-410872 OR TELEPHONE 011-44-1543-268402

BUMPER STICKERS "I BREAK FOR BEANIES BABIES" "BEANIES ROCK" "I LOVE BEANIES" $2 EA. OR 5 FOR $5 (INCLUDES 2 SURPRISE STICKERS) WITH L/SASE TO: RAINBOW, PO BOX 107B, PALOS HTS, IL 60463-0107 ORDERS SHIPPED SAME DAY RECEIVED. DEALERS WELCOME

A SET OF OVER 100 TY BEANIES CAN BE YOURS. WIN OVER 100 RARE, RETIRED, CURRENT & TEENIE BEANIES. INCLUDES GARCIA, PEANUT, BRITANNIA, ERIN, PRINCESS, PEACE, BESSIE AND MORE. SEND $8.00 AND A 1 PARAGRAPH ESSAY ABOUT WHAT YOU WILL DO WITH THE COLLECTION IF YOU WIN.

SEND $8.00 AND ESSAY TO: RFL, PO BOX 346 FOX RIVER GROVE, IL 60021 DEADLINE: DECEMBER 311998

CRITTER CONDOS: Handcrafted, decorative, stackable wooden houses for Beanie type toys. For a brochure and price list call or send a legal size SASE — Kemp's Critter Condos • 203 E. Hickory St. • Lombard, IL 60148 • (630) 932-9509

BRITANNIA, ERIN, PINCHERS, PRINCESS, PEACE, GOLDIE, ECHO, + ALL CURRENTS AND MAY 1998 RETIREDS. OFFERS 860-868-8089 AFTER OCTOBER 1ST.

Attn dealers and collectors! 4x4x7 acrylic display boxes $1.50, 4x4x8 boxes $1.60. Slide on tag protectors, $.07, plastic locket 15 cents, hard plastic locket, 30 cents. Call 919-412-0147 or visit www.coolbeanies.com.

Beanies not included. Not associated with Ty Inc.

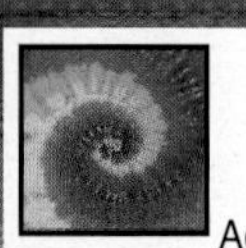

Cosmic Endeavors
Beanie, Bear & Plush Collectibles Show
Open to the public from 9am - 3pm
Admission $5 for adults, kids under 12 FREE

Illinois	September 27	Marriott Hotel - Schaumburg
Arizona	October 18	Embassy Suites Hotel - Scottsdale
Illinois	December 13	Marriott Hotel - Schaumburg

50-100 tables full of huggables! • Door prizes every 15 minutes! Charity raffles too!

For more information, contact Greg & Lisa Koch (847) 590-8908 or tyeduo@aol.com

Visit the Cosmic Shop Online at http://members.aol.com/tyedyeduo

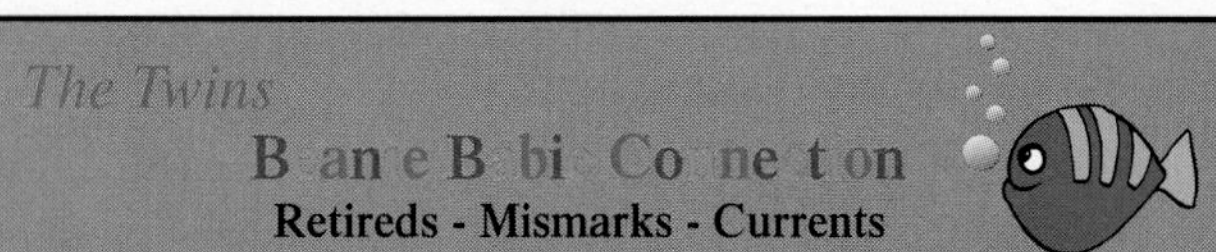

Buying Retireds

Two Locations To Serve You!

Rhea Thompson	**Rita Goodwin**
Denver, CO	**Capistrano Beach, CA**
phone: (303) 429-8785	**phone: (949) 489-3479**

CATHY'S COLLECTIBLES

Selling and Buying Beanie Babies™

Ty and Disney, Ty Plush and Teenie Beanies
Great prices retail and wholesale • Established since 1996
Sav-a-heart tag protectors • 8 colors • new hard acrylic design

Retail AND Wholesale

Hours: Monday - Friday 10:00 a.m. - 6:00 p.m. Eastern time
Flint, MI (810) 655-2654 or Fax (810) 655-2267
E-mail: kiwi@tir.com

October 31-November 1, Durham, NC - '98 Beanie Symposium Toy Show. 10am-3pm (Both Days) Durham Marriott at Civic Center, $5 at Door Dealers-Games-Contests-Raffles-Guests! Visit www.gannglobal.com (910) 350-8272

YOU AND YOUR BEANIE Personalized Horoscopes Suitable For Framing. Send your Beanies date of birth and Your date of birth, along with $4.95 plus $3.00 shipping & handling. Please send check or money orders to: HD Global PO Box 612 Sterling, IL 61081. GREAT GIFT IDEA!

VENDOR SPACES AVAILABLE IN ARIZONA! One of the LARGEST shows in the Southwest! TLC Promotions presents the "BEANIE BABIES & COLLECTIBLES EXPO" at the Phoenix Civic Plaza, Dec. 12 &13, JUST IN TIME FOR CHRISTMAS. There's 30,000 sq. ft. of exhibit hall space!! Sell to thousands of eager buyers in two days. This is a NATIONALLY PROMOTED event! Reserve now! Call toll free 1-877-580-9422

My Display Box™

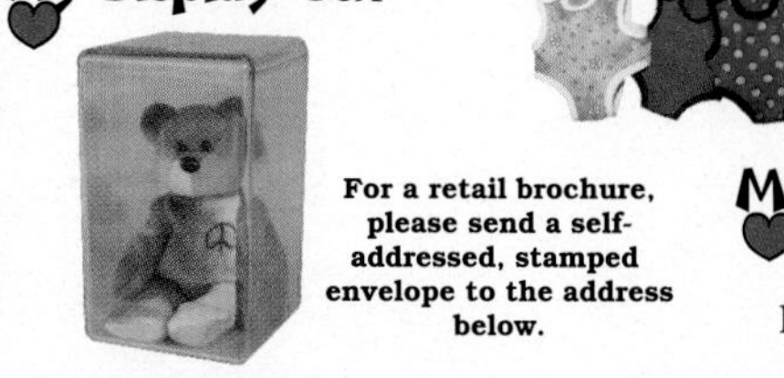

For a retail brochure, please send a self-addressed, stamped envelope to the address below.

My Carrier™ Only $11.95 plus shipping

Order online at: www.mconline.com (800) 203-0900 Wholesale pricing available.

My Collectibles Inc. 17675 SW Farmington Rd. Suite 486 Aloha, OR 97007

Internet Classifieds
Free Giveaways!
Trading Posts!
Chat Rooms!
www.planetbeanie.com

Collectors. Distributors. Retailers. Maniacs.

The best way to buy, sell and trade with the world.

eorlando@planetbeanie.com

Beanie Cards. Save $ buying complete set of 55 Series 1 cards $100 per set. Also limited edition of 9 cards $95. We have loose cards reg set $2 ea, Limited Edition $12 ea, and Bear Cards only $5 ea. To order send check or money order

THIS AD CONTINUES ON PAGE 248

Carousel Critter Cubby™

Displays 8 to 16 Beanie toys

Size 9.5" round x 7.5" high (non-mechanical)

$18.95

Shipping charge per order: $3.00
We accept VISA and MasterCard

Please check our Web site HTTP://www.jacamac.com
JACAMAC™ Inc. • PO Box 72 • New Hope, Virginia 24469
Fax your orders to (540) 363-2687

Custom Made and Personalized for Your Favorite Beanie/Stuffed Pal

Many Colors to Choose From

Many More Styles to Choose From

Checks Accepted

$21.95

Plaques 'N Color

$25.95

Call for Details (209) 522-0242 •Fax (209) 522-0252
Most Major Credit Cards Accepted • Shipping Costs & Sales Tax not included

ROYAL IMAGES

Current – Retired – Hard To Find Pieces

"Ty Attic Treasures - Ty Plush"

Exclusive Acrylic Tag Protectors

Phone: (630) 924-0520 Fax: (630) 924-5755
Business Hours: 9 a.m. to 6 p.m. Central Time
E-mail: RoyalImg@aol.com
Credit Cards Accepted

STUFFED TOY DO-DADS™

Accessories for your favorite bean bag, Miniature stuffed toy or other collectibles

From
L&H Deco-Art Inc.

Display Shelf Tents Bunk Beds Swings Cradles School Desks Cages Hammocks

Visit our Web site www.stuffedtoydodads.com

(You have no computer-No problem)
Call or write us for a printout

998 Victoria Street
Phone: 847-395-2594
E-mail: CoolStuff@stuffedtoydodads.com
Antioch, IL 60002
Fax: 847-395-1451

Beanie Marketplace

to AMC Hobbies, PO Box 36 Columbia, KY 42728
add $3 S+H. Limited Quantities available.

BEANIE BABY WEEKLY NEWSLETTER! THE LATEST PRICE UPDATES! DEALERS BUY & SELL PRICES... THE LATEST NEWS AND VIEWS...THREE MONTH SUBSCRIPTION ONLY $ 24.95. ARUNDEL COINS & COLLECTABLES, 7418 BALTIMORE & ANNAPOLIS BLVD, GLEN BURNIE, MD 21061-3538

---

the Original
Beanie Baggies

Protect your
Beanies... Ty Attic
from
Dirt, Grime, Smoke

100 Beanie Baggies $7.00 + s/h

Clear Collector Baggies are sized to protect your Collectibles.
All have zip closure for easy access.

Send for prices of other Collector Baggies. Mail/fax or E-mail to:

Rainy Day Ltd.
P.O. Box 25203
Federal Way, WA 98093

Fax 253-952-6982

E-mail: rainydayltd@worldnet.att.net
Web Page: http://home.att.net/~rainydayltd

BEANIE BOXES

•Acrylic Boxes
4"x4"x8"
Call for prices

•Clear Vinyl Cases
9"x5"x4"
$.89 each or $79.00 per 100
Lockable & stackable
Comes with labels
S&H included

•Lockett Style Tag Protector
$25.00 per 100
S&H included

•Clear Slide On Tag Protector
$18 per 100
S&H included

The PFM Company
20008 Kelly Rd.
Harper Woods, MI 48225
(313) 521-1002
(800) 661-5111
fax order (313) 521-0212
Money order/check/Visa/MC

BEAN E POLE™
The ultimate way to DISPLAY and STORE your BEANIE BABIES™

The **BEAN E POLE™** stands 5 feet tall and is constructed of durable, white furniture-quality plastic. It is maintenance free and requires little space, no more than a standing coat rack.

The **BEAN E POLE™** will securely hold 28 to 56 Beanie Babies™ with permanently mounted adjustable holders.

ONLY $59.95
(plus $8.75 S&H)

check

To order call
1-800-933-1608

www.beaniebabybeanepole.com

"Bean E Pole" is a trademark of Wenc Industries, Inc. "Beanie Babies" is a trademark of Ty Inc. Wenc Industries, Inc. is not affiliated with or endorsed by Ty Inc.

This month visit **www.eviesbeanieraffle.com** for special guest appearances by

Bubbles, Bumble, Caw, Fortune, Hoot, Lizzy, Radar, Spinner, Spooky and Velvet.

Would you like to add any or all of the above Beanie Babies to your collection? Then hurry over to www.eviesbeanieraffle.com. Want to enter this raffle but you don't have access to the internet? Then fax 773.684.9011 (U.S.A.) to request your entry form via fax or mail a self-addressed stamped envelope to Evie's Beanies, P.O. Box 5750, Chicago, IL 60680-5750.

10 Beanies / 10 Raffles / 10 Winners
10 Tickets / $10 (U.S.)

Evie only features mint condition Beanie Babies with mint condition swing and tush tags, no imitations, no exceptions. Deadline for entering this raffle is 11:59 pm CST October 19, 1998. Visit the site for more details. Tune in to **www.eviesbeanieraffle.com** on October 20, 1998 at 9:00 am CST when the winners will be announced!

A significant portion of this month's proceeds will benefit Breast Cancer Research.

ADVERTISER INDEX